D0936544

Economic policy for
building peace.

DATE		

Economic Policy for
Building Peace

Economic Policy for Building Peace

The Lessons of El Salvador

edited by
James K. Boyce

LYNNE
RIENNER
PUBLISHERS

BOULDER
LONDON

Published in the United States of America in 1996 by
Lynne Rienner Publishers, Inc.
1800 30th Street, Boulder, Colorado 80301

and in the United Kingdom by
Lynne Rienner Publishers, Inc.
3 Henrietta Street, Covent Garden, London WC2E 8LU

Library of Congress Cataloging-in-Publication Data
Economic policy for building peace : the lessons of El Salvador /
    edited by James K. Boyce.
    Includes bibliographical references and index.
    ISBN 1-55587-526-2 (hc : alk. paper)
    1. El Salvador—Economic policy. 2. El Salvador—Economic
conditions—1945–   3. El Salvador—Politics and
government—1979–1992. 4. El Salvador—Politics and
government—1992–   I. Boyce, James K.
HC148.E283   1996
338.97284—dc20   96-12269
                                                       CIP

British Cataloguing-in-Publication Data
A Cataloguing-in-Publication record for this book
is available from the British Library.

Printed and bound in the United States of America

     The paper used in this publication meets the requirements
 ∞   of the American National Standard for Permanence of
     Paper for Printed Library Materials Z39.48-1984.

     5 4 3 2 1

Contents

List of Tables and Figures		vii
Foreword, Anders Kompass		xi
Preface, Victor Bulmer-Thomas, Michael E. Conroy, Hector Dada, Keith Griffin, Gabriel Siri, and Lance Taylor		xiii
Acknowledgments		xvii
1	El Salvador's Adjustment Toward Peace: An Introduction	1
	James K. Boyce	
2	The Historical Background to the Conflict	19
	Carlos Acevedo	
3	The War Economy of the 1980s	31
	Alexander Segovia	
4	Macroeconomic Performance and Policies Since 1989	51
	Alexander Segovia	
5	The Peace Accords and Postwar Reconstruction	73
	Elisabeth J. Wood	
6	Domestic Resource Mobilization	107
	Alexander Segovia	
7	External Resource Mobilization	129
	James K. Boyce	
8	Distributional Implications of Macroeconomic Policy: Theory and Applications to El Salvador	155
	Manuel Pastor, Jr., and Michael E. Conroy	
9	The Financial System: Opportunities and Risks	177
	Colin Danby	
10	Structural Adjustment, the Agricultural Sector, and the Peace Process	209
	Carlos Acevedo	

11 Environmental Degradation and Development Options   233
      Deborah Barry and Herman Rosa
12 Exports and the Consolidation of Peace   247
      Eva Paus
13 Conclusions and Recommendations   279
      James K. Boyce

    Statistical Appendix   285
    Acronyms, Units of Measure, and Spanish Terms   317
    Bibliography   321
    About the Contributors   345
    Index   347
    About the Book   359

Tables and Figures

Tables

2.1 Heads of State, 1898–1994   22
2.2 Composition of Agricultural Production, 1979   23
2.3 Farm-Size Distribution, 1971   23
2.4 Income of Landless Agricultural Workers in Central America, Early 1960s   24
2.5 Average Annual Inflation Rates in Central America, 1950–1979   28

3.1 Businesses Closed Temporarily or Permanently and Jobs Affected, 1979–1985   35
3.2 Economic Assistance Pledged by USAID, 1980–1989   38
3.3 Exchange Rates and Inflation, 1978–1990   39
3.4 Costs of Direct and Indirect Damages Caused by the Armed Conflict and Estimated Reconstruction Costs   45
3.5 Occupational Structure, San Salvador Metropolitan Area, 1978 and 1991   46

4.1 Operations of the International Financial Institutions, 1989–1993   52
4.2 Composition of Exports, 1988–1993   54
4.3 Macroeconomic Significance of Family Remittances, 1979–1994   56
4.4 Real and Nominal Rates of Protection in 1987 and 1993   58
4.5 Basic Economic Indicators, 1990–1994   62
4.6 Urban Poverty, 1988/89–1992/93   64

5.1 Financing the Peace Accords: Investment Requirements, 1992–1996   88

5.2   Funding Priorities and Shortfalls, 1993–1996   90

6.1   Savings and Investment as a Percentage of GDP, 1970–1994   109
6.2   National and Domestic Savings Rates in 83 Developing
       Countries, 1970–1992   112
6.3   Tax Coefficient and Composition of Tax Revenues,
       1970–1994   115
6.4   Financing of the Peace Process, 1992–1995   117
6.5   Evolution of National Defense Budget, 1989–1995   118
6.6   Central-Government Budget Outlays in Selected Areas,
       1991–1995   119
6.7   Commitments Made by the Government of El Salvador to
       the International Monetary Fund in 1992, and
       Achievements   121
6.8   Planned and Actual Capital Expenditure by the Nonfinancial
       Public Sector, 1992–1994   122

7.1   Official External Assistance to El Salvador, 1992–1995   131
7.2   Funding Requirements and Commitments for Programs
       Mandated Under the Peace Accords, 1993–1996   132
7.3   Funding Shortfalls for Higher-Priority Programs as of
       September 1994   134
7.4   IMF Estimates of Central-Government Expenditures on the
       Military, Education, and Health, 1989–1993   144

8.1   Topics and Policies in the Stabilization/Adjustment
       Class/Sector Approach   158
8.2   Alternative Policies in the Equity-Enhancing Class/Sector
       Approach   170

9.1   Absorbing an Inflow   182
9.2   Liquidity of the Commercial Banks, 1989–1994   185
9.3   Financial Assets and Liabilities of Salvadoran Households
       and Firms, 1991   190
9.4   Total Approved Credit from the Banking System, 1985–1993 192
9.5   Bank and Financiera Branches by Department, 1994   193

10.1   Value of Agricultural Production, 1980 and 1993   211
10.2   Indices of Implicit Prices of Agricultural Production and
       GDP, 1980–1993   213
10.3   Value of Agricultural Exports, 1986–1993   214
10.4   Coffee Prices and Exports, 1980/81–1992/93   216
10.5   Prices of Maize and Beans, 1985/86–1992/93   216
10.6   Beneficiaries of Land Reform in the 1980s   218

10.7   Farm-Size Distribution, 1971 and 1987   220
10.8   Agrarian Structure, 1961–1991   222
10.9   Agricultural Credit, 1990 and 1993   224

11.1   Distribution of Coffee Lands, 1971 and 1988   243

12.1   Structure of Nontraditional Exports, by Destination and
        Product, 1992 and 1993   252
12.2   Indicators of Maquila Performance, 1985–1993   253
12.3   Structure of Imports, 1980–1993   253
12.4   Daily Real Minimum Wages, 1980–1993   259

A.1   Central America: Human Development Indicators, 1992   285
A.2a   Gross Domestic Product at Current Prices, 1970–1993   286
A.2b   Gross Domestic Product at Constant 1962 Prices,
        1970–1993   290
A.2c   National Accounts and Government Revenue and
        Expenditure, 1970–1993   296
A.3   Balance of Payments, 1970–1993   298
A.4   External Debt and Net Transfers, 1970–1993   300
A.5   Structure of Government Revenue, 1970–1992   304
A.6   Structure of Government Expenditure, 1970–1992   306
A.7   Total Approved Credit from Banking System, by Sector,
        1985–1993   308
A.8   Area, Yield, and Output of Major Crops, 1970–1993   309
A.9   Merchandise Exports, 1970–1993   310
A.10   Merchandise Imports, 1984–1994   312
A.11   Consumer Price Index by Major Categories, 1980–1993   314
A.12   Minimum Real Wages, 1989–1993   315

Figures

3.1   Terms of Trade, 1975–1989   33
3.2   Growth of GDP and Major Sectors, 1978–1988   36
3.3   Fiscal Deficit, 1978–1989   37
3.4   Inflation, 1978–1989   40
3.5   Composition of Government Expenditure, 1975–1987   43
3.6   Real Salaries, 1980–1988   44

4.1   Composition of Tax Revenue, 1985–1994   59
4.2   Real Exchange Rate, 1970–1993   61

6.1   Private and Public Investment, 1970–1994   111

6.2   National Versus Foreign Savings, 1980–1994   113
6.3   Tax Coefficient, 1970–1993   116

7.1   Potential Trade-off Between Government Budget
       Deficit and Social Tensions Due to Inadequate
       Peace Expenditures   143

9.1   Gross and Net Bank Reserves, 1989–1993   181
9.2   Monetary Aggregates as a Proportion of GDP, 1963–1993   184
9.3   Formal-Sector Interest Rates, 1992–1993   185
9.4   Domestic Credit as a Proportion of GDP, 1963–1993   188

10.1   Relative Prices of Agricultural Goods Compared with
       Nonagricultural Goods and Services, 1970–1993   212

11.1   Population Growth by Selected Zones, 1971–1992   236
11.2   Selected Tributaries of the Lempa River   238
11.3   Harvest Employment for Major Export Crops,
       1979/80–1988/89   239
11.4   Coffee-Harvest Minimum Wages, 1973–1993   240
11.5   Indices of Real Prices of Corn and Beans, 1978–1993   240
11.6   Map of Coffee Areas   242

12.1   Merchandise Exports and Imports, 1980–1993   248
12.2   Nontraditional Exports by Product Type and Destination,
       1981–1993   251
12.3   Inflation and Wage-Adjusted Real Exchange Rates,
       1980–1993   257
12.4   Net Exports of CACM Member Countries to CACM,
       1970–1993   268
12.5   Real Profit Rate and Real Minimum Wage, 1980–1991   272

Foreword

The enormous complexity of peacemaking efforts, particularly in the light of dramatic and seemingly insoluble conflicts around the globe, often diverts attention from the equally difficult issue of the appropriate policies to pursue once peace has emerged. Negotiating an end to devastating conflict can seem nothing short of miraculous; however, once the specter of war recedes, consolidating the peace and making it sustainable is an equally daunting task. Unfortunately, there are few blueprints or existing policy frameworks to provide nations emerging from war with useful input for economic policymaking in the transition from emergency circumstances to long-term development strategies. This study was undertaken to analyze the experience from one country, El Salvador, presently facing this challenge, and to explore some of the dilemmas and alternatives with respect to the special needs of nations emerging from extended strife and seeking to consolidate peace.

The report raises a variety of issues of paramount importance to national policymakers, the international donor community, international financial institutions, development practitioners, the UN system, and most important, citizens themselves. Although there is increasing international recognition of the inextricable relationship between peace and development, what policies should be pursued to promote which development model still remains a source of intense discussion. In commissioning this study the UNDP's underlying objective has been to offer a contribution to this growing national and international debate on postconflict economic policymaking.

This study was carried out by an independent team of international economists whose work was reviewed by an advisory panel of eminent academics and development economists. The views expressed in this report are exclusively those of the team that researched and wrote it and are not necessarily shared by the UNDP. However, we believe the report provides an initial body of important insight and an analysis to stimulate debate on economic policymaking for reconstruction and peace consolidation, a new and challenging area that requires considerable future research and analysis. We look forward to future contributions from other participants in the development policy debate arena that may further enrich this complex discussion.

Anders Kompass
Resident Representative
United Nations Development Programme
San Salvador, El Salvador

Preface

El Salvador offers much to give observers pause. A small nation on the Pacific coast of Central America, it has long been viewed as exceptional for the energy and entrepreneurship of its people, at all social and economic levels, as well as for the deep social inequality and festering political tensions that have characterized most of its history.

Twelve years of civil war, recognized by all observers—from the U.S. Kissinger Commission to the UN Economic Commission for Latin America and the Caribbean—as bred of inequality and fed by injustice, ended in stalemate. The peace process that was then negotiated, with critical UN mediation, has not been completed or fully consolidated as the bulk of the UN personnel who have monitored it are withdrawn. Whether the peace will hold depends now, more than ever, on the nature of the social and economic policies that the Salvadoran government implements—a course of action that could benefit from positive influence by the international community.

Will the space afforded by peace and a relative abundance of foreign exchange be used to design policies for resolving the land claims of former combatants and landholders in the formerly contested areas of the country? Will the government choose economic strategies designed to ameliorate the deep social inequalities that produced the war and worsened in the last decade? Or will it follow narrowly defined stabilization and adjustment policies at the cost of deepening political and economic tension?

This study addresses these questions in a path-breaking contribution to the debate over policy during postconflictual transitions. The study is not a simple or unbridled critique of the present government policies in El Salvador, nor of the international financial institutions. It is not a utopian call for social programs without recognition of their economic costs and consequences. Nor is it a theoretical exercise based on principles that have not been grounded and tested in contemporary Salvadoran reality. Rather, it explores policy alternatives that are realistic and feasible, and that respond directly to the dilemmas of a country emerging from civil war.

The study offers, first, an overview and interpretation of recent Salvadoran history that provides a carefully structured context for understanding the implications of alternative sets of economic policy. The early chapters provide a comprehensive background for evaluating the economic policy needs of the nation as it seeks to consolidate peace. That background emphasizes some of the special features of El Salvador that may permit—and require—economic policies different from those that have become most common. The terrible damage to infrastructure and the environment during 12 years of war, the large-scale internal displacement and the emigration of more than a million people (largely to the United States), and the receipt of nearly a billion dollars per year in remittances from those emigrants are among the most important features covered.

The study's reflection on alternative sets of macroeconomic policy recognizes that a newly emerging mainstream perspective on policy can be brought to bear in the Salvadoran case. Conventional economic theory was built, until recently, on the precept that direct attempts to alter the distribution of income and economic opportunity were likely to inhibit economic growth and reduce the likelihood of fulfilling a nation's social and economic goals. Contemporary policy, strongly influenced for many nations by the international financial institutions, responded to historical patterns of excessive and inappropriate state intervention in the economy by encouraging drastic curtailment of the role of the state.

The new perspective elaborated here, based on both contemporary growth theory and new empirical studies made worldwide, suggests that sustained economic growth is in fact unlikely in conditions of deep and worsening social inequality. Furthermore, the inordinate privatization and liberalization of the economy in reaction to prior state intervention is seen as potentially damaging to the well-being of the poor majority, lessening rather than enhancing the prospects for long-term growth.

The alternatives to current policies in El Salvador proposed and analyzed in this study are drawn from a variety of successful experiences elsewhere in the world. They are adapted to the specific context of El Salvador and compared to the policies recommended by many of the most important international actors.

The new macroeconomic perspective, along with policies recommended for microeconomic and mesoeconomic reforms, grows out of a direct concern for the design of efficient policies that will promote both equity and the consolidation of peace. The redesign and implementation of an agrarian reform of the sort now seen as critical to the success of several of the Asian high-growth countries, the promotion of greater efficiency in the financial sector, and the protection of natural resources for present and future generations are some of the alternative policies the study recommends to enhance El Salvador's prospects for peace, stability, and economic growth.

This study was commissioned by the El Salvador office of the United Nations Development Programme (UNDP) in response to the critical role it has been asked to play in the Salvadoran peace process. During the negotiations leading to the Salvadoran peace accords of January 1992, the government and the FMLN agreed that reconstruction financing would require some mediation. The UNDP was given the task of developing programs for international financial assistance, for coordinating among international donors, and for monitoring implementation of reconstruction, resettlement, and other processes mandated in the peace accords. In the face of financial constraints and conventional macroeconomic policies not directed to the special requirements of adjustment toward peace, the UNDP has sought to promote dialogue on appropriate policy in the post-conflictual transition.

The relevance of the issues examined in this study is not confined to El Salvador. The analysis will, of course, be particularly germane to other countries emerging from civil conflict as they confront very similar dilemmas, but many of its findings are also relevant to the wider range of countries that are at risk of future conflict but still have the chance to avoid it. We commend this study to the reader and look forward to the vigorous debate we hope it will provoke.

Victor Bulmer-Thomas, Michael E. Conroy,
Hector Dada, Keith Griffin, Gabriel Siri, Lance Taylor

Acknowledgments

This volume is the product of a study commissioned by the United Nations Development Programme in San Salvador. Responsibility for the views expressed herein rests with the authors alone, and should not be attributed to the United Nations or to any of its member agencies.

The authors were assisted in the preparation of this volume by an advisory board comprising Victor Bulmer-Thomas, Michael E. Conroy, Hector Dada, Keith Griffin, Gabriel Siri, and Lance Taylor. We are grateful for their many helpful suggestions. We are also grateful to the many individuals in international agencies, in the government of El Salvador, and elsewhere who generously shared time and information with us. We also thank the staff of the San Salvador mission of the United Nations Development Programme, and in particular Anders Kompass and Francesca Jessup, for their unflagging support and encouragement.

James K. Boyce

Economic Policy for
Building Peace

1

El Salvador's Adjustment Toward Peace: An Introduction

James K. Boyce

The transition from civil war to peace poses formidable challenges for economic policy. During the postconflictual transition the goals of economic policy cannot be limited to macroeconomic stabilization and conventional structural adjustment. Economic policy must also promote the adjustment toward peace. The recent experience of El Salvador offers valuable lessons in a world in which civil conflicts are tragically widespread.

The interdependence of peace and development in El Salvador is widely recognized. A failure to achieve broad improvements in living standards would fuel social tensions and heighten the risk of renewed war, and a return to war would shatter hopes for economic revival. Yet there has been little systematic discussion of how economic policy should be reshaped in the special circumstances of a country emerging from civil war. In El Salvador the government and the international financial institutions (IFIs) have pursued essentially the same macroeconomic stabilization and structural adjustment policies they would have followed had the country never been at war. Recognition of the interdependence between peace and development has been translated into the questionable precept that if the peace process were allowed to interfere with economic policy, both would fail. This book is based on the contrary premise that *unless* the peace process is allowed to reshape economic policy, both will fail.

Two broad sets of economic issues arise in the adjustment toward peace. The first concerns the problem of financing the immediate costs of peace, including the establishment of new democratic institutions, the reintegration of ex-combatants into civilian life, and the repair of physical infrastructure. The mobilization of resources for the peace process is a political problem as well as a financial problem. External-assistance actors must deploy appropriate conditionalities if their aid is to support the momentum of the peace process and "crowd in" domestic resources for peace-related needs.

The second set of issues concerns the longer-term interrelationships among economic growth, income distribution, and the consolidation of peace. Income inequalities can jeopardize both peace and growth. Investments in human capital and natural capital are as critical as investment in physical capital. Democratization—in the broad sense of movement toward a more equitable distribution of power—can improve the functioning of both the state and the market. These issues are not unique to countries emerging from civil war, but the postconflictual setting presents them in exceptionally stark relief.

The following section discusses the short-term issues of financing the costs of peace, the next considers the longer-term policy issues, and the final section provides a brief overview of El Salvador's recent history as background for the chapters that follow.

Economic Policy and
El Salvador's Postconflictual Transition

The war in El Salvador had many losers, but no clear victors. The peace accords brokered by the UN and signed at Chapultepec, Mexico, in January 1992 were born of a military stalemate. The 12-year civil war, which claimed some 75,000 lives, had brought neither the government nor the guerrillas of the Farabundo Martí Front for National Liberation (FMLN) the prospect of a decisive victory. Both sides agreed to major concessions to be implemented in phased steps in the ensuing months. The government agreed to recognize the FMLN as a legitimate political party, to disband its paramilitary police forces and replace them with a new, politically neutral police force, to purge the armed forces of those responsible for human-rights abuses, to reform the judiciary and establish new democratic institutions, and to transfer land to ex-combatants and supporters of the FMLN. In return, the guerrillas agreed to lay down their arms and contend for power via free elections.

The far-reaching reforms embodied in the Chapultepec Accords were hailed as a "negotiated revolution" by Alvaro de Soto, who mediated the peace talks on behalf of the Secretary-General of the UN (Golden 1992; Karl 1992). Neither the negotiation nor the revolution ended, however, with the signing of the accords. The peace agreement stopped the shooting, but the conflicts that rent El Salvador's social fabric continue to be fought by other means. The policies of external actors can either strengthen or weaken the political resolve of both sides to implement the accords and consolidate the peace.

Economists and the international financial institutions they staff are generally ill-prepared to operate in such a context. Contemporary economic theory typically takes for granted, as exogenously given, basic underpinnings of the economy that are far from settled in a country torn by civil conflict. These include a well-defined and socially accepted distribution of property or "initial endowments," a legal system to enforce property rights and contracts, and a state able to perform necessary economic tasks not fulfilled by markets, such as the provision of public goods. All of these preconditions are compromised or shattered by civil war, if indeed they existed before it. And they do not spring forth spontaneously upon the signing of a peace agreement. Rather, they must be built gradually in a process regarded as legitimate by all parties to the conflict. Economic theory has little to say about how this crucial process of institutional change is to be accomplished. Indeed, many economists seem oblivious to the need to modify their policy prescriptions in the absence of these fundamentals.

International financial institutions such as the World Bank, the International Monetary Fund (IMF), and the Inter-American Development Bank (IDB), cannot so readily ignore these core issues of political economy. Yet these agencies historically have sought to distance themselves from such political issues, straying as little as possible from the familiar economic terrain in which they can claim technocratic expertise. In recent years the IFIs have widened their self-proclaimed mandate to encompass such previously off-limits topics as military expenditure and "governance." But although these concerns now feature in the IFIs' public pronouncements and public relations, they remain poorly integrated at the operational level of their country programs. In El Salvador they have been notable by their absence.

This lacuna has contributed to a lamentable lack of coordination between economic policy and the peace process. Institutionally this has been manifested in the division of labor between the Bretton Woods institutions (the World Bank and the IMF) and the UN: Economic policy has been the province of the former, the peace process the province of the latter. Writing in the March 1994 issue of *Foreign Policy,* Alvaro de Soto and Graciana del Castillo (1994a) depict the resulting situation by means of a metaphor: El Salvador is a patient on the operating table "with the left and right sides of his body separated by a curtain and unrelated surgery being performed on each side." Like most metaphors, this image is inexact (see Chapter 5), but it dramatizes a critical issue raised by the Salvadoran experience.[1]

Contemporary macroeconomic policy distinguishes between short-run stabilization and medium-to-long-run adjustment. Stabilization involves primarily fiscal and monetary policy; in the division of labor among the IFIs this is mainly the province of the IMF. Adjustment refers to policies designed to alter the structure of the economy, including the relative sizes of the public and private sectors and of the tradeable and nontradeable sectors; this is mainly the province of the World Bank and the regional development banks.

The dominant strand of policymaking at the IFIs maintains that sound economic medicine is basically invariant with respect to time and place. Government budget deficits are assumed to be the root cause of inflation; hence these deficits must be curtailed, regardless of local circumstances such as the need to fund peace programs. Liberalization of trade and of the financial sector invariably promotes efficiency and growth. Structural adjustment is the key to long-run growth, the benefits of which will sooner or later percolate to the poor. If, in the meantime, reforms impose short-run costs on the poor, they should be cushioned by temporary schemes. Land reform is missing from the policymakers' tool kit because asset redistribution would transgress the minimal role accorded to the state.

The special features of the postconflictual transition do not imply that sound economic policies are unnecessary, nor that they should be sacrificed to political expediency. But in the aftermath of a civil war the soundness of policies can be ascertained only in light of the political economy of the peace process.

In the short run, economic policy during the postconflictual transition must support political as well as economic stabilization. Political stabilization requires the successful implementation of the measures negotiated in the peace accords. This in turn requires adequate funding for programs mandated by the accords, and a continuing commitment by both sides to the ongoing peace process. Neither of these conditions is an axiomatic feature of "sound economic policy" prescribed without reference to the peace process.

In some cases it could be necessary to ease macroeconomic stabilization targets so as to permit funding of peace programs through deficit finance. In the case of El Salvador, however, considerably greater domestic resources could be mobilized for the peace process by shifting government expenditure from other uses, notably military spending, and by raising the country's extremely low tax coefficient. The IMF reports that "in the Western Hemisphere, El Salvador allocated the largest share of total [government] spending for defense (16 percent) in 1992, and the smallest share for social security and welfare (3 percent)" (Abdallah 1995, p. 77). The World Bank (1994d, p. 182) reports that total government revenue in 1992 was less than 10 percent of GNP, the lowest of any middle-income country in the world. In recent years IFI-backed policies in El Salvador have contributed to some progress in raising tax revenues, though there remains much room for improvement. However, the IFIs have largely neglected military expenditure.

The failure of the IFIs to promote vigorously a greater reallocation of domestic resources to peace programs has been compounded by their failure to incorporate the maintenance of the political will behind the peace process as a policy objective. Yet large-scale infusions of external assistance, and the conditions attached—or not attached—to them, can significantly affect the priorities of political actors and the balance of power among them. A key lesson of El Salvador is the need for "peace conditionality" as an element of stabilization policies during postconflictual transitions.

Growth, Distribution, and the Consolidation of Peace

In the long run, economic policy after a civil war must promote not only economic adjustment but also a process of political adjustment: the consolidation of peace. In such a context distributional equity cannot be relegated to a lower priority than economic growth—it must be a policy objective of the first order. To promote both equity and growth, economic policy should aim not only to stimulate overall investment, but also to achieve an appropriate balance among investments in human, natural, and physical capital. Rather than focusing narrowly on demarcating the respective roles of the market and the state, economic policy during postconflictual transitions must also promote an equitable distribution of power, without which neither the market nor the state is likely to advance successfully the goals of efficiency, economic equity, and growth.

Growth and Equity Revisited

Recent years have seen a quiet revolution in economists' understanding of the relationship between growth and equity. For many years the dominant view was that there was a "great trade-off" between these objectives: Policies to improve distributional equity would exact a price via lower growth. A revisionist view popularized in the 1970s by World Bank president Robert McNamara, among others, held that "growth with equity" was possible if the income increments from growth could be directed disproportionately to the poor. In the 1990s fresh empirical and theoretical work has advanced a third and strikingly different proposition: Equity not only is compatible with growth, but positively promotes it.

On the basis of a cross-sectional study of more than 40 countries over the quarter-century from 1960 to 1985, Rodrik (1994) concludes that the countries with more equal distributions of land and income experienced more rapid growth. Primary-school enrollment—a rough indicator of equity in the allocation of human-capital investment—also had strong positive effects on growth. One avenue by which equity appears to have fostered growth was the encouragement of investment in physical capital: Land distribution and primary-school enrollment both were statistically significant determinants of the investment/GDP ratio.

In an analysis with clear relevance to El Salvador, Alesina and Perotti (1993) test the proposition that a key link in the causal chain from equity to growth is political stability. They first test whether income inequality increases political instability, then whether political instability reduces investment. To both questions the answer is "yes," a result they term "not only statistically significant, but also economically significant."

A third econometric study, by Birdsall and Sabot (1994), likewise finds that countries with lower income inequality tend to have higher growth. These authors suggest that an important equity-to-growth link is investment in basic education. High income inequality reduces both the demand for primary education and its supply. Demand is limited because poor families cannot afford to send their children to school, and supply is limited because the rich resist paying taxes to subsidize education for the poor. Again, the analysis is quite relevant to El Salvador. Whereas public expenditure on education in "medium human development" countries rose from 2.5 percent of GNP in 1960 to 4.7 percent in 1990, in El Salvador it declined over the same period from 2.3 percent of GNP to 1.8 percent (UNDP 1994d, p. 158).[2]

Writing in the *American Economic Review*, Persson and Tabellini (1994) pose the question, "Is Inequality Harmful for Growth?" They too answer in the affirmative. They present empirical evidence from a long-run historical panel of nine industrialized countries and from a postwar cross-section of 56 countries; in both, econometric analysis indicates that income inequality significantly lowers growth. Investment is again an important mediating variable: Higher inequality leads to lower investment and hence to lower growth.[3]

In a historical study of the Americas since the European conquest, Engerman and Sokoloff (1994) similarly conclude that differences in "the degree of inequality in wealth, human capital, and political power" account for the enormous long-run variation in economic performance. Their analysis highlights the historical link between extreme inequality and the cultivation of certain export crops, including sugar and coffee, a relationship that has featured prominently in El Salvador's history.

A further strand in the recent literature focuses on how inequality can impede growth in the presence of financial-market imperfections. In these theoretical models the poor are blocked from undertaking high-growth activities by their inability to afford the initial setup costs, and owing to imperfect financial markets they are unable to borrow for this purpose. Plausible examples include investment not only in physical capital but also in education. Hence policies to redistribute income and wealth, as well as policies to reduce imperfections in credit markets, can enhance growth.[4]

It is still early to speak of a new consensus on growth and equity in development economics, but signs of an impending shift are evident. In *The East Asian Miracle*, the World Bank's (1993b) widely publicized study of the economic performance of the "high-performing Asian economies," great importance is attached to the role of widespread primary education in laying the foundation for growth. Other dimensions of distributional equity also feature in the analysis. Equity is recognized as a source of political legitimacy (p. 158); land reform in Taiwan is held to have advanced both land productivity and political stability (p. 161); successful land reform in China, Japan, Korea, and Taiwan "helped to lay the foundation for rapid, shared growth" (p. 169); and the failure of the Philippines to share this success is attributed to the fact that "Philippine policy making has historically been captive to vested interests that have shaped economic policy to protect and enhance their privileged position, often to the detriment of national well-being" (p. 169). Despite these insights, however, *The East Asian Miracle* for the most part echoes the McNamara-era view that growth with equity is merely possible, stopping short of the recognition that equity actually promotes growth. Indeed, the legacy of the old trade-off mentality is still apparent in that the successful combination of rapid growth with equity is regarded as "the essence of the miracle,"[5] rather than as the logical, unmiraculous result of causal links from equity to growth.

In November 1994 a delegation from the government of El Salvador visited the World Bank and IMF in Washington, lunched with the principal author of *The East Asian Miracle*, and carried multiple copies of the book back to El Salvador. It remains to be seen whether Salvadoran policymakers will build on the vital lessons of the East Asian experience regarding the importance of equity—notably in land distribution and education—for economic growth.

Investment in Natural, Human, and Physical Capital

Investment in physical capital—the plant and equipment with which labor transforms raw materials—has long been recognized as a basic precondition for economic growth. Investment in human capital—the health and education of the labor force—is now widely agreed to be of comparable or perhaps even greater importance.[6] In El Salvador there is considerable scope for greater public and private investment in both physical and human capital. As a share of GDP, El Salvador's gross domestic investment is among the lowest in Latin America.[7] El Salvador also has the lowest primary-school enrollment ratio of any country in the Western Hemisphere, with the exception of Haiti.[8]

Investment in natural capital—that is, sources of raw materials, and sinks for the disposal of by-products of economic activity—has yet to receive comparable attention from policymakers, despite much recent talk of "sustainable development." In part this is because some regard natural capital as a fixed endowment, something that cannot be augmented by human activity, while others regard physical and human capital as perfect substitutes for natural capital. The first view gives rise to Malthusian pessimism: Humanity is on a one-way road to depletion of its natural capital, and the only question is how quickly we travel it. The second view gives rise to Panglossian optimism: As natural capital is depleted, price signals will induce smooth factor substitution and technological change, ensuring that we continue to inhabit the best of all possible worlds. Neither view recognizes the basic fact that humans can *invest in* natural capital, as well as deplete it.

For example, soil erosion and the depletion and degradation of water supplies are today critical environmental problems in many countries. El Salvador faces them in extreme forms (see Chapter 11). Yet appropriate human interventions can slow and even reverse these processes. Soil conservation measures, including terracing, afforestation, and the cultivation of cover crops and green manures, can restore soils and improve water retention. Integrated pest management can, over time, allow ecosystems to recover from the toxic legacy of indiscriminate pesticide use. Pollution control can allow water quality to recover from contamination by industrial and domestic wastes.

The problem is that many of the returns to such investments in natural capital are external, accruing to others in society, rather than internal to the investor. For example, the campesino who protects soil and water may derive some personal benefit from doing so, but much of the social benefit will be reaped by others. No market mechanism exists by which those others can pay the campesino to invest the "right" amount of time and money in natural capital. In the absence of social mechanisms to correct this market failure, there will be systematic underinvestment in soil conservation, water quality protection, and other types of natural capital. The possible corrective mechanisms include state regulation, taxes and subsidies, community management, and informal norms and sanctions, alone or in combination.

Investments in natural, human, and physical capital are highly complementary; that is, one type of investment can enhance the scale and productivity of the others. For example, investment in the human capital of the poor can lead to greater investment in natural capital by several routes: by reducing their need to degrade the environment for immediate survival; by improving their ability to combat environmental degradation of which they are victims, not perpetrators; and by diffusing knowledge of the relationships between economic activity and the environment (Segura and Boyce 1994).

Investment in physical and human capital forms critical links in the newly recognized causal chain from distributional equity to growth, as noted earlier. Investment in natural capital constitutes a further link. Greater equality of wealth and power can be expected to result in lower rates of environmental degradation by lowering the discount rates of the poor, and by enhancing the ability of the less powerful to resist the imposition of external costs on them by the more powerful (Boyce 1994). El

Salvador offers striking examples of the effects of political and economic inequalities on natural capital, ranging from the environmental damages inflicted by the war itself to the current threat to San Salvador's aquifer from attempts to urbanize disputed lands at the adjacent El Espino coffee cooperative (Barraza 1994).

Democratization: Beyond the Market and the State

In El Salvador, as elsewhere, a central element of the structural adjustment programs backed by the IFIs has been the "modernization" of the state. In practice this has primarily meant efforts to trim the size of the state by privatizing state-owned enterprises and eliminating certain agencies and functions, coupled with attempts to increase the efficiency of what remains. Such efforts are often well justified in terms of both growth and equity. What has been generally missing from IFI prescriptions, however, has been *democratization,* both in the broad sense of promoting a more equitable distribution of power, and in the narrow sense of strengthening democratic institutions such as free elections, the protection of human rights, and the administration of justice.

This omission reflects the widespread tendency among economic theorists and policymakers alike to concentrate on defining the appropriate roles of the market and the state, while abstracting from the political economies within which both are embedded. When the problems posed by the distribution of power are broached at all, the favored solution is "technocratic insulation"—defined in *The East Asian Miracle* as the ability to formulate and implement policy "with a minimum of lobbying for special favors from politicians and interest groups" (World Bank 1993b, p. 167).

Successful economic policy in El Salvador will require critical state interventions that have been underemphasized in the adjustment programs implemented to date. These include interventions to promote a more equitable distribution of income, to correct financial-market imperfections, to redress environmental externalities, to implement agrarian reforms, and to promote competitive industries in the tradeable-goods sector. But these interventions—or, for that matter, any other program of state modernization, whatever its mix of market and state—are unlikely to succeed in the absence of political reforms that establish checks on the use and abuse of power.

Democratization, not only in the narrow electoral sense but also in the broad sense of establishing an equitable distribution of power, is crucial because it provides the only secure foundation for accountability. Democratic accountability is more desirable than technocratic insulation not only because it is a virtue in itself, but also because in its absence there can be no guarantee that technocrats will in fact pursue the public interest.[9] In El Salvador it is also more viable, because technocratic insulation is quite difficult to achieve in the wake of a negotiated settlement to a civil war, the essence of which is the creation of checks and balances on the exercise of power.[10]

Democratic accountability thus can better serve the function ascribed to technocratic insulation in *The East Asian Miracle:* It can foster the formulation and implementation of policies that advance the long-term interests of the society as a whole rather than the short-term interests of a powerful few. Democracy in the broad sense provides the necessary political leverage:

- To protect basic human rights
- To safeguard the property rights of the poor
- To foster the political stability needed to encourage private investment
- To orient public investment toward advancement of the public interest
- To combat corruption
- To prevent the socially injurious exercise of market power, that is, monopolistic or oligopolistic control over input and output markets
- To secure government action to redress environmental externalities, such as industrial pollution and watershed degradation
- To minimize the extent to which selective government interventions, such as subsidized credit or export incentives, are captured by unproductive rent seekers instead of being effectively tied to economic performance
- To implement redistributive policies in pursuit of inclusive economic growth

In sum, medium- and long-term adjustment toward peace requires more than achieving macroeconomic balances between exports and imports, saving and investment, and government revenue and expenditure. It also requires equity, that is, balance in the distribution of income and wealth; balanced investment in human, natural, and physical capital; and democratization to achieve balance in the distribution of power. Economic policy during the postconflictual transition therefore must aim to secure not only stabilization and growth but also equity and the consolidation of peace. Policies that fail to build on the powerful complementarities among these objectives will ultimately fail to achieve any of them.

War and Peace: Learning from El Salvador

El Salvador's civil war provided a dramatic illustration of the potentially debilitating economic impact of great inequalities of wealth and power.

The economic, political, and social changes wrought by war have created the opportunity to at last redress these inequalities and thereby lay the foundation for a more stable and prosperous future.

Inequality and Organized Violence

The roots of war in El Salvador can be traced to the latter half of the nineteenth century, when the country became a major producer and exporter of coffee. The volcanic slopes of central and western El Salvador are admirably suited for growing coffee. Most of these lands were held by indigenous communities in the mid-nineteenth century as communal property. In response to the opportunities presented by coffee, communal property was abolished by state decree in 1882. By the turn of the century the indigenous communities had been forcibly evicted and the country's best coffee lands converted into *latifundia,* large estates owned by the "Fourteen Families" who formed the core of the ruling oligarchy.[11] The result was among the most inequitable patterns of land distribution in the world.

There is no inherent technological reason that coffee must be grown on large estates; in some countries, including Costa Rica and Colombia, coffee is widely grown on small family farms. There was a strong political logic, however, behind the large-estate mode of coffee cultivation that emerged in El Salvador. The advent of the international coffee market presented lucrative opportunities for profit, and these opportunities—and the land to realize them—were seized by those with the political and economic power to do so.

The expropriation and concentration of landholdings "freed" labor to work on the coffee estates. But much of this labor was required only for the harvest. For the remainder of the year, the seasonal laborers survived on *minifundia,* very small holdings where they grew subsistence crops such as maize and beans. A central aim of the coffee oligarchy was to keep this labor available and cheap. The deployment of military forces to maintain rural law and order and suppress intermittent peasant revolts contributed to this end.

El Salvador's agrarian structure thus was forged by a process that bears little resemblance to the stylized theories of social interaction found in neoclassical economics textbooks. It did not emerge from free exchanges among optimizing individuals, in which the more efficient producers bought land at the prevailing market price from others, who then merrily reinvested their capital in alternative lines of production in which they could better compete. Rather, the country's agrarian structure arose through intimidation, bloodshed, and hatred, the scars of which remain visible to this day.

Organized violence was necessary not only to create El Salvador's oligarchical agroexport structure, but also to maintain it. The Great Depression and the attendant slump in world coffee prices hit the Salvadoran economy hard. Coffee growers responded by slashing wages and employment. Discontent mounted, and a peasant revolt broke out in 1932. The Salvadoran Communist Party, founded three years earlier and led by Farabundo Martí, helped to lead the uprising, but it was not a carefully organized affair. The military quickly crushed the revolt, and government forces killed 10,000 to 30,000 people in the *matanza,* the slaughter, an event indelibly imprinted on the country's historical memory.

Fifty years later El Salvador was engulfed in a civil war in which the government confronted the Farabundo Martí National Liberation Front, named after the communist leader executed during the *matanza*.[12] No single event marks the beginning of the war; it gathered force in a rising tide of violence. The October 1979 coup by young army officers brought to power a junta that combined reformist policies with severe repression. In January 1980 the largest demonstration in El Salvador's history—one aim of which was "to pay homage to the *compañeros* who had died in the 1932 uprising"—was fired on by paramilitary forces who killed scores and wounded hundreds (Montgomery 1995, pp. 108–109). In March 1980 the government promulgated an agrarian reform, nationalizing large estates. That same month Archbishop Oscar Romero was assassinated during a mass; a few days later the thousands of people who gathered in central San Salvador for his funeral were attacked with bombs and machine guns by military forces, leaving scores dead. By the end of the year, virtually all avenues for peaceful opposition to the government had been closed.

The junta and its successors, including the government of José Napoleon Duarte that was elected in 1984, received strong backing from the U.S. government, which in a 1981 white paper characterized the Salvadoran conflict as "a textbook case of armed aggression by communist powers."[13] The global rivalry between the United States and the Soviet Union that was being waged in earnest in the 1980s helped to fuel the civil conflict in El Salvador. But superpower contention was not a sufficient condition for civil war. The central role of economic and political inequalities in the origins of the war was implicitly recognized in the U.S.-sponsored doctrine of low-intensity conflict, which coupled military force with economic and political reforms designed to win the "hearts and minds" of the populace.

The combination of repression and reform both reflected and reinforced divisions among political actors in El Salvador and the United States. In the United States, reformist measures were necessary for the Reagan administration to win support in the opposition-controlled Congress for stepped-up economic and military aid. In El Salvador the political opening fostered by reforms permitted some open criticism of government policies. Such criticism in turn was often met by further acts of repression.[14]

Alfredo Cristiani of the rightist Alianza Republicana Nacional (ARENA) party was elected president in March 1989. Cristiani represented what has been variously described as the "agro-industrial," "modern," or "more moderate" wing of El Salvador's ruling elite, and his ascendancy to the presidency marked a shift in the balance of power within the ARENA party.[15] While embarking on a new economic agenda of neoliberal reforms, the Cristiani government continued the low-intensity conflict strategy and the intermittent peace talks with the FMLN begun under Duarte's government.

Two dramatic events in November 1989 intensified the search for peace. The first was an FMLN offensive that brought the war to the capital and dispelled illusions that either side could soon win the war. The second was the murder of six Jesuit priests at the University of Central America in San Salvador.[16] These events helped to precipitate a shift in U.S. policy in favor of a negotiated settlement. By the end of 1990 the United States had cut military aid to El Salvador and imposed conditions whereby military aid would be eliminated altogether if the government failed to negotiate in good faith, and restored to previous levels if the FMLN did not do the same (Whitfield 1994, p. 188).

In a sense, the peace agreement that followed was born of the excesses of violence that had preceded it. Alvaro de Soto (1994, pp. xiii–xiv) expressed this paradox as follows: "The Jesuits had to lose their lives to provide the moral outrage that kept the Salvadoran armed forces on the defensive and forced the concessions at the negotiating table, without which a durable peace could not possibly have been built."

El Salvador's Negotiated Revolution

The Chapultepec Accords, signed in January 1992, aimed not only to end the civil war but also to resolve the underlying causes of the conflict. The potential for organized violence was to be reduced through demobilization of armed combatants, a purge of military officers guilty of human-rights abuses, the disbanding of paramilitary forces, and the creation of a neutral police force, the National Civilian Police (PNC). A more equitable distribution of power was to be achieved through the strengthening of democratic institutions, including reform of the judiciary, free elections open to participation by all parties, and the creation of a permanent human-rights ombudsman's office. The most pressing economic inequalities were to be redressed through land transfers to ex-combatants and FMLN supporters, microenterprise and housing assistance for ex-combatants, and expanded poverty-alleviation programs.

Under the timetable established in the peace accords, each side agreed to implement a series of measures tied to complementary actions by the other. The implementation process was beset by a number of delays, however.

These were sometimes blamed on financial constraints, but the basic reasons for the delays were generally political: The process of negotiation did not end with the signing of the accords. For example, the purge of the army officer corps occurred only after substantial delays and required strong international pressure. A particularly serious threat to the peace process came in October 1992, when the FMLN halted its phased disarmament in response to a lack of progress in the land-transfer program; this dispute culminated in a further UN-brokered agreement designed to expedite the transfer of lands. The establishment of the PNC was also subject to numerous delays. The dismantling of the National Police, originally slated for the end of 1993, in the end was not completed until January 1995.

The March 1994 elections represented a landmark in the implementation of the peace accords. The ARENA party won the presidency, the largest share of seats in the Legislative Assembly, and the vast majority of municipal elections, while the FMLN, participating in elections for the first time, finished second in the presidential race and won a number of assembly seats. Although the elections were marred by incomplete voter registration and polling irregularities, they were peaceful and the outcome was regarded as reasonably fair by most observers.[17]

The land-transfer program established by the accords and the October 1992 supplemental agreement provided for voluntary land transfers to ex-combatants on both sides and to peasant supporters of the FMLN in the former conflictive zones. Landowners who agreed to give up their lands were to be compensated at "market prices." The program was described by many as a land-for-arms exchange. De Soto and del Castillo (1994b, p. 11) observe:

> The land transfer program was certainly not an attempt at land reform or a mechanism for income redistribution as such, but rather the main venue in the Agreement through which ex-combatants and supporters of the FMLN would be reintegrated into the productive life of the country.

The fulfillment of even this limited aim has proven problematic, however: The transfer program is now far behind schedule; agricultural credit and technical assistance have not been readily available; the current macroeconomic environment is very unfavorable to agriculture; and the recipients are saddled with debts for land acquisition they are unlikely to be able to repay.

Failures to fulfill the expectations of demobilized ex-combatants have had serious implications for public security. Ex-combatants are widely cited as a factor in the country's recent crime wave. Moreover, protests by ex-combatants periodically threaten to rekindle organized violence. In January 1995, for example, former soldiers occupied the Legislative Assembly and other government buildings in San Salvador for two days, taking hundreds of hostages and blocking key highways. The weekly journal *Proceso* commented: "The actions taken by the demobilized soldiers demonstrate the extremes to which desperate people, without jobs or a future, can resort" (Center for Information, Documentation and Research Support 1995).

The Chapultepec Accords represent only initial steps toward peace in El Salvador. Further progress will require a deepening of economic reforms to achieve a more equitable distribution of wealth and income, and continued strengthening of democratic institutions to ensure the rule of law. In their absence, the roots of organized violence in El Salvador will remain intact.

Generalizing from the Salvadoran Experience

El Salvador's peace process has been facilitated by two favorable circumstances: the end of the Cold War and an abundance of foreign exchange thanks to external assistance and remittances from Salvadorans overseas.

The superpower rivalry between the United States and the Soviet Union was not the prime mover of the Salvadoran conflict. As President Alfredo Cristiani remarked at the signing of the peace accords, the war in El Salvador had "profound social, political, economic and cultural roots . . . in synthesis, the absence of a truly democratic form of life" (quoted by Whitfield 1994, p. 380). But as noted above, the U.S.–Soviet conflict added fuel to the fire. The end of the Cold War unquestionably created an external environment more conducive to peace in El Salvador.

Remittances and external assistance have cushioned the country's postconflictual transition in three ways. First, ample foreign exchange has prevented shortages of imports.[18] Second, the erosion of the living standards of the poor has been moderated, and for some reversed, by transfers from relatives abroad. Third, external resources have provided a "cushion of governability," easing political pressures and conflicts. Although the volume of these inflows in El Salvador is remarkable, the phenomenon is not exceptional in postconflictual settings: The end of a war often triggers both substantial aid and an influx of private capital.[19]

Apart from these somewhat special circumstances, many aspects of the Salvadoran experience are of general relevance to the formulation of economic policy in postconflictual transitions. A negotiated conclusion to a civil war inevitably poses the short-run problems of securing the financial and political preconditions for implementing the peace accords. In such a context there is a critical need for "peace conditionality" in the policies of the major external-assistance actors, including the international financial institutions. Over the long run, the consolidation of peace in countries emerging from civil war often hinges, as in El Salvador, on the forging of a more equitable distribution of wealth and power. If El

Salvador succeeds in its adjustment toward peace, and if the international community absorbs the lessons of that experience, then the terrible war will not have been entirely in vain.

Notes

1. For a more general analysis of coordination problems between the UN and Bretton Woods institutions, see Childers and Urquhart (1994, pp. 77–87).

2. The composition of public expenditure on education is also important. Birdsall and Sabot (1994, p. 4) observe that in Latin America as a whole the ratio of total public expenditure on education to GDP has been similar to that in East Asia, but that the share allocated to basic (as opposed to higher) education has been notably lower. They attribute this to pressure from high-income families "to channel subsidies to higher education where their children will be the beneficiaries."

3. Persson and Tabellini's theoretical analysis hypothesizes that the reason that greater inequality leads to lower investment is that in democracies the distributional conflicts generated by inequality lead to redistributive policies that tax or otherwise deter investment. They find empirical support for this in the history of Organization for Economic Cooperation and Development (OECD) countries; their postwar cross-sectional analysis also indicates that the negative relation between inequality and growth holds only in democracies. This hypothesis can be questioned. Much of the new growth and equity literature (including Persson and Tabellini's own main empirical results) suggest the opposite conclusion: that redistributive policies can enhance growth. For evidence of a positive association between democracy and private investment in Latin America, see Pastor and Hilt (1993).

4. See, for example, Galor and Zeira (1993). Danby (in this volume) discusses credit-market imperfections in El Salvador.

5. World Bank (1993b, p. 8). "The striking characteristics of the East Asian miracle are rapid and persistent growth in a context of high income equality," the volume's principal author remarked at an IMF Economic Forum. "This unusual combination indeed suggests a miracle" (*IMF Survey* 1995, p. 78).

6. *The East Asian Miracle* (World Bank 1993b, p. 52), for example, concludes that "primary education is by far the largest single contributor to the HPAEs' [high-performing Asian economies'] predicted growth rates." See also Rodrik (1994, pp. 15–22).

7. In 1992, according to the World Bank (1994d, p. 178) gross domestic investment in El Salvador stood at 16 percent of GDP; the only country in Latin America for which a lower ratio was reported was Argentina, at 15 percent.

8. The ratio for El Salvador, according to the UNDP's (1994d, pp. 156–157) *Human Development Report,* was 71 percent in 1990. For comparison, in Nicaragua the reported ratio was 76 percent, in Honduras it was 93 percent, and in Mexico it was 100 percent.

9. One can contrast the voluntarism of *The East Asian Miracle*—in which economic technocrats left to their own devices choose to advance the public interest—to Alice Amsden's (1989) characterization of the South Korean model as one in

which the government disciplined the capitalists, and the student movement in turn "disciplined" the government.

10. This can be contrasted to the situation facing an occupation government installed by external powers after an international conflict, as in postwar Korea and Japan.

11. As Bulmer-Thomas (1987, p. 340) notes, in fact some 60 families, rather than 14, came to dominate the country's economic, social, and political life.

12. The FMLN was formed in 1980 by an alliance of five parties; for details, see Montgomery (1995, Chapter 4).

13. Cited by Whitfield (1994, p. 405).

14. "Between 1983 and 1986," Whitfield (1994, pp. 242–243) remarks, "unions, popular organizations, and social forces tentatively re-emerged from the silence and fear of the early years of the war and first filled and then pushed beyond the narrow margin of legality granted them by a U.S.-driven policy committed to 'democratization' in the midst of war."

15. For discussion, see Wolf (1992), Paige (1993), and Johnson (1993).

16. The six priests, and a housekeeper and her daughter, were slain on the night of 15 November 1989. Suspicions immediately focused on the military. After the war these suspicions were confirmed by the findings of the Truth Commission for El Salvador (1993). For a thorough account, see Whitfield (1994).

17. The Secretary-General of the United Nations reported that "the elections were held under generally acceptable conditions, without any major acts of violence, although serious flaws regarding organization and transparency were detected" (United Nations Security Council 1994b, pp. 2–3).

18. This has not been an unmixed blessing: Inflows of external resources have propelled exchange-rate overvaluation, with adverse effects on producers of tradeable goods.

19. Within three years of its 1971 independence war, for example, Bangladesh received more external assistance than in its previous 24 years as East Pakistan (Hartmann and Boyce 1983, p. 268).

2

The Historical Background to the Conflict

Carlos Acevedo

In the 1980s El Salvador underwent one of the most intense civil wars in the contemporary history of Latin America. The peace agreement between the Salvadoran government and the Farabundo Martí National Liberation Front (FMLN), signed in Chapultepec, Mexico, on 15 January 1992, laid the crucial groundwork for the reconstruction of Salvadoran society and for the establishment of a democratic political system unprecedented in the country's history. But the prospects for a permanent peace in El Salvador remain uncertain.

Macroeconomic stability and growth are necessary conditions for consolidation of the peace process, but they are not sufficient. In the two decades before the war, the Salvadoran economy experienced rapid growth rates with low inflation, but this did not prevent the social crisis that culminated in the armed conflict. As President Alfredo Cristiani has said, the war in El Salvador had "profound social, political, economic and cultural roots . . . in synthesis, the absence of a truly democratic form of life" (quoted by Whitfield 1994, p. 380). If El Salvador's history during the first three-quarters of the twentieth century offers any lesson for the current postwar period, it is that the success of the peace process in the long run will hinge on the country's ability to redress the great inequalities of wealth and power that imperil both economic and political stability.

The Economic Roots of Social Conflict in El Salvador

El Salvador has long had one of the most inequitable social orders in Latin America. The origins of this order lie in the country's agroexport-based economic model, which has centered on coffee production since the last quarter of the nineteenth century. The Salvadoran state played a key role in the development of this model. The decrees of 1881–1882 expropriated the *ejidos,* or community farm lands—ostensibly for the purpose of fostering "modernization" of the country's economy through private land ownership and incentives for coffee growing. This process laid the foundations for the large plantation–small farm (*latifundio–minifundio*) system that formed the backbone of the agricultural-export model in subsequent decades. The principal beneficiaries were the large landowners and merchants who had previously been engaged in indigo production (Lindo 1990), as well as certain urban dwellers who had access to sufficient capital and/or credit to make the initial investments needed to grow coffee (Bulmer-Thomas 1987, p. 22). During this large-scale process of "competitive exclusion" (Durham 1979), the emerging coffee oligarchy gained control over no less than 40 percent of the country's total land area (Menjívar 1980, p. 23); at the same time, thousands of small farmers were driven off the lands they had tilled for years.

Because coffee profits depended heavily on control of labor costs, the state also imposed measures to guarantee the availability of cheap labor. The decrees expropriating and restricting access to land were followed by laws governing agricultural day labor and appointing rural judges, whose primary function was to recruit and control the supply of workers needed to expand coffee production. These laws were complemented by the creation of a rural police force for the coffee-producing departments in 1889 and by the formation of the National Guard in 1912 (Menjívar 1980, pp. 150–151). At the same time, agricultural workers were prohibited from organizing.

As a result of this process, the Salvadoran economy came to be centered almost entirely around the exportation of coffee. From 56 percent of the total value of the country's exports in 1890, coffee's share increased to 96 percent in 1931 (Wilson 1978, p. 209). The country's ties to the international economy, the organization of the financial system, the superstructure of the political regime, and economic-growth and social-development patterns were all largely conditioned by the nature and performance of the coffee industry. The economic power and political influence of the coffee oligarchy grew accordingly.

The world economic crisis of 1929 further intensified the concentration of land ownership as falling coffee prices forced the most vulnerable producers to sell their lands to larger coffee growers (Wilson 1978; White 1973). This phenomenon, coupled with the unrest engendered by electoral fraud in 1931 and rising unemployment, set the stage for the insurrection of 1932. That event was a sequel to earlier peasant uprisings in the coffee-producing regions in 1872, 1875, 1880, 1885, and 1898 (Menjívar 1980, p. 69; Durham 1979, p. 43).

The *matanza* of 1932, in which it is estimated that between 10,000 and 30,000 people lost their lives (Anderson 1971; Wilson 1978, p. 237), was a watershed event in the political history of El Salvador. Until 1931 the coffee oligarchy had exercised direct control over the state apparatus. The army's swift action in quelling the rebellion, however, signaled a change in the system of oligarchical domination as the military took direct control of political power in exchange for defending the interests of the agricultural elite. In subsequent years, as can be seen in Table 2.1, military officers led the government. After suppressing the peasant rebellion, the Martínez government banned all forms of organized political opposition. The Communist Party, which had played a role in organizing the uprising,[1] was banned in the Constitution of 1939. The type of authoritarian regime that emerged in the Martínez era conditioned relations between the military and civil society throughout the next 50 years.

The Bimodal Agricultural Sector

The evolution of world commodity prices after World War II made diversification of the country's agricultural exports increasingly attractive. Cotton and sugar cane joined coffee as major export crops. In the 1950s the country experienced a cotton boom, made possible by the development of more effective pesticides, success in controlling the blights that occurred in the coastal areas where most of the cotton was grown, and state investment in communications and physical infrastructure. Production of cotton increased by more than 12 times between 1950 and 1963 (Browning 1971, p. 235). By 1960 cotton accounted for 15 percent of the total value of El Salvador's exports (Dada Sánchez 1978, p. 31). Production of sugar cane also increased substantially, fueled first by domestic demand and then by increased access to the U.S. market when El Salvador received a portion of the sugar quota previously allotted to Cuba.

Whereas export crops were produced mainly on large estates (latifundios), the bulk of the subsistence crops were grown on small farms (minifundios), as shown in Table 2.2. As had occurred earlier with the expansion of coffee production, the development of sugar cane and cotton plantations exacerbated the concentration of land ownership, forcing small subsistence farmers to move to mountain slopes and to more eroded and less fertile lands. By the 1970s the Gini coefficient of land concentration in El Salvador had reached 0.83, the highest in Central America (Gordon 1989, p. 29) and one of the five highest in the world (Taylor and Jodice 1983, pp. 140–141). The 1971 agricultural census found that 1.5 percent of farms operated 49 percent of agricultural lands, while at the other extreme 87 percent of farms operated less than 20 percent of total acreage (see Table 2.3).

The steady appropriation of the available arable land by the latifundios provides a better explanation than undifferentiated "population pressure"

Table 2.1 Heads of State, 1898–1994

1898–1903	Tomás Regalado
1903–1907	Pedro José Escalón
1907–1911	General Fernando Figueroa
1911–1913	Manuel Enrique Araujo
1913–1918	Carlos Meléndez
1918–1922	Jorge Meléndez
1922–1927	Alfonso Quiñónez
1927–1931	Pío Romero Bosque
1931	Arturo Araujo
1931–1934	General Maximiliano Hernández Martínez
1934–1935	General Andrés Ignacio Menéndez
1935–1944	General Maximiliano Hernández Martínez
1944	General Andrés Ignacio Menéndez
1945	Colonel Osmín Aguirre Salinas
1945–1948	General Salvador Castañeda Castro
1948–1950	Military Government Council
1950–1956	Colonel Oscar Osorio
1956–1960	Colonel José María Lemus
1960–1961	Civilian junta
1961–1962	Civilian-military directorate
1962	Rodolfo Cordón
1962–1967	Colonel Julio A. Rivera
1967–1972	General Fidel Sánchez Hernández
1972–1977	Colonel Arturo Armando Molina
1977–1979	General Carlos Humberto Romero
1979–1982	Revolutionary juntas[a]
1982–1984	Alvaro Magaña
1984–1989	José Napoleón Duarte
1989–1994	Alfredo Cristiani
1994–	Armando Calderón Sol

Note: a. Following the coup against Romero on 15 October 1979, a series of three military-dominated juntas held power.

for the growing social tensions associated with the agroexport model. In the 80 years from 1892 to 1971, according to Durham (1979, p. 48), the availability of land to poor rural households in El Salvador dropped from 7.4 to 0.4 hectares per family. Of that decline, 85 percent can be attributed to the increased concentration of land, whereas population growth accounted for only 15 percent. In the period immediately preceding the outbreak of the armed conflict, the rural landless or near-landless population amounted to 30–37 percent of the country's total work force, one of the highest proportions in the world (Prosterman and Riedinger 1987, p. 143).

The economic growth model coupled development of the agricultural export sector with the underdevelopment of the subsistence sector. A seasonal employment system linked the two sectors. The agroexport sector required hundreds of thousands of migratory workers during the harvest, but it was unable to guarantee them a year-round salary. To maintain a ready supply of seasonal labor, the agricultural export sector relied on subsistence agriculture. During the months of unemployment between harvests, these semiproletarian workers farmed their small plots of land (minifundios),

Table 2.2　Composition of Agricultural Production, 1979

	Percentage of total agricultural value	Percentage of value on 0–10 ha. farms	Percentage of value on 10+ ha. farms
Maize	5.9	77.9	22.1
Beans	1.7	78.3	21.7
Sorghum	2.5	82.3	17.7
Coffee	68.5	17.4	82.5
Cotton	10.9	6.3	93.7
Sugar	4.2	n.a.	n.a.
Total	93.7	23.0[a]	77.0[a]

Source: El Salvador. Ministry of the Economy. *Indicadores Económicos, 1979.*
Note: a. Excludes sugar and other crops not included in table.
n.a. = data not available

Table 2.3　Farm-Size Distribution, 1971

Size of farm (hectares)	1971 agricultural census				
	Farms		Area (hectares)		Average area per farm (hectares)
	Number	Percentage of all farms	Total	Percentage of total area	
Total	270,868	100.0	1,451,895	100.0	5.4
0.7–3.5	234,941	86.7	283,311	19.5	1.2
3.5–14	24,762	9.1	237,446	16.4	9.6
14–35	6,986	2.6	215,456	14.8	30.8
35–70	2,238	0.8	154,164	10.6	68.9
> 70	1,941	0.7	561,518	38.7	289.3

Source: CEPAL 1993c, Table 14, p. 48.

cultivating corn, beans, rice, sorghum, and other subsistence crops. Because most of the cost of reproducing this migratory labor force was covered through the unpaid labor of workers' family members, the agroexport sector could offer wages that were much lower than those it would have had to pay to maintain salaried workers for the entire year. Despite the high productivity achieved by the agroexport economy,[2] the wages of farm workers in El Salvador remained low even by Third World standards.[3] In the early 1970s landless agricultural workers in El Salvador had the lowest income levels in Central America (see Table 2.4).

The bimodal agrarian structure resulted in the underutilization of both labor and land.[4] By the mid-1970s the rate of underutilization of the agricultural labor force in El Salvador was 47 percent, the highest in Latin America (USAID 1977, p. 42). At the same time, land on the latifundios also showed a high rate of underutilization. In 1961, farms larger than 50 hectares accounted for almost 60 percent of the total arable land. Less than 35 percent of this area was classified as being under cultivation; 45.8 percent

Table 2.4   **Income of Landless Agricultural Workers in Central America,**
             Early 1960s

	Annual income per family in U.S. dollars
Guatemala	340
El Salvador	229
Honduras	n.a.
Nicaragua	370
Costa Rica	727

Source: Bulmer-Thomas 1987, p. 162.
n.a. = data not available

of the land on these farms was being used as pasture.[5] In 1971, on the large estates of more than 200 hectares, only 25 percent of the land was being used to grow grain or permanent crops; the rest was being used for pasture or forestland. On farms of fewer than 10 hectares, on the other hand, 72 percent of the land was cultivated (PREALC 1977, Vol. I, p. 316).

The living conditions of the poor majority under this economic growth model were abysmal. In the mid-1970s more than 83 percent of the country's rural population was living below the poverty line (USAID 1977, p. 45). More than 80 percent of rural families had substandard housing; most dwellings had no sewage-disposal system nor electricity (USAID 1977, pp. 20–21). Of the children under five years of age, 73.4 percent showed symptoms of malnutrition (INCAP 1976). The 1971 census revealed that 115 of every 1,000 live-born children died before reaching the age of one year (PREALC 1977, Vol. II, pp. 77–78). The most prevalent diseases in the country were closely related to low income levels—nutritional deficiencies, and infections due to the lack of timely medical care (ibid., p. 85). Illiteracy in the rural population was 50 percent among those aged 15 to 19, and 74 percent among those aged 45 and over (ibid., pp. 37–38).

Faced with the land shortage and unrelenting poverty, hundreds of thousands of rural Salvadorans emigrated to Honduras in the 1950s and 1960s. In 1969, when the so-called Soccer War broke out between the two countries, an estimated 150,000 to 300,000 Salvadorans were farming Honduran land (Bulmer-Thomas 1987, p. 195). In that year Salvadorans made up an estimated 15–20 percent of the total work force in Honduras and some 30 percent of the work force on Honduran banana plantations (North 1985, p. 63). After the war, most of these emigrés were forced back to El Salvador.

The Rise and Fall of the
Import-Substitution Industrialization Model

In the 1950s a process of industrialization was instituted, with the aim of re-placing imports with domestically produced goods. This import-substitution industrialization (ISI) model did not fundamentally alter the concentration of wealth. A large proportion of the initial financing for the industrialization process came from capital amassed by the agricultural-export sector,[6] which received a substantial boost from the increase in prices for raw materials during the decade following World War II (Dada Sánchez 1978, pp. 40–41). As had happened during the initial phase of the agroexport model, the ISI model received active support from the state, which adopted an intensely protectionist policy that provided for tax breaks and discretionary application of tariffs, along with considerable investment in infrastructure works aimed at reducing industrial operating costs.

Despite these inducements, in the early stages the process of industrial development was hindered by a major obstacle: Significant limitations were placed on the growth of the domestic market by the unequal distribution of income and the wage structure associated with the agroexport model. As a result the majority of the population lacked the purchasing power necessary to generate sufficient demand for industrial goods. The General Treaty of Economic Integration signed in 1960 by Guatemala, El Salvador, Honduras, and Nicaragua—a sequel to the various bilateral free-trade agreements entered into by the countries of the region during the 1950s—offered a way to ease this constraint by expanding the potential market for Salvadoran industrial goods to the entire region, through the creation of the Central American Common Market (CACM).

With the advent of the CACM the Salvadoran manufacturing sector grew at an annual average rate of 8.1 percent between 1960 and 1970 (CEPAL 1980, p. 70). During the same period the share of manufactured goods in total value of exports increased from 5.6 percent to 28.7 percent (ibid., p. 94). By the mid-1960s, 64 percent of the country's industrial exports, mainly textiles, shoes, and pharmaceuticals, were going to other Central American countries. The majority of the remaining 36 percent were exported almost entirely to the United States. Of the latter products, a significant proportion were garments and electronic items assembled in El Salvador in plants owned by U.S. firms using imported inputs and parts.

In theory, the ISI model was intended to help the country to maintain its foreign-currency reserves and reduce its vulnerability to external fluctuations through the substitution of locally produced products for imported goods. In practice, however, costs for imported intermediate and capital goods (machinery, equipment, semifinished materials, etc.) added to the pressures on the balance of payments, while fostering a new type of dependency on imported technology needed to keep the country's industries running.[7] This was reinforced by a tariff policy that discouraged the domestic production of intermediate and capital goods (Bulmer-Thomas 1987, p. 192).

The industrialization strategy further exacerbated the concentration of wealth by favoring the establishment of relatively capital-intensive industry. In 1962, firms with more than 50 employees—which made up 8 percent of all firms with more than five employees—held 82 percent of total fixed capital (O. Menjívar n.d., p. 7). In the early 1970s, 12 percent of the firms generated more than 60 percent of total industrial output and absorbed 60 percent of the labor force in the sector (Colindres 1977, p. 129). The result was a distorted form of industrialization that was extremely capital intensive, slanted toward the production of consumer goods, highly dependent on imported products, and lacking in intersectoral links to the rest of the economy.

The ISI model proved incapable of absorbing much of the excess labor force generated under the agricultural-export model. The total number of workers employed in industry and agroindustry increased from 52,000 in 1951 to 248,000 in 1971 (North 1985, p. 53), but the manufacturing sector itself generated relatively little employment. In the early 1970s almost half the labor force classified as "industrial" was still engaged in processing coffee, cotton, and sugar (White 1973, p. 228). Between 1960 and 1970, the proportion of industrial workers in the total labor force actually declined from 13.1 percent to 11.1 percent (CEPAL 1980, p. 18). Services and commerce absorbed the largest proportion of growth in the economically active population, and by the 1970s two-thirds of the urban work force was engaged in these two areas (World Bank 1980, p. 9).

The ISI model also fostered a spatially concentrated urbanization process. Most of the industrial growth took place in the San Salvador metropolitan area, where 75 percent of the country's industrial apparatus and an even higher percentage of the service sector were concentrated in the early 1970s (World Bank 1979, p. 16). The concentration of industry in and around San Salvador provided an additional impetus for the migration from rural to urban areas that had accelerated in the 1950s as a by-product of the intensification of export-oriented agriculture.

The living conditions of much of the urban population were extremely poor. In the late 1970s, 56 percent of urban families resided in overcrowded dwellings (Murillo Salinas 1974a, pp. 431–432), 40 percent of which did not meet the minimum basic standards for habitability set by the Urban Housing Institute of El Salvador. More than 15 percent of the available housing units did not have a reliable water supply, and 25 percent lacked any kind of sanitary service. Inequality in the ownership of urban land, although less acute than in the agricultural sector, was also marked. Whereas the wealthiest 3 percent of the population held 19 percent of the residential land, with a density of seven or fewer dwellings per hectare, the poorest 29 percent of the population was crowded into an area equal to 14 percent of the total residential land, with a density of 57 to 80 dwellings per hectare (Murillo Salinas 1974b). Wage levels, although higher than in rural areas, were not sufficient to enable most urban workers to adequately meet their basic needs. In the late 1970s, 42 percent of urban workers were earning an income that placed them below the official poverty line of 100 colones per month (World Bank 1980, p. 8).

Because the ISI model failed to address directly the income-distribution problems underlying the process of accumulation promoted by the export-oriented agriculture, it reproduced at the urban level the inequalities prevailing in the agricultural sector. Indeed, the model in many ways exacerbated the tremendous social disparities in the country. By 1974 the poorest 20 percent of the population was receiving only 2.8 percent of total income, while the share of the richest 20 percent had risen to 66.4 percent (Rosenthal 1982, p. 33).

The Failure of the Economic Model and Weakening of Authoritarian Rule

Between 1960 and 1978 the Salvadoran economy grew at an average annual rate of 5.4 percent. Gross agricultural output increased by 4.1 percent per year during the same period, one of the most dynamic sector growth rates in all of Latin America (López Córdovez 1994, p. 25). Notwithstanding this vigorous growth, socioeconomic disparities fueled political strife.

The ISI strategy set in motion—albeit unintentionally—a series of social changes that would later have a significant impact in terms of the restructuring of Salvadoran society. One such change was the emergence of an urban middle class, which developed in the course of the expansion of commerce and services associated with the industrialization process. As this middle class gained relative weight within the socioeconomic system, a certain broadening of the political spectrum took place. Meanwhile, beginning in the mid-1960s El Salvador experienced significant growth in the number of labor organizations (almost all of which were urban), although by the end of the decade only a modest 5 percent of the total labor force belonged to these organizations (Menjívar 1982, p. 137).

The inflationary pressures induced by the rapid increase in world prices at the beginning of the 1970s complicated this situation. Following the first oil-price shock of 1973–1974 El Salvador, like the rest of Central America, was faced with double-digit inflation after decades of remarkable price stability (see Table 2.5). In response, Salvadoran industrial groups intensified the trend toward consolidation with the aim of realizing economies of scale that would reduce their operating costs. Small and medium-size firms, which were more vulnerable to the effects of inflation, were driven out of business. These dynamics swelled the ranks of the unemployed in the industrial sector. At the same time, despite the stirrings of organized labor, workers had considerably less power to protect themselves

Table 2.5   Average Annual Inflation Rates in Central America, 1950–1979 (%)

Years	Guatemala	El Salvador	Honduras	Nicaragua	Costa Rica
1950–1960	0.9	3.0	2.0	4.9	1.8
1960–1970	0.7	0.8	2.2	1.9	2.0
1970–1971	–0.5	0.5	2.3	1.6	3.0
1971–1972	0.6	1.5	5.3	1.1	4.6
1972–1973	13.6	6.4	4.5	20.1	15.3
1973–1974	16.6	16.9	13.4	23.3	30.1
1974–1975	13.1	19.2	6.4	2.7	17.4
1975–1976	10.7	7.0	4.8	2.8	3.5
1976–1977	12.6	11.9	8.4	11.4	4.2
1977–1978	7.9	13.2	6.2	4.6	6.0
1978–1979	11.5	15.9	12.5	48.1	9.2

Source: Bulmer-Thomas 1987, p. 202.

from inflation than did business owners. This translated into a rapid decline in real wages.

Unlike the industrial sector, the agroexport sector profited from the increase in world prices, which provided an additional stimulus for export-oriented agriculture. The intensification of export agriculture exerted additional pressure on the land and capital markets, and led to a drop in subsistence agriculture in per capita terms and an even more regressive distribution of agricultural income (Bulmer-Thomas 1987, pp. 150, 200).

This phenomenon was not unique to El Salvador; it occurred throughout the region. However, the other Central American countries had used the Alliance for Progress to undertake at least some restructuring of their land-tenure systems in preceding years. In El Salvador agrarian reform had been considered taboo since the peasant uprising of 1932,[8] and the only escape for the dispossessed peasant population had been migration to Honduras.

Under these circumstances, the 1969 war with Honduras had catastrophic consequences. El Salvador simultaneously lost its principal intraregional export market, access to the land route for transporting its goods to the southern part of the Central American isthmus, and the outlet for its landless peasant farmers. The return of Salvadorans who had been living in Honduras compelled the government to broach the issue of agrarian reform.[9] The Plan for Economic and Social Development for the five-year period 1973–1977, formulated at the start of Colonel Molina's presidency, incorporated agrarian reform as one of its strategic policy lines. But opposition led by associations tied to the agricultural-export sector was so strong that the government was forced to retreat. At the same time, the new government's partiality toward business owners in their conflicts with labor propelled the labor movement toward more radical positions.

The Salvadoran political system was ill-equipped to mediate effectively among contending interests and address demands for greater economic and social democracy. Since 1932 the military had ruled through a series of "official" parties—the Pro-Patria Party, founded in 1934; the Revolutionary Party of Democratic Unity (PRUD), formed in 1949; and the Party of National Conciliation (PCN), established in 1961. The latter party served as an instrument of political control for the regimes of Molina (1972–1977) and Romero (1977–1979). Electoral fraud in both 1972 and 1977 undermined the legitimacy of the political system, which led to greater radicalization of the middle and working classes.

In this context, leftist political-military organizations began to emerge. The first of them, the Popular Liberation Forces (FPL), was founded in 1970 by Salvador Cayetano Carpio from a faction that split from the Communist Party. In 1972 the People's Revolutionary Army (ERP) was established. In 1975, following the assassination of Roque Dalton, the ERP split and the Armed Forces of National Resistance (FARN) were formed. At the same time, the so-called mass organizations of workers and peasants appeared on the sociopolitical scene. The United Front for Popular Action (FAPU) came into being in 1974, followed the next year by the People's Revolutionary Bloc (BPR). Both groups played a crucial role in organizing large demonstrations against the Romero regime beginning in 1977.[10]

The state's increasingly hostile response to its political opponents accelerated polarization and broadened the social base of support for the left. Government repression escalated with the promulgation in December 1977 of the Law on the Protection and Assurance of Public Order, which gave the armed forces carte blanche to seize land, dissolve strikes, suppress demonstrations, and carry out arbitrary detentions (Gordon 1989, p. 246). Romero was ousted in a coup d'état staged by a relatively progressive segment of the military on 15 October 1979. The new government proved unable to curb the process of polarization, however. In 1980 the leftist forces coalesced in the FMLN. Under a state of siege declared in March 1980, the state security apparatus, together with rightist paramilitary organizations, escalated repression of opposition social and political organizations, regardless of their ideological orientation. By the end of the year virtually all legal avenues of social and party organization, mobilization, and protest had been closed.

The military offensive launched by the FMLN on 10 January 1981 marked the formal start of the armed conflict. But this was merely the culmination of the great socioeconomic and political pressures that had been mounting for decades in Salvadoran society, which successive authoritarian regimes were incapable of defusing.

Notes

1. In the course of the insurrection, the military captured and executed Agustín Farabundo Martí, who had helped to found the Communist Party of El Salvador in 1929.

2. In the early 1950s Salvadoran coffee yields were the highest in the world (Bulmer-Thomas 1987, p.154). By 1957–1958, cotton yields were also the highest in the world (ibid., p. 156).

3. In the 1950s, Ivory Coast coffee workers, for example, were earning 20 percent more in real terms than their counterparts in El Salvador (White 1973, p. 123).

4. The underutilization of land and labor—key inputs in any agricultural production function—is an often-observed manifestation of the economic inefficiency deriving from the dichotomy between land ownership and the labor force (see Sen 1975, pp. 60–71).

5. Moreover, 32 percent of the latifundio land classified as "under cultivation" in the early 1970s in fact was not being farmed (Durham 1979, p. 51).

6. Of the 42 major industrial ventures launched prior to 1960, 25 were held by groups of coffee growers (Mena 1976).

7. In 1970, 44.3 percent of El Salvador's industries were operating with imported raw materials and intermediate goods (PREALC 1977, Vol. II, Table 59).

8. In 1967 mere support for an agrarian reform initiative by the Reform Action Party (PAR) was enough to have it declared illegal.

9. The closure of the Honduran border changed the direction of Salvadoran migration. After 1970 the flow of Salvadoran emigrants shifted toward the United States, Belize, Mexico, Nicaragua, and Costa Rica. By 1976 the number of Salvadorans residing illegally in the United States was estimated at 225,000 (Gordon 1989, p. 123).

10. As minister of defense during the Molina administration, General Romero had overseen numerous repressive measures, including the massacre of student protesters in 1975 and the military siege of several rural communities in 1974–1975.

3

The War Economy of the 1980s

Alexander Segovia

In the late 1970s a series of adverse factors of both external and internal origin precipitated the most profound economic and social crisis in El Salvador's history. The crisis was subsequently exacerbated by the devastating effects of an armed conflict that raged throughout the 1980s, costing some 75,000 lives, leaving thousands of people wounded, orphaned, and disabled, and provoking a mass migration out of the country that eventually involved some 20 percent of the Salvadoran population. The war also caused huge material losses: War-related damages are estimated to have totaled some U.S.$1.5 billion in infrastructure alone, with replacement costs calculated at $1.63 billion (MIPLAN 1992b, p. 4).

Adding fuel to this social fire was a series of natural catastrophes in the 1980s, including several droughts and a major earthquake. The latter struck the San Salvador metropolitan area on 10 October 1986, killing 1,200, injuring 300,000, and leaving 300,000 people homeless. The quake also caused enormous material damage, with replacement costs estimated in late 1986 at $1.2 billion (IDB 1987, p. 8).

The damage wrought by these social and natural disasters was exacerbated by the policy response of the government. Falling output, rising inflation, and political instability necessitated attention to the issue of macroeconomic stabilization. The government attempted to apply the typical medicine of government-deficit cutting and currency devaluation throughout the decade, a strategy that was problematic in a wartime setting and imposed its own set of economic and social costs.

This chapter presents an overview of El Salvador's macroeconomy during the 1980s, emphasizing the nature and magnitude of the economic and social crisis and describing the logic and effectiveness of the economic-policy response to that crisis. The chapter contains four major sections. The first analyzes the dominant features of the Salvadoran economy, the characteristics and scope of the crisis of the 1980s, and the impact of that crisis on the primary macroeconomic variables. The second section examines

31

the implications for the Salvadoran economy of a phenomenon that grew increasingly important in the 1980s, namely, the influx of foreign capital, mainly from the U.S. government and, to a lesser extent, from Salvadoran emigrants living in the United States. The third section looks at the principal characteristics, as well as the economic and social costs, of the adjustment that took place in the country during most of the last decade. The fourth section of the chapter explores the economic, social, and political implications of the changes of the 1980s, particularly with regard to the shifting political basis for adjustment and reform. The chapter's coverage extends to 1989, when a new government took the reins of power and began to implement another strategy for macroeconomic stabilization and restructuring.

The Nature of the Economic Crisis of the 1980s

Basic Features of the Salvadoran Economy[1]

In order to comprehend the underlying causes and the specific characteristics of the crisis in El Salvador, as well as the results achieved through the economic policy applied during the last decade, it is important both to review the basic features of the Salvadoran economy in the late 1970s, and to understand the way in which short-term macroeconomic balance is achieved in this sort of economy.

The most prominent feature of the Salvadoran economy is its reliance on external resources, a characteristic it shares with many other Central American countries. The productive apparatus, particularly in manufacturing, depends heavily on imports of intermediate and capital goods, and limitations on the growth of output in the short term are therefore determined by the level of reserves the country has at its disposal at any given moment.[2] Unfortunately, El Salvador's economy has traditionally relied on a handful of primary export products to generate foreign exchange. With international markets for these products volatile, foreign-currency receipts vary from year to year and growth is therefore also volatile, unless the country borrows from foreign sources or draws down reserves in periods of reduced export earnings. Foreign exchange, moreover, plays a key role in the inflation process. Although monetary variables and domestic food prices also matter,[3] most pricing is via markup; increases in the cost of imported intermediates, perhaps due to a foreign exchange shortage, will raise both costs and inflationary expectations.[4]

Thus, foreign exchange is important to both growth and inflation. On the one hand, foreign exchange shortfalls are likely to induce stagflation; on the other, the greater the availability of foreign currency (through reserves, loans, or transfers), the greater the possibility that adjustment measures to any particular external or internal shock can be introduced gradually, thus significantly reducing their costs. Keeping foreign exchange available is particularly important because in an economy like El Salvador's, traditional stabilization policies are not likely to bring a quick recuperation in private investment; indeed, such policies are likely to negatively affect those variables—the real interest rate, effective demand, the availability of credit, and the level of public investment—that determine private investment in the short run. As a result, much of our understanding of the internal behavior of the Salvadoran economy must be built on an analysis of the external sector, a procedure we follow in the next subsection.

The Magnitude of the Economic and Social Crisis, and the Economic-Policy Response

The onset of El Salvador's economic crisis in the late 1970s was directly related to a series of adverse external phenomena. The decline of international and regional demand and a reduction in prices for the country's principal export products were accompanied by a steep rise in petroleum prices and higher world inflation (and hence higher import prices). Hence the country's terms of trade deteriorated sharply (see Figure 3.1). The resulting shortage of foreign exchange was exacerbated by the drop in private foreign financial flows, the increase in service on the external debt that had been amassed in earlier years (BCR 1980, p. 1), and massive capital flight.[5] The latter phenomenon was triggered partly by declines in the value of coffee exports, which led producers to shift their capital assets,

Figure 3.1   Terms of Trade, 1975–1989 (1975 = 100)

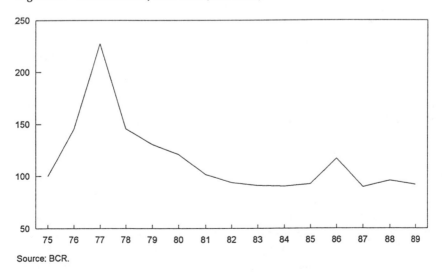

Source: BCR.

and partly by the negative reaction to the government's nationalization of the trade in coffee exports.

The foreign exchange shortage came to a head in 1980. Given the extreme dependence of the productive apparatus on imports of intermediate and capital goods, this resulted in a sharp drop in production and employment. Moreover, the scarcity of foreign currency brought an end to the financial and exchange stability the country had enjoyed for more than 50 years and led to the creation of a large black market in dollars, which was partly fed by funds sent back by Salvadoran emigrants. The black market also became an important vehicle for capital flight, further fueling the cycle of slowing growth and accelerating inflation.

The country's economic plight was aggravated by internal political strife, which manifested itself in takeovers of factories and farmlands, sabotage of production facilities, and abductions and murders of business executives. This situation engendered a climate of widespread anxiety and uncertainty, which grew worse with the institution of structural reforms in 1980, including agrarian reform and nationalization of the banking system and of the export trade in coffee and sugar—measures that were interpreted in business sectors as the start of a process of socialization of the economy.[6]

Table 3.1 reveals the impact of these economic and political pressures on the Salvadoran economy. Between 1979 and 1985, 248 businesses closed temporarily or permanently, affecting a total of 27,413 jobs. The sharpest negative impacts were felt in 1979–1981, the period in which the political-military conflict escalated in urban areas, especially in the country's industrial center of San Salvador.[7] Real GDP suffered a cumulative drop of 24.3 percent over the period 1979–1982, with the industrial, agricultural, and construction sectors experiencing declines of 34 percent, 12.7 percent, and 44.3 percent, respectively (see Figure 3.2). Reduced output, lower import levels, and the climate of political insecurity combined to produce a nearly 90 percent decline in private investment during the period 1979–1981, further worsening the economic scenario.

The government's response during the first years of economic crisis (1979–1980) was expansion oriented and relied on administrative (rather than market) mechanisms. The government attempted to prop up demand by increasing foreign borrowing, hoping to cover the deficit in the current account and relieve the foreign exchange–induced pressures on growth and inflation (BCR 1980, p. 21). To do this, the government sought support from international lending agencies, in particular the International Monetary Fund (IMF).[8] The authorities also implemented an anti-cyclical policy based on public investment projects in order to compensate for the enormous decline in private investment (BCR 1980, p. 29). This approach, embodied in the Emergency Plan instituted in 1980, was financed with external resources and internal credit from the Central Reserve Bank (Banco

Table 3.1   Businesses Closed Temporarily or Permanently and Jobs Affected, 1979–1985

Year	Businesses closed	Jobs affected
1979	29	6,981
1980	108	9,964
1981	84	5,779
1982	16	2,070
1983	2	917
1984	3	28
1985	6	1,674
Total	248[a]	27,413

Source: Ministry of Labor and Social Security.
Note: a. Of this total, 69 subsequently reopened.

Central de Reserva, or BCR), which also devoted considerable resources to financing an ongoing agrarian reform. In 1980 the BCR thus became the principal supplier of credit for the economy as its overall financing reached unprecedented levels (BCR 1980, p. 29). As a result of this anti-cyclical policy, consumption and public investment were virtually the only variables that showed any dynamism during the first few years of the crisis.

On the administrative side, the government sought to relieve the pressure of foreign exchange by subjecting imports to a system of permits, prohibitions, and prior-deposit requirements. The government also attempted to tame inflation by stimulating food production, establishing maximum prices for a series of strategic products, and freezing salaries, wages, and social benefits for workers.[9] Finally, the government sought to implement structural reforms, including agrarian reform. From an economic and social standpoint, this reform program was intended to address long-standing problems relating to the concentration of income and wealth; politically the reforms were aimed at isolating radical groups on both the left and the right.

Regrettably, but predictably, the expansion-oriented public-spending policy and the growing costs of the armed conflict brought an unprecedented increase in the fiscal deficit (see Figure 3.3 and Appendix Table A.2c). This occurred, in part, because public revenues declined during this period as a result of the economic stagnation, increased tax evasion, and lower prices for the principal export products. With production falling and foreign currency scarce, short-term supply was fixed and the widening deficit added to the inflationary pressures on the cost side.[10]

By 1981 the expansion-oriented economic strategy was abandoned. With the armed conflict heating up and public finance under pressure, the government launched an austerity program that called for reducing aggregate demand through tighter monetary controls; curtailing nonmilitary

Figure 3.2   Growth of GDP and Major Sectors, 1978–1988

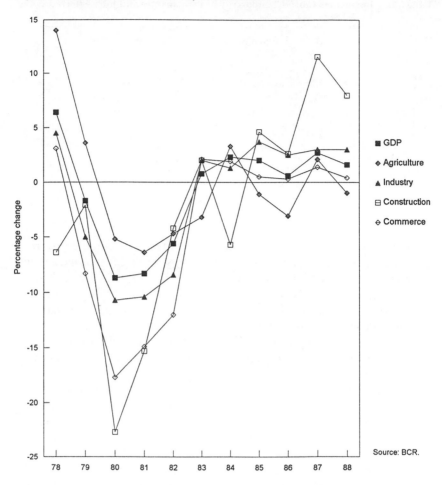

Source: BCR.

government spending, especially public investment; freezing wages, salaries, and the prices of some basic goods and services; increasing charges for some public services; and adopting stricter exchange controls.

This shift toward austerity was consolidated in 1982 when a new Government of National Unity came to power. In July 1982 the new government signed an agreement with the IMF for a standby credit in the amount of $50 million and compensatory financing for $37 million. In return, the government agreed to a one-year stabilization program whose principal features included the creation of a parallel foreign exchange market (designed as a way to move toward a liberalized exchange policy by shifting transactions to the "free" market);[11] differential adjustment of interest rates; reduction of the public-sector deficit, especially that of the central government; and an increase in the price of revenue stamps.[12]

Figure 3.3   Fiscal Deficit, 1978–1989 (As a percentage of GDP)

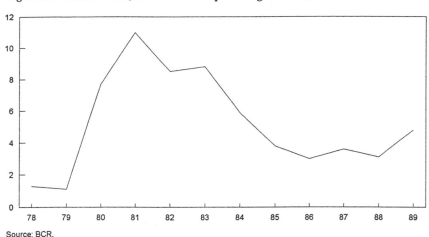

Source: BCR.

The signing of the agreement with the IMF enabled the government to gain access to external financial resources, especially from the United States. U.S. aid began to increase substantially in 1982, reaching its peak level in 1987. Thanks to this influx of foreign aid, the country was able to surmount its foreign exchange crisis, reverse the recessionary trend of earlier years, and even obtain positive growth rates for the remainder of the decade. Unfortunately, the economy's growing dependence on politically determined foreign aid meant that certain underlying macro imbalances—which would become evident if aid was ever to be withdrawn—never really corrected. Thus, the Salvadoran macroeconomy gave a positive, but fragile, image of successful "adjustment."

The country's economic policy underwent another change when the Christian Democratic Party (PDC) came to power in 1984. Recognizing the new flow of U.S. aid, the PDC initially shifted from austerity to expansion, adopting policies designed to increase salaries for public-sector employees and minimum wages for urban workers, to selectively reduce interest rates and increase the availability of credit for the public and private sectors, and to control the resulting inflationary pressure via a temporary law regulating prices for a set of basic goods and services. With regard to foreign exchange, the policy of gradually shifting commercial transactions from the official market to the parallel market was continued—by June 1985 more than half of all imports and exports of goods and services were being channeled through the parallel market (GTZ 1989, p. 36). This prompted an effective depreciation of the exchange rate, triggering a rise in inflation.

Budgetary pressures intensified through 1985, partly because of increasing public employment as well as larger outlays for defense and

Table 3.2   Economic Assistance Pledged by USAID, 1980–1989 (U.S. fiscal years)

	1980	1981	1982	1983	1984	1985	1986	1987	1988	1989	Total
					Millions of U.S. dollars						
Loans	40	71	71	87	81	70	52	53	35	35	595
Grants	13	35	122	175	142	359	266	416	290	258	2,081
Total	59	106	193	262	223	429	318	469	325	293	2,675
					Percentage structure						
Loans	69	67	37	33	36	16	16	11	11	12	22
Grants	31	33	63	67	64	84	84	89	89	88	78
Total	100	100	100	100	100	100	100	100	100	100	100

Source: Rosa and Segovia 1989, p. 235.

Table 3.3   Exchange Rates and Inflation, 1978–1990

	1978	1979	1980	1981	1982	1983	1984	1985	1986	1987	1988	1989	1990
					Exchange rate (Colones per U.S. dollar)								
Official	2.50	2.50	2.50	2.50	2.50	2.50	2.50	2.50	5.00	5.00	5.00	5.00	5.00
Parallel					3.78	4.00	4.80					5.60	7.60
Black market	n.a.	n.a.	n.a.	n.a.	4.15	4.00	4.10	6.50	5.14	5.50	5.30	6.17	8.14
					Inflation rate								
Annual average	13.3	12.1	17.4	14.8	11.7	13.1	11.7	22.3	31.9	24.9	19.8	17.6	24.0

Source: Segovia 1991, p. 18.
n.a. = data not available

Figure 3.4   Inflation, 1978–1989

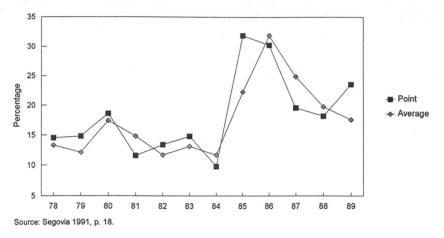

Source: Segovia 1991, p. 18.

security. Since no tax reform aimed at increasing revenues was instituted (with the exception of another increase in the price of revenue stamps in 1985), the government was eventually forced to begin reducing public investment and social spending. By this time the combination of fiscal laxity and exchange-rate depreciation had driven inflation to over 20 percent, a figure without precedent in the country's post–World War II history (see Table 3.3 and Figure 3.4).

In January 1986 the government launched a new stabilization effort, this time under the aegis of the United States Agency for International Development (USAID). The cornerstone of this program was a 100 percent nominal devaluation of the currency, as a result of which the parallel market was eliminated and a single exchange rate of 5.00 colones to the dollar was established.[13] On the fiscal side, the government adopted a temporary, one-year windfall tax on coffee export earnings and a selective tax on consumption, eliminated tax exemptions for government-owned companies, and instituted an income-tax reform. On the monetary side, a ceiling of 100 million colones was placed on public-sector financing, active and passive interest rates were raised, and a broad program of credit to the private sector was implemented.[14]

For various reasons, the stabilization program did not yield the desired results. Exports did not respond to the real devaluation of 32 percent achieved by consolidating the controlled and parallel markets, mostly because the majority of exports was already in the parallel market. The new single rate did benefit those few products such as coffee and sugar that had been subject to the controlled rate, but since the short-run supply elasticity of these items is low, devaluation yielded windfall profits and not an export surge. Moreover, the initial advantage afforded by the devaluation was quite short lived, because inflation soon eroded the depreciation of the exchange rate (Saca and Rivera 1987, p. 341).

Another factor in the program's lack of success was exogenous: The severe earthquake on 10 October 1986 compelled the government to increase spending, making it impossible to meet fiscal and monetary goals. Current expenditures also grew significantly as a result of the rise in inflation and an increase in salaries for public employees. Finally, the program met with political resistance from both business and labor.[15]

As the program's failure became evident, USAID recommended a second devaluation and threatened to withhold aid disbursements if the government did not comply. The government resisted and instead attempted to apply a second fiscal package that included increases in direct taxes, as well as a variable surcharge on the levy on taxable capital assets of 100,000 colones or more. The latter drew strong and effective opposition from the private sector[16] and the government was therefore forced to pursue deeper cuts in nonmilitary expenses, especially in the areas of public investment and social spending, a strategy that reinforced the decadal shift in the composition of government expenditures toward the military. Financial imbalances nonetheless continued, with the sole improvement being some reduction in inflation—largely due to the USAID-opposed policy of fixing the exchange rate.

External-Resource Flows, Adjustment, and the Transformation of Salvadoran Society

As poor as this adjustment record may seem, it would have been worse had it not been for a fundamental shift in the supply of foreign exchange. Beginning in the early 1980s, external nonmerchandise flows—mainly in the form of aid grants from the United States and, to a lesser extent, from money sent back by Salvadorans living abroad[17]—replaced coffee as the principal source of foreign currency in El Salvador's economy. This massive influx of external resources enabled the country to overcome its balance-of-payments crisis (Segovia 1991, 1994a) and maintain some degree of exchange-rate stability. These external financial flows also helped the government maintain a higher level of domestic investment and government spending than would have been possible otherwise. Thus, official foreign aid—and later funds from Salvadorans living abroad—helped to mitigate the social costs of the war and lessen the usual social and economic wreckage associated with stabilization policies.[18]

This positive role for external flows in the short run meant, however, that El Salvador was able to postpone necessary adjustment measures. Indeed, because aid was mostly given for political reasons, there was a much lower level of conditionality in terms of economic policy than is usually applied to developing economies (Rosa and Segovia 1989; Rosa 1993a). Even when the United States did make the adoption of stabilization policies a condition for the allocation of aid, the various Salvadoran governments had considerable leeway for negotiation and were able to obtain favorable terms by raising concerns relating to national security or internal political instability (Segovia 1991; CEPAL 1993a; IDB 1993a).[19] As a result, structural imbalances worsened while external dependence intensified.

This dependence nevertheless allowed the primary donor, the United States, to promote an ambitious program of economic and social remodeling.[20] For example, many of the structural reforms introduced in 1980 by the Salvadoran government (agrarian reform, nationalization of the banking system and of coffee and sugar exports) were strongly encouraged by the U.S. government and fostered the emergence of new economic and social agents.[21] According to CEPAL (1993a), the agrarian reform reduced the average size of large estates from 410 to 190 manzanas and promoted the emergence of cooperatives (which by 1988–1989 controlled 38.7 percent of total production of export crops). These new cooperatives are characterized by their high level of organization and their activism in the political sphere, which have changed the constellation of political forces within the country, particularly in light of the declining relative power of traditional landholders.[22]

After 1984 USAID began to advocate a strategic change in policy: the institution of a new model of development based on the promotion of non-traditional exports. When the Christian Democratic government proved reluctant to adopt this model, USAID began to work from outside the government to establish a social base of support for the model by financing the Foundation for Economic and Social Development (FUSADES), an organization closely connected to the private sector. Between 1984 and 1992, some $100 million was channeled into FUSADES (Rosa 1993a, p. 4). This effort succeeded in enlisting the business sector, especially big business, into a nongovernmental institutional framework prepared to take on the functions abandoned by the state and to serve as counterparts to international cooperation (Barry 1993, p. 1). In short, the United States actively intervened to create both a new economy and the political and institutional constituencies to support it.

One striking contradiction, however, is that U.S. aid, by propping up the Salvadoran colón, was simultaneously undermining the economic basis for a new model of export-led growth. While the "space" provided by external flows softened the need for adjustment and allowed both the U.S. and the Salvadoran governments to engage in a project of profound economic and social restructuring, the failure to bring El Salvador's economy back in line with its own domestic export capacity meant that the supposed goal of policy change—a competitive economy for world markets—was being further undermined.

The Economic and
Social Consequences of Adjustment

The Consequences of the Fiscal Adjustment

Although foreign aid allowed the government to postpone balancing internal and external accounts and to pursue a broader agenda of economic restructuring, there were significant consequences to the adjustment policies pursued. According to USAID (1994b), urban poverty climbed from 50 percent in 1976 to 61 percent in 1988. CEPAL data (1993a) indicate that the proportion of the Salvadoran population living in poverty increased from 68 percent to 74 percent between 1980 and 1990, while the proportion living in "extreme" poverty rose from 51 percent to 56 percent. Together with the war, fiscal retrenchment—as indicated by a fall in public spending from 25 percent of GDP in 1980 to 11 percent in 1990—was a key factor in the increase in poverty, the sharp decline in wages, and the dramatic fall in most economic and social indicators during the 1980s.[23] Public spending could have been less drastically reduced had the government been able to enhance its revenues, but throughout the 1980s the private sector resisted any meaningful tax reform. Meanwhile, the relative share of military spending rose owing to the political-military context, crowding out spending on education and health (see Figure 3.5 and Appendix Table A.6). The government grew increasingly dependent on external funding to do what little it could in the way of social programs.[24]

The fiscal austerity of the 1980s also brought about a deterioration in the country's economic and social infrastructure.[25] By the end of the decade the bulk of current expenditure (more than 60 percent) was being devoted to the payment of salaries—even though the real wages in the public sector had fallen over 30 percent (see Figure 3.6). In the meantime,

Figure 3.5   Composition of Government Expenditure, 1975–1987

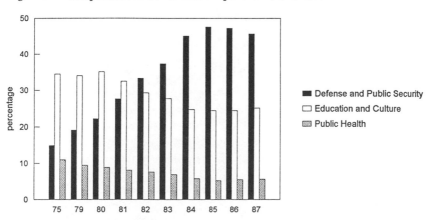

Ministerio de Hacienda and BCR.

spending on physical resources (equipment and supplies) decreased so much that by 1989 only 16 centavos out of every colón was being spent for this purpose (Rivera Campos and Gallagher 1994, p. 21). In short, the Salvadoran government's social expenditures fell, administrative and institutional capabilities were eroded, and growth-promoting public investment was slashed.

The Salvadoran government's austerity measures were thus selective: Defense expenditure was protected; social spending was not. The pursuit of a fiscal adjustment so costly to both social peace and long-run growth was partly due to the pressure of international lenders. The international organizations, often led by USAID, assumed that El Salvador's external and internal imbalances were the consequence of excess domestic demand caused by the fiscal deficit, which in turn had been caused by excess public spending. As a result, the international agencies recommended the application of orthodox stabilization policies aimed at reducing nominal aggregate demand and absorption through monetary and fiscal restraint.

But whereas fiscal deficits at the beginning of the decade may have been linked to excess spending, due to expenses associated with structural reform and the use of public investment as an anti-cyclical mechanism, during the second half of the decade spending as a percentage of GDP fell below the levels of the early 1970s.[26] The orthodox fiscal obsession likely misdiagnosed inflationary dynamics in El Salvador, which have as much to do with costs and inflationary expectations as with monetary expansion. At the same time, the international agencies overlooked the negative distributive effects of the policies they were recommending and failed to propose policies for combating poverty in the country.[27] Social programs were viewed as an "add-on" to be included only when external resources could

Figure 3.6   Real Salaries, 1980–1988 (1980 = 100)

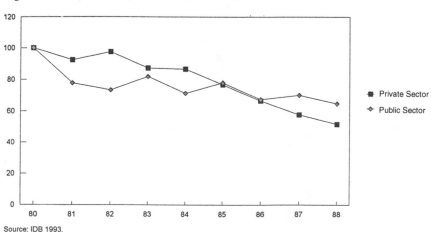

Source: IDB 1993.

be found, leaving such efforts extremely vulnerable in the future—even as they have become more necessary to secure social stability and guarantee the peace.

The War-Related Costs of Adjustment

The costs of Salvadoran adjustment in the 1980s cannot, of course, simply be attributed to the application of stabilization policies. Adjustment costs associated with the war were just as high or even higher during some periods, and more than $1.5 billion worth of social and economic infrastructure was destroyed as a result of the armed conflict (see Table 3.4).

The war also induced a series of changes that have transformed the social and economic structure of the country. Some one million Salvadorans emigrated to the United States, mostly to flee the conflict, and within the country approximately 500,000 people were displaced. The emigration reduced the overall size of the labor force; this may have alleviated social pressures somewhat, but it also implied significant costs for the country in terms of human capital.

Meanwhile, the internal migration due to displacement made the country's population increasingly urban. Whereas the urban population increased from 36.5 percent to 39.5 percent of the total population between 1950 and 1971 (Lungo 1994, p. 5), by 1992 the proportion had climbed to 47 percent. According to UNICEF data cited by the Ministry of Planning (MIPLAN 1991c, p. 8), of the 500,000 displaced persons, half are children;

Table 3.4   Costs of Direct and Indirect Damages Caused by the Armed Conflict and Estimated Reconstruction Costs (millions of U.S. dollars)

Sector	Direct costs	Indirect costs	Total costs	Reconstruction costs[a]
Electricity	63.7	191.1	254.8	310.6
Telecommunications	84.8	242.3	327.0	340.0
Water supply and sewerage	6.0	351.9	357.9	375.0
Railroads	25.3	66.4	91.7	77.0
Roads and bridges	65.4	233.3	298.7	285.0
Airport		26.2	26.2	36.0
Ports		26.6	26.6	26.0
Transportation	43.6	50.7	94.3	66.0
Education	2.1	8.9	11.0	12.5
Health	0.1	17.5	17.6	17.7
Municipal facilities	0.3	1.0	1.3	1.3
Housing	5.0	15.0	20.0	23.0
Agriculture	32.8	20.0	52.6	57.5
Total	329.0	1,250.8	1,579.8	1,627.5

Source: MIPLAN 1992b.
Note: a. Revised figures.

Table 3.5   Occupational Structure, San Salvador Metropolitan Area, 1978 and 1991
(percent)

Sector	1978		1991	
	Formal	Informal	Formal	Informal
Industry	75.5	24.5	59.7	40.3
Construction	94.7	5.3	67.1	32.9
Transportation	82.0	18.0	43.3	56.7
Established commerce	43.9	56.1	32.6	67.4

Source: Briones 1991.

and there are approximately 100,000 children between the ages of six and 18 working on the streets of El Salvador. Forty-seven percent of these children migrated from the departments most affected by the conflict. The phenomenon of internal migration produced pressure on public services, and led to a relative shortage of labor in rural areas.

Partly as a result of this situation, the country's occupational structure underwent profound change. The agricultural sector employed fewer people—the proportion of the economically active population working in the sector declined from two-thirds in 1950 to half in 1980 and 45 percent in 1985. At the same time, employment in the commercial and service sectors grew (IDB 1987, p. 14). Employment stability declined substantially, while employment in the informal economy increased (see Table 3.5). In terms of employment, the 1980s can be characterized as a lost decade (Briones 1991, p. 23).

Conclusions

For El Salvador the 1980s was a time of profound crises and far-reaching structural change. External shocks and internal political strife combined to decimate the Salvadoran economy. The initial government response was to resort to administrative controls and countercyclical expansionary policies. Rising inflation then forced a shift toward austerity, but the usual harsh impact of adjustment measures was softened by a rise in external transfers.

Foreign-currency flows from official aid alleviated the need for external adjustment and allowed the Salvadoran government to meet the financial needs imposed by the armed conflict. With the government unable or unwilling to force significant tax reform onto a reluctant private sector, fiscal deficits were ameliorated through cuts in public spending—mainly reductions in public investment, social spending, and the real wages of public employees. The result of this mode of fiscal adjustment included deterioration in the quality and quantity of social services, a sharp cutback in public infrastructure, and a financial and institutional weakening of the state apparatus. The worsened distribution of income and the debilitated state and public infrastructure would later pose obstacles to consolidating the peace, developing the country, and constructing a genuine democracy.

Two implications of this history for the current era of reconstruction should be stressed. The first is the simple fact that the traumatic economic and social crises of the 1980s produced what can be regarded as the *profile of a new country*. During the decade, the country's social fabric was rent and traditional alliances were replaced by new ones. Power groups linked to the traditional agroexport-based economic model, itself a fundamental cause of the conflict, were weakened, partly because of the agrarian reform. Mass migration—involving at least 20 percent of the total population—profoundly changed the relative proportions of urban and rural population and the occupational structure of the country.[28] In this context of social dislocation and change, the United States, through its economic assistance, was able to help bring about significant shifts within the private sector, creating a new extragovernmental institutional framework and building support for an economic model based on export diversification.

The second key legacy of the 1980s is the contradiction between short- and long-run models and measures. It is certainly true that El Salvador needs to reinsert into the world economy with a less volatile means of earning foreign exchange. Yet U.S. efforts to refashion the country's political economy in this direction were undercut by a continuing aid flow that propped up the colón, and by the insistence of international lenders on spending cuts that threatened social stability, weakened state capacity, and curtailed complementary public investment. There are usually conflicts whenever an economy tries to move from stabilization to growth, but they seem especially difficult in the Salvadoran case—and they are all the more pressing because peace has brought with it high social expectations. In this regard, it may be useful to recall the relative flexibility of international lending agencies during the early and most critical years of the 1980s crisis. When a victory by the insurgent groups was considered possible, these institutions acted on the basis of fundamentally political considerations, allowing heterodox measures, including structural reforms and expansionary fiscal policy, that they subsequently decried as inappropriate. After the insurgency seemed to be tamed, the international lending institutions returned to "business as usual," promoting a type of fiscal adjustment that imposed high social costs and failed to take sufficient account of the special needs of a country divided by war. The current postwar phase, like the early 1980s, is a period of special needs. Although El Salvador has structural problems akin to those of many other countries at a similar level of development, there is one major difference in a postconflictual transition: The country must pursue economic stabilization and reform even as it attempts a double transition from war to peace and from an authoritarian regime to a democratic system. Policy must aim to repair the distributional damage done by both the war and the orthodox model of economic adjustment.

Notes

1. The principal arguments in this section are drawn from Segovia (1991).

2. This role of the foreign exchange "gap" in determining output is modeled in Krugman and Taylor (1978), Taylor (1988), and Pastor (1992b). These models also suggest how foreign exchange shortages can trigger inflation; in Taylor (1988) and Pastor (1992b), for example, inflation is a way of ratcheting down real aggregate demand to the externally determined level of supply. As Taylor notes, the other way to adjust to the external gap is via contractionary monetary and fiscal policy; this is, of course, the route favored by international lending institutions.

3. In El Salvador, the monthly behavior of the inflation rate has traditionally shown seasonal changes linked to the seasonal nature of crops. During the first six months of the year, inflation is generally higher owing to the relative shortage of basic grains and other agricultural food products, which exerts upward pressure on prices until the beginning of the primary harvest season. An effective anti-inflation policy therefore must provide for the establishment of a strategic reserve to compensate for periods in which such products are in short supply. Note that here too foreign exchange plays a role in inflation by enhancing or diminishing the ability to import food and make up for production shortfalls in agriculture.

4. A recent analysis of the causes of inflation in Central America may be found in CEPAL (1994); other works dealing with the case of El Salvador include Saca (1987), Saca and Rivera (1987), Rivera Campos (1988), and Segovia and Pleitez (1988).

5. Because the capital flight took a variety of forms (undervaluation of exports, overvaluation of imports, overvaluation of interest on foreign investment, etc.), it is extremely difficult to determine the exact amount that left the country. Using the traditional method of measuring capital flight through short-term capital movements plus net errors and omissions as an indirect indicator, however, yields a figure of $840 million for the period 1979–1983 (Boyce 1992, p. 19).

6. According to the World Bank (1983, p. 5), after the reforms were instituted the government expanded its role in the economy, gaining control of 9 percent of the gross value of agricultural production (2.3 percent of GDP) and 15 percent of the total farmland, 10 of the 13 sugar plantations, all foreign trade in coffee and sugar, and all commercial banks. The World Bank also pointed out that this situation brought about an increase in public-sector employment, which prior to the reforms had accounted for 8 percent of the economically active population.

7. With the mass closure of businesses, open unemployment during the period January–June 1980 reached 23 percent, while underemployment climbed to 38.9 percent (BCR 1980, p. 15).

8. According to BCR data (1980, 1981), in 1980 the IMF lent El Salvador $13,920,000, in connection with which a stabilization program was implemented and remained in effect until June 1981. In addition, that same year the IMF extended a long-term trust fund loan for $26 million. In 1981 El Salvador solicited

funds under the IMF's compensatory financing facility in order to offset the reduction in its export earnings. The amount received was $32,250,000, a sum equal to half of El Salvador's IMF quota.

9. The Temporary Law on Economic Stabilization, enacted in 1980, regulated the prices of various goods and services and froze salaries and wages.

10. The policy on control and prohibition of imports also intensified the economic crisis by contributing to the decline of the Central American Common Market. The restrictions affected mainly nonessential imports, the majority of which came from the Central American countries. As Bulmer-Thomas (1987, pp. 245–247) has noted, the policy of import bans and restrictions was practiced by all the countries of the Central American region. However, since one country's imports are another's exports, this policy seriously hurt intraregional trade and thus each country's individual output level.

11. A dual system with two exchange rates was created. The official rate remained 2.5 colones per dollar, while the parallel rate was allowed to fluctuate in response to supply and demand. The latter market in fact functioned as a gradual devaluation mechanism as merchandise shifted from the official to the parallel market.

12. As has been pointed out by various authors (Saca and Rivera 1987; Bulmer-Thomas 1988), this stabilization program was extremely flexible (it established no objectives regarding the maximum size of the fiscal deficit as a proportion of GDP, for example). This flexibility, not typical of IMF programs, can be attributed to U.S. foreign-policy considerations.

13. To prevent a dramatic surge of capital flight, exchange controls were tightened as part of the package.

14. The government also took several less orthodox actions, notably selective adjustment of salaries by between 10 percent and 15 percent; temporary freezing of prices for basic market-basket goods, as well as drugs, rent, and transportation; and the establishment of subsidies for producers of basic grains and for public transportation.

15. The private sector opposed the program on the grounds that it was restrictive, interventionist, and tax oriented and that it failed to offer sufficient incentives for production.

16. At the political level, the right-wing parties instituted a boycott of Legislative Assembly sessions that went on for several months. On 22 January business owners organized a work stoppage, paralyzing virtually the entire country. In addition, 25 legal actions were brought before the Salvadoran Supreme Court alleging that the sovereignty tax was unconstitutional. These efforts were ultimately successful, as the court held that the tax did in fact violate the constitution (Pelupessy 1988).

17. During most of the 1980s, remittances from Salvadoran emigrants were not incorporated into the formal system; rather, they fed an extensive black exchange market, which in the context of the war became the main channel for capital flight. This situation changed at the end of the decade, when the government devised a more effective way to channel these resources, and remittances replaced official transfers as the principal source of foreign currency in the country (see Chapter 4).

18. The growing volume of foreign aid also allowed the country to avoid the external debt crisis into which the rest of Latin America plunged in the 1980s

(Rosa and Segovia 1989). Because of El Salvador's geopolitical importance, the United States ultimately forgave $464 million of its debt in late 1992.

19. A 1985 U.S. General Accounting Office report observed, "AID has not been able to insist on more action because macroeconomic reform is not always the top U.S. priority, given the political and security objectives which place a premium on maintaining political stability. The Department of State believes political stability could be undermined by unpopular economic reforms" (GAO 1985, p. iv).

20. As Rosa argues, the massive infusions of aid provided by the United States (some $4.5 billion during the period 1980–1992) enabled it to go considerably beyond sustaining the war effort, mitigating its social costs, and keeping the Salvadoran economy afloat; the United States was also able to bring about far-reaching changes of such broad scope that, taken together, they produced significant change in Salvadoran society (Rosa 1993a).

21. Rosa (1993a) asserts that U.S. support for the agrarian reform was based on two currents of thought. One current conceived of the reform as a fundamental element in the battle against rural poverty and a means of laying a solid foundation for the industrial development of the country. The other current saw the reform as a political tool in the counterinsurgency struggle, applying the logic of the doctrine of low-intensity conflict. In any case, agrarian reform has consistently been a central component of the demands of opposition groups in the country, especially the Christian Democratic Party, which was the party in power at the time the reform was initiated.

22. It is also important to note that the social structure of the agricultural sector was profoundly altered by large-scale migration of the population as a consequence of the conflict.

23. The public-spending figures are from Rivera Campos and Gallagher (1994). Although some social indicators improved during the last decade, especially in the area of health, most of them deteriorated (World Bank 1994b; USAID 1994b; Belt and Lardé de Palomo 1994b; CEPAL 1993a).

24. As USAID pointed out in 1992, many inputs vital for assuring the quality of education and health services were being financed through external grants and loans, which made these programs unsustainable in the medium term unless both internal resources and program efficiency could be increased substantially (USAID 1992, p. 21).

25. For a detailed analysis of public-investment trends and the state of basic infrastructure, see Rivera Campos and Gallagher (1994).

26. See Appendix Table A.6. See also Rivera Campos and Gallagher (1994); Wisecarver (1989); and KPMG Peat Marwick (1990).

27. The World Bank (1986), for a good example, proposed that the adjustment policies included in the 1986 stabilization program be intensified and suggested that the price controls and subsidies provided for in that program be eliminated; however, the proposal included no measures to combat poverty and social problems.

28. As a result of this migration, an autonomous source of foreign currency and consumption appeared to supplement and eventually overshadow foreign aid— the funds sent back by Salvadorans living abroad. This is discussed in more detail in Chapter 4.

4

Macroeconomic Performance and Policies Since 1989

Alexander Segovia

In 1989 the government of Alfredo Cristiani came to power and embarked on a new set of stabilization and adjustment policies. The government's program, which included a major reform in the trade and tax regimes as well as a general thrust toward privatization and liberalization, was backed by the relevant international institutions (see Table 4.1). The World Bank played a particularly key role, substituting for the role USAID had previously played in directing and supervising the Salvadoran economy in the 1980s.[1] The program was, moreover, generally supported by the private sector; this eased the somewhat tense business–government relations that had characterized the previous presidency.

During the period of the adjustment program's implementation, the economy has experienced relatively high rates of growth (of 5 percent or more in recent years) and the rate of open unemployment has diminished, albeit marginally. Although poverty indexes have remained high, they do not appear to have grown worse, and inflation has been controlled. International institutions have thus judged the program as both highly successful on its own terms, and important as a supportive economic basis for the peace process (USAID 1994b, p. 3).

This period of macromanagement has not, however, been an unqualified success. Stability and growth have depended heavily on a very large and increasing influx of remittances from Salvadorans residing overseas. This influx has financed—and indeed can be regarded as the principal cause of—a large and widening trade deficit. Growth in nontraditional exports to countries outside the Central American Common Market (CACM) has been quite sluggish, in part due to the appreciation of the real exchange rate driven by remittances.

At the same time, remittances have mitigated the social costs of adjustment, not only by sustaining growth and checking inflation, but also by directly augmenting the incomes of poor and middle-class households. The fact that poverty has remained so high *despite* these inflows is therefore

Table 4.1   Operations of the International Financial Institutions, 1989–1993

	SDR (millions)
International Monetary Fund	*158.7*
August 1990: 12-month standby arrangement	35.6
January 1992: 14-month standby arrangement	41.5
May 1993: 10-month standby arrangement	34.5
March 1994: Extension and increase of May 1993 arrangement	47.1
	U.S.$ (millions)
World Bank	*204.5*
February 1991: First Structural Adjustment Loan (SALI)	75.0
June 1991: Social-Sector Rehabilitation Project	26.0
July 1991: Power-Sector Technical Assistance Project	11.0
March 1993: Agricultural-Sector Reform and Investment Project	40.0
September 1993: Second Structural Adjustment Loan (SALII)	50.0
September 1993: Technical Assistance Loan (TAL)	2.5
	U.S.$ (millions)
Inter-American Development Bank	*600.3*
1990: Advanced non-university technical training	14.4
1990: Rehabilitation and improvement of rural roads	44.0
1990: Comprehensive multisectoral credit program	60.0
1991: Preinvestment program	7.0
1991: Social investment fund (first phase)	33.0
1991: Major highways program	120.0
1992: Support for rural small business	0.5
1992: Support for low-revenue small business	1.5
1992: Electricity-sector program	125.9
1992: Investment-sector loan	90.0
1992: Rehabilitation of aqueducts and sewer systems	19.0
1993: Support for small coffee producers	1.0
1993: Social investment fund (second phase)	60.0
1993: Credit program for small business	24.0

Sources: World Bank; International Monetary Fund; Inter-American Development Bank; Rosa 1993.

quite troubling. Moreover, the long-term future of the flows is uncertain, particularly given recent changes in U.S. immigration policy. The policy "space" provided by the current foreign exchange bonanza could have been used to develop the infrastructure for competitive exports and to repair the poor distribution of assets and income that was a fundamental cause of the war. Instead, the government chose to push a neoliberal model of economic adjustment that may eventually worsen equity and increase macroeconomic fragility.

The new government that took power in June 1994 has chosen to deepen this neoliberal restructuring and has recently announced a new program aimed at turning El Salvador into *a large free-trade zone with assembly, financial, and market services.* The program, which has as its central pillar a fixed exchange rate and convertibility of the colón (along with further market liberalization) has generated much debate in El Salvador and in the Central American region. In contrast to the reforms applied by the previous government, this new adjustment proposal has neither the unconditional backing of the private sector nor the formal stamp of approval of the international financial institutions.

This chapter presents a general evaluation of the post-1989 adjustment efforts and an initial appraisal of the recently announced reforms. The chapter is organized into five parts. The first section sketches the economic and political context in which the post-1989 adjustment program was applied. The second and third sections analyze the logic and results of that adjustment strategy, and the fourth explains the reform program announced recently. The chapter concludes with general reflections concerning the policy implications of the need to make economic modernization compatible with the consolidation of peace and democracy in the country.

General Context of the Reform Program
(1989–1994)

Macroeconomic policies are never implemented in a vacuum. Negative trends and external factors can often make a coherent adjustment fail, and positive trends can give flawed approaches the aura of success. In our view, at least three background factors are key to understanding the character, achievements, and particularities of the adjustment program initiated in 1989. The first is the reduction in regional and internal political and military tensions, a trend that enhanced social stability and raised private investment because of the attendant reduction in risk. The second factor was the restoration of the alliance between the government and the private sector, a phenomenon that also aided the process of private-capital formation. The final factor was the massive increase in the flow of foreign exchange coming from remittances, a trend that produced a more favorable growth-inflation trade-off. This section briefly discusses each of these factors.

The Amelioration of the Domestic
and Regional Political-Military Crisis

After the guerrilla offensive of November 1989, El Salvador entered a period of relative sociopolitical stability. Peace negotiations began in 1990 and culminated in the signing of the Chapultepec Accords in January 1992. The signing of the peace accords lifted a principal obstacle to economic management of the country—that is, the war—and the relative (and growing) tranquility both improved the investment climate and helped to reactivate some sectors and activities that were depressed during the conflict.

The end of the war and the subsequent reconstruction phase also had a favorable direct impact on the economy. For one thing, the peace effort has required some expansion in public spending;[2] although even more "investment" in consolidating the peace would have been desirable, large sums have indeed been expended and this has had the usual multiplier impacts. Moreover, the end of the war permitted the government, particularly after 1992, to free resources that were dedicated to the war effort and to redirect them to investment in the social sectors. Again, more could have been done, but this spending shift toward nontradeable services also helped domestic employment and income. In sum, peace brought some positive dividends as well as costs.

The positive economic effects of this domestic peace process were reinforced by successful peace negotiations in other areas of Central America. In Nicaragua, for example, the defeat of the contras and the installation of an elected government helped to usher in an era of détente in the Central American region. This resulted, among other things, in a slow but sustained recovery of the regional market. El Salvador has particularly benefited from this, and demand from the Central American Common Market has been one of the principal sources of growth in recent years (see Table 4.2). Thus, the resolution of both the domestic *and* regional crises had positive externalities that helped the post-1989 Salvadoran reform program to achieve better economic results.

Reestablishment of the Private Sector–Government Alliance

The coming to power of Alianza Republicana Nacional (ARENA) in June 1989 also brought a warming of business–government relations, in contrast to the various tensions that had characterized the decade of the 1980s. In a country in which the private sector has the power to make any economic strategy unviable, its almost unconditional support for the government was

Table 4.2   Composition of Exports, 1988–1993 (millions of U.S.$)

	1988	1989	1990	1991	1992	1993
Traditional products	393.5	252.8	296.2	272.0	217.3	283.4
Nontraditional products	215.3	244.7	285.3	316.0	380.2	448.3
Central America	139.8	160.6	175.0	193.7	257.2	309.2
Rest of the world	75.5	84.1	110.3	122.3	123.0	139.1
Total export of goods	608.8	497.5	581.5	588.0	597.5	731.7
Assembly (gross)	n.a.	80.0	81.0	132.0	198.0	278.0

Source: BCR.
n.a. = data not available

decisive in implementing the adjustment program. By its nature the program involved changing the existing economic rules of the game with sometimes negative effects—at least in the short term—for certain sectors (particularly agriculture and certain manufacturing firms). That business was willing to go along with such short-term sectoral pain suggested the depth of the new alliance.

Although private-sector support for the government and its program was partly driven by ideological considerations, it also reflected the impact of U.S. efforts to "modernize" the business community. Such efforts over the 1980s (reviewed in Chapter 3) had created a social base for support of the export model, much of it centered in the new business institutions such as the Foundation for Economic and Social Development (FUSADES). Indeed, FUSADES played a leading role in the design and promotion of the adjustment program, and at least 17 business leaders and persons linked with that institution became part of the new government. Other factors that contributed to business modernization and support for the new government were: (1) the crisis of traditional agriculture, which forced many business persons to explore new opportunities in other areas and economic sectors; (2) the internal political crisis that had spurred an emergent process of internationalization of Salvadoran capital; and (3) generational change in some of the most important economic groups in the country (Segovia 1994a).

The Massive Growth in the Flow of Remittances

During most of the 1980s remittances bypassed official channels. This situation changed toward the end of the decade when the post-1989 government opened currency-exchange shops and established a single exchange rate, the latter move being intended to eliminate the black market. Recorded remittances soon took the place of official transfers as the largest single source of foreign exchange for the country, increasing from 3.5 percent of GDP in 1988–1989 to more than 8 percent in 1992, the year in which for the first time they exceeded the total earnings from exports (see Table 4.3).[3] By 1993, remittance inflows were double the volume of official external assistance, and in 1995 they may surpass 10 percent of GDP.

Perhaps the most important impact of remittances was that they allowed the government to focus on economic restructuring and not simply stabilization.[4] In particular, the size of the remittance flow provided the government with sufficient foreign exchange to finance the trade gap and maintain a stable exchange rate, making it easier to maintain growth and control inflation.

With the problem of short-run stabilization more or less solved, the government concentrated its attention on the actual task of structural adjustment, understood as a general process of economic liberalization.[5] Indeed,

Table 4.3   **Macroeconomic Significance of Family Remittances, 1979–1994**

Year	Remittances (millions of U.S.$)	Remittances as a % of exports	Remittances as a % of net transfers	Remittances as a % of GDP
1979	49.2	4.4	95.7	1.4
1980	59.6	5.5	86.5	1.7
1981	74.7	9.5	92.4	2.2
1982	87.3	12.5	42.0	2.4
1983	97.0	12.8	35.7	2.4
1984	121.0	16.7	38.4	2.6
1985	101.9	14.7	31.9	1.8
1986	134.5	17.8	35.0	3.4
1987	168.7	28.5	29.4	3.6
1988	194.0	31.9	38.1	3.5
1989	203.7	41.0	39.2	3.5
1990	322.1	55.4	56.6	5.9
1991	518.0	88.1	94.6	6.8
1992	686.0	114.7	91.7	8.1
1993	789.0	107.8	89.4	8.1
1994	870.0	104.7	n.a.	9.7

Sources: FUSADES; BCR.
n.a. = data not available

the greatest achievements of the adjustment program, from the point of view of its designers and backers, were advances in installing in the country an economic system based increasingly on market forces. The problem, as will be discussed in the second section, is that the inflow of remittances has resulted in an overvaluation of the Salvadoran currency that works against the achievement of the government's export-oriented growth model.[6]

Remittances also played a fundamental role in cushioning the social costs of adjustment and stabilization. As several studies point out (Montes 1987; CEPAL 1993b; USAID 1993b), remittances have had a strong redistributive effect, because they often represent a direct transfer to the poor sectors of the society. Montes (1987) estimated that one-third of Salvadoran families have at least one relative in the United States, and that the remittances received by each family represent on average 47 percent of their income; USAID (1993b, p. 31) cites studies showing that remittances increase the income of poor urban and rural families by one-third. Thus for many poor families remittances play a crucial role in subsistence.[7] Given the close relationship between income distribution and social tensions, remittances have played a crucial, albeit not consciously orchestrated, role in the Salvadoran peace process, and certainly helped to reduce political opposition to the post-1989 economic restructuring.

In addition to direct effects, remittances indirectly affect the income distribution in several ways. Most obviously, emigration reduces the supply of labor, putting some upward pressure on employment and/or wage rates within the country. A substantial fraction of remittance income undoubtedly translates into demand for food, helping to boost basic grain prices, thereby benefiting net sellers of grain, some of whom are poor. Nevertheless, both real wages and basic grain prices have fallen sharply in recent years, demonstrating that whatever their favorable effects, emigration and remittances have been insufficient to counter unfavorable trends in the current macroeconomic environment. Some remittance income also provides working capital for small businesses (López and Seligson 1989). And although data on this point are lacking, anecdotal evidence indicates that in some communities, taxes paid by small businesses started and sustained by remittances have financed local infrastructure such as roads and bridges (*New York Times* 1994).[8]

Finally, remittances allow the country as a whole to live "beyond its means," importing more than it exports (that is, aside from labor), and they cushion the economy from the need to close its trade deficit. This certainly made the adjustment process easier; as has been pointed out by ANEP (1992, p. 52), remittances have been the key factor preventing the adjustment of the 1990s from producing recession, in that internal investment as well as domestic consumption have been financed with external savings. Thus, increased remittances, encouraged in part by some of the policy changes in the post-1989 period (particularly the decision to unify the exchange market), helped to make the stabilization and adjustment package more successful than it otherwise would have been.

Logic and Content of the
Post-1989 Adjustment Program

Whereas the adjustment program initiated in 1989 had the usual goals of inflation fighting and macro stability, its more fundamental objective was to lay the groundwork for installing in the country an economic model based on private enterprise. This implied eliminating all restrictions and controls that blocked the functioning of market mechanisms (i.e., liberalization) as well as opening the greatest possible space for accumulation of capital by business sectors, principally through privatization and reducing the size of the state. It was assumed that the axis of accumulation of the new model would be located in the external sector, with exports providing the foreign exchange necessary to maintain short-run financial and exchange-rate stability. In contrast with the agroexport model, where the bulk of exports consisted of a few primary commodities facing unstable prices on the world market, the new model would rely on nontraditional agricultural and industrial exports and would be oriented to markets outside the immediate region. Exchange-rate policy was to support export promotion; for this reason, in mid-1990 the single rate of exchange was established and a "dirty float" system was put in place with the objective of maintaining a flexible and realistic exchange rate.

With the aim of increasing the openness of the economy, raising its general efficiency, and eliminating its anti-export bias, steps were taken to design a profound tariff reform. This reform sought to reduce tariffs from a range of 0–290 percent to a range of 5–20 percent. The tariff reductions were carried out in little more than two years, and as shown in Table 4.4, there was a significant impact on the real level of protection.[9] Liberalization also had a domestic face: Interest-rate restrictions were relaxed and price controls were eliminated on approximately 200 products.

An accompanying fiscal reform program included the elimination of export duties, the reduction and simplification of direct taxes, and the introduction of a value-added tax (see Figure 4.1). This package reinforced the regressiveness of the tax system, a topic further explored in Chapter 6.

Partly to reduce pressure on the spending side, steps were taken to design a program for restructuring the public sector. The basic component of the program was reform of the ministries linked to the social sector, particularly education and health. In addition, a privatization program was designed that included the sale of some state property and the privatization of public services.[10]

The central element of the privatization effort, however, involved the financial system. To complement the devolution of banks to private hands, a financial reform was carried out that included making the central bank an autonomous institution, creating a stock exchange, and strengthening oversight and control mechanisms.

A further stated objective of the program was the reduction of extreme poverty. The strategy to combat poverty had three basic pillars: (1) the

Table 4.4   Real and Nominal Rates of Protection in 1987 and 1993 (%)

Sector	1987		1993	
	Nominal	Real	Nominal	Real
Coffee	−25.0	−28.0	0.0	−0.9
Cotton	0.0	−9.8	5.0	4.7
Other agricultural and mineral products	4.8	−0.5	10.6	11.6
Beverages and tobacco	88.5	301.6	20.8	28.1
Textiles	40.5	84.8	13.0	21.4
Garments, leather, and footwear	41.7	75.1	27.7	53.6
Wood and furniture	43.8	87.1	13.5	19.2
Paper and printed matter	27.3	43.7	5.2	4.4
Chemical products	12.2	7.9	5.7	5.5
Rubber, plastic, and nonmetallic products	23.8	38.6	7.2	8.5
Machinery and equipment	21.7	38.6	7.1	7.3
Petroleum and electricity	6.1	2.3	6.6	7.2

Sources: For 1987, World Bank 1989; for 1993, Méndez and Abrego 1994.

Figure 4.1   Composition of Tax Revenue, 1985–1994

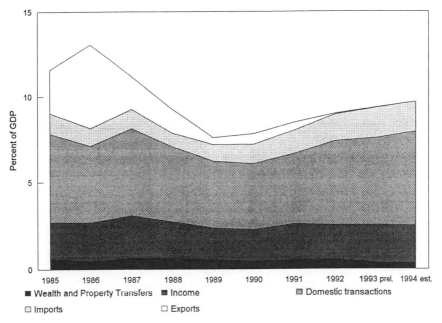

Source: USAID, from BCR.

achievement of strong and sustained growth related to the export drive; (2) investment in human resources; and (3) the implementation of compensatory programs for the most vulnerable groups (Belt and Lardé de Palomo 1994a).

Originally, the adjustment program was designed to be implemented in two phases: the stabilization phase, which at first was envisaged to last 18 months, and then the adjustment (or restructuring) phase in the proper sense of the term. However, the guerrilla offensive of November 1989 prevented the government from developing the program as planned. As a result, in 1990 both types of policies began to be applied simultaneously at great speed, which caused some protest from a disoriented business sector (ANEP 1992, 1993, 1994).

The adjustment program did not undergo substantial changes as a result of the signing of the peace agreements. The National Reconstruction Program (PRN), the result of the agreements, was designed independently from the adjustment program. It was considered by the government and by the international financial institutions as *complementary,* in the sense that its implementation would aid in achieving the objectives of the adjustment program, given its calming effect in the social arena. Moreover, this vision of complementarity followed from the premise that the majority of the PRN would be financed with external resources, so that its implementation would not work against the goals of stabilization and domestic-resource mobilization inherent in the adjustment program (see Chapter 6).

General Evaluation of the Adjustment Program

Progress in Stabilization

One of the successes of the program is the progress achieved in stabilizing the Salvadoran economy. Annual inflation slowed to 15 percent in 1990–1993, versus 25 percent in the preceding five years (see Appendix Table A.11). In our view, this is due principally to the availability of foreign exchange from remittances and international aid.[11] Moreover, this inflation success has been "purchased" with an increasingly overvalued exchange rate, as the central bank has sought to essentially fix the nominal exchange rate in the face of modest price increases (see Figure 4.2). The colón rose in real price by 31 percent between the end of 1990 and May 1994 (IMF 1994b, p. 6). The result has been a dramatically widening trade deficit, notwithstanding strong growth in exports to the CACM, that raises worries for a model supposedly built on export growth and a "realistic" exchange-rate policy (see Table 4.5)

There remains significant debate about how best to resolve the contradiction between a highly valued currency and an export-oriented accumulation model. Both Harberger (1993b) and Hinds (1994) suggest that remittances are long term and structural and that the current real exchange rate is therefore market-appropriate; in this view, nominal devaluation would simply translate quickly into inflation. Other authors, including González Orellana (1994), argue that appreciation of the real exchange rate has come at the cost of a severe deterioration in export competitiveness, and that a real devaluation is needed to promote competitiveness.

Ultimately, what exchange-rate policies should be adopted depends on the permanence of the current remittance flows. It would make sense to force a real devaluation only if remittances were viewed as a short-run phenomenon; devaluation would simply adjust the exchange rate to where the market itself will be in few short years. An IMF official interviewed for this study took an optimistic view, suggesting that in future years remittances are likely to grow at the same rate as host-country (that is, U.S.) GDP. Although this would represent a somewhat lower rate of increase than seen in previous years, it would imply that the current cushion will be maintained for the foreseeable future.[12] A less optimistic scenario, predicted by some observers, is what might be termed a "soft landing." In this view, remittance inflows will gradually decline in coming years as the ties between emigré Salvadorans and their homeland grow weaker and the share of their earnings they are willing to repatriate diminishes accordingly.

Figure 4.2 Real Exchange Rate, 1970–1993 (1980 = 100) (Rise corresponds to depreciation; Salvadoran consumer prices and U.S. wholesale prices)

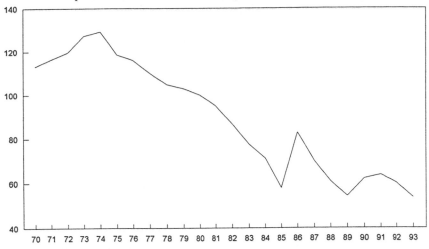

Source: IMF, International Financial Statistics.

A more alarming possibility is a sudden drop in remittances, perhaps precipitated by a change in U.S. immigration policy. Officials at international financial institutions interviewed in November 1994 tended to discount this possibility, but at the end of that month the U.S. government announced plans to terminate the Deferred Enforced Departure program, under which some 180,000 Salvadorans lived in the United States without immigrant visas.[13] Although the affected persons will be able to delay their departures, the termination of the program could affect large numbers of Salvadorans in the next year or two. At the same time, other anti-immigration measures in the United States could lead to the repatriation of Salvadorans residing there illegally.[14] The result could be a "hard landing," in which repatriation and a sharp contraction in remittances lead to shortages of foreign exchange, severe income losses for remittance recipients, and great pressure on labor markets. In such a case, the stabilization victory after 1989 would be exposed as resting on fragile pillars, a result foreshadowed by the recent Mexican collapse.

Progress in Structural Adjustment

If structural adjustment is understood simply as the process of installing a neoliberal economic model, then El Salvador's post-1989 experience may be considered a great success.[15] The Salvadoran economy is now less protected externally and more reliant on market mechanisms for its internal functioning. In addition, the space for accumulation by the private sector has been expanded through the process of privatization and a reduction in the size of the state. In addition to consolidating the support of international

Table 4.5   Basic Economic Indicators, 1990–1994

	1990	1991	1992	1993	1994[a]	Average 1985–1989	Average 1990–1994
Real growth of GDP (%)	3.4	3.5	5.3	5.1	5.5	1.6	4.6
Real GDP per capita (1962 colones)	635	644	663	672	n.a.	624	654
Gross domestic investment (% of GDP)	11.9	14.0	16.9	17.1	18.5	13.3	15.7
Private investment (% of GDP)	8.9	10.3	11.5	12.4	13.5	9.4	11.3
Public investment (% of GDP)	2.9	3.2	4.6	4.6	4.6	3.8	4.0
Deficit in nonfinancial public sector (% of GDP)	2.5	4.5	6.3	4	3.4	3.6	4.1
Deficit of central government (% of GDP)	3.2	4.5	4.8	3	n.a.	3.7	3.9
Public saving of nonfinancial public sector (% of GDP)	-0.3	-0.7	0.2	0.8	n.a.	0.6	0
Exports (millions of U.S.$)	582	588	597	722	797	629	658
nontraditional exports	285	316	380	450	540	199	394
Imports (millions of U.S.$)	1,262	1,406	1,699	1,900	2,067	1,012	1,667
Trade deficit	680	818	1,101	1,177	1,270	382	1,009
Deficit in current account (millions of U.S.$)	330	292	338	266	n.a.	234	306
Net international reserves (millions of U.S.$)	463	471	587	714	790	252	605

Sources: FUSADES, BCR, IMF, USAID.
Note: a. estimate.
n.a. = data not available

financial institutions, this structural change has generally reinforced the confidence of the private sector, with favorable effects reflected in the modest but sustained recovery of private investment.

The process of "modernizing" the market economy has not, however, been free from difficulties and problems. Some of these have clearly contradicted the overall goal of a competitive economy. For example, irregularities in the privatization of banking have produced oligopolization in the financial sector, hindering fair competition and raising real interest rates (including commissions) to borrowers. In this context, the banks have become the de facto financial arms of major economic groups, reflecting and reinforcing the concentration of wealth.[16] This, in turn, has negative effects on the prospects for sustainable economic growth and the strengthening of new economic actors.

Perhaps the biggest conflict, however, is the aforementioned contradiction between the use of the exchange rate as an inflation-fighting tool and the objective of creating a strong and diversified export sector. There have been some advances in terms of creating an institutional network of support for the export sector, fostering greater "export consciousness," and decreasing effective protection, but the performance of nontraditional exports to the rest of the world has remained weak. As can be seen in Table 4.2, the only nontraditional exports that have shown dynamic growth in recent years are: (1) those goods directed to the CACM, and (2) assembly services; a category that was assigned an important role in the strategy from the start, in which gross exports rose from $80 million in 1989 to $278 million in 1993. The assembly industry generated 41,152 jobs in the period 1985–1993 (see Chapter 12). According to USAID (1993b, p. 35), 17 free-trade zones are now under development in El Salvador that could generate more than 100,000 new jobs in the current decade. Impressive performance in the assembly industry is not, however, likely to make up for generally slack growth. Not only is such a strategy limited in its capacity to bring in foreign exchange, given that local value added represents only about 30 percent of gross value (compare the gross values reported in Table 4.2 with net earnings reported in Table 12.2), but also the possibilities for future growth have been reduced since the U.S. Congress has blocked financing for free-trade zones (GAO 1993).

Although a key barrier to generating a new export axis is the appreciated colón, Hinds (1994) and ANEP (1993) have also stressed the *lack of productive investment.* Hinds (1994) attributes this to high interest rates, high operating costs (due to deficient infrastructure, taxes on inputs and capital goods, etc.), the low national savings rate, and the mentality of many business entrepreneurs, who expect high returns without large risks.[17] ANEP (1992, 1993) has repeatedly argued that the weak showing of exports is due not only to exchange-rate overvaluation but also to economic incentives that encourage speculative investment and investment in the commercial and service sectors, rather than in the production of trade-able goods.

There indeed has been an increasing orientation of the economy toward the tertiary or service sector: The share of agriculture in GDP has declined dramatically in recent years, while the share of commerce and services has increased considerably.[18] This shift to nontradeable services is not surprising, however, in light of the real exchange-rate appreciation and the direct boost to consumption due to remittances.[19] In short, the exchange-rate policy and the lack of productive private investment are closely linked. A successful macroeconomic alternative would have to both depreciate the currency in real terms and increase investment.

Finally, the adjustment of 1989–1994 was not able to decrease poverty significantly (nor did this goal figure prominently in its intentions). Indeed, the number of people living in what the Ministry of Planning classifies as "extreme poverty" in urban areas rose from 23.3 percent of the urban population to 29.6 percent in 1992/93 (see Table 4.6). Such progress as has been achieved has been due to government compensatory programs—mostly financed with external resources (see Chapter 6)—as well as economic growth and the redistributive effect of remittances. The positive impact of remittances, probably the main factor in limiting poverty and ameliorating distributional inequities, can hardly be viewed as a deliberate result of government policy, except to the extent that the Salvadoran government helped to persuade the U.S. government to allow emigrés to stay in that country past the date of the negotiated conclusion to the armed conflict. In any case, poverty in El Salvador continues to be far too high and is widely recognized as the most serious threat to the consolidation of peace (see, for example, USAID 1994b; World Bank 1994b).

The lack of major progress in the social sector—not withstanding the positive impacts of the large inflows of remittances—is related to two

Table 4.6   **Urban Poverty, 1988/89–1992/93**
            (number of people and percentages 1989–1993)

	1988/89	1990/91	1991/92	1992/93
Number of people				
Relative poverty	707,356	782,407	751,730	516,567
Extreme poverty	517,570	550,606	573,211	734,552
Total	1,224,926	1,333,289	1,324,942	1,251,367
Percentages of total				
Relative poverty	31.9	32.2	30.4	20.8
Extreme poverty	23.3	21.9	20.8	29.6
Total	55.2	54.1	51.2	50.4

Source: MIPLAN, Multipurpose Household Survey, various years.

factors. First, the government placed a much higher priority on structural adjustment than on social policy (Belt and Lardé de Palomo 1994a). The trickle-down vision underlying the program accepted the old premise that the objectives of growth and distribution are incompatible in the short term, and therefore its proponents argued for growth first and redistribution of the fruits of growth later.[20] This is hardly an auspicious framework for making significant dents in poverty rates. Our own vision of the compatibility of equity and growth, elaborated in Chapters 1 and 8, squares with current research in development economics and permits policy that accords top priority to poverty reduction.

A second reason for slow progress on poverty and inequality was the institutional and financial weakening of the state as a result of the war, economic crisis, and fiscal adjustment. On the administrative side, many of the policies designed to improve social welfare were impeded by the lack of qualified personnel and institutional resources; those policies that were implemented often lacked adequate control mechanisms. This institutional weakness has been exacerbated by the thrusts toward privatization and decentralization, which accorded with the U.S.-supported strategy of building up institutions that were parallel to the state. On the fiscal side, revenues have increased only moderately (see Chapter 6). As a result, social programs often have relied heavily on external funding, a phenomenon that suggests the lack of a deep governmental commitment to building and maintaining appropriate social safety nets.

In sum, the Salvadoran economy has been substantially restructured: The market plays a larger role, the state has less power, and the private sector has more property. But progress toward a diversified export strategy and sustainable growth has been frustrated by an overvalued exchange rate and the lack of productive investment. Progress on the social front meanwhile has been very slow and largely inadequate to meet the demands of a deeply frustrated society. These policy shortcomings point to the need for a new strategy—one that would consciously depreciate the real exchange rate to foster the shift to tradeables, encourage more productive private investment (in part through enhancing public investment), and pay far greater attention to the lot of the poor.

The Reform Program
Announced by the Calderón Sol Government

In early 1995 the Calderón Sol government that had taken office in June 1994 announced its intention to carry out a new economic-reform program. The centerpiece of the program is the proposal to fix the exchange rate at a level of 8.75 colones to one dollar, with total convertibility. This would entail the creation of a currency board, which would eventually take the place of the central bank, because in such a context exchange-rate policy would disappear, and credit policy would effectively be ceded to Washington. The underlying goal appears to be a total dollarization of the Salvadoran economy. The designers of the program anticipate that this policy would have a series of short-term benefits for the country. In the first place it would increase the confidence of national and foreign investors due to the final elimination of the exchange-rate risks associated with devaluation. In the second place, fixing the exchange rate and forcing the dollarization of the economy would hold inflation to levels prevailing in the United States. This, it is argued, would increase El Salvador's competitiveness, promote saving, and contribute to raising real wage levels. Third, the new exchange-rate policy would cause interest rates to drop substantially, preferably close to international rates; this would aid in increasing levels of productive investment. Finally, fixing the exchange rate would reduce the quasi-fiscal deficit that arises due to the exchange-rate losses of the central bank (see Chapter 9).

Accompanying this fixed exchange-rate policy would be a dramatic reduction (over five years) in tariff rates, such that the new ceiling would be 6 percent and the new floor 1 percent (the respective figures are currently 20 and 5 percent). With the goal of giving businesses time to adjust, the government is considering reducing tariffs by stages (rather than a full and immediate cut) and allowing the pace of tariff reduction to differ by sector; agricultural and animal-husbandry sectors, for example, would receive special treatment. It is argued that this move toward more complete trade liberalization would help modernize the business sector, resulting in greater efficiency and greater productivity. Moreover, it would promote productive investment because the virtual elimination of tariffs on inputs and capital goods would reduce costs of production. Finally, it would encourage foreign investment, because the whole country in effect would be transformed into a free-trade zone open to the world.

Because tariff reduction would decrease fiscal revenues, the government proposes both to increase the value-added tax and to step up measures to combat tax evasion. In addition, privatization would be accelerated, with any resulting revenue improvement to be directed toward investment in human capital and the improvement of infrastructure. On the expenditure side, the program prescribes austerity in the public sector, including a program of reduction in public employment and reform of the pension system. The immediate impact on income distribution, particularly on the tax side, is likely to be regressive.

One objective of the program is to transform El Salvador into a financial center, a goal seemingly based on the Panamanian experience with dollarization. To this end, the reform would include the strengthening of mechanisms for financial-system oversight, as well as breaking the bank oligopoly by exposing the system to foreign competition. Along the same lines, the program calls for strengthening market mechanisms through eliminating the restraints and conditions that negatively affect competition. Among the measures proposed to accomplish this are the creation of a Law of Free Competition and the preparation of a new commercial code.

The announcement of the program set off intense debate in El Salvador and in Central America. As of this writing, the principal business organizations have given it conditional support (expressing concerns about higher taxes and worries about the fixed exchange rate), while the opposition parties and the trade unions have declared themselves opposed to it. The other Central American countries have reacted cautiously, particularly because one thrust of the plan is to reorient El Salvador from the Central American market to the larger world economy and because the proposed tariff changes would violate current subregional agreements. El Salvador has formal commitments to the CACM that it cannot abandon lightly. Nor should it do so, for intraregional trade is currently the most dynamic component of the country's export sector (see Chapter 12). In light of these reactions, the specifics of the plan remain highly tentative.

Regardless of its final content, the proposal represents a unique opportunity to begin a serious debate about what kind of economy will be most desirable in the future for El Salvador. The program does seek to respond honestly to three fundamental problems of the Salvadoran economy. First, it attempts to respond to the notable deficiency of productive investment, and hopes that dollarization will reduce risk and attract foreign, as well as domestic, investment. Second, it attempts to discipline a domestic business class accustomed to extraordinarily high rates of profit by tightening competition and financial oversight. Finally, it recognizes the need for the Salvadoran economy to be incorporated within the world economy in a new way, suggesting that the demand originating in the internal and regional markets is insufficient to sustain high growth rates (particularly for the assembly industries) and that therefore the country should pursue a reorientation toward the world market, particularly the North American market.

Although the new program is a welcome opening for debate, however, it offers the wrong policies at the wrong time. One key premise of the program is that receiving remittances from Salvadoran labor is akin to having an assembly zone located in the United States; these earnings are structural in nature and will continue in the medium term. This view suggests that it is useless to try to alter the real exchange rate by means of devaluations; central-bank attempts to depreciate by intervening in the currency market will only generate exchange losses and reduce the real credit available to the private sector.

But declaring defeat in the face of the "Dutch disease" may prove to be a recipe for long-run disaster if and when remittances eventually decline, particularly if this were to occur quickly, as in the "hard-landing" scenario.[21] Sooner or later, El Salvador will have to fall back on exports—and the export infrastructure will only be there if the government combines the right policies (i.e., public investment) with the right prices (i.e., a less highly valued colón). Freezing the exchange rate now against the dollar would instead lay the groundwork for a financial explosion à la Chile in 1982 or Mexico in 1994: Bad news or external shocks could trigger an economic meltdown.

The notion of El Salvador as a financial center is quite unrealistic, particularly in light of the presence of well-established and sophisticated financial centers elsewhere in Latin America. The new proposals also seem to assume that the Salvadoran economy is already in shape to compete with other countries for foreign direct investment (FDI), and that there is sufficient mobility of resources and factors of production inside the economy that those negatively affected by shifting incentives will be able to move rapidly to sectors and activities that show higher profit rates. In our view FDI is likely to be hesitant and the adjustment process slower and more painful. The rush toward complete economic liberalization proposed by the government ignores the lessons of successful developing countries, including Korea and Taiwan, where pragmatic market-supporting interventions did much to make private-sector-oriented models work.

The elements of an alternative strategy are discussed in more detail in Chapters 8 through 12. The key shortcoming of this new program is the failure to incorporate a serious effort to reduce poverty directly and to redistribute assets, opportunities, and income. Poverty reduction is crucial as an end in itself. But the evidence clearly shows also that market economies work best when they start from the precondition of relative equality, for the reasons reviewed in Chapters 1 and 8. Among other benefits, greater equality reduces rent seeking and induces a willingness to share burdens, both of which make it easier to achieve stabilization and adjustment. For El Salvador's new market-oriented strategy to work, the government must *now* launch a committed redistributional and antipoverty program.

The need for such a program is particularly great in a country trying to fulfill the obligations of a peace accord. The success of any economic program depends on creating a climate of political and social stability that can give confidence to national and foreign investors. This in turn presumes the consolidation of democracy and the full implementation of the Chapultepec Accords. It is clear that the country cannot subordinate peace to economic restructuring: Moving ahead with both processes simultaneously is the only viable option for attaining the goals of development and democracy. The best way to ensure such compatibility is to make the more general guarantor of social peace—distributional improvement and the elimination of poverty—the centerpiece of a new economic strategy.

Conclusions

El Salvador's recent economic history offers several lessons for understanding the future. The first is simply that the success of the adjustment program begun in 1989 may be overstated. It was undertaken in a highly favorable context—the beginnings of peace, the growing closeness of business and government, and the increase in remittances—that both cushioned social costs and dampened inflationary pressures. Such a favorable context may not, however, be repeated in the coming years. The costs of implementing the peace are growing, business may be less enthusiastic as the government attempts to improve the private sector's tepid response to market incentives, and, most important, the flow of remittances may taper off. In this sense, the adjustment process is entering a new and more difficult stage.

A second insight from this recent history is that the existence of international aid and remittances allowed the government to concentrate its efforts on installing a more market-based economic model rather than simply stabilizing the macroeconomy. Although the policy achievements on this front have been impressive—liberalization, privatization, and the relative shrinking of the state have clearly gone forward—a more fundamental shift toward export diversification and sustainable growth has been frustrated by an overvalued exchange rate, an oligopolistic banking sector, and insufficient productive investment. The neoliberal model is "all dressed up with nowhere to go"; unless the real exchange rate can be depreciated and investment enhanced, El Salvador will remain highly dependent on transfers and remittances.

A final lesson relates to the social situation. Progress in the fight against extreme poverty in recent years has been minimal; this phenomenon is all the more disturbing in light of the policy space and the direct positive distributional consequences of the remittance flow. This lack of progress is partly due to a now dated stagist notion that growth must come first and distribution only later. The scale and the breadth of extreme poverty in El Salvador require that we move beyond this vision and instead recognize that growth and distribution are not necessarily contradictory goals. What is needed is the simultaneous pursuit of economic growth and equity, particularly because a more equitable underlying distribution of assets and power is the key to making markets work to produce growth. Building on this equity–growth linkage, subsequent chapters specify various institutional and fiscal reforms that would fit into such an inclusive model.

Although the tentative program of reforms recently floated by the government does not point in this direction, the government does seem to have recognized several fundamental weaknesses in the current economy. The new program offers a useful opportunity to debate both interpretations of the past and projections of the future. Such a debate opens up the real possibility of achieving, for the first time in the country's history, a basic consensus on economic and social questions. This will be an indispensable requirement for assuring the continuity and the viability of any development strategy—and for ensuring that any such strategy reinforces, rather than undermines, the democratization of Salvadoran society.

Notes

1. As Rosa (1993b) has pointed out, the institutionalization of this role of guidance and supervision of the structural adjustment process by the World Bank was formalized with the approval of the first structural adjustment loan in 1991 (see Table 4.1).

2. The National Reconstruction Program (PRN) covers approximately 40 percent of the country, including 20 percent of the population most affected by the war. Investments and current expenditures within the scope of the plan vary between $1.2 and $1.6 billion over a five-year period. The average expenditure in each of these years is equivalent to between 4 and 5 percent of GDP (IDB 1993a, pp. 3–4).

3. Orellana Merlos (1992, pp. 5–7) reviews official estimates for the years 1979–1991 and their problems. He estimates the remittance inflow in 1987 at $504 million, compared to the official estimate of $169 million and Montes's (1987) estimate of $1.3 billion. Table 4.3 reports the official estimates that seem to be relatively accurate in the most recent years.

4. Moreover, the government's latitude for defining policies was augmented considerably once it had access to these remittances precisely because they were *autonomous*—and as such not subject to the usual conditionalities attached to foreign aid and international assistance. For example, the government did not have to rely on funds from the IMF, despite having signed four standby agreements (which were considered precautionary).

5. On the World Bank's concept of structural adjustment, see World Bank (1988) and Williamson (1990).

6. Although appreciation of the real exchange rate does not have any strong adverse impacts on traditional exports or on exports to the CACM, it is of major importance to the competitiveness of nontraditional exports outside the region (see Chapter 12).

7. A national household survey, conducted by the Ministry of Planning in 1991–1992, found that 7.1 percent of "extremely poor" and 12.4 percent of poor households received remittances, on average $36 per month and $61 per month, respectively. Remittance income is greatly understated in the survey, however: Total remittances extrapolated from the survey were only $149 million per year, compared to the officially registered inflow of $690 million for 1992. Siri and Abelardo Delgado (1995, p. 6) note that understatement is likely to be especially significant for poor households.

8. On the other hand, emigration that has produced remittances has also had some negative distributional consequences. Survey data indicate that emigrants

tend to have "above-average labor force characteristics" (Funkhouser 1990, p. 23) and the country is now deprived of their human capital. The positive income effects of emigration must also be weighed against the social costs of the disruption of families and communities. And, perhaps most troubling, El Salvador's heavy dependence on remittances renders the economy in general, and the poor in particular, vulnerable to an adverse shock from their sudden contraction, a topic that is discussed later.

9. There was much "water" in the earlier tariffs, thanks in part to competition within the CACM; hence the lowering of tariffs did not result in a wave of bankruptcies (see Chapter 12).

10. For a detailed analysis of the process of privatization in El Salvador, see Segovia (1994c).

11. In fact, the only times that the government had problems in controlling inflation were precisely those at which the exchange rate underwent strong fluctuations (as happened at the end of 1989 and the beginning of 1990 due to the November guerrilla offensive) or when measures were applied that directly affected costs and inflationary expectations. The latter was the case in 1992, when the introduction of VAT and other fiscal measures led to significant price increases. The inflationary spiral of 1992 was particularly serious because the introduction of the VAT coincided with a serious shortage of basic grains (beans) due to the drought that afflicted the country that year.

12. Similarly, Harberger (1993b, p. 17) predicts that the influx of remittances will continue "as long as more than a million Salvadorans live abroad," and that they will probably grow over time, "particularly if those Salvadorans share in the economic growth which is occurring in the United States."

13. The DED program was established to provide temporary protected status in 1990, and was extended on three occasions "based largely on Salvadoran government contentions that the country was not able to assimilate large numbers of its citizens now living in the United States." In deciding to terminate the program, the Clinton administration ignored "strenuous appeals by Salvadoran authorities" (Associated Press 1994).

14. For example, California's Proposition 187, passed by voters in November 1994, seeks to deny public education and health care to illegal immigrants, and requires teachers and health-care providers to report illegal immigrants to immigration authorities.

15. These advances have been highlighted by international institutions as one of the most important achievements of the adjustment program. USAID (1994b, p. 3), for example, maintains that the program has been highly successful in redirecting the economy toward greater dependence on market forces and a competitive private sector. The World Bank (1993b, p. 2) similarly says that reform has been successful in establishing the bases for a modern market economy.

16. For a critical analysis of the process of privatization in banking, see Sorto and Segovia (1992) and Sorto (1995).

17. Harberger (1993b, p. 16) reports that, with the important exception of agriculture, real profit rates in El Salvador are very high, in the neighborhood of 20–30 percent per annum.

18. Changes in relative prices have played the major role in this shift, as can be seen by comparing the percentage composition of GDP at current prices

(reported in Appendix Table A.2a) to its composition when valued at 1962 prices (Appendix Table A.2b). For discussion, see Chapter 10.

19. This investment bias toward the service sector also reflects the oligopolistic structure of the financial system coupled with the existence of strong economic groups tied to this sector.

20. For example, FUSADES (1993) suggests that: "Experience shows that the sequence which eventually makes it possible for a country to eliminate extreme poverty, while at the same time attaining a condition of solvency (i.e., without significant macroeconomic disequilibrium), consists of *sustained growth first in order to distribute the fruits of growth later*" [emphasis in the original]. See also CENITEC (1993).

21. The "Dutch disease" refers to the adverse impact of a foreign exchange bonanza on the competitiveness of other industries in the tradeable-goods sector (Corden 1984).

5

The Peace Accords and Postwar Reconstruction

Elisabeth J. Wood

In their influential contribution to the debate about postwar reconstruction and macroeconomic policy in El Salvador, Alvaro de Soto and Graciana del Castillo decried the lack of coordination between the UN on the one hand and the International Monetary Fund (IMF) and the World Bank on the other. They likened El Salvador to a patient lying "on the operating table with the left and right sides of his body separated by a curtain and unrelated surgery being performed on each side" (de Soto and del Castillo 1994a, p. 74).[1]

The metaphor is a dramatic depiction of the difficult challenge of achieving both the consolidation of peace and economic growth following civil war. If efforts at policy reform—economic and political alike—are not coordinated, either "operation" may undermine the other. Yet the consolidation of peace seems essential to sustained economic growth, and economic growth may stabilize the peace.

The surgical image with its emphasis on the role of the international agencies does not, however, capture important aspects of the political dynamic of peace building in El Salvador and the possible conflicts between peace-building and stabilization processes more generally. Far from a passive and unitary patient undergoing twin surgeries to remedy an underlying illness (presumably the civil war, its causes and consequences), El Salvador is made up of divergent groups whose conflicting interests not only fueled the war but continue actively to shape the peace. Moreover, Salvadoran society has undergone a period of profound change that reshaped the objectives, constraints, and alliances of many groups. Belying the illness metaphor, as a result of these changes—many of which are positive—the country may be able to consolidate a historic breakthrough in its political and economic organization and build a society sharply different from the Salvadoran past in its democratic order and progress toward economic justice.

The negotiation, implications, and uneven implementation of the Chapultepec Accords and their relation to postwar reconstruction is the subject

73

of this chapter. The analysis focuses on the political bargaining between representatives of domestic organizations and institutions that shaped both the agreement itself and its subsequent implementation. The active support and timely intervention of international organizations, particularly the UN and the United States, were critical both to the successful negotiation of the agreement and to its implementation to date. But without sustained reference to the domestic political actors we will not understand the political dynamics of the peace process and their political and economic implications. The political bargaining did not end with the signing of the agreement but continued to shape its implementation and reconstruction generally as the various domestic actors faced new challenges, constraints, and opportunities, attempting to maintain their own organizational cohesion and to extend their political power on the new post-accords political terrain.

For the governing party, Alianza Republicana Nacional (ARENA), the principal challenge was to negotiate and implement the peace agreement without alienating adherents (which include many landlords and military officers), compromising its position as the dominant right-of-center party, or weakening its neoliberal economic agenda. Stability in the transition would depend in part on ARENA's ability to deliver on the terms of the accords lest renewed unrest, armed or not, undermine the party's ability to raise reconstruction funds from international donors and to portray itself in the 1994 election campaign as the deliverer of the peace.

For the Farabundo Martí Front for National Liberation (FMLN) the consolidation of a democratic political process was a necessary but not sufficient condition for success in their transition from insurgent movement to political party. The construction of a postwar organizational and economic base depended in part on delivering an acceptable set of resources to ex-combatants and civilian supporters. Maximizing the transfer of land—in area and economic potential—as well as delivering training and credit programs was therefore a key interest for FMLN negotiators. The FMLN's bargaining power depended in important measure on its option to slow or halt the demobilization of the guerrilla forces. Once the guns were turned in, the FMLN would lose its special stature as an armed force of the civil war and signatory to the peace agreement, and become another out-of-power political party (although one with special relations with international actors).

For the armed forces the principal challenge was to retain as much control of its institutional base as possible, given the extraordinary process of civilian and international intervention in matters hitherto strictly internal that were initiated by the accords. Whether the officer corps would in fact acquiesce to that process was uncertain as the cease-fire began in February 1992.

For peasants in conflicted areas, the agreement provided a clear incentive to establish a claim to de facto tenancy as soon as possible. This sense of an unprecedented historical opportunity was reinforced by the very visible presence of the UN monitors as they patrolled the countryside. Peasant organizations experienced increasing success in mobilizing campesinos for land takeovers.

For landlords throughout El Salvador, and particularly for those owning properties within or near conflicted zones, the agreement occasioned a great deal of uncertainty. Despite the clause reasserting their property rights, many landlords were burdened by debts accumulated during the war and intimidated by the FMLN and the prospect of an organized workforce, and decided to sell.

These political interests and agendas were central to the peace process in El Salvador. There are two central themes emphasized here. First, the agenda of the peace agreement—if fully implemented and consolidated—will lay the institutional foundations of political democracy in the postwar period. However, the agreement does not directly address the profound economic and social inequalities that fueled the civil war. The consolidation of the political reforms is both necessary and urgent if a future process of political bargaining is to define a more equitable model of economic development. Second, the principal impediments to consolidation of a durable peace in El Salvador have been domestic political obstacles, not economic constraints imposed by macroeconomic policy. To the extent that a lack of economic resources constrained some aspects of the peace process, the shortfall itself reflected a lack of political will. International actors, although they contributed significant financial resources and political pressure at key moments, did not compensate for inadequate political commitment by Salvadoran actors, particularly the Salvadoran government.

This chapter is the first of three that address the short-run problems of the implementation of the peace accords. Chapters 6 and 7 analyze the mobilization of domestic and external resources in more detail.

Bargaining Over the Terms of Peace

By the end of the 1980s the Salvadoran civil war was a military stalemate as neither side achieved—nor, in the judgment of many observers, *could* achieve—a military victory under the prevailing political conditions. The situation in the late 1980s was by no means static, however: The quickly changing geopolitical context brought a set of problems and opportunities to the contending Salvadoran parties whose social, political, and economic worlds were also being reshaped by the civil war (Gibb and Smyth 1990; Segovia 1994a; Rosa 1993a; Johnson 1993). By mid-1989 three elements essential to the negotiation process that eventually led to the peace agreement were in place.

First, the FMLN made an unprecedented peace proposal in early 1989 that indicated their acceptance in principle of elections and their willingness to participate in the upcoming elections if they were postponed by six months. The initiative followed an internal political debate that redefined the stated goal of the insurgency from socialist revolution to the construction of a pluralist democracy. According to the FMLN, although the new objective implied some structural reforms (including further agrarian reform), it did not entail a single-party political system or the abolition of private property (FMLN 1989; see also Byrne 1994). That the offer was serious was evident in their abandoning a previous insistence on an interim power-sharing arrangement, and was reiterated in their later dropping a previous insistence on the integration of the two armed forces as well. Despite some degree of internal dissension, subsequent negotiating positions clearly indicated that issues of military, police, electoral, and judicial reform would take precedence over socioeconomic issues (Overseas Development Council 1994; Gibb and Smyth 1990; FMLN 1990; Murray et al. 1994). While asserting the FMLN's readiness to launch a major offensive, guerrilla spokespersons reiterated their preference for a negotiated resolution of the war (Karl 1989; Beretta 1989).

Second, the election of Alfredo Cristiani as president put the ARENA party in the seat of political power. Although the party remained divided between modernizers who favored negotiations and hard-liners who opposed them, as the governing party it was now more vulnerable to political pressure for negotiations and more accountable for their failure; indeed Cristiani had run for office on a platform that included a commitment to some kind of negotiations (Gibb and Smyth 1990). In the judgment of the FMLN, ARENA, as the representative of the political interests of the landed and business elite, was more likely to support a negotiated resolution if ARENA participated directly in negotiating its terms (Beretta 1989).

Third, the Bush administration, in response to the FMLN's initiative, signaled its tentative interest in a negotiated resolution to the war. This indicated that the degree of U.S. military and economic support that the government enjoyed under the Reagan administration was no longer a given (Gibb and Smyth 1990; Karl 1989).

Although a few initial meetings between the FMLN and government representatives occurred in mid-1989, the process ground to a halt by early November in a context of increasing political violence. The FMLN launched a major offensive in San Salvador in November 1989. Their initial success erased any lingering illusion that the changes in Eastern Europe and in Nicaragua would mean a dissolution of the insurgents' military capability. Although the guerrillas did not hold any city for more than three weeks, they brought the war home to the wealthy neighborhoods, which underscored the military's inability to contain the war. But the populace did not join in an insurrection; this strengthened the position within the FMLN of those who saw negotiations as the only resolution of the conflict. The assassination of the six Jesuits and their two women employees by the Atlacatl Battalion, an elite unit of the Salvadoran armed forces, made untenable further U.S. congressional support not conditioned on negotiations.[2] The offensive and its aftermath thus dramatically illustrated the inability of either side to prevail militarily, as well as the ongoing costs of continuing the war (Gibb and Smyth 1990; Byrne 1994).

In the aftermath of these events, the FMLN and the group of Central American presidents separately approached the UN for assistance in reaching a negotiated resolution to the civil war. A series of subsequent agreements, hammered out over a period of more than two years, laid the procedural, constitutional, and institutional groundwork for the final peace accords (signed on 16 January 1992). The FMLN's decision to pursue political and military reform rather than extensive economic reform as a clear priority was consistently demonstrated throughout the process, despite ongoing internal tension over the issue. For example, at the May 1990 meeting in Caracas, Venezuela, the FMLN proposed the elimination of both armies and the establishment of a new civilian police force, as well as the investigation and prosecution of a range of political crimes; the only socioeconomic proposal addressed the needs of demobilized ex-combatants (FMLN 1990).

The first accord of more than procedural significance was signed in San Jose in July 1990, when both parties agreed to the establishment of the UN mission in El Salvador (ONUSAL) to verify compliance with provisions mandating respect for human rights. This role for the UN was unprecedented: Not only was the organization to enter into the internal affairs of a member nation, but it would do so on terms that extended far beyond its traditional peacekeeping role of monitoring military compliance between states.[3]

In April 1991 the parties agreed on a series of constitutional changes; this was a clear signal that the FMLN was prepared to accept the 1983 Constitution (if suitably amended). Despite some opposition by hard-line ARENA party members, the agreements were subsequently ratified by the ARENA-controlled National Assembly. This was an indication of Cristiani's ability to deliver party compliance on at least some of the reforms despite opposition from party hard-liners. The most important constitutional changes concerned the institutional mandate of the armed forces: Civilian control over the military was made explicit, its mission was limited to defense, and a new civilian police force was to be established. The agreements also provided for a Truth Commission under UN auspices to investigate past human-rights violations.

Despite this progress, negotiations subsequently became mired over what UN officials called the Gordian knot: What would be the future of the two armed parties to the war? In part the issue was one of guarantees: What guaranteed the security of former guerrillas and the implementation of reforms once the FMLN turned in its arms? Negotiations stalemated in mid-1991, and fighting intensified as both sides attempted to expand their putative claims to control of geographical areas.

By mid-September 1991 both the United States and the Soviet Union had expressed their support for the negotiations, thus contributing pressure to reach an agreement. The New York Accord, signed on 25 September 1991, untied the Gordian knot. Some of the FMLN members would join the new National Civilian Police (PNC). (According to a secret but soon widely circulated annex, up to 20 percent of the new force would be former FMLN guerrillas.) The armed forces would be reduced, the Treasury Police and National Guard eliminated, and the military officer corps purged by an Ad Hoc Commission. In addition, the National Commission for the Consolidation of Peace (COPAZ), a group composed of representatives of the political parties, the FMLN, and the government, would supervise the implementation of the agreements, verify compliance, and draft necessary legislation. For the FMLN, the guarantee that the agreements would be implemented once its forces were demobilized was twofold. It included the support of the international community (particularly the verification role of the UN) and the supervisory role of COPAZ, which was given the power of access to all sites of implementation.

The New York Accord also included the first outline of the socioeconomic agreements to come. According to a senior UN official close to the negotiations, the government would not consider changes in its economic model; this position was accepted implicitly by the FMLN in April 1991.[4] The FMLN then proposed the minimum conditions to reach an agreement, principally resources for the reintegration of ex-combatants and civilian supporters, a forum for discussion of issues important to the opposition social movement, and a commitment to existing agrarian reform laws. The New York Accord therefore reiterated the constitutional ceiling on landholding, while stating that the existing ceiling would be effectively implemented.

The accord also outlined the "definitive" agenda of still-outstanding issues for negotiation. In addition to the outstanding socioeconomic issues (measures to alleviate the social costs of structural adjustment programs, channels for direct external funding to community development, and the creation of the forum for negotiation of socioeconomic issues), the most difficult issues were the terms of the cease-fire and the terms of the reincorporation of the FMLN. The accord stated that the existing state of tenancy in the conflicted areas would be respected as an interim measure. But it did not (and at that time could not) specify who would get what land; nor was it clear in what areas (the "conflicted zones") tenure claims based on current occupancy would be respected.

In the months after the accord was signed, political tensions in the countryside rose steeply as peasant organizations attempted to consolidate their claims to de facto tenure before the war's end. For example, in the municipality of Jiquilisco, Usulután, members of cooperatives working abandoned land fenced off the most promising parcels, formally notified landlords of the occupation of their property, and instigated armed border patrols against any attempt by the landlords to return (Wood 1995).

In late 1991, as it became clear that Perez de Cuellar would not accept another term of office as UN Secretary-General beyond the end of 1991, pressure on the negotiating parties to reach an agreement was increased, particularly by the United States. Four days before the year's end, it was clear to UN officials that the only remaining obstacle to an agreement was the issue of land; only then did the negotiators convened in New York return to the agenda of socioeconomic issues. A few minutes before midnight on 31 December 1991, agreement was reached, with President Cristiani accepting what became the final draft of the socioeconomic chapter.[5]

The Peace Accords

The extraordinary process of negotiations between the Salvadoran government and the FMLN culminated in the signing of the peace accords at the Chapultepec Palace in Mexico City on 16 January 1992. In essence, the agreement laid out a political compromise in which the left agreed to a democratic political regime and a capitalist economy with only limited socioeconomic reform, and the right agreed to participation by the left in a democratic political regime with some socioeconomic reform. The Chapultepec Accords enshrine a democratic bargain: The two sides agreed to resolve their future differences through a democratic political process (Karl 1992; Vickers 1992; Munck 1993).

The principal achievement of the agreement was an agenda of reforms that would institutionalize the new—democratic—rules of the political game. The main provisions, many of them carried over from the New York Accord, were reforms of the armed forces, accountability for past human-rights violations, the founding of a new police force, and restrictions on the arbitrary exercise of state power. In sharp contrast, negotiators made little effort to finalize the details of the socioeconomic agreement that had been sketched in the New York Accord until the very end of the negotiation process; as a result, it was one of the weakest sections of the Chapultepec Accords. As described earlier, there were two principal reasons for this: First, the FMLN made an explicit decision to pursue as their strong priority the political conditions and institutions that would make democratic politics possible; second, the government refused to discuss any modification of its general economic policy.[6]

The accords also provided a set of guarantees for the transition period. A detailed calendar defined the schedule for the dissolution of the security forces and immediate-reaction battalions as well as the gradual demobilization of the FMLN by October 1992. Although the accords did not explicitly state that each step depended on the completion of others earlier in the calendar, key actions by the two parties were staggered. For example, the National Guard and Treasury Police were to be abolished before the first 20 percent of the FMLN guerrillas were to demobilize. The transition period was to culminate in the general elections of March 1994, with the FMLN competing for executive, legislative, and municipal seats alongside other political parties.

This linkage thus provided some degree of security to both sides: Each was required to take a sequence of significant and costly steps that, if implemented, would signal continuing compliance with the terms of the peace agreement. The calendar did not require definitive and irreversible steps early in the cease-fire period that would have necessitated an unreasonable degree of early confidence in the other party's compliance. The implicit conditionality of the calendar also pertained to programs of economic reintegration: Land transfer and training programs were to be underway as combatants were demobilized. COPAZ, the interparty commission that was to verify compliance with the peace accords, would designate a commission with wide representation by political parties to follow up on the legal issues involved in the mandated reforms.

Political and Public-Security Reforms

The core of the peace agreement—the axis around which its democratic promise revolved—was the agenda of extensive reforms of the coercive apparatus of the state, including changes in the structure, size, ideology, and personnel of the armed forces. In addition to the formal assertion of civilian control and the narrowing of the military's mandate to defense achieved in the constitutional reforms of April 1991, the accords also included the dissolution of the civil-defense patrols, the regulation of private security forces, the institutional separation of intelligence services from the Ministry of Defense, the suspension of forced conscription, and the restructuring of the reserve service. The Treasury Police and National Guard were to be abolished as public security forces and reabsorbed into the army. The counterinsurgency battalions, including the Atlacatl, were to be absorbed into the regular forces. These were key concessions because these institutions had been essential to the military's control over rural areas (Stanley 1995).[7]

On the issue of past human-rights violations, the peace agreement established an Ad Hoc Commission comprising three Salvadoran civilians empowered to investigate the human-rights record of the officer corps of the armed forces and to make binding recommendations that could include their dismissal. Given the military's long-standing impunity for human-rights violations, the review of armed-forces personnel by civilians was an unprecedented breach of its institutional autonomy. The accords also reiterated the commitment of both the FMLN and the government to the Truth Commission established earlier. This second commission, composed of three non-Salvadoran experts in international law supported by a staff of UN personnel, was to investigate past abuses by both sides, issue a public report, and recommend measures to prevent future abuses (Buergenthal 1994). The commission had no authority of prosecution; however, cases that might result from its investigation were specifically exempted from the amnesties declared as the cease-fire began and its recommendations were binding on the parties to the negotiations.

The peace accords mandated the founding of the new National Civilian Police under the Ministry of the Interior, completely separate from the armed-forces chain of command. The accords also established a new National Academy of Public Security (ANSP) for the training of the new force. In the secret annex to the New York Accord mentioned earlier, a quota of 20 percent each was established for former guerrillas and former National Police (PN) officers (in the latter case, after an evaluation of their record; both had to go through the ANSP course). The provisions included a special "transitory regime" during which the PN would gradually relinquish control of successive geographical areas to the PNC until the PNC was fully deployed.

The peace accords also reaffirmed earlier agreements on judicial and electoral reforms contained in the April 1991 agreement. Most important of these was the founding of a new investigative and prosecutorial body, the National Counsel for the Defense of Human Rights. Constitutional reform also transformed the selection of Supreme Court magistrates as a step toward breaking the traditional dominance of the judicial system by the ruling political party.[8] The accords included provisions to strengthen the independence of the National Judicial Council in order to promote judicial reform, including the founding of an institution for the training of judges and other judicial personnel. A new Supreme Electoral Tribunal (TSE) was established with broad political-party representation to supervise voter registration and elections. The accords also mandated the legalization of the FMLN as a political party, recognizing the right to meet, to mobilize, to publish, and to hold licenses for communication (necessary for the legalization of the FMLN's two hitherto clandestine radio stations). In addition, the accords proclaimed the right of return for exiles and promised special security measures for FMLN leaders.

Socioeconomic Reform

The section of the peace accords concerning socioeconomic reform was in places vague and ambiguous, in sharp contrast to the detailed agreements on military reform and public security. Whereas the accords explicitly declared any consideration of the "philosophy and general orientation" of the government's economic policy as beyond the scope of the agreement, the government agreed that stability in the postwar period depended on the transfer of some resources to former guerrillas and their supporters.[9]

Principal elements of the agreement's limited agenda of socioeconomic reform were (1) limited land transfer to ex-combatants and civilian supporters of the FMLN, (2) the extension of credit for agriculture and for small business, (3) measures to alleviate the costs of structural adjustment, (4) "modalities" for external aid to communities, (5) the founding of a forum of labor, business, and government for further negotiation, and (6) a National Reconstruction Plan (PRN), which was to target the former conflicted zones and included programs to facilitate the reincorporation of the members of the FMLN into civilian life.

The peace agreement thus did not include a redistributive agenda; this was a troubling omission in view of the sustained fall in real wages during the civil war and the contribution of social and economic inequality to its emergence. No agreements on wage increases or even the right of unions to organize were included. Notably absent was any significant extension of existing agrarian-reform legislation; indeed, the agreement indirectly affirmed the existing constitutional ceiling on landholding (245 hectares). Nor was poverty directly addressed outside the areas targeted by the PRN except in the vaguest of terms (Vickers 1992). Despite some donor rhetoric to the contrary, neither the government nor the FMLN ever saw the land transfer as a measure to redress distributive concerns that had fueled the civil war. Rather, the land transfer was intended to facilitate the reintegration of ex-combatants and FMLN supporters into the economic and social life of the country.

Redistribution was thus limited to the transfer—more precisely, the sale—of land to ex-combatants and supporters of the FMLN as part of the reincorporation measures. There are perhaps two principal reasons for this (Wood 1995). First, the ARENA government's economic policy emphasized diversification away from a narrow dependence on agricultural production, and integration into regional and international markets—a policy that would be more threatened by wage and labor policies favorable to workers than by the limited transfer of land. That is, for the modernizers in the ARENA party, the price to be paid in land for peace did not look steep—*if* it could be limited to the conflicted zones and did not threaten the political and economic base of the party in the western coffee areas and in business circles. Second, land transfer was critical for the FMLN's internal political cohesion: Given the peasant origins of most of its combatants, to negotiate an end to the war without some transfer of land would have led to traumatic internal difficulties.[10]

Given the importance of the land issue both in the civil war and in the political dynamics of the immediate postwar period, a more detailed understanding of its treatment in the accords is essential. The peace accords identified various categories of properties for potential distribution: properties exceeding the 1983 constitutional limit of 245 hectares, properties belonging to the state, land offered voluntarily for sale to the state, and properties occupied in the conflicted zones by residents and workers. There was no attempt to determine how much land would fall into any category, and initial estimates varied widely.

The transfer of private properties in the conflicted zones was one of the most politically sensitive parts of the agreement. In one controversial passage, the accords stated that "in conformity with the New York Accord, the present state of tenancy within the conflicted zones will be respected until a satisfactory legal solution of definitive tenancy is found" (Government of El Salvador 1992, p. 28). Given the reference to the New York Accord, the relevant date of the "present state of tenancy" was subject to intense debate: Was it therefore 25 September 1991 (when the New York Accord was signed) or 16 January 1992 (when the final agreement was signed)?[11]

Moreover, as discussed earlier, the accords did not define the boundaries of the conflicted zones, despite several references to programs particular to those areas. According to the agreement, within 30 days of the signing the FMLN was to present an inventory of properties it claimed in the conflicted zones; the government was to legalize tenure definitively within six months. The agreement stated explicitly that the current landholders would not be evicted, and defined *tenedores* as present residents and/or workers of the conflicted zones.[12]

The peace accords did little more than sketch the terms of transfer for each category; in general, credit for purchase was to be extended under the terms of the 1980 agrarian reform. In the conflicted zones, the transfer of private property would depend on the voluntary selling of the property by the titleholder; if the landlord chose not to sell, the government was to relocate the occupying tenedores to unoccupied land within the same area whose owners did want to sell. Landlords were to be paid market prices, but what that would mean in areas where the civil war had raged was not spelled out. Nor did the agreement adequately define the process by which these issues would be resolved and the transfer implemented. COPAZ was to be the "guarantor" of the land agreements, but was not given any specific authority.[13] COPAZ was to appoint a Special Agrarian Commission (CEA-COPAZ) to supervise the land-transfer issue, and in particular to "verify" the status of properties and tenedores in the conflicted zones.

The accords stated that the government would present a draft of the National Reconstruction Plan to the FMLN within a month of the signing of the agreement. Although the FMLN's recommendations and requests would be "taken into account," its role was clearly secondary: There was no provision for its participation or for that of program beneficiaries in the development of the PRN (except in the case of credit policy). The principal goals of the plan were the integrated development of "areas affected by the war" (note the absence in this section of any reference to conflicted zones, a legacy of the struggle over the issue), attention to the basic needs of the population most affected by the war and of the ex-combatants of both sides, and the reconstruction of damaged infrastructure. Policies facilitating the reincorporation of demobilized ex-combatants were to include programs such as scholarships, jobs and pensions, housing projects, and business promotion. Appealing to the international community for support, the accords assigned to the UNDP the role of consultant in fund raising, project design, and coordination with nongovernmental organizations (NGOs).

The accords also included brief sections on a few ancillary issues. They decreed that credit should be widely available to farmers and small businesspeople and that target populations should actively participate in policy design. The government agreed to adopt measures to effectively defend consumers and strengthen programs to alleviate the social costs of structural adjustment. The government also agreed that external aid could be channeled directly to communities and popular organizations in conflicted zones. However, details were sorely lacking for each of these issues.

As in the New York Accord, remaining issues—including, importantly though implicitly, negotiations over wages and working conditions—were consigned to the socioeconomic forum. The agenda for further negotiation ranged from redressing the social costs of structural adjustment to "economic and social problems that will arise due to the end of the conflict." In addition, the government agreed to submit revisions to the laws to promote a "climate of harmony in labor relations." However, the resources that the forum would command were quite small.

In summary, the socioeconomic agenda consisted primarily of initiatives that would facilitate the reintegration of ex-combatants and the tenedores into civilian life. Notably absent from the socioeconomic agenda of the accords was any significant extension of existing agrarian-reform legislation. Nor was poverty directly addressed outside the areas targeted by the PRN except in the vaguest of terms (Vickers 1992), a troubling omission in view of the sustained fall in real wages during the war and the widespread conviction that economic deprivation had contributed to the emergence of the conflict. Moreover, the calendar for implementing the socioeconomic agenda was defined by the political logic of the peace process, not by an analysis of its feasibility.

Although the balance of political forces in the country had been sufficient for reaching the commitments enshrined in the peace accords, at the war's end it remained an open question whether the evolving balance of power in the postwar period would be sufficient for their realization.

Bargaining over Reconstruction

As the two armies separated to their designated "points of concentration" after the signing of the peace accords on 16 January 1992, both domestic and political actors became increasingly aware of the difficult challenges of peace building after more than a decade of civil war. Beyond the immediate issue of the effectiveness of the UN's monitoring of the cease-fire, two key issues loomed. First, would the calendar of staggered implementation of the accords, together with the attention of the international community, provide mutual confidence sufficient to engender ongoing compliance? Second, who would pay the costs of peace, given the significant resources required for the implementation of the peace agreement? These two issues were inextricably related: The political implications of the amount and modalities of funding could either reinforce or undermine the political will and capacity of one or both parties to carry out the terms of the peace agreement.

The fundamental challenge was to translate the political commitments of the peace accords into adequately funded programs and policies that would institutionalize the democratic bargain that resolved the war. As argued earlier, a complex conditionality among various elements of the agreement was central to its political logic; their successful implementation would be similarly interlinked. For both ARENA and the FMLN, the challenge was further complicated by internal divisions that would have to be managed if the peace process was to go forward. As the ongoing violence by disillusioned ex-combatants in Nicaragua demonstrated, successful reintegration involved much more than the laying down of arms:

> Strategies for the reintegration of combatants into the political, social, and productive sphere are far more than the need to insure simple economic survival, it is also a much deeper and complex process of sustaining faith among ex-combatants in the content of the peace process and strengthening the conviction that the negotiated settlement brought with it genuine alternatives to a previous grim history of exclusion (UNDP 1993, p. 9).

Contributing to the prospects for successful implementation was the commitment of international actors to the peaceful resolution of the war. The long-standing special relationship between the U.S. and Salvadoran governments—combined with the much more recent commitment of the United States to the negotiated resolution of the war—meant that the United States might make timely contributions (Segovia 1994a). According to a senior UN official close to the negotiations, the United States made explicit assurances to both parties that substantial funding would be forthcoming (interview, see note 4). A significant degree of European interest was also expected.

Many international donors were reluctant to underwrite the peace agreement, however, without assurances that both parties to the war were committed to the agreement—and, in particular, that the government was prepared to finance ongoing costs of reforms once donor funding was exhausted. In addition, substantial funds would be forthcoming only if adequate financial procedures were in place, including detailed proposals and budgets and standard accounting procedures. Yet at the time of the signing of the accords, there existed no overall assessment of the cost of implementing the agreement, but only initial estimates for reconstruction based on a preliminary version of the PRN. During the negotiation of the accords, no attempt had been made to estimate its financial implications (interview, see note 4); such a process probably would have impeded the reaching of an agreement by the end of 1991.

Planning for postwar reconstruction began in mid-1991, half a year before the signing of the peace agreement, with an initial Consultative Group meeting of donors (MIPLAN 1991d). USAID contributed significantly to initial aspects of the government's reconstruction planning. Two teams of consultants to USAID carried out assessments of two aspects of the reconstruction, defining possible priorities and estimated costs for programs of physical infrastructure (Jones and Taylor 1991a, 1991b) and reintegration of ex-combatants (Creative Associates International 1991).

Between August 1991 and the second donor meeting in March 1992, a special group in the Ministry of Planning and Coordination of Economic and Social Development (MIPLAN) issued a series of increasingly detailed documents describing what was to become the National Reconstruction Plan (MIPLAN 1991a, 1991b, 1991c). The documents were presented as preliminary efforts that could be modified after a process of consultation. The purpose of the program, reiterated throughout the various versions, was to support national reconciliation through the reintegration of the FMLN and its civilian supporters into the political and economic life of the country. This reintegration was to take place in the context of the government's policies of macroeconomic stabilization and adjustment that were seen as necessary for economic recovery. The reduction of absolute poverty and the promotion of human welfare were also objectives of the PRN, understood as complementary to the government's overall economic policy.

The political viability of the PRN, according to one preliminary government document, hinged on the participation of the local population, which was seen as complementary to the government's policy of decentralization (MIPLAN 1991a). The pattern of beneficiary participation would be modeled on the Municipalities in Action (MEA) program, a model of community development previously financed by USAID through the Commission for the Restoration of Areas (CONARA). CONARA would be superseded by the Secretariat of National Reconstruction (SRN), which would implement the PRN in two phases: a contingency phase of urgent short-term programs and a second phase of projects lasting up to five years.

The FMLN and allied NGOs strongly criticized the MIPLAN documents on three counts, reflecting the opposition's quite different conception of reconstruction (Murray et al. 1994). First, the avenues of participation were inadequate and would further marginalize the beneficiaries and their representative organizations because the key roles of project development and prioritization were left to the government. The explicit role of the beneficiary population seemed to be limited to advising the mayor in town meetings. The opposition's reaction was perhaps particularly sharp given the linkage of the government's proposed participation procedures to the MEA program, which had been long denounced for its counterinsurgency aims in the civil war. Second, the left argued that the building and repair of infrastructure was overemphasized at the expense of other development needs in the former conflicted zones. For example, in the November version of the PRN, 68 percent of the budget was targeted for infrastructure and only 10 percent for employment-generation and agricultural programs (MIPLAN 1991c). Third, the FMLN argued that the proposed target area was too limited geographically and should be extended. These criticisms were advanced in two short documents, essentially position papers rather than counterproposals, that were circulated in early 1992 by the FMLN and the opposition NGOs.

In February 1992 the UNDP convened an interagency meeting of 60 high-level experts from 14 UN agencies to assess the reconstruction needs of the country. The final report of that meeting argued that the government should take advantage of the experience of opposition NGOs in the conflicted zones and, after evaluation, incorporate some of their innovations into the new reconstruction program (UNDP 1992). As part of its mandate under the accords to provide technical assistance to the reconstruction process, the UNDP sponsored a series of meetings between representatives of the government, the opposition NGOs, and the FMLN. The meetings led to a technical-assistance proposal for the donor meeting and initiated a limited pattern of UNDP-coordinated *concertación* that would subsequently address various reintegration issues. The UNDP subsequently developed major portions of the reinsertion programs, mobilized a significant fraction of international contributions, and coordinated the development of various reconstruction programs.

The government made a number of limited changes to the PRN in response to opposition criticisms and the UNDP recommendations. First, the channels of NGO participation were clarified: NGOs could apply directly to the SRN for funding, for example, without the approval of the local mayor. However, the principal avenue for local projects continued to be MEA projects, and the role of the mayor and municipal council continued to dominate. Second, the geographical coverage was gradually increased from 84 to 115 municipalities.[14] Third, the programs were redefined to give a greater emphasis to human-capital development—although the proposed budgets under the new programs continued to emphasize infrastructure.[15] Although still dissatisfied, the FMLN decided to attend the second donor meeting, fearing that it would be blamed for shortfalls in external funding if they did not (Murray et al. 1994).

At the March 1992 Consultative Group meeting, the government presented three documents outlining programs and budgets for the PRN, the strengthening of democratic institutions, and technical assistance (respectively, MIPLAN 1992b, 1992a, and 1992c). The government argued that it faced very serious fiscal constraints, emphasizing both the need to increase social spending in general (not just in PRN areas) and the absence of a peace dividend given the degree of external financing of the war and the merely gradual reduction of the armed forces (MIPLAN 1992b). Table 5.1 summarizes the proposed budgets.

Table 5.1   **Financing the Peace Accords: Investment Requirements, 1992–1996 (in millions of U.S. dollars)**

Program	Total	Priority
National Reconstruction Plan		
Social sector and human capital	416.9	324.5
Basic infrastructure	200.0	200.0
Infrastructure	354.9	268.1
Productive sector	277.6	137.5
Land acquisition	50.0	33.0
Environment	52.0	15.6
Strengthening Democratic Institutions		
National Civilian Police	223.1	
Public Security Academy	50.0	
Judicial reform	29.9	
General Attorney's Office for the Protection of Human Rights	8.7	
Supreme Electoral Tribune	6.3	
Other institutional reform to strengthen democracy	74.8	
Indemnization of armed forces	40.0	
Technical assistance	33.9	
Total	1,528.0	745.7

Sources: MIPLAN 1992a, 1992e, 1992f.
Note: The figures for strengthening democratic institutions and for technical assistance, drawn from MIPLAN 1992e and 1992f, respectively, do not correspond to the figures for those categories presented in MIPLAN 1992a. The data presented here are based on the former as the more detailed of the source documents.

The international community pledged some $600 million in response ($800 million if previous commitments are included). By June 1992 more than $200 million in commitments were in process (SRN 1992a), almost all of it from the United States. In addition to other funding, USAID provided the 116 million colones needed for the contingency phase of the program to the newly founded Secretariat of National Reconstruction (SRN).

In the months after the meeting, two issues of particular importance continued to dominate the reconstruction debate: the reintegration of ex-combatants in general and the transfer of land in particular. As described earlier, neither the scope nor the terms of the land transfer were clearly spelled out in the agreement. Negotiations collapsed in mid-1992 over the amount of land to be transferred, the number of beneficiaries, and the applicability of "special conditions" versus "market prices." Nor were the promised training and credit programs—the necessary complements to land transfer—in place.

The impasse threatened the peace process itself as the FMLN suspended its demobilization process and political tensions increased. In an extraordinary instance of its "good offices" mandate, the UN sent a team of agrarian specialists to evaluate the situation and subsequently offered the two parties a take-it-or-leave-it settlement. The proposal, later considered by the UN as an addendum to the peace accords, defined the scope of the transfer: the number of beneficiaries (47,500 comprising 7,500 ex-combatants of the FMLN, 15,000 ex-combatants of the armed forces, and 25,000 tenedores) and the amount of land per beneficiary (depending on soil quality). If the agreement had been fully funded *and* fully implemented, the transfer of land would have amounted to 12 percent of Salvadoran farmland (a bit over half of the amount distributed under the 1980 agrarian reform). However, subsequent agreements pared down the amount to be transferred, as will be discussed further.

Development of the reinsertion programs trailed the negotiations over land. Representatives of the FMLN and the government began negotiations to define the reinsertion programs for ex-combatants by mid-1992, with the UNDP acting as an observer. While discussion continued, the UNDP coordinated an emergency appeal to international donors to address the pressing needs of the FMLN combatants, ranging from shelter to medical assistance. These were later expanded to include a package of household goods and, in the case of those turning to agriculture as their postwar employment, farming tools as well (Weiss Fagen 1995).

The FMLN's initial reintegration proposal included training programs for thousands of people that ranged in duration from one to five years, employment guarantees for two years, as well as housing for 12,000 households, for a total cost of $258 million. By May 1992 the proposal had been scaled down to little over $200 million, but this did not yet include figures for land purchase. In September 1992 the government offered a counterproposal that defined two tracks available for lower-ranking ex-combatants (SRN 1992c). The proposal distinguished between short-run and medium-run projects for the two tracks, on the grounds that resources and programs for immediate needs (including documentation, household goods, and living expenses during initial training) should be underway while remaining programs were being designed. The proposal listed some estimated costs but gave no estimate of the total cost (but see Table 5.2 for the government's estimated costs as presented at the 1993 Consultative Group meeting).[16]

After a series of discussions facilitated and coordinated by the UNDP, the two parties agreed on three reinsertion tracks (in addition to the PNC track for those ex-combatants who joined the new police force). For those pursuing agriculture, training programs by NGOs were to begin immediately; once they had received land through the land-transfer program, agricultural

Table 5.2   Funding Priorities and Shortfalls, 1993–1996 (in millions of U.S. dollars)

Programs	Requirements, CG budget 1993	GOES commitment (April 1993)	Expected int'l contribution (April 1993)	Shortfall (April 1993 est.)	Shortfall (January 1994 est.)
Priority Programs					
National Civilian Police	173.0	35.4	6.0	131.6	} 182.0
Public Security Academy	104.7	28.0	9.9	66.8	
Judicial reform	219.8	162.3	15.0	42.5	
Counsel for Human Rights	16.8	6.4	1.1	9.3	} 66.6
Elections tribunal	20.0	0.6	4.0	15.4	
Reintegration (PRN)	316.8	26.6	80.0	210.2	177.8
Pensions for disabled	8.2	0.7	0.0	7.5	—
Land transfer	142.5	23.3	47.5	71.7	62.7
Housing	77.1	2.6	12.5	62.0	—
Agricultural credit	62.0	0.0	10.0	52.0	—
Microenterprise credit	27.0	0.0	10.0	17.0	—
Poverty alleviation (PRN)	310.2	57.2	147.4	105.3	93.7
Subtotal	1,161.3	316.5	263.4	581.1	520.1
Other Programs (PRN)					
Social and productive sector	120.0				−14.6
Infrastructure	530.1				161.0
Environmental sector	17.5				15.4
Total	1,828.9				681.9

Sources: MIPLAN 1993a; GAO 1994; January 1995 UNDP figures.

Note: For further details see Table 7.2. A negative shortfall indicates a surplus. The report to the 1993 CG meeting also included a priority request for poverty-alleviation funds for non-PRN areas ($372.2 million). Because these figures are not included in other documents, they are ignored here as well. In addition, a separate document requesting $20.4 million for technical assistance (MIPLAN 1993b) accompanied the principal document; this request is treated in the text but is not included in the table.

credit, including a five-year loan to capitalize the farms, was to follow (UNDP 1993). Those ex-combatants preferring a nonagricultural future would have access to credit for the founding of "microenterprises" after technical-vocational training; university scholarships were also available if appropriate.

The third track was for the approximately 600 midlevel commanders and leaders of the FMLN. The track consisted of credit and training in technical and administrative skills, to enable the participants to start their own businesses or to join existing ones. Initial academic-equivalency courses contributed to the further refining of the track; in their aftermath, the UNDP coordinated a set of NGOs in the design and implementation of three subtracks: technical-vocational training (33 percent of the participants), business administration (58 percent), and executive training (9 percent) (UNDP 1994b).

Throughout the negotiations, the government maintained that reintegration benefits should be equally available to both sides. Parallel programs (except for the midlevel commanders' program, for which there was no parallel group) for ex-combatants of the armed forces were developed both for agricultural and technical-vocational training. In the process of project development and implementation the programs were quite separate although the opportunities were roughly similar.

In April 1993 a third Consultative Group meeting of international donors was convened by the World Bank. The government presented a revised proposal that emphasized the reinsertion programs and poverty alleviation, with updated figures of estimated needs, and existing government and donor commitments. A funding gap of still-unfinanced programs was substantial (summarized in Table 5.2).[17]

In addition to the overall shortage of funds, the inadequate funding of many priority programs judged essential to the consolidation of the peace process—particularly the new public-security institutions and the reintegration programs—troubled many observers and intensified the debate about the relationship between economic and political reform (de Soto and del Castillo 1994a; Segovia 1994b). Moreover, progressive lack of confidence in the National Reconstruction Secretariat by donors resulted in its programs being almost exclusively funded by USAID, with other donors opting to channel bilateral assistance through other ministries and through the UNDP. We return to this debate in the following two chapters.

The Uneven Implementation of the Peace Accords

In the three years since the signing in Mexico City, remarkable progress has been made in some aspects of the agreement. The FMLN participated in the general elections of March 1994, making a respectable showing at the presidential and legislative levels. The military was restructured, purged, and reduced in size; the new civilian police force is deployed throughout the country. However, implementation of the peace agreement has been incomplete and uneven in several areas, including a number essential to the consolidation of peace in El Salvador.

The implementation of the cease-fire itself was remarkably successful; both sides withdrew without exchanging a shot. The dissolution of the Treasury Police and the National Guard did not occur without substantial resistance, but they were formally abolished by mid-1992. The absorption of the irregular battalions into the regular army occurred with little deviation from the programmed dates. The reduction by half in the size of the army was achieved well before the deadline. Although some critics report that the initial number of soldiers had been inflated (Weiss Fagen 1995), the current size of the armed forces is well below the level mandated in the peace accords, according to a U.S. Department of Defense official (interview, December 1994).

The demobilization of the FMLN was completed two months behind schedule, on 15 December 1992. The reasons for the delay were twofold. Not until late 1992 was it clear that Cristiani would implement the purge of the officer corps recommended by the Ad Hoc Commission. In addition, the FMLN conditioned their demobilization on progress in land and reintegration programs that suffered long delays throughout 1992.

The explosion of an arms locker in Managua in June 1993 confirmed the existence of substantial clandestine arms caches, one of the most serious violations of the peace accords, according to the UN. The deposit included anti-aircraft missiles and sufficient arms to re-arm the Popular Forces of Liberation (FPL), the group responsible for the cache, to its full strength at the end of the war.[18] The incident deepened doubts on the part of the many right-wing elements about the adequacy of ONUSAL's verification of the FMLN's demobilization, as well as the FMLN's commitment to the peace process. Subsequently a number of additional arms caches were identified and destroyed.

The purge of the officer corps following the report of the Ad Hoc Commission occurred only after substantial delays and required extraordinary international pressure. The United States played a key role; high-level military officers visited El Salvador to reiterate the U.S. position that the commission's recommendations be implemented. The 103 officers named in the commission's report were finally dismissed by the end of 1993. This was a step toward the abolition of impunity unprecedented in the history of El Salvador. The reform of the judicial system was by many accounts one of the weakest aspects of the peace accords (Popkin, Vickers, and Spence 1993). However, the agenda of reform was expanded as a result of the investigations of the Truth Commission. In March 1993 the Truth Commission released its report examining the history of human-rights violations during the civil war.[19] The report named those deemed responsible for those cases for which adequate evidence had been amassed and recommended their exclusion from political office for 10 years. The commission made a series of binding recommendations for judicial reform—in addition to those reforms mandated by the peace accords themselves—to break the institutionalized impunity for human-rights violations.

Few of the Truth Commission's recommendations were acted on in the months that followed as controversy swirled over the report, particularly its recommendation that the entire Supreme Court resign. Nonetheless, by mid-1995 progress on several issues had been made. Despite long delays, a new Supreme Court was inaugurated in mid-1994 whose breadth of political representation is unprecedented in El Salvador; this may make possible serious reform (UN Security Council 1994f; Popkin 1994).

One key recommendation of the Truth Commission was that a further investigation be made of the existence (both past and present) and funding of armed networks for the purpose of political violence (death squads). In the wake of a rising tide of political assassinations, the UN sent Under-Secretary General Marrack Goulding to El Salvador in November 1993. As a result of his visit, a Joint Group was convened to investigate the death squads' continued existence (Economist Intelligence Unit 1994). In the report issued in July 1994, the Joint Group reported the evolution of death squads into organized crime with some political overtones (Spence, Vickers, and Dye 1995, p. 9). Although the group's recommendations have had little impact, the violence did subside after the 1994 elections.

Despite initially inadequate funding and support, both the National Counsel for the Defense of Human Rights and the National Judiciary Council have showed recent signs of increasing institutional capacity, thanks in part to increased international tutelage as the departure of ONUSAL (with the exception of a few staff members) in April 1994 became more imminent (Popkin 1994). In addition, a process of judicial review and training began under the new Supreme Court.

The founding of the Civilian Police Force has been one of the most troubled aspects of the peace process. As one expert observes,

> Because the accords provided for a completely new institution, it was more likely that a new organizational culture and adequate guarantees for civilian rights can take hold. Yet the very features of the PNC project that made it so promising also created serious obstacles to success (Stanley 1995, p. 8).

Among those obstacles were the financial challenge of building a new institution from scratch, the repeated reluctance on the part of the National Police to cooperate with the PNC in the transition period, and the crime wave fueled in part by delays in the reinsertion programs. As a result, the training and deployment of the PNC was subject to extraordinary delays and problems (Stanley 1993; Stanley 1995; UN Security Council 1994a, 1994f).

A lack of initial funding impeded adequate training and deployment of the new force on the original schedule.[20] After the New York Accord was signed, initial steps to begin the founding of the National Academy of Public Security and the PNC itself should have been taken, but President Cristiani did not name the responsible interim officials until the end of 1991. Moreover, facilities and equipment belonging to the former security forces were retained by the armed forces and the PN, forcing costly delays as the PNC was built from scratch. Although the UN, the UNDP, Spain, and the United States participated in the development of curriculum and organizational plans, adequate international funding was not forthcoming. One analyst suggests two reasons for the reluctance to fund an institution so obviously key to the peace process: the general lack of programs and interest in funding police, and the reluctance to fund an institution to which the government seemed inadequately committed (Stanley 1995).

One reason for donor skepticism about the government's commitment to the new force was its reluctance or inability to end the continuing efforts on the part of the PN and elements of the former security forces to undermine the autonomy and capacity of the PNC. The penetration of the new force by more members of the PN than was allowed for in various agreements outlasted frequent ONUSAL attempts to enforce those agreements. The issue was complicated by high and rising levels of crime that were attributed by many to demobilized combatants of both sides. In December 1992 the FMLN and the government agreed to expand the number of PN agents admitted to the PNC, provided they were evaluated and attended the academy (UN Security Council 1994e; Spence, Vickers, and Dye 1995, p. 7). The number of former PN agents to have joined the new force exceeded those levels; the government's long-standing refusal to supply ONUSAL with lists of former combatants made enforcement of the agreements extremely difficult. Two entire units of the PN were transferred into the PNC in 1993 with neither the evaluation nor retraining agreed to in the December 1992 agreement. Nor were they integrated into the new *civilian* line of command; rather they began exercising command control outside their divisions (Washington Office on Latin America 1994). The close working relationship between the ONUSAL police division and the PNC was disrupted for several months by a new deputy director of the PNC, who was eventually dismissed (see Chapter 7; see also Washington Office on Latin America 1994; Weiss Fagen 1995). Moreover, the training center for the PN continued to produce new recruits well after the opening of the ANSP, in clear violation of the spirit if not the letter of the accords. The new PNC director's attempt to implement ONUSAL's recommendation that all those transferred in excess of the December 1992 agreement be dismissed led to a month-long strike by one of the units in early 1995. The situation was eventually resolved: Over 150 members of the unit retired with a year's severance pay (Spence, Vickers, and Dye 1995, p. 7; El Salvador Information Project 1995).

In late 1994 the government of the newly elected president Calderón Sol decided to dissolve the PN by the end of the year. Some observers attributed this willingness to accelerate the process to evidence of involvement of high-level PN officers in organized crime.[21] The PN was disbanded on 31 December 1994 and its facilities turned over to the PNC in mid-January 1995. Moreover, the government recently increased its funding of the PNC by a substantial fraction.

Ongoing and unresolvable delays in the transfer of land—an essential aspect of the rural reintegration—continue to present serious threats to the consolidation of the peace process. Despite an agreement to scale back the number of beneficiaries from 47,500 to approximately 40,000, as of 16 March 1995 more than 50 percent of the reduced number of beneficiaries had yet to receive land.

According to Ken Ellis, a senior USAID official, the problem was not one of funding for the implementing agency, the Land Bank, but rather one of political will (interview, December 1994). The Land Bank had adequate interim funding from USAID; the bottleneck from month to month in the transfer of land was not due to a shortage of cash. Rather, the recurrent delays were due principally to two factors. First, the titling process remained remarkably cumbersome, despite repeated agreements to streamline it (which could have been done by presidential decree). The government consistently took a bureaucratic approach to the process, insisting until recently that only originally verified tenedores would receive land, and refusing to extend credit until legal title was demonstrated.

Second, the FMLN and its allied peasant organizations found it extremely difficult to construct a stable list of beneficiaries for each property to be transferred. In part this reflects the substantial mobility in the countryside in the aftermath of the war and in part the FMLN's inadequate organizational resources. The instability in the lists of beneficiaries was reinforced by the delays in titling, leading to a vicious circle fueled by insecurity as some beneficiaries decided the delays and terms of transfer were too hard a bargain. As a result of the ongoing delays and problems, representatives of the government and the FMLN agreed in mid-1994 to scale back the number of ex-combatants and tenedores to benefit from the land transfer from 47,500 to 40,648. In May 1994 the former administration agreed to accept nonverified beneficiaries and to extend the duration of the land certificates past the deadline, but as yet little acceleration of titling has resulted. The government announced in May 1994 that adequate funding for the scaled-down version of the land-transfer program had been secured (UN Security Council 1994e).

The Calderón Sol administration took a number of positive steps to accelerate the land transfer, but progress remained slow despite extended deadlines. The replacement of the president of the Land Bank and the hiring of more than 100 members of the FMLN as Land Bank staff may assist the transfer. In mid-March 1995 the government, the FMLN, and the splinter party from the FMLN agreed to close the list of beneficiaries at under 40,000 persons. As of that date, 52 percent of the 29,266 former FMLN tenedores had received land, as well as 35 percent of the former soldiers.

The delays in the transfer of land continue to undermine the reinsertion process, as beneficiaries of the rural reintegration program endure continuing uncertainty. Nonetheless, despite the delays, the training programs of the various reinsertion programs were completed in 1994 (UN General Assembly 1994). Between August 1993 and May 1994, 5,280 ex-combatants of the FMLN, 5,031 former soldiers, and 1,220 tenedores participated in agricultural training; through 1 July 1994, 1,685 FMLN ex-combatants and 6,239 former soldiers completed training as part of urban reinsertion programs. The training for the midlevel commanders was completed in March 1994, with 190 receiving technical training, 350 training in business administration, and 60 training in executive-level business administration. In addition, some 1,200 ex-combatants, of which about 700 are former members of the FMLN, continue to receive scholarships, almost 80 percent for university studies.

However, delays and problems in the extension of credit for reinsertion continue. Beneficiaries of the urban program are presently in the process of applying for supplementary credits. The process has been delayed by the cumbersome application forms and the lack of feasibility studies to help beneficiaries identify potential projects (UNDP 1994). Funding for some programs remains inadequate, perhaps due to donor reluctance to commit funds without clear signals that the necessary commitment to land transfer is in place (Table 5.2; UN Security Council 1994c).

Although three-quarters of the beneficiaries of the rural reinsertion program had received five-year credits to capitalize their farms by mid-1994 (UN General Assembly 1994), the program to extend annual production credit did not receive adequate financial and organizational resources. According to GAO estimates, the need for agricultural credit on the part of potential beneficiaries of the land-transfer program was at least double that available in 1993. An ongoing problem has been bank requirements that applicants have clear title or landlord's permission and records clear of any accumulated debt. These requirements have been difficult for many beneficiaries to meet and have recently been weakened (UN Security Council 1994b; interview with USAID official, December 1994). Although some distribution of emergency housing has occurred, projects to develop permanent housing suffer delays due both to the problems with land transfer and to a lack of funding (UN General Assembly 1994).

In mid-1994 the parties to the agreement negotiated a rescheduling of the implementation of the accords (UN Security Council 1994c). The agreement addressed several of the reinsertion issues: ONUSAL was given more explicit authority to oversee the PNC, the government was to guarantee access to credit by beneficiaries of the land-transfer program, and a timetable for the reinsertion programs was defined. However, delays continue, particularly in the transfer of land.

Reinsertion benefits remained a hotly contested issue; demobilized members of the National Police, security forces, and civil-defense patrols paralyzed the government on a number of occasions, most recently in January and February 1995, when thousands of protestors occupied the National Assembly and other government buildings demanding land and indemnity payments. Many of the demands clearly exceed the commitments of the peace accords (in particular, civil-defense patrol members were never considered in any of the negotiations to be eligible for the reinsertion benefits). Under the mediation of ONUSAL, the government agreed to a compromise set of programs to be implemented in the subsequent two months.[22] The specter of ongoing unrest by ex-combatants of both sides in neighboring Nicaragua offers a cautionary lesson to Salvadoran observers, many of whom associate the increasing crime rate with the demobilization of combatants of both armies and the inadequacy of the reinsertion programs.[23]

The debate over beneficiary participation at the local level continues as some opposition NGOs report their marginalization from the town-meeting process (Murray et al. 1994).[24] Many NGOs had little success in direct application to the SRN; most of the opposition organizations that received SRN resources participated in agricultural credit programs coordinated by Catholic Relief Services or technical-assistance programs coordinated by the UNDP (SRN 1994). Particularly troubling was the experience of Suchitoto, where an innovative experiment in local concertación was subsequently squashed by SRN and ARENA officials (Yariv and Curtis 1992; Murray et al. 1994). Recent efforts by the new administration may indicate a greater openness toward opposition-NGO participation. However, the cancellation of a meeting of mayors of various parties to explore the potential for a regional-development plan for their areas of San Vicente, due to death threats by the apparent resurgence of a notorious death squad, indicates the continuing political tensions surrounding local reconstruction initiatives (El Salvador Information Project 1995).

A global evaluation of reconstruction efforts in El Salvador, and the National Reconstruction Plan in particular, has yet to be conducted (but see Murray et al. 1994 for the most thorough attempt to date). Although the SRN has issued periodic assessments of its programs (for example, SRN 1993b), a significant amount of reconstruction funding does not pass through the SRN (for example, some $200 million in Japanese funding for major reconstruction), nor are institutional self-evaluations as illuminating as an overall assessment might be. The task is difficult: The categories of funding and the assigning of particular funding to particular categories have undergone continuous redefinition in the various reconstruction documents, with the consequence that tracing program design and funding is complicated in most cases. In addition, available government reports often do not adequately clarify the standing of financial commitments (how much has been committed, how much disbursed, how much assigned to the executing agencies, how much expended; see Murray et al. 1994). A comprehensive evaluation of the reconstruction process to date should be based in part on case studies of a representative group of municipalities in order to assess the incidence of various programs and the adequacy of co-ordination among them, as in Murray et al.'s study (1994). The fundamental issue is whether or not the efforts will impel a new distinct pattern of economic and human development in the postwar period.

Finally, although the socioeconomic forum did not become an arena for wide-ranging negotiations over broader social and economic issues, as some of its supporters had hoped it would, some revisions to existing labor law were made after labor organizations succeeded in making credible the possibility that the United States would revoke Generalized System of Preferences (GSP) status to Salvadoran exports (Economist Intelligence Unit 1993, 1994). Although provisions for the founding of a labor council as a consultative body to the Ministry of Labor were included, the revisions concerning the right of free association were not (UN Security Council 1994b). There have been no agreements on wages to date.

The Outstanding Agenda of the Peace Accords

Although much of the agenda mandated by the peace accords has been accomplished, some aspects of the agreement essential to the consolidation of peace in El Salvador are not as yet adequately implemented. The further consolidation of the National Civilian Police and the reintegration of ex-combatants and tenedores are the most pressing of the outstanding agenda, all the more urgent after ONUSAL departed at the end of April 1995.[25] A small team of specialists (MINISAL) remains in the country to continue the verification of the remaining agenda's implementation, coordinating with the UNDP in ongoing reinsertion programs.

The PNC faces formidable challenges to the consolidation of its role in the postwar period. The ongoing crime wave, fueled in part by the demobilized ex-combatants, has led to a trend toward remilitarization of public security, such as military troops patrolling the streets as a deterrent under Operation Guardian in early 1995 (Spence, Vickers, and Dye 1995, p. 9; Fundación Flor de Izote 1995). The organized and at times violent protests of former members of the armed forces, the security forces, and the civil-defense organizations would intimidate even an experienced police force.

Despite efforts by the UN and a number of donor countries, including Spain and the United States, to fortify the judiciary and the PNC, investigation and prosecution of serious crimes remains largely a goal, not a reality (Popkin 1994; Spence, Vickers, and Dye 1995). According to a 1994 UN report, not one of the 75 most serious violations of the right to life after July 1992 resulted in a trial (UN Security Council 1994d, pp. 11–13). Indeed, in over half of the cases there was no police investigation at all; this indicates the inability of the new PNC to adequately enforce the rule of law as yet. In some cases in which investigations did lead to the identification of suspects, judicial authorities did not act promptly to issue warrants and on occasion released suspects despite evidence. Although serious deficiencies continue, the present process of judicial review and training under the new Supreme Court should result in a strengthened judiciary. Ongoing technical assistance to the National Counsel for the Judiciary and other judicial bodies is essential for the consolidation of an impartial judicial system to eradicate impunity.

The PNC has a range of resources upon which to draw to meet this challenge. According to one expert, the law and doctrine of the PNC, as well as the curriculum of the National Public Security Academy, conform to modern standards for police conduct, accountability, and civilian control (Stanley 1995, p. 7). The training in police methods in the academy exceeds the training previously available in El Salvador; accumulating field experience will also help. Although training and retraining of PNC members by international instructors at the academy may continue in the short run, the training of Salvadoran instructors would contribute to the long-term viability of the force. The recent retirement of a number of former members of the PN from overly autonomous units of the PNC may contribute to the consolidation of the civilian nature of the new force.

A range of legislation addressing the various institutional reforms mandated by the peace agreement and the Truth Commission has yet to be passed. The constitutional reforms have yet to be ratified by the new Legislative Assembly as required by law. In addition, the government has not yet ratified various international human-rights agreements (including a recognition of the compulsory jurisdiction of the Inter-American Court of Human Rights), a binding recommendation of the Truth Commission (UN Security Council 1994f). Finally, the nomination of a new National Counsel for the Defense of Human Rights met stiff resistance in the Legislative Assembly (*Proceso* 1995b).

The adequate reintegration of ex-combatants is essential for the consolidation of peace and democracy. According to the UN, approximately half of the demobilized members of the armed forces were not attended to by any reinsertion program (UN General Assembly 1994, p. 10). More than 50 percent of the reduced number of beneficiaries of the land-transfer program have yet to receive title to properties. Those beneficiaries who have received title need ongoing programs of training and credit if their reinsertion is not to reproduce long-standing patterns of rural poverty. The remaining properties are myriad smallholdings in the northern departments; their transfer poses particularly challenging problems (Spence, Vickers, and Dye 1995, p. 13).

In addition, the transfer of the numerous small properties underlying communities of repatriated refugees, such as Segundo Montes and San José Las Flores, remains an urgent and challenging issue. The "human settlements" pose special problems because the social and productive infrastructure developed during the civil war would be undermined if only a piecemeal fraction of the underlying properties was transferred. In the judgment of the UN, the resolution of the issue requires special treatment and the transfer of property rights en bloc (UN Security Council 1994e, p. 8).

Although the completion of the presently defined programs is necessary, it is not sufficient for successful reintegration. Additional training, and the extension of credit and ongoing technical assistance for the participants in the urban reinsertion programs, including the midlevel commanders of the FMLN, would also contribute to reconstruction and the consolidation of peace. As the UN Secretary General stated:

> The development of programs established in the accords that attend to ex-combatants, demobilized soldiers, and tenedores between determined dates does not in itself guarantee the sustainability of their reinsertion. It is necessary to support these actions with development projects that guarantee the generation of permanent jobs, the securing of sufficient income to provide for minimal necessities and to support the reknitting of the social fabric. The sustainability in the medium and long run of the process requires substantial changes in the programs providing attention to the ex-combatants of the FMLN, the demobilized soldiers of the armed forces, and the civilian population resident in the formerly conflictive areas. It is necessary to complement the initiatives presently underway with new projects of economic, social, and political reinsertion and reintegration that will allow a change in emphasis from an emergency to sustainable development. There exists a high risk of social decomposition if the basic needs of the population of the ex-conflictive areas do not receive integral attention (UN General Assembly, 1994, p. 6; author's translation from the Spanish).

The provision of housing for ex-combatants remains an outstanding part of the reinsertion programs.

The documentation of voters and the construction of an accurate electoral roster remain key issues for the transparency and legitimacy of future elections. The newly constituted Electoral Tribunal is presently considering a range of reform to electoral procedures, including the issuance of a single-identity electoral and social-security document, the construction of a new roster, voting by residence, and procedures for broader representation on municipal councils (UN Security Council 1994e).

Increasing unrest by workers protesting labor conditions and wages in the *maquilas* of the free-trade zones underlines the need to reconstitute the socioeconomic forum to address labor issues (Fundación Flor de Izote 1995; *Proceso* 1995b). Although the recent inauguration of the Labor Council provides one venue for discussion, some observers doubt that it will address many of the forum's outstanding issues.

In the long run the financial burden of the various programs and institutions established as part of the peace process will be increasingly assumed by the Salvadoran government. Prospects for funding the 1995 shortfall of approximately $138 million to finance the remaining costs of the peace process are uncertain at present (Government of El Salvador 1995; reproduced in Table 6.2). These issues are addressed in Chapters 6 and 7.

Domestic political support for the consolidation of the outstanding agenda of the peace accords is complicated by the present decomposition and realignment within and between the political parties. Two parties, the FMLN and the Christian Democrats, split in the aftermath of the 1994 elections. Nor has ARENA been immune to the present tendency toward internal division: the Calderón Sol administration mustered only lukewarm support for its economic policy of radically opening up the economy, and allegations of corruption by members of the former and present administrations continue to be made by a splinter party of ARENA.

Conclusions

The peace accords hold out the prospect not only of ending the war but of achieving a transition to political democracy. The importance of the agreements on political reform for the relation between the consolidation of peace and economic policy go well beyond the obvious issues of the implied fiscal burden imposed on the postwar state and the desirability of democratic objectives per se. The consolidation of democratic politics is necessary if stable patterns of investment and economic growth are to be achieved. The consolidation of democratic politics is also crucial if bargaining over the results of economic growth is to lead to the emergence of a more inclusive economic model.

The course of the implementation of the accords was determined by a process of political bargaining that overlapped with the negotiation of the accords themselves. In that bargaining, domestic political actors hammered out agreements and concessions on the various issues that reflected the evolving balance of power among the contending interests. International actors—particularly the UN and USAID—contributed resources, mediation, and general accountability that shaped the evolving balance of power in ways ranging from ensuring that some resources went to opposition organizations, to conditioning funds on compliance with the accords, to providing various forums for ongoing negotiations. Yet international pressure was not itself sufficient to ensure timely and adequate implementation of three of the most difficult issues: deployment of the PNC, land transfer, and the purging of the military.[26] Progress on those issues required extraordinary international pressure, with limited results (except in the case of the purge, which was eventually completed, though far behind schedule).

Although significant change in key institutions has been achieved, the implementation of other commitments remains uneven and precarious. Contributing issues include the daunting complexity of the problems themselves, lacunae in the peace accords (especially on judicial and land issues), the difference between the political logic of the negotiation process and the economic logic of some of the mandated reforms, the declining bargaining power of the FMLN, the insufficient institutional capacity of organizations key to the process, and enduring, profound social and economic inequalities (de Soto and del Castillo 1994b; Segovia 1994b; Weiss Fagen 1995). In addition, the pace of implementation was frequently subordinated to the economic goals and policies of the government (UN General Assembly 1994, p. 5).

However, contrary to some analyses, it has been argued here that funding constraints have not been the principal obstacle to the timely implementation of the peace agreement.[27] Only the development of the PNC and the extension of agricultural credit suffered significantly for this reason; even in the first case, the lack of an initial public commitment by the government contributed to the initial lack of international funding (Stanley 1995), and the extension of credit suffered as much for the lack of administrative capacity on the part of the implementing agencies. The delays in the land-transfer program—and hence in other reinsertion programs as well—were not due to budgetary problems. The pattern of ongoing delays and inadequate measures for the police and reinsertion programs points to a more fundamental problem: a lack of political will on the part of the government at crucial stages of the reconstruction process. That the delay affected the new police force and the land-transfer program is particularly troubling: According to de Soto and del Castillo (1994b), "on their success rests the entire peace process"—and its sustainability in the long run.[28]

In the first year of the Calderón Sol administration some progress was made.[29] The durability of the reforms to date, as well as the further implementation of outstanding reforms, will depend on the government's commitment as well as its ability to mobilize adequate domestic resources to finance the new institutions, develop adequate credit channels, and consolidate the investments in the former conflicted zones of the country.

Although much has been achieved, neither the peace accords—even if fully implemented—nor the government's economic policies contain adequate distributive measures to alleviate poverty effectively and promote human development. An agenda of broader economic participation through well-designed redistributive measures is likely to be a condition for inclusive economic growth as well as the consolidation of the peace. In the long run, the success of El Salvador's peace process will hinge on the following question: To what extent, and on whose terms, will distributional issues be addressed on the postwar political terrain? Future political bargaining over both further implementation of the peace accords and economic policy will determine the outcome.

Notes

1. The author would like to express her gratitude for comments on earlier versions to James Boyce, Hector Dada, Richard Fagen, Francesca Jessup, Terry Karl, Anders Kompass, Kevin Murray, Eva Paus, Alexander Segovia, and William Stanley, and her appreciation for financial support to the San Salvador office of the United Nations Development Programme and the Harvard Academy of International and Area Studies. Remaining errors are of course solely hers.

2. See Whitfield (1994) for a definitive account of the Jesuit case and its consequences for U.S. relations with El Salvador. U.S. support was further undermined by subsequent detailed allegations of human-rights violations and corruption on the part of high-level military and government officials (U.S. House of Representatives, Arms Control and Foreign Policy Caucus, 1990).

3. See Holiday and Stanley (1993) and Weiss Fagen (1995) for analysis of the UN's role in the implementation of the peace accords.

4. Interview with senior UN official, November 1994.

5. Interview with senior UN official, November 1994. As the deadline approached in late December, the difficult issue of the definition of "conflicted zones," which had been a stumbling block throughout the negotiations, surfaced once again. In relation to the cease-fire negotiations, the question was one of geography: Which forces would be concentrated where? In addition, the issue concerned the transfer of land to ex-combatants and their supporters in the conflicted zones. While negotiators never reached agreement on the conflicted-area boundaries, enough confidence was marshaled that the parties agreed not to delay signing the agreement on that basis. This as well as other ambiguities in the socioeconomic accord proved to be very difficult issues in the implementation of the agreement.

6. Despite the limitations of the socioeconomic chapter, the Salvadoran peace agreement was more detailed than many other agreements ending civil wars (Segovia 1994b).

7. The accords also provided for civilian participation in curriculum development in the military academy.

8. Magistrates are now selected by a two-thirds majority of the National Assembly and serve staggered nine-year terms (Popkin 1994).

9. Salvadoran elites were well aware of the difficulties in neighboring Nicaragua posed by disgruntled ex-combatants on both sides, which without doubt contributed to the inclusion of reintegration programs.

10. One indication of the depth of conviction on this issue: FMLN field commanders in Usulután—many of them of peasant origins—repeatedly conditioned the concentration and demobilization of their forces on progress in the transfer of land, at times without authorization from their central command (Wood 1995).

11. The issue was further confused by a clause in which the government reserved the right to apply the law (i.e., carry out evictions) on land occupied after 3 July 1991, the date of the agreement between the government and the Democratic Peasant Association (ADC).

12. Because tenedores did not necessarily occupy property, I will use the Spanish term rather than the literal translation "holders."

13. The agreement specifically mentioned two government agencies, the Land Bank and the Salvadoran Institute for Agrarian Transformation (ISTA), but did not clarify their role in its implementation; nor did it define the overall line of authority among the various governmental organizations.

14. The eventual target population consisted of 35,400 former soldiers, 11,000 former guerrillas (including war veterans), 60,000 displaced persons, 26,000 repatriates, and 800,000 residents of the PRN municipalities (SRN 1992a).

15. Combining the categories of (major) "infrastructure" and "basic infrastructure" (under the rubric of "social sector" and "human capital"), infrastructure accounted for 63 percent of the proposed budget of priority needs (see Table 5.1).

16. With the help of hindsight to approximate the missing estimates, a comparison of the two proposals shows that—excluding land—the government's proposal was roughly half that of the FMLN (author's rough estimate).

17. For a more detailed breakdown of funding recommendations by program and commitments by donors, see Table 7.2. For less detailed but more recent estimates, see Tables 6.4 and 7.3.

18. William Stanley, personal communication, February 1995.

19. See Buergenthal (1994) for a detailed account by a commissioner of the investigative process and internal debates that informed the report.

20. A U.S. State Department official argues that the deployment of the PNC as early as it did occur was important, despite inadequate training and equipment, because it was important to capitalize on the euphoria of the signing of the accords (interview with U.S. State Department official, December 1994).

21. In June 1994, the lieutenant in charge of the criminal-investigations division of the PN was identified on a videotape of a bank robbery in San Salvador (Popkin 1994).

22. *Proceso* 1995a.

23. See Collier (1994) for evidence linking rising crime rates in some districts of post–civil war Uganda with landlessness of ex-combatants.

24. The winner-take-all nature of municipal elections impedes local concertación; there are recent reports that the Elections Tribunal is considering reform on this issue. In addition, the tribunal may initiate a new electoral roll (voter list) before the next elections, in answer to a frequent complaint as to the inaccuracy

of the existing roll in the March 1994 elections (Spence, Dye, and Vickers 1994; Spence and Vickers 1994).

25. Beginning in October 1994, an interagency commission constituted by the UNDP and ONUSAL began developing plans for continued technical assistance for priority areas, including the strengthening of the new democratic institutions, the reinsertion programs, electoral reform, and the fund for war veterans and their families.

26. See Holiday and Stanley (1993) and Weiss Fagen (1995) for detailed analysis of the role of the international organizations, particularly the UN.

27. This argument therefore differs from the emphasis given by other analysts to macroeconomic policy in delaying implementation of the agreement (e.g., Overseas Development Council 1994).

28. Whether international actors could have contributed to the construction of a deeper commitment to the implementation of the peace agreement, either through more funding or different conditions on its donation, is explored in Chapter 7. The constraints and opportunities for domestic-resource mobilization are explored in Chapter 6.

29. On this point, after noting the encouraging evidence of sustained political will by government officials to comply fully with the remaining elements of the peace accords, a recent UN Security Council document went on to state:

> However, it must be matched by concrete action and the capacity to activate still recalcitrant sectors within the administration. Delay in implementation of the outstanding commitments has also been due to a lack of organization and expertise—a common phenomenon in developing countries—and in some instances, a lack of financing (UN Security Council 1994e).

6

Domestic Resource Mobilization

Alexander Segovia

As peace has come to El Salvador the need to mobilize domestic resources has grown. Although international agencies and foreign governments have welcomed the end of the armed conflict, external aid has nonetheless fallen. Domestic savings remain low, as does government revenue. The foreign exchange gap has been filled by remittances from Salvadoran emigrants, as noted in Chapter 4, but it cannot be assumed that this windfall will be permanent. In this context, a crucial task for Salvadoran policymakers is to devise mechanisms that will allow the economy increasingly to use domestic resources to finance the costs of peace and to achieve economic growth with social justice.

Domestic resources consist of public and private savings. The public, or fiscal, side has been a major focus of attention—and conditionality—for international financing agencies in recent years. This has been due, on the one hand, to the need to redress fiscal imbalances in order to ensure macroeconomic stability and, on the other hand, to the recognition that increases in public savings are needed in order to make more domestic resources available for social spending and infrastructure improvements, as well as to satisfy specific commitments under the Chapultepec Accords of January 1992.

To help on the fiscal side, the government instituted a sweeping tax-reform initiative (Gallagher 1993). Although the reform has produced some favorable results in terms of simplification and improved efficiency of the tax system, it has not fully yielded the expected increase in fiscal receipts. Given the rigidity of public spending, there has been a constant potential conflict between the need to fulfill the commitments contained in the peace agreements and the need to maintain and strengthen macroeconomic stability. The threat that in this trade-off the "adjusting variable" would be peace expenditures has been raised in requests for external assistance. Yet it is by no means clear that the potential for the mobilization of domestic resources for peace through expenditure shifting and increased tax revenues has been exhausted.

The government's role would perhaps be less important if the country enjoyed a relatively high level of private savings and an efficient financial system to intermediate these savings into private investment. The resulting private investment could, in turn, prompt the sort of growth that provides for greater social stability and improved tax revenues. Unfortunately, domestic savings are extraordinarily low, at 1.8 percent of GDP, and private investment is both well below historical standards and heavily reliant on external transfers and remittances by Salvadorans abroad. The savings-investment structure in the country is weak and fragile.

This chapter examines the issues of domestic-resource mobilization. Although we devote some attention to private savings and investment—partly because we believe that a healthy uptick of private investment is critical to the goal of sustainable growth in El Salvador—we focus here on the fiscal side. We specifically look at the government's efforts since 1992 to mobilize sufficient domestic resources to enable it to live up to the commitments made in the peace agreements, and explore the effect that the conditions imposed by international financing agencies have had on this process. We assess the tension between the fiscal requirements associated with the peace accords and the fiscal imperatives associated with economic stabilization policies.

The chapter is divided into five parts. The first section analyzes historical trends in savings and investment in El Salvador. The second section provides an overview of the basic features of the tax-reform initiative and its principal results. The government's efforts to mobilize domestic resources following the signing of the peace agreements are discussed in the third section. The fourth section examines the tensions that have developed as the government has endeavored to meet the requirements of the peace accords while simultaneously trying to stabilize the economy. The final section presents some conclusions regarding the need and potential for mobilizing a greater volume of resources in the coming years in order to meet the obligations and challenges of a lasting peace.

Historical Trends in Savings and Investment

During the 1970s total investment (excluding inventory changes) in El Salvador averaged 18 percent of GDP, with private investment equaling 12.5 percent, and public investment 5.4 percent of GDP. With the crisis of the 1980s, the total investment rate fell dramatically, with the decline led by a pronounced drop in private investment (see Table 6.1). The 1990s have seen a recovery of private investment. Public investment has shown some dynamism with the implementation of the National Reconstruction Program (PRN), but it remains well below past levels.

The relationship between private and public investment in developing countries has been the focus of much research. There is a growing consensus

Table 6.1 Savings and Investment as a Percentage of GDP, 1970–1994

	1970	1971	1972	1973	1974	1975	1976	1977	1978	1979	1980	1981	1982	1983	1984	1985	1986	1987	1988	1989	1990	1991	1992	1993	1994
National savings																									
Private	14.1	14.3	15.2	15.2	14.0	17.0	19.7	24.5	14.5	18.7	14.1	7.3	10.8	10.6	9.8	8.7	16.2	7.2	8.3	8.8	6.6	9.5	10.7	12.0	
Public	0	0	0	0	0	0	0	0	0	0	0	0	0	0	0	0	0	0	0.3	-1.6	-1.4	-0.7	n.a.	n.a.	n.a.
Total	14.1	14.3	15.2	15.2	14.0	17.0	19.7	24.5	14.5	18.7	14.1	7.3	10.8	10.6	9.8	8.7	16.2	7.2	8.6	7.2	5.2	8.8	n.a.	n.a.	n.a.
Domestic savings	13.5	13.6	15.1	15.2	14.2	16.9	18.7	24.1	14.6	17.9	14.2	7.3	7.5	6.6	5.2	3.3	8.9	5.2	6.3	4.9	0.7	1.5	0.5	1.8	
Foreign savings	-0.8	1.3	-1.1	3.1	8.6	5.1	0.2	-1.1	9.3	-0.6	-0.8	6.9	2.4	1.4	2.1	2.1	-2.9	5.2	4.2	8.1	6.6	5.0	5.1	3.9	
Gross domestic investment																									
Private	9.2	9.7	12.0	11.3	12.9	15.0	14.3	13.9	15.6	11.5	6.4	6.2	6.5	7.0	7.5	8.7	10.6	10.7	9.5	9.8	9.5	10.9	12.3	12.9	13.7
Public	2.8	3.5	4.4	4.3	5.3	8.0	6.2	7.3	5.8	6.1	7.1	7.3	6.1	4.6	3.9	3.3	2.5	2.9	3.1	3.5	2.3	2.5	3.6	3.6	3.4
Inventory changes	1.3	2.3	-2.3	2.6	4.4	-0.9	-0.5	2.2	2.4	0.5	-0.3	0.7	0.6	0.4	0.5	0.1	0.1	-1.3	0.2	2.9	0.0	0.4	0.5	0.1	0.2
Total	13.2	15.6	14.2	18.3	22.6	22.1	20.0	23.4	23.8	18.1	13.3	14.2	13.2	12.0	12.0	10.8	13.2	12.4	12.8	15.3	11.8	13.8	16.5	16.6	17.3

Sources: BCR; USAID.
n.a. = data not available

that the two are complementary rather than contradictory. Although some still argue that public investment "crowds out" the private-sector counterpart (either because it diverts material or financial resources or because it challenges the dominant position of private capital and hence reduces investor confidence), others suggest that public investment actually enhances private investors' expectations by providing infrastructure and a more buoyant aggregate market (Taylor 1988, 1989; Greene and Villanueva 1991).

Econometric results on the issue are generally supportive of the latter "crowding in" position. Tun Wai and Wong (1982) separately estimated private-investment functions for five developing countries from the early 1960s to the mid-1970s; their results suggest an important role for government investment. Blejer and Khan (1984) used a pooled approach to examine the effects of government investment and other variables on private investment in 24 developing countries over 1971–1979; the results suggest positive effects of public-sector investment, albeit with evidence of crowding out in some cases. Subsequent analyses by Greene and Villanueva (1991), Pastor (1992b), Pastor and Hilt (1993), and Serven and Solimano (1993), all of which use pooled cross-sectional and time-series data, likewise find a positive impact from public investment.

The impact of public investment on private investment is likely, of course, to vary from place to place. Even if the relationship is positive in most settings, there could be cases in which an ill-planned or poorly executed program of public investment fails to stimulate or even deters private investment.

An examination of the investment data for the past 25 years suggests that the relationship between public and private investment in El Salvador is complex and has varied over time (see Figure 6.1). In the 1970s the two variables were positively correlated ($r = 0.8$); and though correlation does not prove causation, this observation is consistent with the logic of crowding in. Private investment dropped sharply with the onset of the political crisis at the end of the decade, suggesting that instability is indeed an important deterrent to investment. During the 1980s private investment recovered somewhat while public investment fell, with the latter itself being in effect crowded out by military expenditure.[1] The challenge in coming years will be to ensure that public investment effectively stimulates private investment.

During the 1980s a significant change occurred with regard to the sources of financing for investment. In the 1970s investment was financed primarily out of national savings, of which domestic savings were the major component. This situation changed radically during the 1980s. On the one hand, foreign savings (mostly official loans) became an important source of investment financing. On the other hand, remittances from Salvadorans living abroad became the principal component of national savings, with domestic savings falling from 16.4 percent in the 1970s to 6.9 percent in the 1980s and only 1.1 percent in the 1990s.[2]

Figure 6.1   Private and Public Investment, 1970–1994 (As a percentage of GDP)

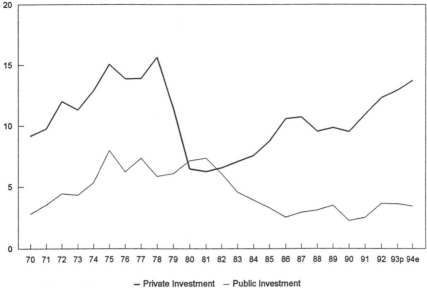

— Private Investment   — Public Investment

Source: USAID, from BCR.

El Salvador's situation has differed strikingly from that of most other developing countries (see Table 6.2). In almost all other regions of the developing world (including Latin America), domestic savings exceed national savings, mainly due to the need to finance foreign transfers related to debt and foreign direct investment. Moreover, El Salvador's *national* savings (which includes the influx of remittances) actually rose in the course of the 1980s, thanks to the export of earners to higher-income economies, primarily the United States. The Salvadoran economy has thus deepened its external dependence; external resources have become the principal way to finance both the foreign exchange gap and the other "gap" with regard to domestic investment.

The relationship between foreign savings and national (or domestic) savings in developing countries has also been a topic of considerable research. The earlier view that foreign savings, in the form of external loans or foreign direct investment, are simply additional to domestic savings was challenged by Griffin (1970) and others, who argued that foreign-capital inflows could discourage both private and public domestic savings. Public-sector savings, in particular, could be deterred if external loans provide a "soft option" for governments, compared to the harder options of raising tax revenues or cutting public-consumption expenditures.

Econometric analyses have confirmed that in many cases foreign savings do, in effect, crowd out domestic savings, although the direction of causality as well as the magnitude of the effect varies among countries

Table 6.2   **National and Domestic Savings Rates in 83 Developing Countries,
1970–1992**

Indicator/Region	1970–1980	1981–1984	1985–1988	1989–1992
Gross national savings/GDP				
Africa	0.11	0.06	0.06	n.a.
Asia	0.18	0.18	0.19	n.a.
Europe/Middle East/Northern Africa	0.15	0.14	0.12	n.a.
Latin America and the Caribbean	0.17	0.12	0.11	n.a.
El Salvador	0.17	0.10	0.14	0.12
Total	0.14	0.10	0.10	n.a.
Gross domestic savings/GDP				
Africa	0.11	0.06	0.08	n.a.
Asia	0.19	0.19	0.21	n.a.
Europe/Middle East/Northern Africa	0.15	0.16	0.15	n.a.
Latin America and the Caribbean	0.20	0.17	0.17	n.a.
El Salvador	0.18	0.04	0.03	0.01
Total	0.15	0.12	0.13	n.a.

Source: Rivera Campos 1994.
n.a. = data not available

(see, for example, Bowles 1987). In the case of El Salvador, as Figure 6.2 shows, the correlation between foreign savings and national savings in the period 1980–1994 is quite strongly negative ($r = -0.8$). Although one should not regard this simple statistical relationship as conclusive,[3] it does suggest that foreign savings have tended to reduce national savings (including savings out of remittances as well as domestic income).[4]

When national savings are broken down into private and public savings, it becomes apparent that over the years public savings have played only a minor role in financing investment in El Salvador (see Table 6.1). The public sector's meager participation in national savings can largely be attributed to the low tax ratio, which historically has been below world standards and is now making only meager progress upward. It is critically important that the state be able to raise revenues for four reasons: first, to finance peace-related expenditures; second, to prepare for the eventual diminution of foreign transfers and foreign savings; third, to permit the expansion of public investment that complements private investment; and fourth, to be able to selectively finance private investments through official credit mechanisms. It is to this issue of revenue performance that we now turn.

The Principal Features and Results of the Tax Reform

Recognizing the need to both enhance and stabilize tax revenue, the adjustment program implemented in 1989 attempted to establish a more

Figure 6.2 National Versus Foreign Savings, 1980–1994 (As a percentage of GDP)

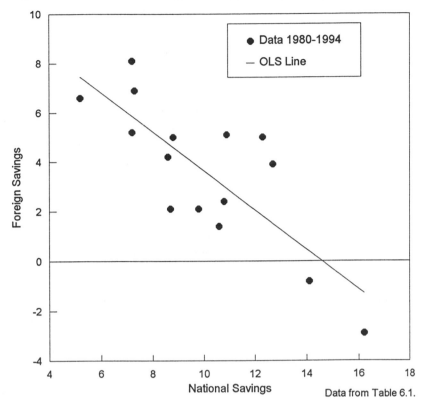

Data from Table 6.1.

modern and equitable tax system and to reduce the state's reliance on volatile export income.[5] Among the most important measures implemented were: (1) a total overhaul of the tax system, including the elimination of all taxes on exports, elimination of the tax on net worth, simplification of personal and corporate income taxes, reduction of the top income-tax rate from 60 percent to 25 percent, and replacement of revenue stamps by a value-added tax (VAT); (2) creation of a unit focusing on collecting from large taxpayers; (3) enactment of a law on tax fraud; (4) improvement of the computer, auditing, and control systems; (5) simplification and reduction of taxes on imports; and (6) elimination of the majority of tax exemptions.

This reform in the structure and composition of tax revenues has had a profound impact. First, the elimination of export taxes—which had traditionally been the most significant source of government revenues—and the introduction of the VAT has indeed made the tax system more stable (see Table 6.3 and Figure 4.1). Second, the reform simplified the tax system so that the bulk of state revenues now come from three taxes: the VAT, the income tax, and the tax on imports. This change has made the tax system much easier to administer and has permitted greater administrative control, particularly because of the tremendous enhancement in computer, auditing, and control systems.[6]

Despite the merits and achievements of the reform there are problems. First, the new system, by reducing direct taxes and increasing reliance on indirect taxes, has made the overall taxation structure more regressive, worsening the already severe inequality of incomes and making the achievement of social justice more difficult. Second, the reform has not had the expected results in terms of increasing revenues, partly because of an extraordinarily high degree of tax evasion.[7] Although the tax ratio (ratio of tax revenues to GDP) did increase by two percentage points during the period 1989–1993, rising from 7.6 percent of GDP in 1989 to 9.7 percent in 1994, it continues to be very low in comparison to that of other underdeveloped countries,[8] and remains low even by the standards of recent Salvadoran history (see Figure 6.3).

Rivera Campos (1994, p. 11) suggests that "official transfers [of foreign savings] are allowing a lower tax burden." In other words, while the formal conditionalities and less-formal policy dialogue of the international donors have sought to encourage an increased tax effort, the financial resources they provide may in themselves have had the opposite effect. In such a context, the strength with which conditionality is exercised becomes critical.[9]

The low level of tax revenues has been largely responsible for the government's failure to achieve its original goal of eliminating the fiscal deficit by 1994 (BCR 1989, p. 20). In fact, the deficit during the period 1989–1994 was higher on average than during the preceding five years (see Appendix Table A.2c). Such modest results illustrate why the fiscal area continues to be called the Achilles' heel of the Salvadoran economy (USAID 1994a, p. 14). It also helps to explain why the state has become increasingly reliant on external resources to finance social spending, especially for programs related to poverty alleviation and investment in human resources. This is particularly worrisome because external assistance is expected to decline in coming years.

The Peace Accords and Domestic Resource Mobilization

Bringing a formal cease-fire and peace to conflict-torn El Salvador was a process that required courage and vision on the part of both sides. Consolidating the peace likewise requires courage, as wary ex-combatants learn to struggle not with arms, but within an agreed-upon political process. It also requires money, devoted both directly to implementing the terms of the peace accords and to the social and human capital-building programs that can yield social harmony. The cost of peace is indeed high, but as the 1980s showed, the cost of war is even higher.

Table 6.3 Tax Coefficient and Composition of Tax Revenues, 1970–1994 (as a percentage of GDP)

	1970	1971	1972	1973	1974	1975	1976	1977	1978	1979	1980	1981	1982	1983	1984	1985	1986	1987	1988	1989	1990	1991	1992	1993	1994
Tax revenues	10.2	10.2	10.5	11.2	11.6	11.8	13.6	15.7	12.5	13.2	10.8	11.3	10.6	10.6	11.5	11.6	12.8	11.0	9.1	7.6	7.8	8.5	9.0	9.4	9.7
Income	1.5	1.6	1.8	1.7	2.1	2.4	2.5	2.2	2.4	2.0	2.4	2.4	2.4	2.3	2.2	2.1	2.0	2.2	1.9	1.8	1.8	2.0	1.9	2.1	2.1
Sales	0.4	0.7	0.8	0.8	1.0	1.0	1.0	1.0	1.0	1.0	0.9	1.6	1.7	2.5	3.2	3.0	2.8	3.0	2.6	2.4	2.5	2.7	n.a.	n.a.	n.a.
Imports	2.5	2.5	2.5	2.4	2.4	2.1	2.0	2.3	2.0	2.1	1.1	1.0	0.9	0.9	1.1	1.2	1.0	1.1	0.8	1.0	1.1	1.3	1.5	1.8	1.7
Exports	1.9	1.4	1.6	2.3	2.4	2.5	4.2	6.4	3.2	4.6	3.1	2.7	2.2	1.9	2.1	2.5	4.9	1.9	1.4	0.4	0.6	0.5	0.1	0	0
Other	3.9	4.0	3.8	4.0	3.7	3.8	3.9	3.8	3.9	3.5	3.3	3.6	3.4	3.0	2.9	2.8	2.1	2.8	2.4	2.0	1.8	2.0	n.a.	n.a.	n.a.

Source: BCR; 1992–1994 from USAID.
n.a. = data not available

Figure 6.3   Tax Coefficient, 1970–1993

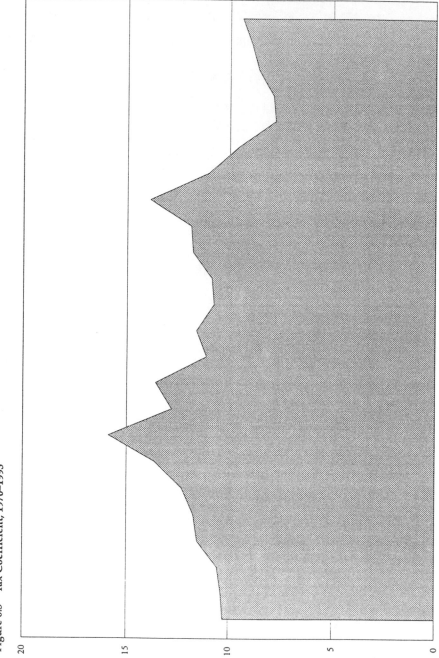

Source: IMF, International Financial Statistics and Government Finance Statistics; 1993 tax revenue drawn from USAID.

As noted in Chapter 5, the United States General Accounting Office (GAO 1994) estimated that it would cost U.S.$1.8 billion to fulfill all the commitments made under the peace agreements through the year 1996. Of this total, the Salvadoran government had committed itself to contribute $408 million (or 22 percent), a figure the GAO viewed as feasible in light of the September 1992 introduction of a VAT and the reduction in debt service resulting from the United States' forgiving $464 million of El Salvador's foreign debt.

In January 1995 the government of El Salvador reported that financing to date for executing the peace agreements totaled nearly $1.4 billion, of which the Salvadoran government had provided $476 million (see Table 6.4). The vast majority of the funds contributed by the Salvadoran government have been used to pay direct costs, especially those related to the strengthening of democratic institutions and population-reintegration programs; in contrast, over half of foreign funds have been used for indirect costs such as infrastructure rehabilitation and social programs.[10]

Table 6.4   Financing of the Peace Process, 1992–1995 (millions of U.S. dollars)

	Foreign financing			Domestic financing	Total available financing
	Loans	Grants	Subtotal		
Direct costs[a]	44.9	362.4	407.3	456.0	863.3
Democratic institutions[b]	1.1	57.2	58.4	343.4	401.8
Reintegration programs	38.6	193.9	232.5	95.8	328.3
Other projects	5.1	111.2	116.4	16.9	133.2
Indirect costs[c]	352.2	155.4	507.6	20.1	527.8
Rehabilitation and replacement of infrastructure damaged in the conflict	339.3	64.8	404.1		404.1
Social and productive support program for population groups most affected by the conflict	12.9	90.6	103.5	14.3	117.8
Debt service				5.9	5.9
Total	397.2	517.8	914.9	476.2	1,391.1

Sources: Calculations made on the basis of information in the publication: Government of El Salvador. *Acuerdos de paz: costo y déficit financiero.* January 1995. Exchange rate used: ¢8.75 = U.S.$1.

Notes: a. Includes the cost of activities scheduled for execution under the peace agreements.

b. Does not include recurrent expenses of democratic institutions that are to be financed by the Salvadoran government under the regular budget.

c. Includes rehabilitation of the infrastructure of basic services and programs designed to boost production, aimed at the people most affected by the conflict.

The peace has, of course, brought dividends as well as costs. Indeed, one of the key factors that explains the successes of the post-1989 structural adjustment program is the peace process itself. Recall that the guerrilla offensive of 1989 was followed the next year by the initiation of the negotiations that eventually culminated in the January 1992 peace accords. The long negotiation process—which made it possible to first de-escalate and then put an end to the armed conflict—fostered a climate of greater stability, which in turn engendered a slow revival of private investment and eventually facilitated a shift of public funds away from military spending.

Table 6.5 shows that since 1991 the defense budget has declined by around 50 percent in real terms and as a proportion of GDP; since 1993 the budget has been frozen in nominal terms at 866.5 million colones (roughly $100 million).[11]

The decline in defense spending has been accompanied by an increase in budget allocations for the social sectors and for activities related to the strengthening of democratic institutions. As can be seen from Table 6.6, allocations for education and health have increased since 1991 both in real terms and as a percentage of GDP. The same has occurred in the case of the budget allocated for the administration of justice and for public safety, which includes the budget of the newly created National Civilian Police.

Whereas the peace has raised new demands for resource use, particularly to implement programs mandated by the accords, it has also made possible economic revival and a realignment of budget priorities. The needs and demands have exceeded the domestic resources committed by the government, however, and hence it has been heavily reliant on foreign help. Securing further external support and improving the mobilization of domestic resources for the peace both remain critical tasks for guaranteeing the sustainability of the Salvadoran polity and economy.

Table 6.5   Evolution of National Defense Budget, 1989–1995

Year	Millions of current colones	Millions of constant colones[a]	Nominal change	Real change	Percentage of GDP
1989	947.0	947.0	—	—	2.9
1990	997.0	807.1	5.0	−14.8	2.4
1991	1,020.3	712.8	2.3	−11.7	2.1
1992	1,183.4	660.9	13.8	−7.3	2.2
1993	866.5	432.1	−36.6	−34.6	1.3
1994	866.5	388.9	0.0	−10.0	1.1
1995	866.5	357.8	0.0	−8.0	1.0

Sources: National budgets and author's own calculations.
Note: a. CPI used deflator, 1989 = 100.

Table 6.6   **Central-Government Budget Outlays in Selected Areas, 1991–1995**

	1991	1992	1993	1994	1995
Nominal (millions of colones)					
Health	404.8	530.0	730.0	881.9	1,204.5
Education	755.9	928.5	1,106.3	1,405.6	1,740.9
Administration of justice[a]	174.7	271.8	376.1	499.2	752.5
Public safety[b]	—	254.7	448.4	572.5	1,068.0
Defense	1,020.3	1,183.4	866.5	866.5	866.5
Real (millions of 1991 colones)					
Health	404.8	441.8	542.8	596.2	740.2
Education	755.9	774.0	882.6	950.2	1,069.8
Administration of justice[a]	174.7	226.6	279.6	337.5	462.4
Public safety[b]	—	212.3	333.4	387.0	656.3
Defense	1,020.3	986.4	644.3	585.8	532.5
As a percentage of total spending					
Health	8.1	7.8	9.6	9.2	10.2
Education	15.2	13.7	14.5	14.7	14.8
Administration of justice[a]	3.5	4.0	4.9	5.2	6.4
Public safety[b]	—	3.7	5.9	6.0	9.0
Defense	20.5	17.5	11.3	9.0	7.4
As a percentage of GDP					
Health	0.8	1.0	1.1	1.1	1.4
Education	1.6	1.7	1.7	1.8	2.1
Administration of justice[a]	0.3	0.5	0.6	0.6	0.9
Public safety[b]	—	0.5	0.7	0.7	1.3
Defense	2.1	2.2	1.3	1.1	1.0

Sources: Ministry of the Treasury and author's own calculations.
Notes: a. Includes the court system, the offices of the inspector general and attorney general, the office of the public prosecutor for human rights, and the judiciary.
　　b. Includes the National Civilian Police force and the national corps of fire fighters.

Fiscal Targets, the Peace Process, and Economic Adjustment

Planning for Peace: Fiscal Targets and Financing the Accords

Public finances were in a precarious state in 1992, when the peace agreements were finalized and signed.[12] The fiscal deficit of the nonfinancial public sector (NFPS) had climbed to 4.4 percent of GDP in 1991—much higher than the figure for 1990 (2.5 percent) and the 1991 target of 2.6 percent. The central government's fiscal deficit had risen from 3.2 percent in 1990 to 5.1 percent in 1991, again above the targeted goal of 2.5 percent.[13] Alarmed by the fiscal imbalances, the IMF insisted on a greater fiscal stringency, including a reduction in the general NFPS deficit by over 2 percent of GDP.[14] The central government itself was supposed to adjust revenue and expenditure by close to 1 percent of the GDP, with expenditure reductions leading the way.[15]

The spending projections were discussed by the IMF's Executive Board on 6 January 1992—two weeks before the formal signing of the Chapultepec Accords. However, the projections made no allowance for the financial implications of peace. The IMF did recognize the problem this might cause:

> . . . according to highly tentative calculations from the outline of a National Reconstruction Plan . . . expenses for the demilitarization of the opposing forces, rehabilitation of refugees and displaced persons, employment and training programs, and infrastructure investment would far exceed any amount that could be reassigned from the 1992 budget (IMF 1991b, pp. 18–19).

After noting that the 1992 government budget contained "no provisions for new spending programs that will be necessitated by the end of the armed conflict," the IMF's Memorandum on Economic Policies stated:

> In principle, the Government will be prepared to reassess and possibly redirect budgeted expenditures (including military outlays) to meet new priorities. Additional outlays that could not be accommodated by the 1992 budget as currently presented would need to be financed entirely by foreign resources, preferably in the form of grants, in order to preserve the price and balance of payments objectives of the program for 1992 (IMF 1991a, Attachment III, pp. 59–60).

Evidently the assumption was that the expenses associated with the peace agreements and national reconstruction would be financed primarily or entirely through foreign resources, in addition to some transitory financing from the central bank (see also USAID 1993b, p. 25).[16]

When peace did come, the failure to account fully for its financial implications produced a worsening of the country's fiscal situation. The NFPS fiscal deficit rose from 4.4 percent of GDP in 1991 to 5.9 percent in 1992 (as contrasted with the target of 2.3 percent). Although the central government's fiscal deficit declined somewhat in 1992 (from 5.1 percent to 4.7 percent), it remained considerably higher than the 2.8 percent objective. The central government also failed to meet its targets for current savings and expenditures (see Table 6.7).

In mid-1992 a World Bank mission visited the country and concluded that:

> Despite the Government's continued commitment to tight monetary and credit policies, the situation remains fragile, particularly on the fiscal side. This is even more problematic as the fiscal implications of the peace

Table 6.7   Commitments Made by the Government of El Salvador to the
International Monetary Fund in 1992, and Achievements

	Target level	Actual level
Percentages of GDP		
Overall deficit (excluding grants)		
of the nonfinancial public sector	2.25	5.9
Central government deficit (3.75% of GDP in 1991)	2.25	3.0
Current savings	1.5	0.4
Total central-government revenues	10.0	11.7
Current expenditure	10.0	11.4
Percentages of government expenditure		
Military spending (22% in 1991)	20.0	15.0
Spending on health and education (22% in 1991)	25.0	19.0

Sources: IMF 1991b, Attachment III, pp. 57–59, and government budget data.

have not, to date, been fully quantified. . . . As the 1992 Budget did not incorporate peace expenditures, the macroeconomic projections for 1992 . . . will need to be revised in the upcoming months. *The authorities should formally incorporate the "peace" impact into [the] monetary program without further delay* (World Bank 1992a, pp. I, 1; emphasis added).

The IMF, however, continued to insist that tight fiscal and monetary targets were still achievable. Visiting El Salvador in July, an IMF mission offered a positive assessment of the macroeconomy, arguing that "economic activity strengthened in the first semester of 1992, inflation continued to ease and [the] net international reserve position strengthened, notwithstanding the slump in international coffee prices" (IMF 1992). The IMF did note shortfalls on the fiscal side but attributed these to the government's delay in implementing planned measures (the VAT, an increase in electricity rates, and the establishment of the large-taxpayers unit), as well as to the effect of the drought on the electric company's deficit and the impact of the drop in coffee prices on fiscal revenues. The mission held to the original objectives for the overall public-sector and central-government deficits—even though the mission foresaw a significant increase in peace-related expenditures during the second half of the year, 45 percent of which could not be covered by foreign resources—and suggested that the government adopt a series of fiscal measures aimed at raising an additional 1 percent of the GDP. Many of the IMF's suggested revenue enhancements were never, however, implemented and others were not put into effect until September 1992 (introduction of the VAT and increase in electricity rates). As a result, the fiscal goals for the year were not attained.

Thus the Salvadoran government and the international financial institutions did not really "plan for peace." Even as rising peace-related expenditures derailed fiscal targets, the IMF's macroeconomic priorities remained firm. Although economic stability and inflation reduction were worthy and shared goals, unrealistic assessments that failed to incorporate the costs of peace threatened to make peace the adjusting variable. At the same time, as documented in the next chapter, the international financial institutions did not themselves fund high-priority programs mandated by the peace accords, nor did they exercise what we term "peace conditionality" to encourage the government to increase further its domestic resource mobilization for peace-related needs. The peace process thus remained largely tangential to fiscal policy, rather than becoming integral to it.

Planning for the Future: Fiscal Targets and Public Investment

The failure to make fulfillment of the accords a primary economic as well as social objective has been compounded by a tendency to achieve fiscal balance through short-sighted reductions in public investment. In 1993 the Salvadoran government achieved the majority of fiscal targets specified in yet another standby arrangement with the IMF, this one also supported by the World Bank and USAID. The tax-to-GDP ratio, for example, rose to 9.3 percent, the highest achieved during the government's term in office. The NFPS and central-government deficits were reduced to 3.9 percent and 1.4 percent of GDP, respectively, and NFPS current savings improved compared to 1992.

This success, however, was largely achieved because capital spending—particularly that associated with the National Reconstruction Program—was lower than planned. As can be seen from Table 6.8, public-sector investment was substantially below projected levels in 1993, a trend that continued in 1994. The principal mechanisms for public investment cutbacks were: (1) execution of programs on a smaller scale than planned, and (2) deferral of program execution until sufficient funds from the international community were available.

Table 6.8   **Planned and Actual Capital Expenditure by the Nonfinancial Public Sector, 1992–1994**

	Planned Expenditure		Actual Expenditure		Percent of planned expenditure realized
	Billions of colones	Percentage of GDP	Billions of colones	Percentage of GDP	
1992	2.214	4.1	2.856	5.7	129
1993	4.145	6.2	2.767	4.6	67
1994	4.013	5.3	2.844	4.0	71

Source: BCR.

Conditioning capital spending on the availability of foreign funds has been accepted by international financing agencies, in the interest of maintaining macroeconomic stability. Yet even the IMF's Executive Board has recognized that although cutbacks in public investment contributed to the attainment of fiscal targets, they may also have jeopardized the achievement of long-term development objectives at a time when the country is in the midst of rebuilding (IMF 1994a, 1994b). As with the failure to take account of peace-related current expenditures, this acceptance of delays in public investment may ultimately harm macroeconomic stability itself, by undermining growth, improved income distribution, and the consolidation of peace.

Why the Gap Between Economic Stabilization and Peace?

The macroeconomic strategy has thus conflicted with the peace process in El Salvador in several ways. There have been broad contradictions: Cuts in social spending, slowdowns in agrarian reform, and reductions in public investment have impeded progress on distributional concerns and dampened future growth prospects, eroding the basic conditions for prosperous and peaceful development. But there have also been more specific problems stemming from the failure of the international financial community to apply peace conditionality much as it has applied the usual economic conditionality.

This failure has been of two types. On the one hand, international agencies did not initially relax fiscal discipline despite the clear awareness that implementing the peace accords would be expensive. On the other hand, when foreign resources were subsequently forthcoming, the international agencies did not sufficiently pressure the domestic authorities to increase their mobilization of domestic resources, and to shift public spending in the direction of short-run programs mandated by the peace accords and long-run investment needed for the consolidation of peace.

The de facto subordination of the peace agreements to economic stabilization can in part be attributed to the fact that the peace process and the economic-reform process have largely been carried out independently of one another.[17] The Salvadoran government itself has not wanted to delay the achievement of economic reform and the refashioning of a new export-oriented model; linking the peace process to economic policy could have produced such a delay. With the exception of some UN agencies—which maintain that fulfillment of the peace agreements should take precedence over the fulfillment of other commitments[18]—international institutions have at least tacitly encouraged the government's subordination of the peace process to economic reform by making progress in stabilization and structural reform the key prerequisite for external financing.[19]

It is true that viability of the peace process in the medium term depends on the achievement of economic stability and the consolidation of structural reforms. At the same time, however, there are finite and politically critical time frames for implementing the peace accords, and if these time frames are not respected serious problems of social and political instability and loss of the government's ability to govern could result. Among other things, this would hamper structural-reform efforts.

One way to respect both macroeconomic and peace imperatives is to apply peace conditionality, which would encourage shifts in government expenditures and enhancements in the revenues via a more progressive tax system (see Chapter 7). Such conditionality would be entirely consistent with a longer-term macroeconomic strategy that pursues a conscious depreciation of the exchange rate (to encourage tradeables production and long-run self-sufficiency), enhanced public investment, and real improvement in the lot of El Salvador's poorest citizens. Unfortunately, this has not been the general thrust of either international lenders or the Salvadoran government; in economic policymaking, peace and public investment have instead been eclipsed by, and at times subordinated to, macroeconomic stabilization.

Peace and public investment, however, can actually lead the way to economic recovery by guaranteeing social stability, providing necessary infrastructure, and stimulating productive private investment. Moreover, the Salvadoran economy, for the moment, faces little danger of inflation as long as the flow of remittances continues. The real issue is how to prepare for the possibility of an eventual slowdown in such external flows—that is, how to take advantage of the current policy "space" provided by the abundance of foreign exchange to consolidate the peace and to build the infrastructure for sustainable growth.

Conclusions

In guaranteeing El Salvador's future, the mobilization of domestic resources is key. Current savings and investment levels are clearly insufficient to ensure high and sustainable economic growth rates. On the saving side, it is important to encourage the continuing flow of remittances from Salvadorans living abroad because these funds have become a significant component of national savings. At the same time, the government needs to prepare for any fall-off in such remittances by boosting savings from domestic residents and laying the groundwork for increases in public savings. Increased savings are necessary for the crucial task of raising private and complementary public investment.

The Salvadoran government naturally has had to start in this area of resource mobilization with its own fiscal house. With the support of international financial agencies the government has endeavored to mobilize greater domestic resources. Tax reform has produced rising and more stable revenues, and advances have been made in improving the auditing and control capabilities of the Treasury Ministry. Nonetheless, the tax-to-GDP ratio remains very low by both historical and comparative standards, the tax structure is quite regressive, and the government faces a significant problem of tax evasion. Most domestic actors recognize the latter problem, and there is a broad consensus in the country on the need to raise revenue. Indeed, during the electoral campaign all the presidential candidates—including Armando Calderón Sol, who won the election—signed a document drawn up by UNICEF in which they agreed to raise the tax ratio to around 15 percent during the period 1994–1999 in order to be able to increase social spending.

Various studies have concluded that given the prospects for economic growth over the next few years and the modernization of the tax, auditing, and fiscal control systems, it is feasible to raise tax revenues by between 0.5 percent and 1 percent each year for the remainder of the century. This would mean a tax ratio of 14 percent by the year 1999, making electoral promises not unreasonable. Yet the government and FUSADES have projected a tax ratio of only 10 to 11 percent. In addition to vigorous implementation of existing tax reforms, the tax ratio could be raised by further taxes on the nonproductive transactions of luxury goods and high-value property transfers. These would also improve the distributional incidence of the tax system.

Assuming that tax revenues can indeed be raised to levels closer to international norms, there will be a need to insure that much of this projected increase actually finds its way into social spending. This implies the need to hold the line on military expenditures, and a need for active peace conditionality on the part of international lenders. Whereas the government has reduced military spending below civil-war levels, further substantial reductions are possible. One reasonable goal would be to reduce military spending to the preconflict level—i.e., well below 1 percent of the current GDP. Such a level would allow both social spending and public investment to rise, even if tax revenues lag, thus contributing to both the country's peace and its economic future.

Why should international financial institutions, usually focused on macroeconomic issues, place an emphasis on ensuring that the Salvadoran government fulfill its peace-related obligations? Even if macro stability remains the paramount goal, research (reviewed in Chapter 8) suggests that such stability is short-lived in the presence of significant inequality and political turmoil. This implies, in turn, that the peace accords should no longer be treated as an afterthought or a "remainder"; macroeconomic strategy must be designed to be consistent with and supportive of the goal of consolidating peace.

Pursuing peace will require the further mobilization of both external and domestic resources, raising taxes in a more progressive fashion, and shifting expenditures toward social policies. Such an alternative program could also make productive use of public investment and existing stocks of foreign reserves, preparing El Salvador for the day when it will have to rely primarily on exports and not remittances as the main source of foreign exchange. We outline such a future-oriented program in the following chapters, stressing the need to elevate public infrastructure and social spending, and to redistribute assets, opportunities, and income. The most pressing immediate objective, however, is to implement fully the programs mandated by the peace accords. The current economic strategy adopted by the government and the international agencies remains inadequate to these tasks.

Notes

1. The World Bank (1993c, p. 1) observes that after 1979 the conflict "diverted public resources from infrastructure and the social sectors to military expenditures."

2. National savings are composed of domestic savings plus foreign transfers, which in this case are mainly remittances from Salvadoran nationals. Domestic savings are therefore calculated as national savings minus foreign transfers. Since much remittance income is in fact consumed, the apparently precipitous decline in domestic savings is partly the result of this accounting convention. Using alternative data, Rivera Campos (1994) reports that domestic savings have actually been negative in recent years.

3. There are two main reasons for caution in interpreting the negative correlation between foreign and national savings in El Salvador. First, the quality of the savings data is uncertain. Second, both national savings and foreign savings could have been influenced (in opposite directions) by other variables, such as the war.

4. In a multivariate analysis of the determinants of private savings in El Salvador, Rivera Campos (1994, p. 9) estimated that every dollar of foreign savings reduced private national savings by 27 cents.

5. The most important measures included under this reform were instituted over a period of slightly more than two years, making El Salvador one of few countries in the world to have executed such extensive tax reform so quickly (Gallagher 1993).

6. Under the joint sponsorship of USAID, the IMF, and the IDB, a tax-system-modernization project, known as MOST, was implemented in 1991. According to USAID (1994b), the Ministry of the Treasury now has "a state-of-the-art tax information system and enhanced administrative capabilities."

7. CENITEC (1993) and Méndez and Abrego (1994) report that tax evasion may be as high as 50 percent, with evasion of the VAT running near 57 percent.

8. The World Bank (1994b, p. 39) observes that El Salvador's tax-to-GDP ratio "remains one of the lowest in the world."

9. Analogous issues arise with respect to "peace conditionality" (see Chapter 7).

10. The data in Table 6.4 omit government commitments toward financing infrastructure projects. For an earlier estimate of such commitments, see Table 7.2; for a discussion of the reasons for differences in priorities among donors and the government, see Chapter 7.

11. The defense budget allocations reported in Table 6.5 are based on national budgetary data. These differ somewhat from expenditure data reported by the IMF (see Table 7.4 and Appendix Table A.6); the reasons for the discrepancies are unclear. Detailed data on Salvadoran military expenditures are not available. Under a special article attached to the National Budget Law in 1983, national defense expenditures approved directly by the president were exempted from investigation and verification (Dalton 1994).

12. During 1991 the country experienced a drought, as a result of which the Rio Lempa Hydroelectricity Commission (CEL) experienced severe losses when the thermal power station was put into operation and the government was obliged to effect larger-than-expected transfers to the commission. In addition, consolidation of the internal public debt in 1989 and 1990 provoked a substantial increase in interest payments in 1991. The situation was further aggravated by the increase in interest payments on the external debt that resulted from the finalization of the debt-restructuring period provided for under the Paris Agreement of 1990.

13. In September the government, in conjunction with the IMF, revised the original goals, raising the target fiscal deficit for the nonfinancial public sector from 2.6 percent to 3.4 percent and that of the central government from 2.5 percent to 3.8 percent. The final results proved that these targets were too ambitious (USAID 1992).

14. The government was also supposed to reduce the total public-sector deficit (including BCR losses) from 4.3 percent of GDP in 1991 to 3.0 percent in 1992, and generate positive savings of 1.5 percent of GDP in the current account of the NFPS. For details see *Memorandum on the Economic Policies of El Salvador* (IMF 1991b, Attachment III).

15. The program also envisioned a shift in the composition of spending, with military spending declining and spending on education and health rising.

16. The economic program of 1992 assumed that the country would receive U.S.$160 million in gross loan disbursements from multilateral institutions and $320 million in loans and grants from bilateral sources (IMF 1991b, p. 42, Appendix VI).

17. Alvaro de Soto and Graciana del Castillo (1994a, p. 72) have remarked: "The adjustment program and the stabilization plan, on the one hand, and the peace process, on the other, were born and reared as if they were children of different families. They lived under separate roofs. They had little in common other than belonging roughly to the same generation."

18. See, for example, CEPAL (1993a).

19. "There is also a heightened awareness that the various elements of the Peace Accords would be impossible to implement without the full support of the donor community and that continued progress in stabilization and structural reforms is a precondition for this support" (World Bank 1993c, p. 21).

7

External Resource Mobilization

James K. Boyce

External assistance has played a critical role in El Salvador's peace process. Grants and loans from bilateral and multilateral agencies have been the main source of finance for many programs mandated by the peace accords, including the land-transfer program, the reintegration of ex-combatants, poverty-alleviation programs, and infrastructure projects. External-assistance actors have also influenced the political momentum of the peace process. Aid has affected not only the balance of payments, but also the balance of power.

Aid can be an important complement to limited domestic resources. It can, however, also become a substitute for them. In attempting to ensure that their assistance "crowds in" domestic government spending, rather than supplanting it, donors often seek to make their aid conditional on policy actions by the recipient government, including expenditure commitments. At the same time, the donors know that some programs will not succeed in the absence of external finance. Hence they must strike a delicate balance.

This dilemma has been quite apparent in El Salvador. External assistance unquestionably has contributed greatly to postwar reconstruction and to the consolidation of peace. But external-assistance actors have been less successful in prompting the government to mobilize greater domestic resources to finance peace programs. Indeed, virtually no internal fiscal reforms were undertaken specifically with a view to financing the peace.

This chapter analyzes the mobilization of external resources for the Salvadoran peace process in both financial and political terms. The first section reviews data on external assistance: How much has been provided, by whom, and for what purposes. These data reveal striking discrepancies between the priorities established under the peace accords and those of many donors. Several possible explanations for these discrepancies are considered.

The second section examines aid conditionality, including formal performance criteria and informal policy dialogue. The absence of conditions

129

can be as critical as their presence. If access to external resources is conditional on the fulfillment of commitments under the peace accords, the political resolve of internal actors to maintain the momentum of the peace process can be strengthened. If, on the other hand, external resources are provided without such conditions, the political will to implement difficult but necessary measures may be weakened. Aid can ease internal pressures for action, fortify the capacity of reluctant parties to resist those pressures, or divert attention and resources to other issues. In this respect, the record of the external-assistance actors in El Salvador has been mixed.

The final section offers recommendations for economic policy in El Salvador specifically and during postconflictual transitions more generally.

Official External Assistance

Resource Commitments

In March 1992, two months after the signing of the Chapultepec Accords, the Consultative Group (CG) for El Salvador met in Washington, D.C. The government of El Salvador's team was led by the planning minister, who made it clear that the government expected the external-assistance actors to finance the costs of peace:

> Minister Lievano de Marques emphasized that the reconstruction effort would not be used as a pretext for abandoning disciplined macroeconomic policy. She stressed that the Government seeks to finance the effort with foreign assistance and noted that she hoped the funding would be additional, thus allowing the Government to continue its important efforts in redressing other social and economic needs (World Bank 1992b, p. 5).

In the words of a U.S. official, the government's stance was, "If you want it to happen, you pay for it."[1]

The donor response was substantial. Since the signing of the accords, El Salvador has received about $400 million per year in external assistance from bilateral and multilateral agencies. Table 7.1 presents a breakdown of total commitments for the years 1992–1995 by donor, as reported by the UNDP.[2] These data include aid not specifically related to the peace accords. Among the bilaterals, the largest donor was the United States, accounting for more than three-quarters of bilateral aid in 1992–1995. Among the multilaterals, the Inter-American Development Bank (IDB) has been the largest single donor.

Table 7.2 presents data on the financing of specific programs mandated by the peace accords for 1993–1996. Estimated funding needs, and the categorization of programs into higher and lower priority, are drawn

Table 7.1   Official External Assistance to El Salvador, 1992–1995
(Completed, ongoing, and planned projects)

Source of funds	Millions of dollars
United States	535.9
Germany[a]	75.4
Japan	19.7
Italy[a]	17.0
Spain	16.7
Canada	14.1
Sweden	11.0
Norway	5.1
Netherlands	1.5
Others	2.5
Bilateral subtotal	698.9
IDB	558.8
CABEI	119.8
World Bank	100.3
EEC[a]	82.7
WFP	39.4
UNDP	7.4
PAHO/WHO	6.1
IFAD	5.0
UNICEF	3.3
Others	6.5
Multilateral subtotal	929.4
Total	1628.3

Source: UNDP 1994a, pp. 3–4.
Note: a. Imputed from data on total project costs (see end note 2).

from the Government of El Salvador's report to the April 1993 CG meeting. In the case of poverty-alleviation programs, the data refer to the National Reconstruction Plan (PRN) zones only. In the case of infrastructure, no attempt was made to separate out that component directed to PRN areas; the data thus refer to infrastructure projects in the country as a whole. Estimated funding needs totaled $1.8 billion. The government's commitment of domestic resources to these programs was $408 million. Two sets of data on external funding are reported: The first is drawn from the same report to the CG meeting; the second, drawn from a January 1994 report by the U.S. General Accounting Office (GAO), includes some additional subsequent commitments but provides a less detailed programmatic breakdown. Donor commitments reported by the GAO totaled $739 million, leaving a funding gap of $682 million.

Speaking in September 1994 before the UN General Assembly, Salvadoran president Calderón Sol stated:

Table 7.2   Funding Requirements and Commitments for Programs Mandated Under the Peace Accords, 1993–1996 (millions of U.S. dollars)

Program	Estimated requirement	GOES commitment	As of March 1993							As of January 1994		
			U.S.	Germany	Japan	IDB	EEC	Others	Gap	U.S.	Others	Gap
Democratic institutions	256.6	169.3	19.0				0.5	0.6	67.2	19.0	1.7	66.6
Judicial system strengthening	219.8	162.3	15.0						42.5			
Human-Rights Ombudsman	16.8	6.4					0.5	0.6	9.3			
Elections Tribunal	20.0	0.6	4.0						15.4			
Police	277.7	63.4	10.9					5.0	198.4	25.8	6.5	182.0
Public Security Academy	104.7	28.0	4.9					5.0	66.8			
National Civilian Police	173.0	35.4	6.0						131.6			
Land Bank	142.5	23.3	35.0				12.5		71.7	44.0	12.5	62.7
Support to demobilized personnel	174.3	3.3	20.0	12.5					138.5	35.0	20.9	115.1
Agricultural credit	62.0	0.0	10.0						52.0			
Housing	77.1	2.6		12.5					62.0			
Microenterprise credit	27.0	0.0	10.0						17.0			
Pensions for disabled	8.2	0.7							7.5			
Poverty alleviation (NRP only)	310.2	57.2	94.5			34.4	18.8		105.3	106.1	53.2	93.7
Housing	76.2	40.9				15.8			19.5			
Municipalities in Action	65.2	0.0	62.5						0.0			
Maternal and child health	55.3	5.3	8.0				12.0		30.0			
Social Investment Fund	52.6	4.8				18.6			29.2			
Other	60.9	6.2	21.3				6.8		26.6			
Subtotal: Higher priority	1,161.3	316.5	179.4	12.5		34.4	31.8	5.6	581.1	229.9	94.8	520.1

Table 7.2   Continued

Program	Estimated requirement	GOES commitment	As of March 1993							As of January 1994		
			U.S.	Germany	Japan	IDB	EEC	Others	Gap	U.S.	Others	Gap
Productive and social sectors and human capital	120.0	10.9	25.7	5.5	3.8		3.7	16.4	53.5	44.1	79.6	(14.6)
Productive sector	55.5	4.8					3.7	9.7	41.0			
Programs for disabled	14.6	2.0	8.9	5.5					0.0			
Scholarships for demobilized	16.5	1.5	9.5						0.0			
Other education and training	20.7	2.6	7.3						10.8			
Other	12.7				3.8			7.2	1.7			
Infrastructure	530.1	78.3	20.5		93.1	161.7		6.0	170.5	30.0	260.8	161.0
Energy	287.6	48.6			63.0	142.7		5.0	28.3			
Roads and bridges	162.3	17.4			20.1				124.8			
Water	34.0	4.0			10.0	19.0		1.0	0.0			
Other	46.2	8.3	20.5						17.4			
Environment	17.5	1.9							15.6		0.2	15.4
Subtotal: Lower priority	667.6	91.1	46.2	5.5	96.9	161.7	3.7	22.9	239.6	74.1	340.6	161.8
Total	1,828.9	407.6	225.6	18.0	96.9	196.1	35.5	28.5	820.7	304.0	435.4	681.9

Sources: MIPLAN 1993a, pp. 49–63; GAO 1994, p. 5.

The offer for assistance made by the international community for the implementation of the Peace Accords raised great hope in our country. Part of this has been delivered, for which we are very grateful. However, some has not yet materialized ... and could be the cause of unnecessary social tensions (El Salvador Information Project 1994).

Table 7.3 reports the estimated shortfalls for a number of higher-priority programs at that time.

The need for further external resources was reiterated in January 1995 by Salvadoran vice president Enrique Borgo Bustamante, speaking at the UN jointly with Salvador Sánchez Ceren, the secretary-general of the FMLN. Citing a $137 million shortfall, the vice president said:

Peace is not enough. We need social peace. We need to remake whatever was El Salvador. We need to walk that last part of the road, and we feel so short of breath.

At the same time, government officials maintained that "they cannot provide any more money without levying new taxes or cutting into education and health programs" (Crossette 1995). However, there remains considerable

Table 7.3   Funding Shortfalls for Higher-Priority Programs as of September 1994 (millions of U.S. dollars)

Program	Needed	Available	Shortfall
Armed-forces demobilization	31.0	25.0	6.0
Public security			
National Police demobilization	9.8	0.0	9.8
Other programs	1.0	0.0	1.0
Land programs			
FMLN land transfer	97.1	78.7	18.4
FAES land transfer	42.5	29.1	13.4
Agricultural credit	44.2	18.9	25.3
Technical assistance	1.1	0.0	1.1
Reinsertion of ex-combatants			
Microenterprise credit and technical assistance	11.7	8.1	3.6
Scholarship program	14.8	14.8	0.0
Leaders and midlevel commanders program	4.1	0.0	4.1
Wounded combatants program	11.1	0.4	10.7
National Police reinsertion	16.5	8.0	8.5
Total	284.9	183.0	101.9

Source: Data provided by the Ministry of Planning, Government of El Salvador.

Note: Not all higher-priority programs are included. For example, estimates for the human-settlements program were unavailable, but it is believed that these would significantly increase the total deficit.

scope in El Salvador both for increasing tax revenues and for shifting government expenditures from other uses besides education and health.

The fact that a substantial, and increasing, fraction of external assistance to El Salvador takes the form of loans rather than grants is a further reason to intensify efforts to mobilize domestic resources to finance peace programs and public investment. More than 40 percent of foreign finance for peace-related programs has come in the form of loans, primarily for infrastructure projects. Loans in general—and loans from international financial institutions in particular—must one day be repaid with interest.[3] Positive net transfers on debt today lead inexorably to larger negative net transfers tomorrow; that is, debt-service payments (interest and amortization) must eventually surpass new borrowing. The question is not *if* this will occur, but *when*.[4] It would be an unfortunate irony—and, in light of the potential for greater domestic-resource mobilization, an unnecessary one—if El Salvador's postwar reconstruction efforts were to sow the seeds of a future debt crisis.

Donor Priorities

The data in Table 7.2 suggest striking discrepancies between the priorities defined by the government (in consultation with UN and U.S. officials) and the priorities of the major non-U.S. donors as revealed by their financial allocations. This is attributable not only to the fact that individual donors had their own agendas, but also, in part, to the fact that the government's own priorities were not always clearly established. Whereas the government and the United States allocated more than 75 percent of their funding to "higher-priority programs"—the National Civilian Police (PNC), judicial and democratic institutions, the land-transfer program, the reintegration of ex-combatants, and poverty-alleviation programs—the other donors devoted 78 percent of their funding to "lower-priority programs." Funding from non-U.S. donors for the PNC, judicial and democratic institutions, and land transfer amounted to only $21 million; together these programs had an expected shortfall of $311 million. At the same time, these donors committed $261 million to physical infrastructure. If we had comparable data on external assistance for non-peace-accord programs, the apparent divergence in priorities would be even sharper.[5]

Several factors may help to explain the reluctance of donors to commit greater financial resources to the programs mandated by the peace accords: (1) constraints on the aggregate volume of aid; (2) the "free-rider" problem in coordination among aid donors; (3) legislative, political, and institutional impediments to the funding of certain types of activities; and (4) skepticism regarding the likelihood that programs will succeed. These factors are not mutually exclusive, and their relative weight varies among donors and across programs.

Aggregate constraints. In the 1990s worldwide official development assistance began to contract, as donor governments curtailed foreign-aid programs in response to fiscal constraints and changing domestic priorities.[6] At the same time, Eastern Europe and the former Soviet states began to compete for external assistance. And with the end of the Cold War, the national-security motivation for U.S. foreign aid in Central America and elsewhere waned. Together these factors led to a 44 percent cut in U.S. economic assistance to Central America during 1991–1993, and to a further 42 percent cut in 1994.[7]

For the United States, however, El Salvador remains a high-priority country. El Salvador was the fifth-largest recipient of U.S. aid in the 1980s (after Israel, Egypt, Turkey, and Pakistan),[8] and in the 1990s it has continued to receive more U.S. aid than any other country in Latin America, virtually all of it in the form of grants. The signing of the Salvadoran peace accords was also followed by a large influx of new lending by the multilateral development banks. Compared to other countries, therefore, El Salvador has retained a rather generous slice of the aggregate external-assistance pie.[9]

The free-rider problem. Insofar as foreign aid is intended for developmental and humanitarian purposes, it has the qualities of a public good: If one donor provides assistance, all reap the benefits. Individual donors, particularly those with relatively modest budgets, may believe that their own marginal impact is negligible; it is the decisions of the other donors that determine the humanitarian or developmental outcome. Hence donor governments may be tempted to "free ride" on the assistance provided by others, devoting their own resources to less disinterested purposes.[10] Aid-coordination mechanisms, such as the Consultative Groups, provide a means to defuse this problem, but their effectiveness is a matter of degree.

In El Salvador the overwhelming preponderance of U.S. official assistance during the war years both simplified and complicated matters. Alone among the donors, the United States had both an established institutional presence in El Salvador and a broad vision of a desired course of political and economic reform. The United States responded quickly to the signing of the peace accords; indeed, the United States helped to design the PRN prior to the signing of the accords. The United States had accumulated large reserves of local currency during the war, as counterpart funds for its Economic Support Fund (ESF) and food aid (Public Law 480) programs, and these provided a ready and flexible source of cash.[11] In addition, USAID had a number of ongoing development projects that could be redirected toward the reconstruction effort.

Many other donors, by contrast, had no substantial on-the-ground presence in El Salvador at the time of the signing of the accords. Moreover, there was a sense among some of them that the United States, having done so much to finance the war, now bore the main responsibility for financing the costs of peace. At the same time, however, the U.S. government sought to encourage other agencies—notably the UN and the international financial institutions (IFIs)—to invest resources in El Salvador's peace process and postwar reconstruction effort. On balance the U.S. presence may have "crowded in" more external assistance to postwar El Salvador than it "crowded out."

Legislative, political, and institutional impediments. Certain types of assistance are difficult for some donors to provide. Assistance to police forces, for example, is legally barred by some donor governments. The purchase of land for redistribution may face domestic political opposition, both from critics of land reform and from critics of compensation to former landowners. Multilateral development banks, which have traditionally financed physical infrastructure and, more recently, "social" programs, may regard the strengthening of democratic institutions as an activity outside their mandate or competence. These impediments do much to explain the apparent discrepancies between donor priorities and those of the Salvadoran peace accords. In the absence of reassessment and reforms in the external-assistance agencies, similar discrepancies are likely to recur in other postconflictual settings.

The main source of external assistance for El Salvador's new National Civilian Police force has been the United States. Since USAID is prohibited by law from providing direct assistance to police forces, this required a special arrangement. With the permission of congressional oversight committees, USAID transferred the funds in question to the State Department, which then contracted the Justice Department to provide assistance through its International Criminal Investigation and Training Act Program. The governments of Spain, Sweden, and Norway also provided some support to the PNC. But for many donors, police funding remains politically untouchable. The fear is that the police will become involved in political repression and human-rights abuses. Yet a central aim of the creation of the PNC was precisely to guard against such eventualities.

More generally, institution building is a slow process, often more intensive in time than in money. "There are two types of donors," commented a donor official, "those with patience and little money, and those with no patience and plenty of money." The strengthening of democratic institutions appeals more to the former type of donor than to the latter.

Much of the infrastructure assistance received by El Salvador in recent years is not directly related to the consolidation of peace. Rather, it is the kind of lending that would have taken place had there never been a war, although the volume of loans after the signing of the peace accords was perhaps augmented by pent-up supply, because much lending was deferred during the war. Some postwar infrastructure lending was redirected toward the former conflictive zones, but in most respects these projects represent business as usual.

Donor preferences for "trade-related" assistance may help to explain the relatively generous funding of physical infrastructure as opposed to higher-priority programs under the Salvadoran peace accords. A common objective in external-assistance programs—in some instances the overriding one—is the promotion of exports from the donor country. Such tied aid not only inflates nominal project costs (because the same inputs often could be obtained on the world market at a lower price), but also biases assistance toward "projects requiring major imports in areas of particular export interest to the donor" (OECD 1985, cited by Jepma 1994, p. 73).

External assistance provided for one purpose can free domestic resources for other purposes. Such fungibility means that aid earmarked for lower-priority programs could indirectly help to finance high-priority programs by easing competing demands on the government budget. This assumes, however, that the government would have otherwise felt compelled to finance those lower-priority activities, and that the government reallocates any resources so liberated to peace programs. Neither assumption is self-evidently true.

Balance-of-payments support—whereby the government receives hard currency, sells it to importers, and can then use the local currency proceeds as it wishes—is particularly fungible. Furthermore, such loans can be disbursed much more quickly than project lending. The conditions attached to balance-of-payments assistance in El Salvador, as elsewhere, have centered on macroeconomic stabilization and structural adjustment. The possibility of using such aid to finance peace-accord programs was recognized, however, in the World Bank's Second Structural Adjustment Loan.[12] Germany's decision to contribute $9 million in cofinancing for this loan was reportedly prompted by this consideration.

The institutional impediments to direct support of peace-accord programs by some major donors, including the IFIs, are formidable but not insurmountable. In a precedent-setting departure from its usual project profile, the IDB is currently considering a $20 million loan to El Salvador to support the judicial reform. Such a loan would, in effect, expand the notion of infrastructure considered appropriate for IDB lending beyond the traditional foci on physical works and human-capital investment to include the strengthening of democratic institutions. This suggests that the logic of the Salvadoran peace process has the potential to catalyze institutional change in the IFIs themselves, with implications extending well beyond El Salvador.

Donor skepticism. Skepticism among some donors as to the government's political will to comply fully with the letter and the spirit of the peace accords may have posed a further constraint on the mobilization of external resources.

From the outset of the peace negotiations there were two opposing views as to how aid should be channeled to intended beneficiaries in the former conflictive zones. The U.S. position was that aid should flow through the sovereign government. The government likewise was keen to avoid any power sharing with the former guerrillas. In the words of a donor official involved in the negotiations:

> The government wanted some consultation, but nothing so participatory as to be co-government. They didn't want to repeat the Nicaraguan experience. They kept using the phrase *co-gobierno* as something to be avoided.

Other donor officials, particularly from some of the European bilateral agencies, believed that at least part of the aid to the former conflictive zones should be channeled outside the government—for example, through nongovernmental organizations (NGOs) that had worked in these areas during the war. With intimate knowledge of the local terrain and established links to communities, the NGOs were seen as a valuable complement to the state. The UN-brokered compromise allowed some aid to be channeled through the UNDP and NGOs, but the vast bulk of reconstruction aid has been channeled through the government.[13] Concerns over politicization in the distribution of these resources may have dissuaded some donors from providing greater support.

In interviews, a number of donor officials expressed concern about the El Salvador government's unwillingness to commit greater domestic resources to peace programs, and cited this as a reason for their own reluctance to do so. "The priorities of the government should be reoriented in favor of constructing an acceptable social infrastructure," said one. "The government should not leave responsibility for this to the donors." Another official took the view that the relatively large allocations of external assistance to physical-infrastructure projects reflected the actual (if not stated) priorities of the government as well as of some major donors.

Several officials expressed particular skepticism about the government's commitment to the creation of the new National Civilian Police. On the PNC's equipment needs, one remarked:

> We have no tradition of handing out weapons. But the Salvadoran army has huge stocks, even though some of these are not easy to use for civilian purposes. The army has vehicles, too. Many needs of the PNC could be met by taking from the army. This is a political question: how to persuade the army to give up equipment. We do not want to help the army hold onto its equipment by financing purchases for the PNC.

The government's reluctance to finance even mundane items for the PNC, such as soap and towels, reinforced this skepticism.

Such reservations are grounded in the specific circumstances of El Salvador. But similar problems can be expected in other postconflictual settings. Peace accords may end the shooting, but the divisions that precipitate civil wars do not vanish instantly. They constitute the setting—and the challenge—for the consolidation of the peace.

Peace Conditionality?

In development circles, "conditionality" often is regarded as something of a dirty word. As Schoultz (1989, p. 410) remarks, "many observers reject as unethical and perhaps immoral the notion of establishing conditions upon aid disbursements." Some external-assistance agency officials are reluctant even to discuss the matter. "We have no conditionalities on our assistance," insisted a senior European Economic Community (EEC) official interviewed for this study. But he then added: "Our only conditionality is respect for democratic institutions." As the qualification suggests, the absence of conditionality can be as problematic as its presence.

Aid conditionality is here taken to be a fact of international life. The issue is not whether external-assistance actors should wield power, but rather what they do with it.[14]

In general, balance-of-payments assistance affords scope for broader conditionality than does project assistance: The conditions govern what the recipient will do not *with* the money but *in return* for it. In El Salvador, the external-assistance actors most able to exercise conditionality, by virtue of the volume and types of assistance at their disposal, have been the United States, the World Bank, the IMF, and the IDB.[15] Accordingly, this section focuses on their policies.

Macroeconomic Conditionality

In El Salvador, as elsewhere, the primary goals of aid conditionality in recent years have been macroeconomic stabilization and structural adjustment. These are not the only goals conceivable in theory, nor are they the only ones that major external-assistance actors ever embrace in practice. Other goals that have been discussed, and at times pursued, include poverty reduction, good governance, and reductions in military expenditure. Although these other goals seem particularly germane to countries in postconflictual transitions, they have not featured prominently in aid conditionality in El Salvador.

Since 1989 there has been a close correspondence between the macroeconomic policy preferences of the government of El Salvador and those of the donors. Both parties favored government budget deficit reduction, low inflation, privatization of the financial sector and of agricultural exports, trade liberalization, and streamlining of the state. The macroeconomic conditionalities embodied in the World Bank's structural adjustment loans (SALs) and IMF standby arrangements therefore have not been impositions on a recalcitrant government.

"In both SALs, the government came to us with the program," recalled a World Bank official. "We just worked out the details. Of course, we were very happy with what they proposed. But there is nothing in these agreements that we invented." An IMF official described target setting in El Salvador as a "very iterative" process: "We're on the phone with them a lot. We're dealing here with a government that shares the same philosophy." In a reversal of the conventional scenario elsewhere, the government in some instances proposed tighter targets than were initially suggested by the Bretton Woods institutions. Nothing prevents a government from pursuing tighter targets on its own. But the inclusion of such targets in formal agreements with the World Bank and the IMF can serve to deflect criticisms of unpopular measures to the external agencies.

The close working relationships between IFI officials and their counterparts in the government of El Salvador are not unusual. Jacques Polak (1991, p. 66), the former economic counselor of the IMF, remarks:

> The country's team, typically composed of senior treasury and central bank officials, will often seek alliances with the Fund staff in order to strengthen its own policy prescriptions. Not infrequently, letters of intent contain commitments put there only because the country wanted them.

In the case of multilateral development banks, there is a further basis for alliances: The job of bank officials is to make loans, and the job of government officials is to obtain them. Congenial relationships carry the risk of "clientitis," a sense of identification that inhibits lending institutions from proposing and implementing conditionalities not welcomed by the borrower.

Economic Stabilization Versus Political Stabilization

The goals of economic stabilization and political stabilization are complementary: In the long run neither is possible without the other. In the short run, however, conflicts between these objectives can arise and pose difficult trade-offs.

One evident possibility is that in the absence of adequate external finance, budget-deficit targets may be incompatible with the need to fund peace-related programs. An August 1993 study on the "Economic Consequences of Peace in El Salvador," undertaken by the secretariat of the UN's Economic Commission for Latin America and the Caribbean, concluded:

> It might be necessary to explore the possibility, should the situation arise, of slightly extending the deadline for reducing inflation or of pursuing trade liberalization less vigorously. Within limits, setting more flexible quantitative goals for the stabilization programme might be an acceptable sacrifice, since it would secure the higher goal of ensuring the governability of a society that has, for years, been in the throes of a disastrous civil war (CEPAL 1993a, p. 12).

When queried on this point, IFI officials offer two responses: First, a relaxation of budget-deficit targets would jeopardize macroeconomic stability, ultimately endangering the peace process itself; and second, in practice the budget constraint has not been binding in El Salvador. Neither argument can be lightly dismissed.

The first argument proceeds from the assumption that larger government budget deficits would trigger higher inflation. This would reduce the competitiveness of the export sector (given a de facto policy of maintaining a fixed exchange rate), and would harm the poor, who are least able to maintain their incomes in the face of rising prices. Hence IFI officials stress the need to finance peace expenditures by other routes: via increased tax revenues, government-expenditure shifting, and external resources.

There is a large intermediate terrain, however, between rigid adherence to the macroeconomic targets on the one hand, and profligate deficit financing of peace-related expenditures on the other. Analogous to the trade-off between inflation and unemployment depicted in macroeconomics textbooks, there may be a trade-off between the size of the government budget deficit and the social tensions arising from inadequate peace expenditures. This situation is depicted in Figure 7.1.[16] Faced with such a trade-off, prudent policymaking does not restrict the choice set to points *A* and *Z*.

The second argument points to government fiscal priorities, rather than the aggregate expenditure ceiling, as the explanation for inadequate funding of peace programs. This argument is well founded: There is considerable scope in El Salvador for both shifting expenditure and increasing tax revenues. But this raises a further issue. If economic development is the overriding objective of the IFIs, if the consolidation of peace is necessary to economic development, and if successful and timely implementation of the programs mandated by the peace accords is necessary for the consolidation of peace, then it logically follows that the IFIs should include the latter in their conditionalities.

Yet in El Salvador the IFIs have for the most part limited their purview to more conventional macroeconomic concerns. They have not extended their conditionalities to the peace process—for example, by setting targets for greater reallocation of government spending to programs mandated by the peace accords. Instead the IFIs have supported the government's efforts

Figure 7.1   Potential Trade-off Between Government Budget Deficit and Social
Tensions Due to Inadequate Peace Expenditures

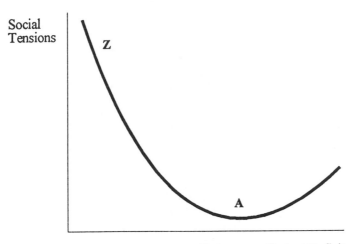

to shift the costs of peace onto the external assistance agencies. The World
Bank (1992c, p. 9) set the tone at the March 1992 CG meeting:

> Adequate external financial support for the NRP [National Reconstruc-
> tion Plan] is the critical condition for NRP's implementation within a
> framework of macroeconomic stability and sustainable growth. Without
> sufficient external resources the Government will face two alternatives:
> (i) maintain macroeconomic stability by curtailing NRP implementation,
> with likely severe political and social consequences or (ii) finance the
> NRP predominately with domestic resources sacrificing macroeconomic
> stability and longer-term growth.[17]

This statement again reduces the potential trade-off between macroeconomic instability and inadequate peace expenditures to a binary all-or-
nothing choice; and, more important, it ignores the scope for further reallocation of domestic resources to peace programs.

Faced with the fiscal requirements of peace, and limited external resources, the government in fact has three options: (1) to run a larger budget deficit; (2) to increase domestic-resource mobilization by shifting government expenditure from other uses and/or increasing tax revenues; and
(3) to accept shortfalls in the funding of peace-related programs. In postwar El Salvador the second option has much to recommend it. Although
there is some limited room for easing the budget-deficit targets, excessive

relaxation would prove costly in terms of macroeconomic stability. There is considerable scope, however, for further mobilization of domestic resources to finance the costs of peace.

Military Expenditure

Military expenditure is an obvious candidate for budget cuts to free more domestic resources for programs mandated by the peace accords. Although Salvadoran military spending has declined since the war, it continues to absorb a substantial amount of scarce government resources. The share of Salvadoran GDP devoted to the military in 1993 was 1.7 percent, according to the IMF (1994b, p. 45).[18] This compares unfavorably with the 0.5 percent for health and 1.6 percent for education (see Table 7.4), and remains far above its prewar level of 0.7 percent of GDP.[19]

According to a senior IMF official interviewed for this study, the IMF has not engaged in discussions of military expenditure in El Salvador.[20] Instead it has maintained its traditional focus on aggregate government expenditure rather than its composition: "We tend to leave that [expenditure composition] to the World Bank and IDB. When asked, we make certain analyses, for example, of the share of the wage bill in the public sector. But generally we rely on others."

A World Bank official closely involved with El Salvador policy stated that the World Bank "never discussed explicitly" the issue of defense expenditure. This official maintained that the issue lies outside the Bank's mandate and competence, and that a change in the Bank's mandate in this respect would be undesirable because it "would risk damaging the credibility of the Bank as an objective, apolitical institution."[21]

An IDB official expressed the view that donor pressure on the Cristiani government would have been counterproductive:

> There are political realities. The peace accords were delayed by Cristiani's problems with the military. I have no doubt that he would have liked to cut their budget more, but those guys are powerful. Had Cristiani not been able to postpone the sacking of 100 top military officers, the peace process might be in shambles now.

Table 7.4   IMF Estimates of Central-Government Expenditures on the Military, Education, and Health, 1989–1993 (percentages of GDP)

	1989	1990	1991	1992	1993
Military	3.7	3.0	2.6	2.2	1.7
Education	1.8	1.6	1.5	1.5	1.6
Health	0.8	0.8	0.8	0.8	0.5

Source: IMF 1994b, pp. 26, 45.

Following the signing of the peace accords, U.S. military aid was scaled down to $23 million in 1992.[22] Cutbacks in U.S. military aid were accompanied by substantial U.S. funding for peace-accord programs, as documented earlier. Initial U.S. conditionalities were not as strong as they might have been, however. "We could have leveraged more from the government in the early 1990s, on land, the PNC, and other peace-related issues," a U.S. official remarked. "Our policy at the time was that we were getting as much as we should extract. I personally believe we could have gotten more, but *we ourselves* didn't have the political will." The situation changed somewhat under the Clinton administration (that is, after January 1993), but at the same time the volume of U.S. aid decreased.

The efficacy of recent U.S. pressures on the government has also been limited by the lack of support from the IFIs. Although the World Bank, IDB, and USAID have negotiated cross-conditionality on macroeconomic issues, they have not done so with respect to implementation of the peace accords. A senior USAID official stated that he personally approached World Bank and IDB officials to seek backing for efforts to reorient government spending toward peace-accord programs, without success:

> The IFIs have steadfastly refused to talk about military expenditure targets in El Salvador. They say: "This is political conditionality, and we are apolitical organizations. We cannot include budgeting sufficient funds for the PNC or land transfer in our conditions. The U.S. government can do that because it has a political agenda, but we don't." There has been a concerted effort by the Banks to stay completely away from these issues.

The reluctance of the IFIs to venture into this terrain in El Salvador is not entirely consistent with the public posture of these institutions. There has been much debate in recent years as to the appropriate policies and role of the IFIs with respect to military expenditures.[23] In an April 1991 address to a World Bank conference, former World Bank president Robert McNamara called for reductions in military expenditures in developing countries and endorsed the use of conditionality to further this goal (McNamara 1992). In December of the same year—a month before the signing of the Salvadoran peace accords—newly retired World Bank president Barber Conable, Jr., called on the international community to present a "united front" against excessive military spending:

> Weak or uncertain civilian governments may publicly protest, as invasion of their sovereignty, admonitions that arms expenditures be reduced. I speak from experience when I say that such pressure may be privately welcomed by the new democracies. It can be a decisive element in strengthening civilian hands in the internal battle to allocate available resources to economic growth and quality of life investments rather than unproductive military hardware.[24]

A December 1991 memorandum presented to its board of directors codified World Bank policy and was incorporated in the Bank's operational directives. The memorandum called on World Bank staff to "raise issues of unproductive expenditures where they are significant, as part of its policy dialogue and public expenditure reviews, rather than to impose conditionality related to military expenditures" (World Bank 1991a, p. 2). An accompanying opinion by the World Bank's general counsel concluded:

> The discussion of public expenditures for economic and social purposes and the degree of their adequacy for these purposes may therefore be considered . . . as matters relevant to the Bank's mandate, as it is now envisaged, and they obviously fall within the Bank's competence. In addressing these issues, the Bank will be indirectly addressing the issue of non-productive expenditures but without having to get involved in the politically sensitive matter of what is an appropriate level for a country's military expenditures. After all, these are two sides of the same coin (World Bank 1991b, pp. 2–3).

Although apparently ignored in the case of El Salvador, these guidelines reportedly have been put into practice elsewhere:

> The World Bank has confronted the issue of military expenditure in the case of several countries in which such allocations seemed excessive relative to spending on development programs and when important social and physical infrastructure programs were being starved of resources. Because of the sensitivity of the topic, the dialogue has been at the level of Bank senior management and country leaders (World Bank 1994c, p. 48).

These have "tended to be countries with a relatively high dependence on external aid flows" (ibid., p. 49). An example is Uganda, where reportedly "demilitarization came only after prodding from the World Bank" (Carrington 1994).

The IMF has also moved in recent years to place military expenditure on its institutional agenda. An April 1991 communiqué of the IMF's Development Committee raised "the need to re-examine the possible reallocation of public expenditure, including excessive military expenditures, to increase their impact on poverty reduction."[25] In the same year, at the joint World Bank/IMF annual meeting, IMF managing director Michel Camdessus announced that military budgets are "a proper subject for our attention," and characterized this as "just an extension and intensification of our traditional work to help countries improve their macroeconomic policies."[26]

To this end the IMF staff has produced several research papers examining data on military spending and its economic impact.[27] In addition, according to former IMF economic counselor Jacques Polak, the IMF in a few cases "has exercised pressure to reduce military expenditures as part of a program of fiscal adjustment." Polak explains:

> Action of this nature by Fund missions does not show up in letters of intent and thus does not form part of the Fund's formal conditionality. But the Fund and the Bank can be expected to use their financial clout to steer government finance in client countries from military toward development outlays (Polak 1991, pp. 29–30).

There appears to be ample space, therefore, for officials of the Bretton Woods institutions to place military expenditure squarely on the policy agenda. The fact that they have failed to do so in El Salvador suggests that the importance of this issue has yet to be widely affirmed within these institutions at the operational level.

Similar room for maneuver is emerging at the IDB, where the new emphasis on social sectors in recent years has led to heightened awareness of the constraints posed by excessive military spending. A recent assessment of its lending program commissioned by the IDB observed:

> It is crucial that the IDB, through policy dialogue and conditionality linked to social sector lending, persuades governments to allocate a higher proportion of *their own spending* to expenditure which favors the poor (and a lower proportion of their spending to, for example, military spending). . . . Tranched disbursements, linked to policy conditionality and especially dialogue, may be particularly effective for encouraging such changes in government spending structure (Griffith-Jones et al. 1993, p. 69; emphasis in original).

Once again, however, there is no evidence that IDB officials have raised the matter of military expenditure in the case of El Salvador.

Governance

Turning to the other side of the budget-reallocation coin, it would appear that here, too, there is ample institutional scope for peace conditionality in countries like El Salvador. Whereas the legal framework, judicial reform, and the strengthening of democratic institutions were once regarded as outside the purview of the IFIs, in recent years these have been incorporated into the IFIs' definition of their mandate under the general rubric of "governance."

In April 1992 World Bank president Lewis Preston termed good governance "an essential complement to sound economic policies" (World Bank 1992d, p. v). The glossy cover of a 1994 World Bank publication titled *Governance* features the terms "legal framework," "military expenditures," "accountability," "participation," "judicial reform," and "human rights." The document states:

> Good governance is epitomized by predictable, open, and enlightened policymaking (that is, transparent processes); a bureaucracy imbued with a professional ethos; an executive arm of government accountable for its actions; and a strong civil society participating in public affairs; and all behaving under the rule of law (World Bank 1994c, p. vii).

Speaking in June 1994, IMF managing director Camdessus similarly included "good governance—that is, publicly accountable and participatory government that serves the interests of all of society rather than sectional interests" as a crucial ingredient in the "recipe for success" in structural adjustment and economic development (*IMF Survey* 1994, p. 209).

It would appear, therefore, that the central political and military reforms of the Salvadoran peace accords fall within the legitimate purview of the IFIs as redefined by these institutions in recent years. Yet the practice of the IFIs in El Salvador has failed to live up to this potential. In their own project lending, the IFIs have contributed nothing to the various high-priority programs mandated by the peace accords.[28] Nor have they deployed formal conditionality or informal policy dialogue to support these programs indirectly.

The Role of the United States

The United States has attempted to wield conditionality on behalf of the peace process in El Salvador with varying degrees of commitment and with mixed results. As early as 1991, the United States included in its ESF program measures to strengthen democratic institutions, especially the judiciary. According to USAID officials, "the combination of conditionality and provision of resources through project assistance increased the allocation of public expenditures to democratic institutions" (Belt and Lardé de Palomo 1994b, p. 7).

Despite the very large volume of U.S. aid to El Salvador during the war, U.S. influence was circumscribed by the "reverse leverage" wielded by the Salvadoran government vis-à-vis the United States. The Reagan administration needed a moderate civilian government in El Salvador to ensure continued U.S. congressional backing for the counterinsurgency campaign. "As the case of El Salvador suggests," writes Schoultz (1989, p. 415), "at times the donor is more dependent on the recipient than vice-versa." With little credible threat of significant aid reductions, U.S. aid conditionality was less effective than the sums involved might otherwise suggest.

With the end of the Cold War, recipient governments presumably have less scope to wield reverse leverage. Although the volume of U.S. aid to El Salvador has diminished compared to the war years, it is conceivable that the effectiveness of U.S. conditionality has been enhanced because the withholding of funds is now a more credible possibility.

As a relatively successful instance of donor leverage, observers cite the U.S. response to the June 1993 appointment of Oscar Peña, former head of the National Police's Narcotics Unit, as deputy director of the PNC. This appointment was widely perceived as a threat to the integrity of the new civilian police force. The United States withheld deliveries of police vehicles and equipment until Peña finally resigned, almost a year later, in May 1994.

In the case of the land-transfer program U.S. leverage has been less effective. The administrative impediments to land transfers—such as the need to ensure that all back taxes on the land have been paid, or that all joint owners (some of whom cannot be traced) sign the various transfer documents—could be removed, for example, by presidential decree, if there were the political will to do so. Moreover, the land could be transferred as an outright gift, rather than saddling the new owners with a debt for its purchase.

The Salvadoran government has been politically unwilling to take these steps. A U.S. official with long-standing experience in El Salvador explained:

> The smartest and easiest thing they could have done at the beginning would have been to say, "You're farming it? Okay, here is the title." The GOES is not paying anything for the land transfer program—it's all U.S. and EEC money. But the government made it complicated because they don't want to give the opposition a gift. Their attitude is, "We fought these people for twelve years—why should we reward them now?"

Perhaps donor conditionality could have countered this lack of political will. But the United States, the main financier of the land-transfer program, chose not to exercise it. "The U.S. was not in any mood to force the government into a land give-away program," recalls the official:

> That would smack of subsidies. And to a lot of people on Capitol Hill, land reform is a dirty word. It's seen as stealing land from one person and giving it to someone else. Of course, in this case that is pretty far from the truth. It's not stealing. You can even compensate the owner, if you can find him. But lack of political will *here in the U.S.* was a problem, too.

The result was a land-transfer program "doomed to failure because, quite simply, it is designed to fail."[29]

In sum, during a postconflictual transition external-assistance actors must be prepared to exercise peace conditionality. Whereas the support of the international community has played a crucial role in the Salvadoran peace process, that role could have been strengthened by more active peace conditionality. The conditionalities of major aid donors—in particular, the international financial institutions—for the most part were not deployed in support of such objectives as the reallocation of government spending from the military to the new democratic institutions, or the timely implementation of such key programs as the creation of the PNC and land transfer.

In a sense, then, rather than impeding the consolidation of peace by being "too tight," donor conditionalities failed to advance it, by being "too loose." The need to mobilize more effectively the political resources of the external-assistance actors—in addition to their financial resources—is a key lesson of the Salvadoran experience for future cases of postconflictual transition.

Conclusions

External assistance has done much to fund the costs of peace in El Salvador. In general, implementation of the programs mandated by the peace accords has not been seriously hampered by a lack of external resources. The explanation for delays must be sought elsewhere, in administrative bottlenecks and inadequate political will, one symptom of which has been the inability or unwillingness of the Salvadoran government to mobilize greater *domestic* resources for peace-related needs.

El Salvador will need further external assistance in support of peace-related programs in coming years. But a continued willingness on the part of donors to provide resources for the consolidation of peace must be coupled with a greater willingness to withhold them as a penalty for failure to implement provisions of the peace accords. To be effective, aid conditionality must be backed by a credible link between funding and the conditions embodied in formal commitments and informal policy dialogue. This linkage is particularly important in the case of peace conditionality, where (unlike macroeconomic conditionality in postwar El Salvador) there may exist differences of interest and philosophy between external assistance actors and the government. In this important sense, aid conditionality must be tighter, rather than looser, in the context of a postconflictual transition.

External-assistance actors sometimes conflate a country with its government. Yet the government is clearly only one among several internal political actors. The distinction between the government and the country as a whole is particularly important in the aftermath of a negotiated end to a civil war. In providing postwar assistance, donors must seek to maintain the balance among different internal actors on which the momentum of the peace process depends.

A more active policy of peace conditionality in El Salvador would include formal performance criteria and/or informal policy dialogue, with the following objectives:

- Reduction of military expenditure in the next two years to its prewar fraction of GDP, that is, 0.7 percent.
- Reduction of military expenditure in the next five years to a fraction of GDP similar to that in Mexico and Costa Rica, that is, 0.3–0.4 percent.
- More vigorous efforts to raise the tax coefficient to 15 percent of GDP within the next three years and, at the same time, to make the incidence of taxation more progressive. In addition to further improvement in the administration of income-tax collection from high-income individuals, such efforts should include taxes on luxury-goods consumption (in the case of goods that are exclusively imported, this could be accomplished through tariff policy), and taxes on high-value property transfers.
- The commitment of adequate domestic resources on a priority basis to the National Civilian Police, and the implementation of strict measures to prevent human-rights abuses by the new force.
- Steps to streamline and expedite the land-transfer program.
- Direct lending in support of the strengthening of democratic institutions, translating concern for "good governance" into tangible action.

In some postconflictual settings the need to finance peace-related expenditures may require relaxation of macroeconomic conditionalities—for example, if the only feasible way to fund particular programs is through deficit financing. In the case of El Salvador, however, the problem has not been one of insufficient aggregate resources; rather it has been inadequate mobilization and allocation of domestic resources for peace-related needs. Hence there is no compelling argument at present for substantially looser fiscal targets.

During the Cold War, issues of democratic governance and military expenditure were often subordinated to security concerns in the practice, if not always the rhetoric, of the major external-assistance actors. The post–Cold War era has seen a pronounced shift in the stated policies of the IFIs, but this shift has yet to be reflected in their actual practice in El Salvador. In this sense, the consolidation of the peace remains an uncompleted task not only in El Salvador, but in the international financial institutions as well.

Notes

1. Unless otherwise noted, all quotations in this chapter are from interviews with officials of external-assistance agencies conducted in New York, Washington, D.C., and San José, Costa Rica, in October and November 1994.

2. In addition to 1992–1995 assistance, the UNDP reports "total project cost," which includes expenditures prior to 1992 for projects begun before the signing of the peace accords. In the cases of Germany, Italy, and the EEC, only total project cost is available. German and Italian assistance for 1992–1995 is here estimated by multiplying their total project costs by the average share of these years in the total project costs of other bilateral donors (48.9 percent). EEC assistance for 1992–1995 is similarly estimated using the average share of these years in the total costs of other multilateral donors (52.0 percent).

3. The "preferred creditor" share of El Salvador's public debt service is expected to surpass 60 percent in the late 1990s, with the World Bank's share exceeding the 20 percent guideline (World Bank 1993c, p. 20). Bilateral donors occasionally write off their loans, as when the United States forgave $464 million in Salvadoran debt in 1992. In the wake of the 1980s debt crisis, commercial bank loans sometimes have also been, in effect, partially written off (for example, through buy-backs at a discount). Loans from IFIs, however, remain sacrosanct.

4. For discussions of the net transfer cycle, see Griffin (1978, Ch. 3) and Reisen and von Trotsenberg (1988). A recent study for the IDB forecasts negative net transfers from Latin America as a whole to the IDB, perhaps "at quite a high level," by the end of the decade and into the new millennium (Griffith-Jones et al. 1993, p. 77).

5. Because the data in Tables 7.1 and 7.2 do not cover exactly the same time periods, it is not possible to measure precisely non–peace accord external assistance simply by subtracting the latter from the former. It appears, however, that more than half of external assistance to El Salvador in the postwar years has been earmarked for purposes other than programs mandated by the accords.

6. Official development assistance from OECD members peaked in real terms in 1990, at $55.6 billion (World Bank 1994d, p. 196).

7. Total U.S. economic assistance to Central America fell from $824 million in FY 1991 to $462 million in FY 1993 and to $268 million in FY 1994. The decline is even sharper if dated from the peak of FY 1990, when U.S. economic assistance reached $1.3 billion. These figures include development assistance, the Economic Support Fund, and Public Law 480 food aid (data supplied by USAID).

8. From 1980 to 1989 El Salvador received $3.6 billion in U.S. aid. The second-largest recipient of U.S. aid in Latin America was Honduras, with $1.6 billion (Kan 1993, p. 44).

9. In 1991 the net disbursement of official development assistance to El Salvador was $55 per capita, equivalent to 4.9 percent of GNP; the comparable figures for middle-income countries as a whole were $16 and 0.7 percent (World Bank 1994d, p. 198).

10. For discussion, see Mosley (1985).

11. From 1980 to 1991 the United States provided $1.8 billion to El Salvador under the ESF (data provided by USAID). The dollars were deposited at the central

bank, which sold them to importers for colones; an equivalent amount, in colones, was then placed by the central bank in a counterpart fund jointly programmed by the government and the United States. Similarly, local currency from sales of Public Law 480 food generated counterpart funds.

12. The loan document notes that "although pledged donor support for the NRP [National Reconstruction Plan] has been generous, much of it has been in the form of slow-disbursing project financing, and most of it has not been directed toward the areas of highest political priority such as training and equipping the new national police, facilitating land transfers, etc." In response to this problem, the government is said to be "intensifying its outreach to the donor community and is making efforts to obtain more balance of payments support, the local currency counterpart of which can be used to finance NRP expenditures" (World Bank 1993d, p. 5).

13. The ability of NGOs to provide an alternative vehicle for large-scale reconstruction programs was limited by their lack of experience in such activities and by procedural requirements of the donors. For example, USAID became more willing over time to channel limited resources through opposition-linked NGOs, but the agency's ability to do so was constrained by its own bureaucratic rules and procedures. For a discussion of the role of the NGOs, see Washington Office on Latin America (1993).

14. The term "conditionality" here refers to informal policy dialogue as well as formal performance criteria. For a review of recent practice, see Nelson and Eglinton (1992, 1993).

15. El Salvador's agreements with the IMF in recent years have been "precautionary": The country has not actually drawn on the IMF resources available under the standby arrangements. The government sought IMF agreements for two reasons: (1) for technical advice on the relationships between policy instruments and macroeconomic objectives, and (2) for the "catalytic effects" that IMF cooperation gives to relations with other creditors. For the latter reason, IMF conditions carry considerable weight even in the absence of actual drawings on IMF resources.

16. The curve drawn in Figure 7.1 is backward-bending, to allow for the possibility that beyond some point (beyond point *A*) the net effect of increased government budget deficits may be to fuel social tensions—for example, by sparking hyperinflation.

17. At the April 1993 CG meeting, the World Bank representative reiterated that "adequate external financial support to finance priority peace-related expenditures is the critical condition for the consolidation of peace and social progress within a framework of macroeconomic stability and sustainable growth" (World Bank 1993d, Annex IV[a], p. 6).

18. Different sources provide conflicting data on defense expenditures. Compared to the IMF data reported in Table 7.4, government budget data generally show somewhat lower defense expenditures and somewhat higher education and health expenditures.

19. The problem of excess military spending is not confined to El Salvador. Data compiled by the Stockholm International Peace Research Institute (SIPRI) indicate great variation among countries in the region in the percentage of GDP devoted to military expenditure (averages for 1988–1990):

Honduras	4.0	Guatemala	1.4
El Salvador	3.4	Costa Rica	0.4
Panama	2.5	Mexico	0.3

These are calculated from data presented by Happe and Wakeman-Linn (1994, Table 3). In the case of Honduras, estimates from the U.S. Arms Control and Disarmament Agency are substituted for the SIPRI figures, which appear to be anomalously high. The SIPRI data generally exclude foreign-aid–financed expenditures, and hence indicate the "domestic opportunity cost of government appropriations to the military" (Hewitt 1991, p. 22).

20. The government's November 1991 Letter of Intent included a commitment to reduce military spending from 22 percent of recurrent expenditure in 1991 to 20 percent in 1992 (IMF 1991a, p. 58). This provision does not appear to reflect an IMF initiative, however.

21. Similar objections were raised by the executive board of the World Bank when SALs were first proposed in 1980:

> The Board did *not* want to use loans to "buy" policy change, to persuade reluctant developing countries to undertake reforms, to induce waverers to do what they feared would be politically painful or to strengthen the hands of reforming groups in developing countries at the expense of their opponents. Using loans as leverage in this way was meddling in developing countries' internal politics; it would damage the Bank's stance of political neutrality and, to be successful, it would require political skills which the Bank did not possess (Mosley, Harrigan, and Toye 1991, pp. 35–36).

As in the case of SALs, it is conceivable that current objections to World Bank involvement in military-expenditure reductions and other "governance" issues will prove transitory.

22. The United States had been the principal financier of the Salvadoran military during the war, providing over $1 billion of military assistance during the 1980s (Congressional Research Service 1989, p. 26). This figure includes only direct support via the Military Assistance Program, Foreign Military Sales Program, and International Military Education and Training Program.

23. For reviews, see Ball (1992) and Kan (1993).

24. Conable (1991). Conable cautioned against using rigid formulas for determining where military spending is excessive, but he cited governments that spend more on the military than on health and education combined as an indicator. That year the government of El Salvador spent 1.26 billion colones on defense and 1.12 billion on health and education (IMF 1994b, pp. 26, 44).

25. IMF (1991b), cited by Polak (1991, p. 52).

26. Quoted by Ball (1993, p. 2).

27. These include Hewitt (1991), Bayoumi, Hewitt, and Schiff (1993), and Happe and Wakeman-Linn (1994).

28. The proposed IDB loan for strengthening the Salvadoran judicial system, mentioned earlier, is a noteworthy exception.

29. The latter quote appears in a May 1994 USAID memorandum titled "Land: The impossible dream."

8

Distributional Implications of Macroeconomic Policy: Theory and Applications to El Salvador

Manuel Pastor, Jr., and Michael E. Conroy

Although the years of intense armed conflict in El Salvador seem to have finally come to an end, peace in El Salvador is far from assured. Even the principal UN negotiator in the Salvadoran peace process has suggested that the "proclamation of success is premature, and the nature and scope of the unfinished business . . . of the Salvadoran peace process is cause for grave concern" (de Soto and del Castillo 1994b). Consolidating the nascent peace and building civil society require that the dialogue and bridge building that ended the civil war continue; and, while there have been shortfalls and setbacks, the current trends in Salvadoran politics, especially the relatively pacific conclusion of a difficult electoral process, provide a basis for hope.

The economic counterpart to political negotiations and dialogue involves the development of, and commitment to, economic strategies that can reduce social gaps, build common ground, and lead to environmental and political sustainability. Unfortunately, past development and stabilization strategies in El Salvador have generally worsened income distribution and exacerbated poverty, fueling the tensions that produced the war that raged throughout the last decade. If El Salvador is to attain a lasting peace and economic progress, it must pay attention to matters of distribution and poverty. To do this its leaders must realize two things: first, that improved equity and increased efficiency can be compatible rather than conflictual; and second, that there are viable alternatives that are both macroeconomically rational and distributionally superior to those that have been practiced in recent years.

This chapter offers such an alternative argument for the complementarity of economic stabilization and social equity. We begin by considering the general logic and distributional implications of traditional macroeconomic policy, reviewing the historical tension between macroeconomic adjustment and poverty alleviation, especially in El Salvador, and drawing important distinctions between policies of stabilization and of structural adjustment. We focus particularly on the nuances that must be introduced when macroeconomic policy is, as in El Salvador, being made in the context of a relative foreign exchange bonanza.

We then develop the case for a positive link between improved social equity and increased efficiency, reviewing the emerging literature that suggests that a better distribution of income can actually improve the conditions for long-term economic growth and short-term macroeconomic policy. We stress that distributionally sensitive policies are *not* synonymous with a populist-style reflation of the economy. Lack of macroeconomic restraint would be detrimental to the society as a whole and to the poor in particular. It is also clear that growth itself is important for poverty reduction and improved living standards. Private and public investment together with export growth have to be the pillars for sustained economic growth. Structural adjustment is needed that promotes exports, relieves the foreign exchange constraints on growth, and respects the power of markets to allocate resources and reward initiative. Within these general parameters, however, there is much that can be done to promote improved social equity, alleviate poverty, and, in the context of El Salvador, contribute to the consolidation of peace. The chapter ends with an outline of specific interventions that might be considered in contemporary El Salvador.

The Distributional Implications of Traditional Macroeconomic Policy

Since the 1980s macroeconomic policy in El Salvador has been guided by what John Williamson has termed the "Washington consensus," an informal agreement among policymakers in U.S. agencies, international financial institutions, and Latin American capitals that government deficits should be small, exchange rates competitive, and trade and investment flows deregulated.[1] In El Salvador the IMF stabilization agreements of 1990/91 and 1992/93, the World Bank structural adjustment packages of 1990/91 and 1993/94, and the thrust of U.S. aid conditionality have all pushed economic policy in this general direction, albeit with some tolerance for relatively large fiscal deficits due to the war and continuing upward pressure on the exchange rate due to external aid and remittances.

The results on the macroeconomic side have been neither stellar nor dismal. Inflation has been high relative to El Salvador's historical experience but low relative to most of Latin America. Economic growth has been positive for four years in real per capita terms; but real income levels at the end of 1993 were still 20 percent below those of 1978 (USAID 1993d), and the fragmentary evidence suggests that social inequity continues to worsen and poverty continues to deepen. The percentage of the population living in poverty and extreme poverty, for example, grew from 51 percent in 1980 to 56 percent in 1990, while the share of income accruing to the wealthiest 10 percent of all households rose from 31 percent to over 38 percent between 1977 and 1990–1991.[2] Some of the factors behind these trends may have been one-time occurrences, connected to the production disruptions and capital flight prompted by the war; and they may fade in the medium term of a future with peace. However, there is consensus across the political spectrum that significant inequality in access to land is the principal source of endemic poverty for the 73 percent of the Salvadoran population living outside the San Salvador metropolitan area and defined by USAID as rural (USAID 1994c). This underlying structural factor will not be eliminated by any simple set of macroeconomic policies, but macro policy can either exacerbate or ameliorate inequalities. Unfortunately, redistribution upward (i.e., toward greater concentration) has been characteristic of much of Latin America through the 1980s, especially as countries adopted Washington-consensus–style stabilization and adjustment programs.[3]

Attempts to sort out the distributional impacts of conventional (or orthodox) macroeconomic policy and to distinguish those policy effects from more structural elements, such as the allocation of land, have often been plagued by a failure to make clear exactly what is meant by macroeconomic adjustment. There are, in fact, two different aspects to the adjustment process in developing countries: *stabilization,* by which we mean the short-run balancing of demand and supply on both the internal and external fronts; and *structural adjustment,* by which we mean the shifting of resources such that short-run macroeconomic balance becomes consistent with a higher level of long-term output and income.[4] Although the distinctions can be overdrawn, the former has traditionally been the province of the International Monetary Fund and reflects the "expenditure-reduction" part of adjusting to external shocks; the latter has recently become linked with the World Bank and reflects, in a broad sense, the "expenditure-switching" part of adjustment, where changes in relative prices and market efficiency are supposed to make the tradeable-goods sector competitive internationally.

The debate over the effects of adjustment on equity has been equally plagued by a failure to distinguish carefully among different types of income distributions. For example, some argue that orthodox adjustment is regressive because it can reduce workers' wages, while others claim that market-based approaches can be progressive in that they can raise agricultural incomes (which can accrue to workers, owners, or independent producers).[5] The more useful distinction, we believe, is between: (1) *social or income classes* (as long defined by the "functional" distribution of income between workers, owners of capital goods, and owners of land) where the key variables of concern are wage share, the rate of profit, and other such measures; and (2) *sectors of production* (or the relationships between various industries such as agriculture and industry, tradeables and nontradeables) where the key variables are relative prices. These intermediate steps of class and sector are crucial because they provide an analytical route to mapping the effects on the household distribution of income and societal poverty rates. Moreover, it is at the class and sectoral level that groups generally organize to struggle over policy decisions, and it is therefore here that stabilization and adjustment policies are either cemented or frustrated.[6] For that reason we organize our analysis of the distribution-macroeconomy relationship along the categories of stabilization/structural adjustment and class/sector, as shown in Table 8.1.

Stabilization and Distribution

The conventional case. Macroeconomic stabilization usually occurs in the context of excess demand, the signs of which are accelerating inflation, widening trade deficits, and an imbalance in the government budget. Conventional strategy focuses on restraining demand to restore macroeconomic balance. Whereas structuralist critics might point to supply-side shocks—adverse terms of trade, shrinking capital flows, or bad harvests— as the real cause for the internal and external balances, demand restriction is still deemed necessary in the short run. The traditional medicine consists of decreases in government spending and increases in taxes to provide balance on the domestic side; and, concomitantly, a real devaluation to relieve pressure on the external side. Expanded exports are supposed to offset the economic drag from fiscal tightening. However, export volume, the import coefficient, and nonportfolio foreign-investment flows are usually unresponsive in the short run. Short-term portfolio investment, also known as "quicksilver" investment for the speed with which it moves to and from, requires high interest rates whose effects on the domestic market are also

Table 8.1   **Topics and Policies in the Stabilization/Adjustment Class/Sector Approach**

	Classes	Sectors
Stabilization	• wages • devaluation and pressure on wage share • demand reduction and unemployment • budget cutbacks • consumer subsidies	• devaluation and tradeables • devaluation and agriculture • public-investment cutbacks
Structural adjustment	• labor-market liberalization • credit-market liberalization • privatization	• relative price shifts • tariff reductions and increased competition • export promotion

negative. As a result, growth tends to slow. And because domestic prices are usually sensitive to the exchange rate, inflation tends to rise in line with the rate of depreciation. This rather pessimistic pattern certainly seems to fit the Salvadoran case as described in Saca and Rivera (1987) and Segovia (1991).[7]

Orthodox economists and international financial institutions generally argue that the effects of such stabilization programs on the poor could be either positive or neutral. After all, many government subsidies tend to go to middle-class consumers. Moreover, if tradeables are a small proportion of the average worker's consumption basket, devaluation can be consistent with an increase in the real consumption wage.[8] In reality, however, the conventional package often tends to have regressive impacts. Wages (as reflected in the wage share) tend to fall, both because of rising unemployment caused by demand contraction and because of real devaluation that raises the costs of imports (and the import share) and puts pressure on the money wage. Indeed, from the point of view of conventional stabilization theory, such a reduction in labor income can be a positive contribution to the task of curtailing domestic demand.[9] Fiscal retrenchment, in the form of increased taxes and reduced government subsidies, tends to have a regressive effect, because the easiest taxes to raise and collect are often sales and value-added taxes, which fall more heavily on lower-income consumers.[10] Moreover, upper- and middle-class consumers are more likely to be able to protect "their" subsidies against attack in the political process. This inequality in political power, combined with preexisting inequality in income distribution, ensures that the political determination of the incidence of budget cuts often reinforces social inequity, rather than alleviating it. This would seem to be especially true in countries, such as El Salvador, with very wide disparities in both wealth and political access. In short, conventional stabilization, particularly when "filtered" through the real world of domestic politics, should be expected to worsen the distribution of income.

Fiscal tightening associated with conventional stabilization may have other negative economic consequences as well. Public investment is reduced, because cuts in current spending are often more sensitive politically.[11] Such reductions in capital outlays can damage employment and dampen private investment, because in the developing world the latter tends to be "crowded in" and not "out" by its public-sector counterpart.[12] Shortfalls in both public and private investment, in turn, mean that the redistribution of income toward the wealthy, produced by conventional stabilization, may not yield the expected return of higher capital formation, at least in the medium term. Indeed, private investment in El Salvador seems to have responded little if at all to conventional policies during the tightest years of stabilization, 1990 and 1991, when gross private domestic investment averaged only 10 percent of GDP. Of course, those were also years of high political instability. The resurgence of private investment since 1992, though still far below what might be desired, appears to be responding as much to the reattainment of some modicum of social stability (due to the negotiated end to the civil war) and to the concomitant modest expansion of social spending as to more conventional stimuli.

With respect to the "sectoral" effects of conventional stabilization, a real devaluation can raise returns for the producers of tradeable goods, particularly of exportables. Whether the devaluation leads to any real increase in production depends on the actual supply elasticities and the confidence that investors have in the durability of the new exchange rate. A real devaluation should, in theory, also help agricultural producers by raising the price of imported foodstuffs and exportable agricultural commodities. Whether this helps poor farmers, however, depends on the structure of land ownership and on marketing opportunities in the rural areas. In El Salvador, where there are not many small rural property owners well connected to the export trade, we might expect a further concentration of income toward the wealthiest in the rural sector.

Also working against positive effect of devaluation on agricultural producers is the reduction in total demand associated with stabilization, a macroeconomic turn of events likely to dampen any increase in domestic agricultural prices. For example, the initial years of Latin American adjustment to the debt crisis were marked in many countries by declines in relative prices and incomes in the "flex-price" informal and agricultural sectors, probably caused by the general contraction in income and demand (Pastor and Dymski 1990). Thus, despite the theoretical possibility of raising living standards in agriculture, the net effect of a real devaluation combined with shrinking aggregate demand can be quite negative; and the distributive consequences, though complex and contradictory, can lean toward a regressive outcome.

Application to El Salvador. What we have presented is the usual picture of the effects of stabilization on the distribution of income across social classes and sectors.[13] To apply this to the Salvadoran case requires understanding two important nuances. First, orthodox or conventional stabilization theory and practice has changed over the 1980s, particularly in its view of the exchange rate. Whereas the traditional perspective has always stressed devaluation as a tool to attain short-run external balance, exchange rates have increasingly been used to fight inflation. Such exchange-rate targeting has been particularly important in Bolivia, Mexico, and, most recently, in Argentina. Each country has experienced a spectacular and sustained decrease in inflation due to the coupling of an exchange rate "anchor" with fiscal discipline.[14] Such a strategy might lower short-run pressure on wages. In Mexico, for example, the stabilization package of late 1987, which coupled incomes policy with a nearly fixed exchange rate, finally slowed the decline in real wages that Mexican workers had suffered over the first part of the decade.[15] On the other hand, when exchange-rate pegging removes depreciation as a tool to balance trade, the pressure might increase to compress nominal wages in order to maintain export competitiveness. In addition, there may be further downward pressure on agricultural incomes because of the effects noted earlier: Overvaluation makes foreign food cheap and dampens profitability in the tradeable part of the rural sector.[16]

Yet the use of the nominal exchange rate as an anchor for inflation generates the potential for instability and unsustainability in other areas, particularly with respect to the current account deficit. The 1994–1995 financial crisis in Mexico illustrates that using the exchange rate as an inflation-fighting tool does have distributional disadvantages in the medium term. When the exchange rate is held more or less fixed and inflation is still in the process of decelerating, the real exchange rate can become overvalued. This has been a common problem in the cases noted earlier and it implies that internal balance (or inflation reduction) can soon be at odds with external needs for promotion of exports and curtailment of imports. All this, of course, sounds familiar in the Salvadoran case, in which low inflation prior to the 1980s was linked to a remarkably stable exchange rate. The 100 percent nominal devaluation of 1986 prompted an inflationary spiral; and, fearing a repeat, policymakers were slow to devalue again (not until 1989), with the result that the real exchange rate appreciated again.[17]

The relative abundance of foreign exchange resulting from the combination of workers' remittances and official aid is the second key feature relevant to understanding the distribution-stabilization relationship in El Salvador. This influx of foreign exchange, rather than deliberate exchange-rate policy, has led to an increasing real appreciation of the colón in recent years, thus contributing to a reduction of inflation in the country. The distributional impacts of this foreign exchange bonanza are straightforward: Money inflows from Salvadoran emigrés to their family members have surely mitigated the distributional pressures from both orthodox adjustment and the war, while foreign-aid flows have also helped to prop up the exchange rate with the short-run effects discussed earlier. The policy challenges and opportunities posed by these phenomena will be discussed further. The key point here is that the external inflows probably moderated the distributional damage associated with conventional stabilization policy. A large-scale repatriation of Salvadoran nationals in response to anti-immigrant policies in the United States, or a major reduction in their remittances, would have immediate negative consequences on *both* income distribution and economic growth.

Structural Adjustment and Distribution

Economies *stabilize* by reducing demand to a point at which it is compatible with the prevailing foreign exchange constraint. Economies *adjust* by "persuading" exporters to generate the foreign exchange flows that will allow higher demand to persist without triggering inflation. Persuasion in the economy often comes down to prices and profits; so structural adjustment is often focused on shifting relative prices such that internal and external balance are achieved simultaneously, and the basis for economic growth becomes firmly rooted in the export sector.

The Washington consensus on structural adjustment suggests that "liberalization" should be the primary method for changing the incentive structure. The basic view is that freer markets—particularly ones in which the domestic prices mirror international relative prices (accounting for transport and other relevant costs)—are likely to promote the desired change in resource allocation such that a higher level of output, at least in terms of foreign exchange needs, is achievable. The evidence that liberalization can actually do this is, however, less secure than many suppose. Sebastian Edwards (1993), the senior economist in the Latin America division of the World Bank, has pointed out that the earliest studies arguing that liberalization promotes exports and growth focused on the degree of anti-export bias, and not the extent of government intervention. As a result, an economy in which significant export subsidies counteracted import restrictions could be deemed "liberalized" even though it was subject to extensive government involvement in trade and other policy areas. Indeed, the East Asian export success, often pointed to by aficionados of liberalized markets, is hardly based on a reluctant state (World Bank 1993b; Amsden 1990; Sachs 1985). Rather, active, direct, and significant state intervention in setting prices, including subsidies and direct transfers, was the hallmark of their success.[18] Nevertheless, liberalization is advocated as the usual route of structural adjustment programs; and this has been the basic strategy in El Salvador.

The realignment of domestic prices promoted by structural adjustment goes far beyond the broad categories of tradeables/nontradeables; and, hence, the sectoral effects are quite complicated. For example, although a devaluation that is part of a macroeconomic stabilization package may affect the broad distribution between tradeable and nontradeable industries, liberalization of trade—which removes the quantitative restrictions and nonuniform tariffs that cause *certain* importable products to be more expensive—could have an impact on the composition of industries within the tradeable sector. These effects are not frequently distinguished in the literature, but it can be quite important to do so in practice.

Liberalization refers to more than just a trade opening, although this has been the principal component in recent years. Domestic liberalization could also involve the removal of price restraints on agricultural products, which raises farmgate prices and generally encourages the agricultural sector. Financial liberalization removes financial repression (government interventions designed to control interest rates and channel credit) and allows firms previously "rationed out" by administrative mechanisms to borrow. Finally, liberalization is often associated with the privatization of public enterprises and the general shrinkage of state activities. All these elements have been a part of economic strategy in El Salvador since 1989.[19]

The distributional implications of such structural change are usually more complicated than the broad effects of a stabilization program. To some extent, the introduction of market discipline in pricing can improve the distribution of income, primarily because such discipline eliminates the economic rents (benefits attributable to noncompetitive pricing) that arise due to government intervention. Removing tariffs on specific products, for example, can eliminate excess profits and perhaps excess urban wages, shifting income toward consumers. Raising prices of domestic foodstuffs can help small farmers oriented toward the local market. Lifting ceilings on interest rates will make credit more expensive, but it may also mean that access to loans is less determined by political connections. Allowing the market to determine allocation should, in the conventional perspective, mean significant welfare improvements for consumers, nonunionized (or unprotected) workers, poor agricultural producers, and small borrowers who were once forced to the informal market.

To understand the real impacts of using market mechanisms to replace or frustrate rent-seeking behavior, however, we need to first understand the political factors that determine the kinds of intervention a government has pursued. The relative strength of groups in civil society, and the penchant of the government to favor the interests of each group, becomes an important determinant of the distributive outcome from state policies and, by contrast, market liberalization. Populist or left-leaning governments have tended to use their influence to benefit the working class, small farmers, government workers, etc. Conservative governments, such as the successive administrations in El Salvador, have been seen to favor domestic and foreign businesses and their often wealthier constituencies. Removing the protective strategies of each sort of government will therefore have quite different effects on the distribution of income.

Moreover, although conventional theory suggests that market liberalization and the elimination of various regulations and interventions should generally improve social equity, in practice those already enjoying significant assets may do better in the ensuing market competition. In more open world markets, economies of scale often determine the ability to succeed, implying that trade liberalization may induce higher concentration ratios in key industries.[20] In the absence of government programs to provide small farmers with credit, market access, and technology, the long-term gains from higher food prices may accrue to larger and better-positioned agriculturalists. And since market-based credit rationing is a feature of financial markets, especially in developing countries, simply alleviating financial repression does not guarantee that other discriminatory mechanisms such as excess collateral requirements will not continue the pattern of unequal access to loans.[21] In short, without attentive monitoring of the entire liberalization process, the theoretical benefits of structural adjustment on sectoral distribution *may never actually occur*. This point is now widely acknowledged, and has informed the efforts by international financial institutions and USAID to pay more attention to social equity in the adjustment process in El Salvador.

One key policy associated with conventional adjustment, privatization, is especially important from a distributional standpoint; but again the effects are complex. In theory, devolving a firm from state control should improve efficiency, yielding general benefits to consumers even as costs are imposed on the dismissed workers of a restructured enterprise. On the other hand, privatization involves the most profound possible shift in welfare: Public assets are being shifted to private hands and, as noted earlier, those with existing assets to trade—those therefore best positioned to purchase former state firms—are most likely to benefit. In several countries this has meant an effective reward to those who had engaged in capital flight, since their wealth has retained its value in foreign markets and they therefore have more purchasing power. There is also a fiscal downside: Although privatization revenues can, as in Mexico, be used to support some social-welfare programs, rapid privatization can result in "fire sale" prices, which implies both that the public sector will need to cut back its spending more than was necessary and that already wealthy buyers will obtain a better return.[22] Again, tracking these impacts requires careful study of the concrete cases.

Privatization processes in El Salvador have taken place much less rapidly than in much of Latin America. The most important privatizations have been of the financial system and of export marketing, especially with respect to coffee. The nature of the coffee industry, with many small- and medium-scale producers, has led to mixed distributive impacts. But privatization of the financial sector, combined with continued intervention by the state to maintain much higher interest rates designed to draw short-term international capital, has left many of the poorest rural areas of El Salvador without effective access to financial institutions, either for credit or for savings functions (see Chapter 9).

Liberalization, we should also note, can affect the *class* distribution of income, particularly if the labor market itself is liberalized.[23] In theory, trade liberalization should raise the wage share in developing economies; after all, such economies tend to be labor abundant and capital scarce, and the usual logic of factor-price equalization implies an increase in demand for the abundant factor. In dualistic economies, however, a large supply of labor could mean that wage improvement is a long time coming. Also, if land is the relatively abundant factor, then comparative advantage theory predicts an increased return to the landholder upon liberalization. The impact on the mobile factor, labor, is ambiguous. Finally, shrinking the state can produce declines in the "social wage"—the collection of benefits a person can claim by simple virtue of being a citizen—lessening the relative shares of workers in total income.[24]

The distributional effects of restructuring are also affected by its relationship to stabilization. Although stabilization and structural adjustment are analytically separable, they have often been united in practice: Trade liberalization, for example, was an important component of the anti-inflation program in Mexico because import competition, coupled with a controlled exchange rate, provided a second level of price control to the program. Furthermore, liberalization and stabilization sometimes occur simultaneously for political reasons. Liberalization is a fundamentally "Schumpeterian" event: It forces business to scramble to find new economic roles (see Dornbusch 1992) and weakens old political or distributional alliances. This, in turn, reduces the resistance to policy change and allows major reforms to stick.[25] In our view, this may be "good" politics but it is bad economics: A gradualist approach minimizes economic disruption and likely minimizes negative distributional effects. Although it does not appear to have been a major concern of Salvadoran policymakers, stabilization in the country has in fact preceded liberalization (see Chapters 3 and 4).

The hope, of course, is that structural adjustment will eventually produce an economy that is growing rapidly and that this economic expansion will have a positive effect on both per capita income and the distribution of income (due to the tightening of labor markets).[26] Enhancing national income is a goal shared by all observers, but the key issue is whether the path toward growth should and can be paved with less austerity and a less regressive income distribution.

Toward a Distributionally Sensitive Macroeconomic Alternative in El Salvador

The negative distributional patterns apparent in El Salvador are not primarily a function of recent macroeconomic policy. As we have already stressed, the preexisting distribution of income, assets, and power strongly influences whether a particular policy has progressive or regressive impacts.

Data on the shares of income that accrue to different proportions of the total population are available for only a small number of years. Moreover, they are subject to significant problems of interpretation, not the least of which is the problem of second guessing whether individuals surveyed underestimate or overestimate their reported income and, if so, by how much in each income bracket. The most reliable comparative data presently available for El Salvador are based on two income and expenditure studies undertaken in 1977 and 1990–1991. As reported by Gregory (1992) in a study commissioned by USAID/El Salvador, in 1977 the poorest 20 percent of the Salvadoran population received 5.5 percent of total household monthly income; by 1990–1991 that share had fallen to 3.4 percent. At the same time, the share of income accruing to the wealthiest 20 percent rose from 43.9 percent in 1977 to 54.2 percent in 1990–1991. If we also recognize that per capita income declined over this interval by roughly 25 percent, we can see, as Gregory (1992, pp. 5–6) noted, that the decline in the share of income flowing to the lower deciles "would not begin to provide a true measure of the deterioration of living standards among the country's poor."

Virtually all modern observers of the sociology and economics of El Salvador agree that income distribution in the country is driven fundamentally by the structure of land tenure and by the impact that the rural landless and land-poor have on urban and industrial labor markets as well. Notwithstanding the agrarian reforms of the 1980s, land ownership remains highly concentrated. The high proportion of landlessness and near-landlessness depresses wages and unskilled labor incomes throughout the economy.

Although these underlying microeconomic factors have played a paramount role in generating the maldistribution of income in El Salvador, macroeconomic policy has often exacerbated distributional problems for the reasons laid out earlier. Distributive concerns are often set aside, however, by economists who suggest that a bit less justice might be needed for a bit more growth. We suggest, in contrast, that inequality can actually damage the functioning of the economy, and that lessening the maldistribution of income should be a guiding objective for reasons of efficiency and macroeconomic performance as well as equity.

In the following section we outline the case for elevating equity as a *macroeconomic* and not just a *social* concern. We then suggest elements of an alternative that is politically realistic and macroeconomically feasible. We recognize, for example, that although external aid may ease the pains of restructuring, huge enhancements in the aid flow are presently unlikely. Any alternative should therefore focus on changing the nature of the current aid, making better use of domestic resources (including remittances), and rethinking the general logic of macroeconomic stabilization and restructuring. Simple calls to "ease the pain" by speeding growth and risking significantly higher inflation can become an irresponsible form of populism that, in fact, may worsen the lot of the poorest sector of society. A genuine alternative must honor budget constraints, minimize inflationary pressures, *and* push in the direction of a more progressive income distribution.

Income Distribution, Economic Growth, and Reform

Since Kuznets's pioneering studies, it has been a staple of development
theory that income inequality tends first to rise as economic development
proceeds, then to decline after various measures of such development (for
example, per capita GDP) reach a threshold.[27] This "inverted U hypothesis" generally has an acknowledged direction of causality, in which income
distribution is a function of the growth process. But the pattern of causation is sometimes inverted as well. For if it is true that distribution initially
worsens with growth, then premature efforts to improve it may be inconsistent with further development.[28]

There is, however, an emerging literature that contends not only that
a more egalitarian distribution of income is consistent with macroeconomic stability and restructuring, but that it is conducive to higher long-
term growth as well. The argument has several components. First, more
equal distributions of income lead to lower levels of conflict-driven inflation and fewer political struggles over relative prices—for example, tensions between farmers and city dwellers, between exporters and producers
for the domestic markets, or between workers and the owners of their
firms. Combating this conflict-driven inflation dynamic enhances stabilization, while reducing the decibels of complaints about relative price
changes makes the process of adjustment smoother. Second, when structural or stabilization-related measures are introduced, a more equitable
starting point means that any negative consequences on distribution take
place against a baseline context of less social conflict. Countries, in short,
have more room to adjust when social equity has been a long-standing social goal and outcome (Sachs 1987). Third, more egalitarian distributions
may lead to fewer stabilization delays caused by various classes attempting to "outwait" each other in order to insure that the costs of stabilization
are imposed on another group (see Alesina and Drazen 1991). Finally, a
more equal distribution of income and wealth can lead to higher growth
because of increased market size and greater political stability. Both factors provide a more conducive context for private investment, and thus
higher growth (see Rodrik 1994; Alesina and Rodrik 1994).

The empirical work on these issues has established the plausibility of
a positive relationship between improved social and income equality and
more rapid economic growth. The first efforts were simple comparative
studies (for example, Sachs 1985, 1987) that focused on how the superior
distribution in East Asia (notably, from the Salvadoran perspective, as a result of significant land reform) allowed the government to pursue growth-
oriented policies; as Sachs puts it, "the relatively equal income distributions in East Asia free the hand of governments to focus on issues of
efficiency" (Sachs 1987, p. 323). A second set of empirical studies provided indirect evidence of the positive growth–equality relationship by

demonstrating that countries with a more problematic distribution of income have had a higher likelihood of running into foreign-debt problems, primarily because of social conflict over adjustment burdens (see Berg and Sachs 1988; Dymski and Pastor 1990). The most recent empirical exercises have tackled the issue directly, putting together recent developments in the theory of endogenous growth with political models of policy formation, to suggest that less equal societies produce "counterreaction" policies that are less conducive to individual property rights and innovation. The result is a negative link between inequality and growth (see Persson and Tabellini 1994; Rodrik 1994; Alesina and Rodrik 1994).[29]

One of the key factors highlighted in these studies is the importance of an initially fairly equal distribution of assets for subsequent economic growth. The World Bank (1993b), in this context, stresses the importance of widespread human-capital acquisition. In a regression analysis of the determinants of GNP growth in developing countries, primary-school enrollment in 1960 (taken to be proxy for the distribution of human capital) has a positive and statistically highly significant coefficient (World Bank 1993b, p. 61). Rodrik (1994, p. 20) adds initial wealth distribution to the picture. Including a Gini coefficient for initial land concentration (around 1960) in the growth-accounting equation yields a statistically significant negative coefficient (that is, higher inequality of landholdings leads to lower growth), and improves the fit of the regression considerably. Including a Gini coefficient for initial income distribution improves the fit even further. The empirical analysis in Alesina and Rodrik (1994) likewise provides strong support for the critical role of a fairly equal distribution of land in subsequent economic growth.

Although more research is needed on the precise nature of the causal linkages between distribution and growth, the importance and relevance of this emerging research to the Salvadoran case is clear. There is little doubt that a poor distribution of land and income in the country produced the social tensions that provoked both a war and a downfall in the macroeconomy. Moreover, the recent recovery has been driven in part by the achievement of peace and by some level of social consensus; indeed, the private-investment boomlet of the last two years was as much a result of this political phenomenon as of the concurrent structural adjustment program. [30] Achieving a superior distribution of income should therefore be a major goal of stabilization and adjustment in El Salvador, among other reasons because this can be expected to contribute to both medium-term stability and long-term economic growth.

Specific Suggestions for a Macroeconomic Alternative

When distributional pressures build up, Latin Americans have often chosen to flee. The flight takes several forms: flight of capital abroad, flight to other countries or into the hills to wage armed revolution, or a flight of fancy involving the adoption of unsustainable macroeconomic policies. The latter is of most immediate concern here, particularly because those worried about the poor often suggest that macroeconomic expansion, "growing the economy out of its poverty and inequality," is the least conflictual route. Risking a little more inflation, it is sometimes suggested, is a small price to pay for more growth and increased incomes at the bottom of the income distribution. The argument may be especially appealing in El Salvador, where the budget deficit is sizable but not excessive, and where foreign financing of both the current account overrun and the budget shortfall has been available throughout the 1980s and early 1990s.

The history of such efforts suggests, however, that they fail to face the difficult underlying distributional issues: Rather than devise mechanisms to confront directly the maldistribution of income at any given level of output, the hope is to use aggregate demand (mis)management to raise output and therefore improve all incomes. This pattern of "macroeconomic populism" has often failed on both the macroeconomic and the distributional fronts. One recent extreme case, Alán García's Peru, resulted in hyperinflation, a deterioration in the absolute and relative position of the poor, and a handoff in power to a particularly rigid form of orthodox economic management that has likely further worsened the distributional picture.[31] While there may, in fact, be some room for macroeconomic expansion in El Salvador, the key task is to design programs that offer reasonable amounts of macroeconomic restraint yet generate superior distributional outcomes. This implies that difficult institutional changes may be necessary, particularly in the distribution of income-producing assets, and this suggests, in turn, that the microeconomics of reform may be key to macroeconomic success.

We also wish to caution against attempting to solve El Salvador's distributional and economic problems simply by pleading for more foreign support. The case for more aid is certainly strong. The country has shown a commitment to macroeconomic reform, it has come successfully so far through a difficult peace process, and it is still in need of significant external financing for its National Reconstruction Plan. El Salvador, however, has actually received very high levels of external support for both its balance of payments and budget shortfalls since the early 1980s; and the levels of official external assistance can be expected to decline. Moreover, there is reason to argue that external aid should not be used to paper over distributional conflicts but rather to make politically and economically possible the permanent changes that will create the basis for sustained and distributionally sensitive growth.

Following the general categories outlined by Stewart (1987) and the pioneering work of Cornia, Jolly, and Stewart (1987), we sketch here seven general classes of policies that will enhance, rather than detract from, fundamental macroeconomic equilibrium. Their class and sector impacts are outlined in Figure 8.2. These policies can help to bring to El Salvador, from the ashes of war and severe adjustment, both improved equity and increased efficiency and growth, laying the economic foundation for the consolidation of peace. We should note further that all are consistent with the overall macroeconomic strategy recommended by the Adjustment Toward Peace project in this volume: increases in public (and private) investment, a simultaneous tightening of fiscal discipline on the revenue side, and a conscious effort to maintain a more competitive real exchange rate.

Reduced military expenditures. Although political and diplomatic concerns among the international financial institutions (IFIs) have long frozen out discussion of the need for reduced military expenditures, there are encouraging signs of a post–Cold War thaw. At the most senior levels of the IFIs, the taboo has been broken (see Chapter 7). The challenge is to translate this at the operational level. There is little doubt that the policy space for more creative programs that can benefit *all* Salvadorans could start with significantly reduced budgets for the military. Identifying the sectors that benefit will depend upon the uses to which those savings are put.

Increased focus on environmental concerns. The massive environmental deterioration experienced by El Salvador during and since the war represents a threat to present and future productivity for all Salvadorans (see Chapter 11). Although there are likely to be heavier health and welfare impacts upon the nation's poor, the full class-specific incidence remains to be examined. Dramatically increased consciousness of environmental issues, equitable across-the-board legislation for the protection of natural resources, and improvement in workplace conditions will benefit all sectors. In the absence of such policies, the country is at risk of undermining the

Table 8.2   **Alternative Policies in the Equity-Enhancing Class/Sector Approach**

Policies	Classes benefited	Sectors benefited
Reduced military expenditures	all groups	all sectors
Increased focus on environmental concerns	all groups	all sectors
Selective tradeable-goods interventions	all export workers	selected tradeables
Increased public investment in human capital	rural and urban poor	all sectors
Stronger tax enforcement and progressive taxes	rural and urban poor	domestic goods; nontradeables
Enhanced agrarian reform	rural poor	foodstuffs; nontraditional tradeables
Employment-guarantee programs	rural and urban poor	depends on programs

physical bases of growth, and of becoming an environmental pariah, with negative consequences for the foreign-trade sector and the economy at large.

Selective tradeable-goods interventions. A rapidly growing body of literature recognizes the tactical importance and political appropriateness of industrial policies to promote selective specialization in tradeable goods (see Conroy and Glasmeier 1995). The new international-trade theory provides coherent justification for programs designed to expand the production of exportables, particularly through technical assistance to internalize significant training, learning, and scale externalities, especially as they relate to small-scale rural and urban producers. There is, no doubt, room for unproductive rent-seeking behaviors in countries with less transparent governments. But the fundamental attractiveness of such policies has been well established in the growth experiences of the Asian "minidragons" (Amsden 1989).

Increased public investment in human capital. One of the clearest "imperatives" of the new global industrial order is that investment in human capital is the single policy most closely linked with improvements in both income distribution and global competitiveness. In the case of El Salvador this recognition bolsters the case for international support for the expansion of primary education throughout the country, but only if the government agrees to raise additional revenues in nonregressive fashion to match international contributions, and to intensify efforts to increase local participation and accountability. A renewed emphasis in this direction can also be expected to produce immediate improvements in the family living standards of the poorest sectors of Salvadoran society, as well as to help lay the foundations for long-term inclusive growth.

Stronger enforcement of more progressive taxes. The Salvadoran tax structure has an extremely low overall rate of taxation and, as enforced, is highly regressive. If, as is reasonable to assume, one of the most significant sources of profits and high incomes within Salvadoran society is rents earned from export earnings (especially during the renewed coffee bonanza), higher and more progressive taxes would benefit those portions of society previously subject to heavier regressive burdens and those sectors more focused on domestic and nontradeable production.

Enhanced agrarian reform. We suggest that the current land-distribution programs be modified so as to *give* the land to ex-combatants of both sides, freeing them of the land-related financing constraints and permitting them to function within current credit markets for operating capital. This would be one of the simplest and most important steps toward both enhancing equity and consolidating the peace. Reimbursement of previous owners can come from the donated funds already promised by USAID and other sources, assuming rational corrections of distorted land-pricing policies (see USAID 1993d). Furthermore, in light of our earlier discussion of the key role of initial conditions in the equity-growth nexus, it is of paramount importance to consider an expansion of the land-distribution program beyond the specifics of the peace accords.

Employment guarantee programs. For both the urban and the rural labor force, the expansion of nonfarm and seasonal rural employment through infrastructure projects, including road repairs, forest replanting, and environmentally beneficial community projects under expanded FIS aegis may be the next most important fiscally responsible equity-enhancing program available. Programs of this sort have been increasingly advocated for their poverty alleviation value in numerous studies (World Bank 1991d; Ravallion 1991; Echeverri-Gent 1988). They yield immediate employment impacts, particularly for rural workers, as well as positive results for medium-term sustainable growth.

Further policy measures. Measures that fundamentally alter the institutional structure in favor of equity enhancement might also include the following:

- Government investment in programs of microlending and microenterprise development, with special focus on women, woman-headed households, young workers, and ex-combatants
- Programs to encourage the channeling of foreign exchange derived from remittances into projects that preferentially benefit the poor, and that promote the use of remittances for productive purposes by the poor
- In line with the first two points, the use of privatization revenues to generate or subsidize projects with direct positive impacts on the poor, thus directly coupling efficiency-enhancing measures with equity-promoting programs

In El Salvador, sustained future economic growth has to be driven by investment-cum-exports in the context of improved distribution. The foregoing discussion suggests a twofold role for the government in meeting such a challenge. The first role is to manage the size and nature of public investment that complements private investment and has positive distributional impacts, such as investment in primary education, infrastructure, and environmental restoration. The second key aspect of government action involves possible changes in initial endowments. One of the lessons of the East Asian success stories is the pivotal role played by a more equal distribution of income and wealth in setting the stage for rapid economic growth. This issue is politically highly sensitive, especially given recent history. But if the economic development of the country is to be put on a different trajectory, everybody in El Salvador should have a long-term interest in following in the East Asian footsteps.

Macroeconomic stability and growth are no substitute for the necessary *microeconomic* and *institutional* restructuring outlined earlier and further elaborated in Chapters 9 to 12. Macro policies do not write across a blank slate, and growth alone will not solve distributional inequities. The social question is now paramount in El Salvador. New alternative strategies can be key to lifting those at the bottom of the income distribution from poverty—and distributionally progressive policies can, in fact, encourage growth.

The importance of the "social question" is increasingly recognized by even the traditional international organizations. Writing in *Finance and Development,* the journal of the Bretton Woods institutions, Bernstein and Broughton (1994) observe:

> If an adjustment program is designed without regard to its effects on the poor, its insensitivity may become the subject of protests, and it will be unlikely to command the broad support (either within the country or among potential creditors and donors) that is essential for sustained success. . . . The [IMF's] growing emphasis on targeting the poor has emerged from an explicit recognition that great importance must be attached to equity and to the full development of human resources if programs are to be viable in the long run.

With specific regard to El Salvador, the World Bank (1994b, p. 1) states, "Remaining widespread poverty is a major threat to peace and political stability."

The crucial goal is to translate emerging consensus on the appropriate analysis to workable policy alternatives to ameliorate inequality. We have offered one approach above: attempting to respect macroeconomic constraints even as we push for improved equity. Certainly, our own policy list is merely a starting point for an important debate on how best to tackle the social "deficit" in El Salvador and elsewhere. Whatever path is chosen, the key point is to recognize and explore the complementarity of economic efficiency and social justice. With a full commitment to both these objectives, the nascent but still uneasy peace in the political sphere can find its economic counterpart in prosperity, and an era of true consolidation of civil society can begin.

Notes

We acknowledge the support for this chapter received from Anders Kompass and Francesca Jessup of the UNDP office in El Salvador and the leadership on this project provided by James Boyce. Thanks to the various members of, and advisors to, the Adjustment Toward Peace project for their helpful criticisms (especially those of Elisabeth Wood, Eva Paus, Keith Griffin, Lance Taylor, and Victor Bulmer-Thomas). Finally, special thanks to Lori Snyder for her usual able research assistance.

1. See Williamson (1990) for a listing of the elements of the consensus. Although Taylor (1993) offers a point-by-point critique, particularly with regard to how quickly and smoothly adjustment can take place using market mechanisms, he supports the need for reasonable exchange-rate and fiscal policy.

2. Evidence for the shifts in poverty and extreme poverty come from CEPAL (1993a, p. 7). The changes in household distribution are detailed in Gregory (1992).

3. For reviews of the distributional experience of Latin America over the 1980s period of adjustment, see Pastor and Dymski (1990) and Paus (1994a).

4. The importance of distinguishing between stabilization and adjustment in analyzing their distributional consequences is also stressed by Bourguignon, de Melo, and Morrison (1991). Their article summarizes an OECD project that constituted one of the first attempts to systematically study the distributional impacts of the 1980s adjustments in six developing countries. For a less formal but still useful attempt to determine the impacts of the 1980s adjustment on poverty in Latin America, see Cardoso and Helwege (1992).

5. For example, Pastor (1987) criticizes IMF programs on the grounds that their most consistent and statistically significant effect in Latin America in the pre–debt crisis era was the dampening of wage share. Johnson and Salop (1980), meanwhile, make much of the potential increase in agricultural prices that can result from IMF-style adjustment. The two "sides" are clearly talking past one another.

6. For a view of how these class and sectoral distinctions matter for understanding the political economy of policy choice, see Frieden (1992).

7. Saca and Rivera (1987) estimate elasticities for Salvadoran imports and exports that are extraordinarily low while Segovia (1991, p. 18) argues strongly that inflation tracks the exchange rate. Bourguignon, de Melo, and Morrison (1991, pp. 1488–1492) rightly stress that the output loss and redistribution tend to be more severe in an economy characterized by such rigidities than in one that is more flexible in both its production response to price changes and its pricing rules.

8. For the argument that removing subsidies is distributionally progressive, see Sisson (1986, p. 35). As for the consistency of devaluation and rising real living standards, note that the intent behind a devaluation is to increase the profitability of export goods by reducing the real wage in the export sector; although this means that the government must ensure that nominal wages do not keep pace with devaluation, the real living standard need not fall if nontradeables are a large share of the consumption basket. More formally, let the real consumption wage, w^r, be equal to the nominal wage, W, divided by the price index, P, where P equals $(P_N)^b * (e)^{(1-b)}$ and $* P_N$ is the price of nontradeables, b is the share of nontradeables in the consumption bundle, e is the exchange rate, and we limit the notation by assuming that the dollar price of both exports and imports equals one. w^r can be re-expressed as $(w^X)(e^r)^b$ where w^X is the real product wage in the export sector (W/e) and e^r is the real exchange rate (e/P_N). Orthodox policies require a fall in w^X

but they also imply a rise in e^r and b, the share of expenditure devoted to non-tradeables. Hence, the total effect on the real consumption wage is ambiguous (see Cline 1983, p. 180; Dornbusch 1980, pp. 77–78). It should be stressed, however, that stabilizing economies are not usually at full employment and, if devaluation lowers output, wages should be expected to fall as suggested in the text.

9. Pastor and Dymski (1990) offer a regression analysis that suggests a negative relationship between the real exchange rate and the real wage, squaring with the discussion here, which is itself based on Krugman and Taylor (1978). For alternative evidence on the distributional impacts of devaluation (more specifically, of devaluation episodes), see Edwards (1989).

10. For example, the fiscal adjustment that helped to end Bolivia's hyperinflation consisted largely of the introduction of a value-added tax, of known regressive impact, as well as hikes in state petroleum prices that fell heavily on transit-dependent workers. See Pastor (1991).

11. Bourguignon, de Melo, and Morrison (1991, p. 1494) also note the tendency to cut public investment disproportionately, both to ameliorate the immediate impact on poverty and because of the political resistance of bureaucrats.

12. The actual impact of public-investment cuts on private investment depends on whether the public-sector spending is directed toward infrastructure or toward bloated state enterprises from which some workers benefit disproportionately. But the general complementarity of private and public investment has been a consistent result in a recent series of econometric studies of private investment in the developing world (see Greene and Villanueva 1991; Pastor 1992a; Serven and Solimano 1993).

13. We should acknowledge that the distribution of income prior to stabilization is almost always unsustainable; if it were not creating problems with regard to internal and external balance, there would likely be no need to adjust. In this sense, the simple before-and-after comparisons of the text are less valid than a presentation of reasonable counterfactual behavior for class and sectoral income had stabilization been entirely avoided. Unfortunately, such a task is extremely complicated. Moreover, as will be seen in the final section of this chapter, we accept the general need to stabilize a macroeconomy and we focus instead on the possibility for a less regressive strategy to pursue that goal.

14. In contrast, the heterodox experiments in Argentina, Brazil, and Peru in the mid-1980s coupled fiscal laxity with an extreme reluctance to devalue; when the currency eventually had to be depreciated, hyperinflation followed.

15. The economic growth that then occurred in Mexico may have resulted, in part, from the fact that the 1987 *pacto* in Mexico then froze wages at those heavily depressed levels.

16. There may be an asymmetry in which upward movements in the real exchange rate are not passed down to increases in the agricultural wage but downward movements (i.e., overvaluation) induce agricultural enterprises to respond firmly to wage demands in order to protect past levels of profitability.

17. See also Segovia (1991, p. 15) and Chapters 3 and 4 of this volume.

18. For a debate on the relative importance of selective government intervention in the "economic miracle" of the East Asian success stories, see, for example, the World Bank (1993b), Rodrik (1994), Amsden (1994), and Lall (1994).

19. See Chapter 4 of this volume. For a comparison to other Central American reform efforts, see Buttari (1992).

20. In the Mexican case, for example, it is widely expected that larger companies will benefit disproportionately from the North American Free Trade Agreement because economies of scale, and scope in production and marketing, leave them better positioned to weather the competitive storm and successfully restructure in the face of foreign competition. See Dussel Peters and Kim (1992) and Conroy and Glasmeier (1993).

21. For more on credit rationing in an unregulated financial market, see Stiglitz and Weiss (1981); for more on credit rationing in developing countries, see Stiglitz (1986a). For a critique of some of the theoretical assumptions behind the benefits of financial liberalization and a discussion of the fiasco of financial liberalization in the late 1970s in the Southern Cone countries, see Taylor (1993), Ramos (1986), Díaz Alejandro (1985), and Foxley (1983).

22. For more on privatization in Latin America, see Cardoso (1991), and Baer and Conroy (1993, 1994).

23. This was quite important in the Bolivian case, in which the lifting of numerous labor-market regulations in 1985 caused a sharp initial decline in wages; see Pastor (1991).

24. To see why the market wage would track to social wage or social benefits, note that the "fall back" position from unemployment is some probability-weighted combination of the wage at an alternative job, and income when out of work, that is, the social wage. The lower is the latter, the less likely employees are to ask for higher wages or to shirk while at work. For more on the effect of the social wage, see Bowles and Gintis (1990), and for more on "shirking" models, see Stiglitz (1986b).

25. Indeed, some economists argue that policymakers may tend to go overboard to gain credibility from doubting economic agents (Rodrik 1989). Pastor (1991) argues that the simultaneous pursuit of stabilization and liberalization in Bolivia in 1985–1986 was done specifically to break the back of the political opposition to a new economic program.

26. For a discussion of the management of the transition from stabilization to growth, see Dornbusch (1990).

27. See Kuznets (1955) for the original argument and Ahluwalia (1976), Paukert (1973), and Lecaillon et al. (1984) for various restatements.

28. That income inequality might be essential to growth is not an assumption limited to neoclassical theorists; see, for example, the profit-squeeze discussion in Taylor (1983).

29. Whether the negative impact of inequality on growth is more pronounced in democratic states is still a matter of debate. Persson and Tabellini (1994) find evidence for a more pronounced effect in democratic regimes, while Przeworski and Limongi (1993) and Alesina and Rodrik (1994) find little consistent impact. See also Pastor and Hilt (1993) on democracy and private investment.

30. A danger, of course, is that policymakers will ascribe too much of the credit for the investment rise to the economic and not the social policy, particularly since the boomlet tends to validate the policy reforms and make them appear to be successful. For more on the two-way relationship between private investment and the sustainability of reform, see Rodrik (1991).

31. For a survey of recent experiences and explanation of the political conditions that produce populism, see Kaufman and Stallings (1991). For reviews of the Peruvian experience, see Pastor and Wise (1992) and Lago (1991).

9

The Financial System: Opportunities and Risks

Colin Danby

The transition to peace offers El Salvador the opportunity to construct a financial sector capable of supporting a more equitable pattern of development. Unfortunately, this opportunity is being squandered. The government is hastily deregulating commercial banks, pursuing a standard financial liberalization policy that makes no allowance either for the country's special development needs or for its anomalous macroeconomic situation. The provision of financial services to the poor majority has been largely left to a patchwork of donor-funded programs in which credit tends to function as palliative transfers to the poor, working against both sustainable real activity and the development of sustainable financial links to undergird it. Whereas external assistance for the peace accords' commitment to equitable development was part of the bargain that ended the war, such assistance has left a critical gap in terms of financial development.

A financial system is simply the collection of institutions, formal and informal, state run and private, by which financial instruments are created or traded. By providing individuals with the opportunity to hold their savings in financial form, and by providing credit to worthy projects, financial institutions play a critical role in development. In El Salvador financial-sector policies must address two main challenges: (1) the threat posed to macroeconomic stability by the fragility of the liberalized commercial banking system, and (2) the insufficient development of financial institutions able to provide deposit and lending services to small businesses and to the poor.

The first issue results from the combination of financial liberalization and a foreign exchange bonanza. The Salvadoran government has been trying to reduce the real appreciation of the colón—which hurts exports—by sterilizing the inflow, a policy that has helped to drive domestic interest rates substantially above foreign interest rates (taking into account the current stability in the nominal exchange rate). This attracts foreign short-term capital and encourages banks to borrow abroad and relend domestically.

Liberalization of commercial banks has also permitted a great surge in their lending, and has provoked worry that some of it may be unwise if not speculative, in particular burgeoning credit for construction. Given the crossborder mobility of deposits, and the possibility of serious misallocation of credit by inexperienced and eager-to-expand banks, more vigilant and muscular prudential regulation of the banking system is urgently needed.

The second issue arises because even if the country's commercial banks were more prudently run and better regulated, they would continue to serve only a narrow segment of Salvadoran borrowers.[1] Small businesses and the poor are not well served by the existing financial institutions. El Salvador needs to expand categories of financial institutions that can provide financial services to small and medium-sized businesses in rural and urban areas. Services means *both* savings instruments and loans; indeed, the former may be more important. Financial savings ease the accumulation of resources for investment, reduce vulnerability to household or business crises, and improve an individual's standing as a potential borrower. Consolidating peace and promoting *sustainable* equitable development requires promoting institutions, within appropriate regulatory frameworks, that both fund themselves from and provide credit to presently ill-served groups. El Salvador already has several significant institutions of this kind, but work is needed to nurture new ones, improve the regulatory framework, and move away from the currently dominant credit-channeling model.

The credit-channeling variety of development banking funds loans to local recipients with loans from foreign donors, rather than with local savings. Although superficially attractive as a means of quickly dispensing claims on resources, this approach has in fact stunted the development of local institutions that can meet the needs of the poor majority. Foreign resources can crowd out local savings and discourage the very difficult institutional development needed to mobilize local resources. Often, such programs have been no more than palliatives, efforts to use lending to put off confronting serious real-sector problems.

This last point needs to be stressed. Many potential small borrowers who are not now receiving credit *should not* receive it. They are not creditworthy and do not have good investment projects available to them. Without addressing the real-sector roots of poverty—including access to factors of production and difficulties in marketing—there are important limits to what better financial institutions can do.[2] On the whole, finance follows commerce (Bell 1988, p. 796). Efforts to lead with finance, in the absence of conditions for profitable production, are likely to waste resources.

This chapter explores these issues in greater detail. The following section discusses the postwar macroeconomic policy context and the pressures it puts on the banking system; the next section examines the main segments of the Salvadoran financial system; and the final section draws policy conclusions.

Monetary Policy and Financial Liberalization

Liberalization

Salvadoran authorities, supported by the IMF and the World Bank, have moved quickly in the last three years to liberalize the country's financial sector. The main idea behind financial liberalization is that allocation of credit should be left to the "market," with government controls over financial institutions limited to prudential regulation. The government should interfere with neither prices (interest rates) nor quantities allocated (McKinnon 1973; Fry, 1988; World Bank 1989b).

The record of financial liberalization in recent decades has been mixed. Several East Asian countries, most notably South Korea, Indonesia, and Taiwan, have gradually liberalized with apparently favorable results, particularly in terms of increased availability of credit to previously rationed-out firms. On the other hand, in the early 1980s, Argentina, Chile, Uruguay, Turkey, and the Philippines all suffered damaging financial crises within a few years of liberalizing their financial systems. From the extensive literature on these successes and failures a few lessons can be drawn. First, if there are no exchange controls or other restrictions on capital movements into and out of a country, then a liberalized financial system imposes a double burden on the domestic interest rate: It both influences the allocation of credit domestically and affects capital movements into and out of the country. Policy goals in the two areas may easily conflict.[3]

A second broad lesson is that financial liberalization should not precede real-sector adjustments in a "sequence" of liberalization, because financial markets adjust much more rapidly than goods markets. High and variable inflation is particularly damaging to a financial system. The real-sector reforms most commonly emphasized are reducing the fiscal deficit, which is seen as the most important source of inflationary pressure in orthodox theory; privatization, which is seen as both reducing the fiscal deficit and encouraging better resource allocation; and trade liberalization, which is supposed to eliminate the bias against exporting. Just how far these reforms need to go, and whether they do provide an adequate basis for financial liberalization, especially in small, trade-dependent countries, remains open to debate.

A third lesson is that prudential regulation is extremely important. Not only does liberalization usually require regulators to develop capacities that they were not previously required to exercise, but it may also create opportunities for highly risky lending and even outright fraud by private bankers, as happened most notably in the case of Chile in the early 1980s. Real-sector turmoil and domestic interest rates significantly higher than foreign interest rates increase the temptations and opportunities for banker malfeasance.[4]

These lessons suggest that El Salvador's financial liberalization has been premature. Salvadoran policymakers and their advisors in the Bretton Woods institutions have been rightly worried about the kind of system they were moving away from, but may have taken inadequate measures to adapt liberalization to the peculiar circumstances of postwar El Salvador.

Sterilization and Interest Rates

El Salvador is receiving substantial resource flows through remittances and foreign aid—in excess of $1 billion a year into an economy with a GDP of less than $8 billion. Most of the funds arrive in dollars and are exchanged for colones. The increased demand for colones will tend to bid up their dollar price—an appreciation of the currency that will hurt exports, particularly those with important locally supplied inputs.[5]

Because export promotion is a priority for Salvadoran authorities, the central bank, the Banco Central de Reserva (BCR), has stepped into the market to buy dollars as needed to prevent further appreciation. It thereby issues new colones. But the effect of this is to increase the domestic money supply, which, other things being equal, might lead to inflation (and thus to a real appreciation of the colón). In order to avoid that the central bank must simultaneously soak up liquidity by pulling cash into nonspendable forms, such as bonds or bank reserves. This combination of issuing local currency to meet an inflow and then issuing bonds to absorb the increase in the money supply is called "sterilization."[6]

The most direct way to soak up liquidity is through very high reserve requirements on banks. Reserve requirements are currently 30 percent on sight deposits, 20 percent on time and savings deposits, and 50 percent on deposits in foreign currency. Although these nominal reserve ratios are only slightly higher than those of the late 1980s, effective or net reserve ratios—net assets with the central bank—have risen sharply (Figure 9.1), because in the late 1980s credits from the BCR to banks actually exceeded the reserves the banks held with the BCR. The central bank has also at various times over the last two years compelled banks to purchase monetary-stabilization bonds (discussed below) equivalent to a certain percentage of deposits. Current reserve requirements are, however, substantially in excess of what would generally be considered necessary for prudential requirements. This violates the canons of financial liberalization, which hold that banks should allocate credit freely.[7]

Figure 9.1   Gross and Net Bank Reserves, 1989–1993 (As a percentage of deposits)

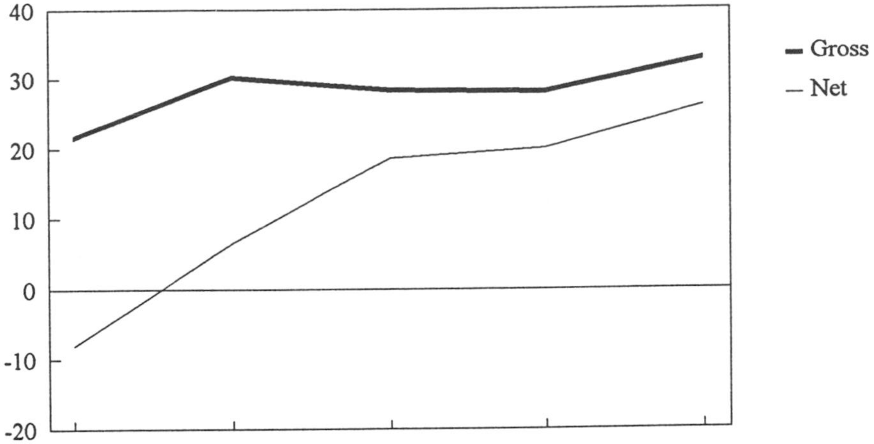

Source: IMF, International Financial Statistics.

Another way to reduce liquidity is through minor regulatory constraints on banks such as raising the discount rate or restricting access to
the discount window, or more stringent enforcement of reserves against
doubtful loans, which can curtail bank lending. Most of these were applied
during the course of 1994, including a virtual closing of the discount window (IMF 1994a). But these are fine-tuning measures, and are of little use
in reining in the credit expansion characteristic of euphoric booms.

Given that other available means are exhausted, the Salvadoran central
bank is pursuing open-market operations, that is, selling bonds in order to
soak up liquid money. Most central banks do this by dealing in bonds issued by their government's treasury. But because the Salvadoran treasury
does not issue bonds, the BCR has to issue its own Certificates of Monetary Stabilization (CEMs).[8] According to BCR figures, private holdings of
BCR-issued securities rose from levels of under 40 million colones in December 1992 to 841 million colones by the end of 1993.[9]

The recent results of this policy can be seen in Table 9.1. The balance-
sheet changes for the central bank show the sharp recent rise in international reserves, and the major role that increased liabilities to the banking
system have played in absorbing that increase so that there is little growth
in liquid money. The table shows that currency in circulation has remained
roughly constant, and that sight deposits have grown only modestly.[10]
Under the central bank's liabilities to (commercial) banks, one can see the
increased use of both reserves and holdings of CEMs to absorb liquidity.
The central bank has also used some of its foreign-currency bonanza to

Table 9.1   Absorbing an Inflow (millions of colones[a])

	December 1992	June 1993	December 1993	June 1994
Central Bank				
Net international reserves	4505	5367	5804	6954
Domestic credit	7923	7708	8580	7562
Liabilities to banks	5338	6517	7632	8306
Currency	215	239	336	430
Deposits	2931	3818	4977	5312
Monetary-stabilization bonds	904	1220	1128	1528
SAFOR bonds	1289	1240	1192	1036
Liabilities to nonmonetary financial institutions	1222	1548	1856	1838
Liabilities to private sector (currency in circulation)	2438	2078	2645	2304
Medium- and long-term foreign liabilities	2400	1973	1841	1620
Other liabilities	1029	958	411	447
Banks				
Net international reserves	195	−15	26	−442
Monetary reserves and currency	5338	6517	7632	8306
Domestic credit	10789	10699	14676	16149
to businesses and individuals	11217	10705	14286	15733
Other	−428	−6	390	416
Liabilities to private sector	14152	15364	20004	21618
Sight deposits	2951	2944	3412	3650
Time and savings deposits	9965	10915	14834	16030
Foreign-currency deposits	804	650	841	1010
Miscellaneous	432	855	917	928
Other liabilities[b]	2171	1838	2330	2394

Source: IMF

Notes: a. Figures have been adjusted by the IMF to correspond to a uniform exchange rate of C9.0 = U.S.$1.

b. Mainly to central bank and nonmonetary financial institutions.

reduce its own medium- and long-term foreign liabilities, which declined by about 800 million colones during this period.

Persuading people to buy CEMs requires offering competitive yields, and the more the central bank needs to sell, the higher the interest rate is pushed.[11] Another consequence of open-market operations is that the central bank has to create money to pay the interest on these bonds. A substantial stock of bonds paying interest of over 15 percent per year constitutes a further source of money-supply expansion in itself, which may in turn require issuing even more bonds, and so forth.

Thus, although high interest rates on time/savings deposits and CEMs have for the time being reduced liquidity and hence inflationary pressures, the BCR has left hostages to fortune: If "confidence" flags, the BCR might have to expand the monetary base very rapidly (so as to avoid financial crisis), thereby losing monetary control. Holders of CEMs and time/savings deposits may indeed be filled with confidence in the country's future and inspired by the government's sound macroeconomic policies, but they may also be simply speculating that the exchange rate will hold up for the time being.[12] The effect of recent monetary policy can also be seen in the rise of M2 and M3 (see Figure 9.2).

Interest Rates and Financial Stability

Because the central bank is competing with commercial banks for financial savings by issuing CEMs, commercial banks will have to pay higher interest rates for their deposits and will therefore have to charge higher lending rates to remain profitable. The cost of credit to local firms rises, and to the extent that exporters tap local credit markets for working capital, higher interest rates make Salvadoran exports less competitive. The consequences may go further: First, higher lending rates of interest can also have an adverse selection effect, as safer borrowers leave the market, actually discouraging some potentially profitable capital investment. As banks find it harder to assemble safe loan portfolios providing an adequate return, they may be more tempted to gamble, particularly on the rising asset values of real estate and real-estate development. Such loans are large, the collateral is visible, and profits can be substantial if asset prices do not collapse. Construction spending in El Salvador has risen from about 2 percent of bank lending in 1989–1990 to almost 14 percent in 1993 (Table 9.4).[13] In these circumstances financial institutions can misallocate credit (and hence real resources) in damaging ways, such as building of fice buildings that nobody will use, as occurred with U.S. savings-and-loan institutions in the 1980s (Stiglitz 1993). Salvadoran bankers have also tended to hold substantial excess liquidity in recent years (Table 9.2), suggesting that difficulty in finding appropriate borrowers, not high reserve requirements, represents the binding constraint on new lending.

Second, the current combination of interest rates and exchange-rate policy encourages short-term, "quicksilver" capital to flow into the country whose owners, whether foreign investors or wealthy Salvadorans, are prepared to withdraw it the moment they see better returns elsewhere. As shown in Figure 9.3, formal-sector nominal interest rates in El Salvador have not been far above inflation, so that real interest rates have been relatively low. They were actually negative in 1993, and even their current level, at less than 10 percent, is not high by recent Latin American standards. But for a foreigner investing in Salvadoran securities, the key question has

Figure 9.2   **Monetary Aggregates as a Proportion of GDP, 1963–1993**

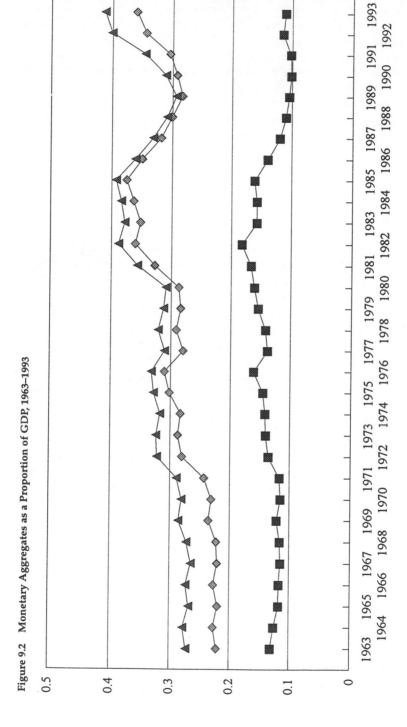

■ M1/GDP   ◆ M2/GDP   ▲ M3/GDP

Source: IMF, International Financial Statistics.

Table 9.2   Liquidity of the Commercial Banks, 1989–1994 (millions of colones)

	1989	1990	1991	1992	1993	June 30, 1994
Total deposit liabilities	7374	9925	11668	15502	19791	22811
Required reserves	1475	2040	2067	2700	3995	4585
Total liquid reserves	1525	2874	2691	2779	4634	5197
Deposits at BCR	1435	2754	2516	2564	4309	4768
Currency	91	120	175	215	325	430
Excess over statutory liquidity[a]	−40	715	450	136	315	183
Excess liquidity[b]	50	834	625	79	640	612

Source: IMF 1994b.
Notes: a. Deposits at BCR less required reserves.
b. Total liquid reserves less required reserves.

to do with expected exchange rates. Given that a devaluation of the colón is unlikely in the near future and that nominal interest rates exceed 15 percent, Salvadoran securities are attractive.[14]

This inflow from foreign wealth holders adds to the flows of dollars from aid and remittances and means the central bank must redouble its sterilization operations to avert the twin dangers of currency appreciation and local inflation. Clearly, if the increase in interest rates needed to sterilize a given inflow attracted an even greater inflow, a point could be reached at which sterilization becomes impossible. It is unlikely that El Salvador has yet reached such a point, and available data do not permit us to distinguish hot money from other inflows. Nonetheless, speculative inflows may be part of the reason for the unusually strong jump in foreign

Figure 9.3   Formal-Sector Interest Rates, 1992–1993 (Percentage per annum)

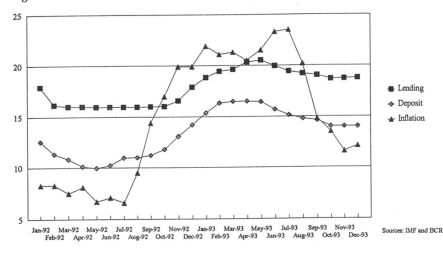

Sources: IMF and BCR.

reserves, by 1.15 billion colones, recorded during the first half of 1994 (Table 9.1), and influential policy analysts take the problem seriously.[15]

Foreign wealth holders are not the only ones tempted to arbitrage this interest-rate difference. Table 9.1 shows that Salvadoran banks have substantially increased their foreign borrowing, which not only increases the dollar inflow but also makes them vulnerable to any future devaluation. The BCR has sought to rein in dollar borrowing by banks, but apparently with little success. We lack data on borrowing by Salvadoran firms, but a feature of similar situations in Mexico and the Southern Cone has been that large firms with the standing to borrow abroad also succumbed to the temptation to arbitrage interest-rate differentials by borrowing cheaply abroad in foreign currency and lending locally at high local interest rates. Because large Salvadoran firms are an important source of credit to smaller firms, this subject merits further investigation.

Hence the bind for the central bank: In the short run, the colón is too strong, and efforts to avoid further strengthening through sterilization run the risk of pulling in even more foreign funds. In the end, sterilization may become self-defeating. Yet, a further real appreciation of the colón has to be avoided, if exports are to be a key to future economic growth.[16]

Conclusions

Experience, backed by considerable theory, shows that premature financial liberalization can have disastrous consequences. If the capital account is open, the economy is small, and newly liberalized financial markets are shallow, the danger is substantially increased. To argue that El Salvador's financial liberalization was *not* premature requires strong faith that (1) Salvadoran real-sector reforms have been thoroughgoing and sufficient to inspire investment and real-sector growth; (2) the current financial sector is sufficiently mature, cautious, and vigilantly regulated that it will not speculatively misallocate; and (3) the broader international macroeconomic environment will be favorable and the country will not be unduly buffeted by major real or financial shocks from outside.

The fact that the central bank is already accumulating such high amounts of domestic debt suggests that this bet is not justified. Not only is this a barren use for the savings involved, but by being an exchange of more liquid money later in return for not spending money now, it raises the danger of greater inflation and/or higher interest rates in the future. If one looks at the loanable funds remaining available to the commercial banks after the central bank has drawn off liquidity—and they are substantial—the signs are less than encouraging. Banks are not fully lent, and there are signs of speculative lending for construction.

An alternative financial-sector policy can only be worked out in coordination with real-sector policies. But given the difficulties being encountered by current policies, and the costs of failure, a prudent near-term policy would probably include: (1) pegging deposit rates so they stand just above inflation, but do not rise too high in real terms;[17] (2) using required reserves rather than open-market operations to soak up liquidity; (3) tightening bank examination and requiring increased accumulation of loan-loss reserves, and imposing sharply higher average and/or marginal reserve requirements against foreign-currency deposits (over 50 percent on the existing stock of deposits, plus as high as 100 percent on any new dollar deposits); and (4) nurturing a market in government bonds, with appropriate guarantees, so that savings can be channeled into infrastructure development or other useful crowding-in public investment, rather than into central bank liabilities.

Steps 2 and 3 would reduce bank profitability and should be regarded as transitional rather than permanent recommendations. The same could be said of step 1 if more attractive homes for savings emerged. But the dangers of the current situation do not permit the luxury of basing policy on what economists call "first-best" solutions, *optima optimorum* that assume a stable and well-ordered world.

Anatomy of the Financial Sector

Recent Background

El Salvador's commercial banks were nationalized in 1979.[18] During the war the formal banking system—the central bank, commercial banks, and development banks—was used for three policy priorities. The most important was wartime government finance, achieved by offering relatively high yields on savings accounts at commercial banks, which were then used (channeled through the commercial banks and central bank) to finance the government's budget deficit. The explosion of credit to the government is evident in Figure 9.4. Second, it was necessary to ensure that certain priority segments of the private sector, especially export agriculture, received loans. The central bank used rediscounts to channel credit to coffee, cotton, and sugar production, through both the commercial banks and the main agricultural development bank, the Banco de Fomento Agropecuario (BFA). This was not a great change: Most of the Salvadoran financial system was constructed to support export agriculture, which had long been the major recipient of lending, in turn backed by rediscounting. But the need was more pressing in the 1980s, especially because the government had nationalized coffee and sugar exporting. Support to agrarian-reform beneficiaries, the third priority, was more of an innovation: The reform was a cornerstone of U.S.-promoted counterinsurgency strategy, and the United States Agency for International Development (USAID) channeled credit to beneficiaries through the development banks.[19]

Figure 9.4   Domestic Credit as a Proportion of GDP, 1963–1993

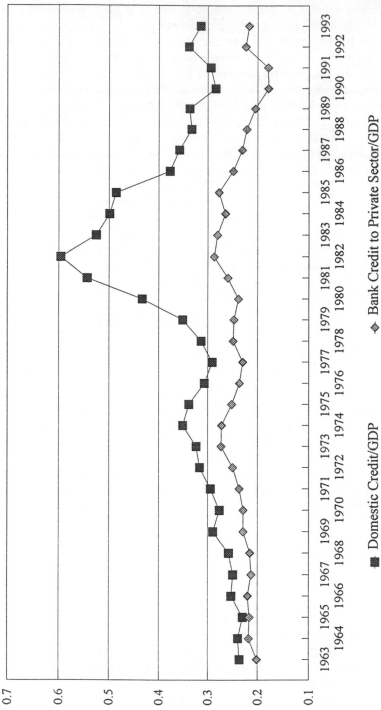

■ Domestic Credit/GDP   ◆ Bank Credit to Private Sector/GDP

Source: IMF, International Financial Statistics.

These policies of channeling credit to export- and reform-sector agriculture (along with some other, smaller categories of favored recipients) were a convenient way of transmitting resources, but bad banking. In the difficult conditions of the war the recipients had trouble repaying loans, but the government was unwilling to foreclose on these favored groups. Instead, it rolled over loans, and refinancing became a larger and larger part of total commercial-bank and (especially) development-bank portfolios.[20] Furthermore, the concessional rates of interest charged for loans and refinancing often made it advantageous to delay repaying. The entire financial system ended the war with enough uncollectible loans that it was technically bankrupt. The memory of this lugubrious process of piling up bad debt has had an important influence on recent policy reforms, and explains some of the difficulty that post-1989 governments have had in defining an operational role for the development banks.

Commercial Banking

This sector includes both full-service commercial banks, which accept sight deposits, and the *financieras,* which formerly functioned as savings and loans, but which are now allowed to lend to a broader variety of borrowers, although their liabilities are still limited to time deposits. Based on legislation passed in April 1990, the government liquidated the weakest commercial banks and financieras, merged others, and attempted to cleanse balance sheets of bad loans. Five banks and three financieras were sold to private shareholders between 1991 and 1994. The regulatory framework governing these institutions was liberalized in November 1992, meaning that restrictions on interest rates offered and charged, and on the allocation of credit, were removed (though high reserve ratios can be regarded as an allocational control). Use of targeted rediscounts has also fallen off, reflecting a genuine retreat by the authorities from efforts to allocate credit, though rediscounting continues through the Banco Multisectorial de Inversiones. Some "moral suasion" is still used by the central bank to influence interest rates (IMF 1994b, p. 26).

These institutions still lend mainly to relatively large, urban firms, to large-scale agribusiness, and to the public sector. Allowed to offer competitive interest rates, the banks have seen their liabilities rise sharply in the last two years (Table 9.1)—so sharply, in fact, that in 1994 they held more deposits with the central bank than the law requires (Table 9.2). They have reported healthy profits (Dimas Quintanilla 1994, Appendix 7) but within the constraints of their institutional bias toward large borrowers, there may be a limit to the profitable lending opportunities available to them. It remains unclear (1) how effectively the regulatory authorities are enforcing provisioning against bad loans, and (2) how restrictive is the

Table 9.3   Financial Assets and Liabilities of Salvadoran Households and Firms, 1991[a]

Households	Rural		Urban		Urban high/ medium income		Urban low income	
	% of total	% participation	% of total	% participation	% of total	% participation	% of total	% participation
Financial assets	100		100		100		100	
Loans to others	15	22	4	24	4	28	13	23
Deposits in formal institutions	84	8	96	53	96	69	86	45
Deposits in organizations/groups	1	1	0	5	0	7	1	3
Liabilities	100		100		100		100	
Institutional credit	34	10	59	17	60	21	57	14
Noninstitutional credit	66	45	41	59	40	62	43	58
Firms	47	28	25	47	24	47	26	46
Cooperatives	0	2	5	6	7	11	2	4
Individuals	19	18	11	17	9	12	14	19
Total assets/total liabilities	0.86		6.65		9.56		1.13	

Firms—users	All firms		Micro firms		Small firms		Medium firms		Large firms	
	% of total	% participation	% of total	% participation	% of total	% participation	% of total	% participation	% of total	% participation
Financial assets	100		100		100		100		100	
Commercial loans	61	50	39	40	16	34	56	55	62	84
Other loans (mainly to employees)	7	60	1	26	4	51	12	80	6	100
Deposits in formal institutions	32	64	59	52	78	56	33	80	31	82
Deposits in organizations/groups	0	22	1	24	3	22	0	18	0	2
Liabilities	100		100		100		100		100	
Institutional credit	71	44	63	27	63	34	89	52	68	77
Commercial credit	27	69	31	56	31	66	11	72	30	87
Noninstitutional credit	2	29	7	32	6	32	1	18	2	20

Table 9.3 Continued

Firms—users

	All firms		Micro firms		Small firms		Medium firms		Large firms	
	% of total	% participation	% of total	% participation	% of total	% participation	% of total	% participation	% of total	% participation
Firms	0	8	1	3	0	9	0	9	0	14
Cooperatives	1	5	0	7	2	4	0	6	1	2
Individuals	0	17	6	22	3	21	0	12	0	7
Total assets/total liabilities	0.67		0.64		0.42		0.46		0.71	

Firms—intermediaries

	All firms		Micro firms		Small firms		Medium firms		Large firms	
	% of total	% participation	% of total	% participation	% of total	% participation	% of total	% participation	% of total	% participation
Financial assets	100		100		100		100		100	
Commercial loans	83	98	58	99	56	100	75	96	85	94
Other loans (mainly to employees)	4	45	1	28	4	68	2	75	4	61
Deposits in formal institutions	12	68	39	57	39	79	23	92	11	89
Deposits in organizations/groups	0	5	1	3	0	9	0	4	0	6
Liabilities	100		100		100		100		100	
Institutional credit	66	45	21	34	53	55	63	67	68	78
Commercial credit	32	80	61	73	42	94	24	79	31	83
Noninstitutional credit	2	23	18	24	5	21	13	17	1	28
Firms	1	5	0	3	0	2	12	8	0	28
Cooperatives	0	6	1	7	1	6	0	4	0	0
Individuals	1	19	16	22	4	17	1	13	1	6
Total assets/total liabilities	1.92		0.82		1.12		1.49		2.02	

Source: Cuevas, Graham, and Paxton 1991.
Note: a. Percentage of sample's aggregate asset or liability holdings in a given instrument, and percentage of respondents in sample holding the instrument.

definition of "capital" that banks must hold. Increased provisioning or need to supplement capital would quickly reduce profits. A recent development that raises some concern over regulatory vigilance is that central-bank officials apparently lost track of a spurt in commercial bank lending in the first half of 1994, especially for construction, and only belatedly sought to reduce it (IMF 1994a).

Bank and financiera offices are heavily concentrated in San Salvador and other large towns, with little presence in rural areas, especially in the north. Restricting attention to commercial bank branches, El Salvador has a national average of 39,747 people per branch (60,511 outside San Salvador). Comparable figures are roughly 18,000 for Mexico and 4,000 for the United States. Of 218 bank and financiera branches in the country, 58 percent are in the department of San Salvador, and a further 26 percent are in the five largest towns outside San Salvador. Table 9.5 provides departmental breakdowns. Mainly rural Morazán, Cabañas, and Chalatenango are particularly ill-provided with bank branches, though that may be partly a result of the war. The scant accessibility of commercial bank branches to rural savers is reflected in the very low number of rural households holding financial savings, reported in Table 9.3.

The two most pressing problems affecting Salvadoran commercial banks—the quality of their loans and the extent of their dollar-denominated liabilities—were discussed in the previous section and will be revisited in the next section. Reforms that might improve access to commercial banking services are important, though less urgent, and should be considered in conjunction with the future role of development banking and smaller-scale financial institutions.

Table 9.4   Total Approved Credit from the Banking System, 1985–1993 (millions of colones)

	1985	1986	1987	1988	1989	1990	1991	1992	1993
Agriculture	976	908	1070	938	1303	1434	2001	3007	3539
Mining	5	3	5	13	7	0	5	2	11
Manufacturing	667	864	1034	1256	1163	1762	2685	4964	4766
Construction	239	257	229	283	252	180	440	1639	2600
Utilities	13	7	2	3	2	15	5	4	7
Commerce	3606	4078	3233	4588	6780	5810	5731	7419	6199
Transport	33	53	46	51	51	48	161	254	478
Services	143	128	143	208	195	150	206	525	589
Refinancing	717	775	758	864	1000	977	980	1210	1003
Other	7	1	2	8	2	14	9	78	20
Total	6407	7074	6520	8212	10756	10390	12223	19102	19212

Source: BCR.

Table 9.5   Bank and Financiera Branches by Department, 1994

Department	Branches of banks	Branches of financieras	Population per bank or financiera branch
San Salvador	68	58	11,728
San Miguel	11	6	22,379
Usulatán	6	4	31,708
Santa Ana	9	5	32,259
Ahuachapán	4	4	32,570
Sonsonate	6	4	35,464
La Unión	5	2	35,878
La Libertad	7	5	43,506
San Vicente	2	1	45,157
La Paz	4	1	49,229
Cuscatlán	2	1	55,763
Cabañas	1	0	136,293
Morazán	1	0	166,772
Chalatenango	1	0	180,627
Total	127	91	23,156

Source: BCR 1994b.

Development Banking

The three main state-run financial institutions are, in descending order of importance, the BFA, the Federación de Cajas de Crédito (FEDECREDITO), and the Fondo de Financiamiento y Garantía para la Pequeña Empresa (FIGAPE). All emerged from the 1980s technically bankrupt. The government has been able to provide enough new resources to the BFA and FEDE-CREDITO, by means of capital contributions and assuming bad loans, to restore them to financial health, but it has not decided clearly what to do with them next (Dimas Quintanilla 1994). One former development bank, the Banco Hipotecario, has been privatized, and there is discussion of doing the same with the remaining three. FIGAPE may simply be liquidated.

The BFA is the oldest and largest development-banking institution, with a loan portfolio of just over a billion colones in 1993 (more than 20 percent of which is nonperforming). Its balance sheet was cleaned up in 1991. It continues to lend mainly to large-scale export agriculture, but it is also the government's favored intermediary institution for channeling credit for other agricultural purposes, and it is handling the credit to beneficiaries of the land-transfer program. The BFA has two institutional advantages: It can accept deposits, though it has been slow in doing so, and it has a network of rural offices, giving it the most substantial rural presence of any Salvadoran financial institution. However, NGOs and others who have dealt with the BFA find it bureaucratic, overstaffed (current staff exceeds 1,500), inefficient, and given to long delays in approving loans (Wenner and Umaña 1993, pp. 163–164; Ladman et al. 1986, p. 97; interviews).

FEDECREDITO was restored to a measure of financial health in 1993, but it suffers from problems similar to those that afflict the BFA. It consists of a national office and 42 agricultural credit unions around the country, and it had a loan portfolio of just over 200 million colones at the end of 1993. Total staff exceeds 800. Bad loans appear to be an enduring problem, although no estimate of the nonperforming portfolio is available. FEDECREDITO does not take deposits from the public; it can accept deposits from its members and has begun to do so, but mainly in the form of required deposits (compensating balances) from loan recipients.

Both the BFA and FEDECREDITO are channeling programs par excellence, funding themselves in recent decades mainly from government contributions and foreign aid or borrowing. For this reason they have had little incentive to try to fund themselves via deposits. Although the BFA is allowed to take deposits, it did not set up the administrative machinery to do so until the mid-1980s, and even then only in a few offices (Ladman et al. 1986, p. xxiv). A series of USAID consultant reports recommending greater deposit taking have had little apparent effect on policy. The current government may also not be anxious to have a state institution compete with the newly private commercial banks for deposits. The BFA is presently overcapitalized in the sense that it could legally more than double lending (assuming it could fund it) without having to expand its current capital base. There may be a more basic problem, which is that administrators are afraid that greater lending would bring greater defaults: Like the commercial banks, they may now see insufficient demand for credit from borrowers they consider qualified.

While the development banks are still recovering from wartime problems, it is unclear what their future is or should be. The national networks and regulatory advantages of the BFA and FEDECREDITO remain attractive. Nonetheless, given our critique of the credit-channeling model, which we will elaborate, these institutions will require, at minimum, extensive reform. If a clear public-policy purpose cannot be defined for retaining them as state institutions, then greater autonomy, decentralization, or privatization may be appropriate.

In August 1994 the central bank's rediscounting functions were spun off into a separate Banco Multisectorial de Inversiones (BMI), initially capitalized with 300 million colones. Although operating as a "second floor" institution (rediscounting loans made by "first floor" commercial banks), it should be considered in the same broad category as development banking. The BMI operates a set of about 20 rediscount lines for specified purposes, most of them at nonconcessional interest rates. These include a 1.1 billion colón line of credit to finance industrial investment, opened in 1990. This is a model of development banking that has become popular in recent years (Mexico's famous Nacional Financiera has made a similar conversion to second-floor status), because it does not compete directly with commercial banks and indeed benefits them, but it should be underlined that it does assume that the market does not allocate credit adequately without state-added inducements, specifically the rediscounter's willingness to provide the bank with additional liquidity in exchange for lending to certain kinds of borrowers. Given the newness of the BMI little can be said about its management or activities, but it is to be hoped that it will work transparently.

Informal Finance

To some degree informal finance is like a photographic negative of the formal financial sector, filling in areas that legally recognized institutions do not reach. Thus informal finance flourished in El Salvador during the 1980s, as formal-sector credit to the private sector declined. But this is also a highly heterogeneous category, much of which in fact operates in close complementarity with formal finance and commerce. Informal institutions help us better understand the working of the entire system, and show us where, and in what ways, the gaps left by formal-sector institutions have been filled.

In terms of the volume of resources mobilized, the most important informal channel is through nonfinancial firms. Large firms, which have access to bank lending (and perhaps even credits from foreign customers or suppliers), lend to smaller firms, mainly in the form of trade credit. Although statistics are lacking, a survey suggests that total lending by firms is roughly half the amount of commercial lending (Cuevas, Graham, and Paxton 1991). The chain of credit from banks to larger firms to smaller firms is clearly visible in Table 9.3.[21] This chain actually overcomes some of the effects of the segmentation created by bank lending policies, but at a price: Trade credit is usually significantly more expensive than bank lending. Firms also often make small loans to employees. During the 1980s, as bank credit grew scarce, the larger firms at the top of this chain opened an informal money market in which they accepted interest-bearing deposits (though only in large amounts). The end of this chain is the main channel of credit to small producers in rural areas, other than intrafamily transfers.[22]

A further example of the principle that finance follows commerce is that there exist vigorous markets in short-term lending to urban vendors. Indeed, both government and NGO microenterprise credit programs have had some success in luring this category of borrower away from informal lenders. There is also an active urban market in longer-term loans, segmented by maturity. A recent report finds one-month loans of the equivalent of $100–$300 costing 21–28 percent per month and secured by a bill of exchange; 2- to 12-month loans for the equivalent of $1,000–$3,000 with a bill of exchange or chattel mortgage security with interest rates in excess of 100 percent on an annualized basis; and loans of $3,000 and over a year, usually guaranteed by a mortgage, with interest of about 60 percent per year (IDB 1993b).

These data suggest that profitable opportunities for informal-sector lending exist in urban areas at least, albeit at very high interest rates. But such opportunities are clearly not ubiquitous. One study of small businesses that received remittance income suggested that rather than helping to build up profitable microenterprises, this income was being used to sustain unprofitable businesses (López and Seligson 1989). Recipients of remittances want to diversify income sources so as to avoid depending on remittance inflows to cover future consumption. For them, an unprofitable business, which might become profitable in the future, may well be better than no business plus higher current consumption. The study suggests, however, that on the whole the return to investment on capital (albeit working capital) in this sector may really be quite low. This has implications for microenterprise credit programs: Although a small-scale institution might be able to imitate the moneylender's local knowledge and allocate efficiently, efforts to simply channel credit to poor people, without other policy reforms affecting the terms of their access to product and factor markets, may be of little benefit.

The picture in rural areas is bleaker. Whereas informal credit is always difficult to pick up in surveys, what is striking is the apparent weakness of both formal *and* informal financial links in the countryside. Cuevas, Graham, and Paxton (1991) do not stratify their rural-household sample by income, as they do their urban sample, but a comparison of the entire rural sample with the urban low-income sample is nonetheless instructive: Forty-five percent of the urban low-income households reported holding some kind of deposit in a formal-sector financial institution, versus 8 percent for rural households. Informal deposits were insignificant in rural areas (Cuevas, Graham, and Paxton 1991, p. 68).[23] In the samples surveyed, average levels of financial assets and liabilities for rural households were less than a quarter of those of urban low-income households.

This phenomenon is understandable given the recent strains to which rural society has been subjected, as well as the absolute poverty of most rural Salvadorans. A centuries-old pattern of forcing indigenous agriculturalists off good land, and policies that tended to make people flee villages for isolated and scattered settlements, have provided poor conditions for the development of formal or informal financial institutions in the countryside (Deere and Diskin 1984; Browning 1971). This pattern was compounded by the accelerated pauperization of the rural population in the 1970s, and war during the 1980s, which displaced more than a million people from their homes (Pearce 1986). What we know about informal financial institutions, from research in a great many countries, is that stable social networks are essential for the functioning of various kinds of savings clubs as well as the work of small-scale moneylenders, because it is the closeness of social ties that enforces repayment. The rural poor use kin networks as a survival strategy. Transfers made within these networks are often called "loans" but frequently are not repaid (Kaufman and Lindauer 1984).

Although informal institutions should certainly not be suppressed, there appear to be scant opportunities to advance Salvadoran financial development by aiding informal financial networks and linking them to formal finance, as has been advocated in some countries with stronger informal institutions. The strength of commercial credit flows from larger to smaller firms suggests that financial liberalization may have some positive effects for smaller firms even if they do not receive credit directly. But most generally, examination of informal finance points up the weaknesses of the economic activities undertaken by much of the urban and rural poor, and suggests that availability of finance, however important, is only a necessary, but by far not sufficient, condition for equitable and sustainable development.

Opportunities

Investment and Savings

We conclude with a discussion of four areas of policy concern. The broadest argument is that *if* there is some rough correspondence between opportunities for investment (in working or fixed capital) on the one hand, and savings capacity on the other hand, *then* the development of different financial institutions appropriate to different segments of the real sector should have important benefits. But what we see in El Salvador is, on the one hand, an excessive flow of (foreign and domestic) savings into the formal sector, encouraged by a premature liberalization of the banks, which seems to be exceeding the capacities of the commercial banks and financieras to allocate credit wisely (to the segment of the market they deal with). On the other hand, the counterpart of this spurious deepening is a relatively shallow financial market for smaller firms. This reflects both their difficult real conditions and the effects of a credit-channeling model in the operation of development banks and most NGO projects that has discouraged the growth of small-scale institutions that could fund themselves from local resources, and has limited the ability of small producers to accumulate any financial savings of their own. At both the large-scale and small-scale levels, then, simply increasing an institution's capacity to lend, absent other changes, can do more harm than good. In the formal sector such efforts risk financial crisis; at the development-bank and NGO level they risk becoming mere transfer programs, palliatives, and substitutes for genuine reform.[24]

Thus we begin by underlining the point made earlier that, on the whole, El Salvador suffers more from a lack of profitable investment opportunities than from a lack of financing for them. Formal-sector institutions have an excess of loanable funds. In the informal sector there may be profitable opportunities, and an expansion of smaller-scale financial institutions may help to locate them, but it cannot be denied that on the whole the country's poor face crippling obstacles in terms of access to land and problems in buying inputs and selling output. Thus measures are urgently needed to improve the profitability of both formal- and informal-sector investment, rural and urban.

With that context established, we can turn to efforts to encourage financial saving, particularly in rural areas. There are two reasons to do this. First, for savers there are advantages to having access to secure financial-savings instruments that pay a rate of interest that is positive in real terms. Although the poor do not save large amounts, they do have the capacity to save.[25] *Financial* savings mitigate insecurity and ease access to credit. These benefits are important both to households and to small firms. Providing a better range of asset choices to a broader range of individuals may also somewhat reduce demand for nontradeables, which tends to push up their prices.

Second, as will be argued, sustainable small-scale financial institutions should be able to fund themselves from local savings. To the extent that such institutions cannot expand quickly enough, there are a variety of other methodologies for making savings instruments from large institutions more accessible, including (1) encouraging or compelling commercial banks to establish more branches in rural areas, and to offer accounts for small savers with relatively low fees, and (2) establishing a government-run savings scheme on the model of Japan's postal savings systems or Indonesia's rural development banks. The BFA's deposit-taking capacities might be expanded.

In the context of deposit taking and increasing savings, the large influx of remittances provides a unique opportunity and a particular challenge. The private transfers of close to $1 billion annually have to be targeted more directly as a source of domestic savings. Siri and Abelardo Delgado (1995) provide excellent suggestions for mechanisms that could be institutionalized to that effect.

Stability of the Formal Financial System

Effective prudential regulation of banks is important under any circumstances, but particularly when banks are only recently independent and rapidly expanding. This has been recognized by Salvadoran policymakers to the extent that they have taken legal steps in the right direction. The Superintendencia de Servicios Financieros (SSF) has been separated from the central bank, and there are hopes that appointing board members from professional associations will limit political interference, though the SSF's director remains a presidential appointee. There are efforts underway, some supported by foreign donors, to train bank examiners, to buy them computers, and so forth. The new banking law tightens formal requirements on commercial banks, requiring provisioning against bad loans and larger capital requirements. Nonetheless there is cause for concern, for two reasons.

First, the SSF lacks the power to mandate provisioning by banks and, most important, to liquidate or take over management of banks threatened with insolvency. Effective prudential regulation requires the ability and political muscle to close down banks that are becoming insolvent, and to do so quickly (see Cho and Khatkhate 1989; and especially Morris et al. 1990, pp. 53–70). Delay usually means that losses mount, because owners with an insolvent bank may be tempted either to loot it or to make very risky loans. But bank owners can be counted on to oppose such takeovers, because they involve claiming some or all of shareholders' equity. Thus even when bank regulators have the formal ability to liquidate, measures to insulate them from political interference and to foster an ethos of independence and professionalism are essential. In the absence of even the formal power to intervene in banks, Salvadoran bank regulators may become good at heading off and coping with small problems, but unable to confront large ones. At a minimum, therefore, the SSF needs the power to take over or liquidate banks, plus better insulation from political interference.

Second, even if prudential regulation is highly effective, it is usually not good at heading off problems arising from macro shocks. Given the macro strains described in the first section, there is considerable cause for worry about the health of the commercial banks over the next few years. The consequences of bank failures, especially if regulators are slow to step in, would be substantial misallocation of loanable funds. Measures that might be useful in reducing those macro strains, and coping with their effects, were discussed at the end of the first section; the importance of high reserve requirements and other measures to discourage the rapid accumulation of foreign-currency liabilities bears repeating here.

Expansion of a Second Tier of Financial Institutions

Commercial banks prefer to lend to large customers, and there are limits to what can be done to make them behave differently. Recent efforts to provide loan guarantees to small borrowers in El Salvador, for example, which tried to overcome the traditional problem that such borrowers usually lack the kinds of securities that banks want, have proven to be costly and difficult to administer. Without giving up on efforts to extend the reach of commercial banks, it should be a policy priority to foster a tier of smaller-scale, locally based financial institutions that can both offer local savings instruments and provide credit based on knowledge of local conditions and borrowers. El Salvador already has an impressive level of NGO-level institutional experience in this area (Fuentes Meléndez and Cuéllar Aguilar 1993a, 1993b; Dimas Quintanilla 1994). But there are three main difficulties: (1) the genuine regulatory problems that arise when institutions begin to offer deposits, (2) the government's enduring lack of sympathy for cooperative organizations, and (3) foreign donors' enduring predilection for credit-channeling programs (discussed in the next subsection).

The BCR, like any conscientious central bank, places capital and regulatory requirements on any institution that accepts deposits. This prevents small institutions from funding themselves based on deposits from the general public, though some larger NGOs are moving in the direction of "formalizing" themselves in order to be able to take deposits. The concerns are well founded because of the danger that fraudulent or ill-managed institutions will steal or lose depositors' money. At the moment, smaller institutions that want to draw on local resources, and remain legal, need to set themselves up as cooperatives of some variety. Cooperative members contribute to the organization's capital and can then make deposits; because of their capital stake they presumably have some incentive to ensure that the institution is well managed. But forming a group of people, each willing to contribute to an institution's capital, is administratively burdensome, and such institutions cannot mobilize large quantities of funds quickly. Donors with funds to disburse have generally preferred to concentrate energies on the lending side. This is one reason that lending has tended to far outstrip deposit taking as a feature of NGO initiatives.

The most prominent institutions of the cooperative variety are credit unions, of which El Salvador has roughly 100; 44 are members of the Federación de Asociaciones Cooperativas de Ahorro y Crédito de El Salvador (FEDECACES), which receives fees from and provides administrative services to its members.[26] Although most of its affiliates are urban, it has a better presence in rural areas than do the commercial banks; for example, it has three affiliates in Chalatenango. FEDECACES is now trying to assume some of the functions of a national bank, through innovations that would allow a member of one affiliated cooperative to carry out transactions at another. Its operational efficiency and loan-recovery record are commendable, and the model of a national association linked to local cooperatives has obvious advantages in combining a national organization's ability to mobilize administrative expertise and training and management services, with a local unit's closeness to its area's conditions.

The Servicio Crediticio de la Asociación de Medianos y Pequeños Empresarios Salvadoreños (CREDIAMPES) has focused mainly on petty commerce. It has achieved good repayment rates and returns based on meticulous observation of its clients' needs, and by adopting a credit-granting procedure—reducing paperwork, coming to the client's place of business, making many short-term loans—that imitates the financial technology of traditional moneylenders. It is now extending its reach to rural lending, and is seeking to formalize itself as a financiera, which would allow it to attract time deposits, and to reduce its dependence on donor financing.

Dimas's suggestion of a special regulatory unit for smaller institutions should be pursued and might provide an appropriate framework for expanding their ability to accept deposits.[27] Foreign aid can offer support through guarantees and capital requirements, but providing training might be one of the most useful contributions, because human capital is clearly an important constraint. But direct channeling of credit through these institutions should be avoided or at least sharply limited, for reasons that will be explained.

Avoiding Transfers Disguised as Credit

The practice of using local institutions as channels for foreign lending to local recipients has on the whole worked against making them sustainable and able to absorb local resources. One reason is simply that foreign resources tend to arrive in lump sums and at concessional interest rates, so that they are, for a development bank or an NGO, a much easier way to fund lending. There has been little incentive to try to change regulations on deposit taking, and even development banks that were allowed to take deposits have shown little interest in doing so. Interviews showed that among government policymakers the myth endures that the poor cannot save.

A related but more subtle reason has to do with the political economy of aid. Aid is seen by donors as a tool of influence, whether the object is to shape a government's foreign policy or an individual farmer's soil-conservation practices. It is the transfer of the donor's resources, as opposed to using locally mobilized resources, that provides policy leverage.

It frequently happens, however, that such transfers are disguised as loans. Foreign-aid donors may wish to appear hard-headed to their own constituencies back home. Or governments may want to cloak a transfer to some favored domestic group, and find using concessional credit or credit guarantees simpler than going through the more transparent budget process. In some cases, recipients may be weak enough to accept formal indebtedness in exchange for resources, giving the donor bargaining power over them in the future.

This is not to suggest that every instance of development-related lending is encumbered by these issues. But when credit is granted in exchange for something beside a credible future commitment to repay, it ceases to be credit, and institutionalizing this kind of quasi-credit works against establishing locally sustainable credit channels. This becomes especially salient in El Salvador because of the broad range of NGO antipoverty efforts. A frequent complaint among Salvadoran NGOs is that when credit is handed out without efforts to affect productive technologies, it is wasted, but that when it is associated with technical assistance and training, recipients do not repay with the excuse that the technical assistance was faulty. These complaints illustrate a more basic problem with the idea of channeling funds from outside donors to local recipients in the form of credit. Two examples follow.

In 1990 the Food and Agriculture Organization (FAO) commissioned a study on the effects of agricultural credit-granting programs aimed at Salvadoran small farmers (Salinas, Cerén Dueñas, and Cardoza López 1993). The authors reported that many credits were not being repaid, and that, after defaulting on a loan from one NGO, a farmer could often borrow from another. In addition, the effects of small-farmer lending had frequently been to encourage planting on steep hillsides, which contributed to soil erosion. The loan programs also encouraged overuse of agricultural chemicals. The main policy conclusion of the FAO study was that future credit programs should have strict conditions for environmentally sustainable production attached to them, and that credit should not be provided on a concessional basis but at "market" rates so as to instill "discipline" among recipients.

With due respect to the excellent analytical work done by the FAO team, this is an inadequate policy response. First, the phenomena reported suggest that beneficiaries correctly understood credit-granting programs as palliative transfers, and saw no reason to repay. Second, deprived of access to good land and secure ownership of even bad land, the impoverished recipients of loans had no reason to farm in environmentally sustainable ways. Even if credit is now provided in exchange for a change in productive technology, it is still, if effective, going to be an exchange of resources for better agricultural practices—a complex and difficult-to-enforce exchange. Raising the interest rate may simply make the credit less attractive, or make recipients even less likely to repay.[28]

Implicit in the FAO recommendations is the notion that small farmers are rationed out of the credit market, and that they are willing to pay a rent—using a more expensive agricultural technology—to be rationed in. This is a slender basis on which to build policy, given that there may be good reasons as well as bad for the existing rationing out, and that the point of a credit policy aimed at enhancing equity should be precisely to *reduce* rationing out, and hence the value of those rents. It would be far better, if the aim is environmentally sustainable production, to use a combination of direct subsidies to reduce the costs of environmentally sustainable technologies, plus regulation to prevent irresponsible practices. If production, thus assisted, is genuinely profitable, then informal or local credit should be forthcoming. If necessary, recipients could be started out with a direct transfer of working capital. If production is *still* unprofitable, it is likely so because of commercialization and land-tenure problems, and efforts to sustain marginal small-scale production under these circumstances may be only expensive palliatives.

Rather more disturbing is the use of credit in the current land-transfer and microenterprise programs for ex-combatants. Beneficiaries can choose between careers in farming and microenterprise. Those opting for agriculture are eligible to receive land and the accompanying debt to the government to pay for it. They are further eligible for a loan of 15,000 colones, at a mildly subsidized rate. (Those choosing microenterprise take a series of classes in business and are eligible for a 20,000 colón loan.) The problem with this program is that there is a political necessity to make payments to ex-combatants, who have experience in using organized force to resolve their problems. Thus, with the land titling program proceeding slowly, agricultural loans are being made to people who do not yet have land and who therefore cannot be expected to use the loans for agricultural improvements. Even for those who can get title, it is far from clear that under existing conditions they are likely to be able to farm successfully enough to pay off their loans. This may explain some of the difficulty in finding enough people willing to claim these benefits: By any rational calculation they may not be benefits at all (Spence and Vickers 1994). It may also produce an "adverse selection" effect, in which only those who do not intend to repay are willing to accept the lending package at the terms offered.

Similarly, people with experience in the field report that many of the recipients of microenterprise loans are simply consuming their capital. In this case, then, pressures have vitiated measures that were intended to improve the likelihood that loans would go to productive investment.

The land transfer should be recognized as a cost of ending the war; especially given the fact that the funds backing it are grants from outside donors, land should be given unmortgaged. As matters stand, recipients will not only have difficulty paying off the debt they assume, but the overhang of debt in future years will make it more difficult for them to qualify for any credit available locally.

Final Notes

It is a mistake to look at the contribution of finance to development simply as a matter of "access" to credit, as one would speak of access to clean water. Finance means exchanges—of money now for money later—requiring willing participants on both sides of the bargain, and an institutional framework that links the two and provides lenders (or savers) with some confidence that they will be repaid. Far from being a simple input, credit and debt are essential coordinating mechanisms of any economy, especially when real resources are scarce. Finance is integral to the real economy, and it entails interlocking relationships that cannot easily be unlinked.

Adjustment toward peace requires that financial-sector policy be tightly coordinated with real-sector policy. Simply pushing credit, whether to large firms through private commercial banks, or to poor people through NGOs, is unlikely to promote sustainable, equitable development. El Salvador's pattern of financial liberalization, and many of its credit-channeling programs, have been guided by an orthodox policy model that is inappropriate for a country facing El Salvador's grave difficulties. The pattern is characterized by partial equilibrium thinking—an unwillingness to trace through the changes that reforms in one area have on another. Hence financial liberalization, which might be well advised in some situations, turns out to be potentially dangerous given large dollar inflows and an exchange-rate policy that avoids nominal appreciation for reasons of promoting exports. Credit to small farmers, in the absence of other conditions for successful agriculture, creates only bad debt and ill will. To recapitulate the main points:

1. Because fiscal, monetary, and exchange-rate policies shape the environment in which commercial banks operate, banking regulation must keep pace with those changes to head off speculative overlending as well as excessive dollar borrowing.
2. Different kinds of financial institutions are needed for different segments of the real sector. Support and appropriate regulation are needed for a second tier of institutions that can serve small firms and rural communities.
3. Availability of financial savings instruments to the poor is as important as availability of credit.
4. Points 2 and 3 are best achieved by promoting local institutions that fund themselves largely from local sources.

Although the financial-sector policies recommended here are necessary complements to real-sector policy reforms, they are not substitutes for them.

Notes

1. Commercial banks are usually the most important institutions in any country's financial sector, but they have important limitations. Evaluating loan applications is costly, and for small firms the profit the bank could make on the loan is unlikely to exceed these costs. Smaller firms are also less likely to be able to pledge assets as guarantees of repayment. Thus smaller firms are generally screened out of the market for commercial loans. There is a broad policy literature on ways either to encourage commercial banks to lend to smaller firms, or to develop other kinds of institutions, public or private, that can provide them credit. Some of this literature has looked to the informal finance that does serve these

firms for institutional models and practices to emulate; for example, Bouman and Hospes (1994) and Adams (1992).

2. In a similar vein, Salinas, Cerén Dueñas, and Cardoza López (1993, p. 13) emphasize "development of a structure of profitability"; Cruz Letona (1991, p. 11), writing on agricultural-development banking, is particularly clear on the importance of integrating credit policy with other agricultural policies, criticizing the tendency of development banks to emphasize credit at the expense of "coherence [of credit policy] with policies affecting producer prices, commercialization, land tenure, and macroeconomic policies such as tax, exchange rate, trade and wage policy. Experience has shown that this level of coordination is a prerequisite for the success and effectiveness of development banking. In other words, where the combined effect of macroeconomic policies is unfavorable for agriculture, the opportunities for the success of credit and financial policy will be reduced."

3. McKinnon (1973) warned of the damage that foreign capital could do to a program of liberalization. His work over the last 10 years, in the context of the sequencing literature, has been consistent with that warning: The myopia of foreign lenders and implicit or explicit government guarantees can foster overlending; arbitrage between foreign and domestic lending may fuel financial crisis. Thus in McKinnon's optimal sequence of liberalization, opening the capital account comes last (McKinnon 1991). Whereas the basic problem of the dual role of the interest rate is commonplace and affects wealthy countries as well, its effects are much more disruptive in trade-dependent countries with shallow financial markets.

4. McKinnon (1991) and Morris et al. (1990); see also discussion in World Bank (1989b) and a critical view in Arestis and Demetriades (1993).

5. This effect will be mitigated by any increased import demand, which will extinguish colones as they are traded back to the central bank for dollars.

6. Good recent discussions of the problems associated with sterilization in Latin America can be found in Leiderman and Reinhart (1994) and Larraín (1994); see also Calvo (1991).

7. The IMF (1994a) has already indicated unhappiness with the level of required reserve, and warned the Salvadoran authorities against pushing them higher.

8. These are mostly 91-day notes, but the central bank sells some with maturities as long as 360 days, and it is trying to lengthen the average maturity.

9. The higher figure in Table 9.1 includes nonprivate holdings. It is not clear in this set of figures how much of the CEM holdings by banks and nonmonetary financial institutions are actually voluntary private-sector holdings. Individuals may be purchasing securities through repurchase agreements or other means by which ownership remains formally with a financial institution.

10. Nevertheless, the funds in time/savings accounts can be converted into liquid money with relatively little difficulty. Moreover, the CEMs are, probably, in practice highly liquid as well. If previous history in other Latin American countries is any guide, there is an implicit agreement that the BCR, in order to keep the market relatively liquid, will buy them back if the need arises. Otherwise, a large sell-off would both raise the interest rates sharply and damage confidence in an instrument the central bank has tried hard to promote.

11. A small securities exchange has been created in recent years whose main function has been to provide the central bank with a place to sell these instruments. But the exchange is not really big enough to make them highly liquid, so the central

bank has to offer a premium of one or two percentage points over deposit interest rates to attract buyers. In mid-1994 these bonds were paying 17.25 percent while time deposits paid about 15 percent (Dimas Quintanilla 1994, p. 4).

12. Of a roughly 7.5 billion colón increase in private-sector liabilities over the 18 months from December 1992 to June 1994, 3 billion was absorbed by the BCR through reserves and bond sales. Credit from these institutions, however, grew by almost 5.4 billion colones, funded both by the remaining 4.5 billion colones in loanable funds and by a somewhat alarming rise of over 600 million colones in foreign liabilities. The remaining 300 million colón increase in credit is funded mainly by a 200 colón rise in BCR rediscounting to the banks. Earlier such rediscounting had fallen (between 1989 and 1992 central-bank credit to the commercial banks fell by over 50 percent) from roughly 2.6 billion colones to 1.2 billion, before rising to about 1.4 billion by mid-1994.

13. High interest rates may also make speculative real-estate development more attractive for lending, because the returns are high as long as property prices continue to rise (as happened with U.S. savings and loans). Similar remittance-fueled construction booms have occurred in Pakistan and the Indian state of Kerala. The problems of currency appreciation and speculative lending are surely important parts of the explanation for the minimal, if not adverse, impact recent capital inflows to Latin America have had on capital accumulation. Indeed, a recent Group of Thirty study notes that "for the Latin American region [capital] inflows during 1990–93 are primarily associated with a decline in saving and higher consumption" (Leiderman and Reinhart 1994, p. A10).

14. Lower inflation would reduce the difference between U.S. and Salvadoran rates, but that is difficult to achieve quickly, and the real-sector effects of the remittance and aid inflow are inflationary. The inflow of spending power raises demand for goods within the country. The increased demand for locally produced goods may be expected to begin pushing up their prices. To the extent that local production responds quickly to these rising prices, it will tend to pull factors of production (land, labor, capital) away from export industries. To the extent that production of local goods does not keep pace with higher demand (and some local goods, like real estate, are clearly in fixed supply) then a general rise in prices, or inflation, may ensue. Such inflation will tend to raise the price of domestic factors (especially labor) and also to undermine the competitiveness of exports. The consequences for both inflation and export promotion are unfavorable.

15. Harberger (1993b) explores this possibility. He and Hinds (1994) call for the central bank to allow appreciation; this position is also implied in an internal IMF document reporting on a staff visit to El Salvador in mid-1994 (IMF 1994a). Although it is novel to see the IMF urging appreciation rather than devaluation, it is actually consistent with the organization's basic opposition to government efforts to manipulate exchange rates, and indeed its original efforts to discourage competitive devaluations.

16. It has been suggested in some circles that a "currency board" system would provide El Salvador with a devaluation-proof currency. The reasoning is specious. A true currency board requires (1) a fixed exchange rate, plus (2) a commitment that base money will never exceed foreign reserves. The latter requirement eliminates the central bank's "lender of last resort" capacities to lend freely to meet liquidity demands in times of financial unease. In other words, monetary

authorities would allow commercial banks to fail and asset values to collapse in the face of rising liquidity demand, rather than increase base money. True currency boards are often confused with fair-weather currency boards, of the sort that Argentina has adopted in recent years, in which base money is limited to dollar reserves *except* when banks are in trouble. This was demonstrated clearly in early 1995 when, in the face of scarce liquidity and short-term interest rates reaching 90 percent, Argentine monetary authorities used overnight lending to shore up commercial banks, circumventing formal currency-board rules. This bimodal policy is really just another restrictive monetary rule, hardly an impregnable defense against speculative runs on the currency.

17. A policy defended in Stiglitz (1993) and, for at least some circumstances, by McKinnon (1988, p. 408).

18. Nationalization of the banks was decreed by the October 1979 civilian-military junta and took effect in March 1980. It was presented as a way to "democratize" the previously inequitable distribution of credit and came at the same time as measures to nationalize the foreign marketing of coffee. Clearly the October junta was seeking to gain control over the institutions most associated with the concentration of wealth and economic power in the country. Equally clearly, as the *juventud militar* lost influence, and civilians inclined to more radical reform left the junta, control over the banks was, once obtained, not used for redistributive ends. Bank lending in fact followed much the same patterns as before, the main difference being higher reserve requirements and purchases of government securities, used to finance fiscal deficits.

19. In the early 1980s the reformed sector got 18 percent of agricultural credit and 32 percent of BFA lending (Ladman et al. 1986, pp. 71 and 97).

20. Ladman et al. (1986, pp. 18–39, 54–61); this source also covers the role of rediscounting.

21. The pattern is also evident in MIPLAN figures cited by Dada Sánchez (1994).

22. See additional discussion in Ladman et al. (1986, pp. 64 and 175–177), and Wenner and Umaña (1993, p. 52).

23. This fits with the pattern observed in most countries, that informal savings instruments are rare. Christensen (1993) provides a theoretical explanation.

24. Discussed further in the final subsection; Adams (1992) and Adams and Von Pischke (1992) provide a similar critique.

25. There is a substantial literature on this; see Adams (1992).

26. FEDECACES has also served as an administrator and channel of credit for foreign donors, though not without difficulty. The abrupt 1986 devaluation of the colón created severe difficulties in repaying a dollar-denominated loan from USAID.

27. Dimas Quintanilla (1994); Fuentes Meléndez and Cuéllar Aguilar (1993b) also provide very useful discussion on this sort of reform.

28. This is characteristic of confusion in much recent development-policy writing about "market" interest rates, as though financial markets were like the market in, say, eggs—clearing at one price that should obtain across the economy—and a program that charged this "market" interest rate involved no distortion of allocation, while a different interest rate would cause ill effects. The "market" rate referred to in, for example, the FAO study is a rate reported by the central

bank based on a survey of commercial banks and financieras. It is representative of dealings between a small group of large financial institutions and a small group of large, well-established customers. It does not indicate anything about the conditions faced by an urban microenterprise or a peasant farmer seeking credit. Indeed the very fact of government or NGO lending to these groups suggest that the "market" is not meeting their needs. Most likely the rate of interest at which these borrowers could obtain loans from a private and competitive entrepreneur—a moneylender—is either much higher than the formal-sector rate, or in fact nonexistent. In the latter case, transaction costs and default premiums can drive up the interest rate that a lender would charge, to a point at which the "adverse selection" effect—by which higher interest rates screen out safer borrowers and leave those who have highly risky projects or no intention of repaying—makes lenders unwilling to lend at all.

10

Structural Adjustment, the Agricultural Sector, and the Peace Process

Carlos Acevedo

Discussions of agricultural policy in developing countries have long been characterized by two fundamentally different approaches. One view sees farming as a business like any other, and land simply as one input or factor of production. It notes that agriculture's share of national production and of the labor force declines as economies develop, and is generally agnostic about the appropriate arrangements for land tenure. The other view regards land ownership as something of more transcendent importance. Some variants of this view celebrate the status quo of land ownership, others urge the return to some past allocation, or demand egalitarian redistribution of land among some subset of the population.

This study adopts a middle position. We argue that farming is indeed a business, but that there are compelling social, political, and environmental reasons to aim for a large sector of relatively small but economically viable farms. In pursuing this goal it is important to avoid a simplistic focus on land tenure exclusively, for two reasons.

First, farmers participate in commercial and credit networks. Their economic viability is determined not only by the quantity and quality of the capital (above all, land) they possess, but also by the opportunities presented to buy, sell, borrow, and lend. As this chapter documents, world market conditions and current macroeconomic policies have created a situation in which farming in El Salvador is now a highly tenuous enterprise. Indeed, it might be concluded that in El Salvador today a small farm (particularly one encumbered by debt for its acquisition) and access to agricultural credit is an economic curse to be wished only on one's worst enemy. Nevertheless, historic ties to agricultural land in El Salvador are such that land redistribution is bitterly opposed by many owners, and fervently desired by many among the poor. In the current macroeconomic setting, however, to focus only on land-tenure reform would prove a barren exercise.

Second, agriculture in El Salvador, particularly on the hillsides that form the watersheds for the San Salvador metropolitan area and other cities, has enormous environmental impacts that must be fully incorporated into agricultural policy. Chapter 11 documents these impacts and analyzes their policy implications. A central conclusion of that analysis is that there is an urgent need for social governance of land use in El Salvador; that is, for the design and implementation of policies to establish a framework of rules and incentives whereby individual economic decisions take into account social benefits and costs. To focus only on land tenure in this environmental setting would prove barren in another, more literal sense.

The agricultural-sector policies advocated in this study aim to advance three principal goals:

1. *Macroeconomic growth and stability:* Agriculture provides products, including wage goods, to the domestic market. Agricultural exports are and will remain a major source of foreign exchange earnings. And the agricultural sector provides a market for nonagricultural goods and services. Prosperous farming is thus linked to a variety of other economic activities, while profitless farming depresses them. Furthermore, the capacity to meet food-consumption requirements through domestic production minimizes the risk of imported inflation during periodic episodes of tight supplies and high prices in international markets.

2. *Sustainable livelihood security:* For a large number of people agriculture remains the main source of livelihood. Many of these people are among the poorest strata of the population. We do not believe that migration to San Salvador or to Los Angeles offers a feasible or desirable alternative to the strengthening of rural livelihoods in El Salvador.

3. *Environmental sustainability:* Agriculture involves the joint production of crops and environmental services. The latter profoundly affect the long-run viability not only of agriculture, but of the economy as a whole. Policy must be grounded on appreciation of the sector's dual role.

This chapter will argue that current agricultural policy in El Salvador cannot be judged a success by any of the above criteria, and that what growth there has been in agricultural output in recent years has come largely despite government macroeconomic policy, not because of it. In particular, as discussed in the following section, macroeconomic policy has turned relative prices sharply to the disadvantage of the agricultural sector as a whole. Changes in the composition of output toward nontraditional agricultural exports cannot be expected to redress fully the adverse effects of the macroeconomic environment. The plight of the rural poor is further exacerbated by continuing inequities in the agrarian structure, described in the second section. The final section discusses alternative policies to address the first two goals identified above; Chapter 11 discusses policies to address the third.

Macroeconomic Policy and Agricultural Profitability

Agriculture historically has been the most important sector in the Salvadoran economy, in terms of its shares of national income, foreign exchange earnings, and the labor force. Though this began to change in the 1960s with economic diversification (see Chapter 2), the 1980s brought the most dramatic decline in the relative importance of the agricultural sector, coupled with considerable growth in commerce and services. This decline was due in part to the war, and in part to a sharp shift in relative prices against agriculture.

The share of agriculture in the GDP nevertheless remains significant, particularly when value added in animal husbandry and agroprocessing industries is included. In 1993 agriculture and animal husbandry accounted for roughly 9 percent of GDP and agroprocessing for 11 percent, bringing the combined total to 20 percent of GDP (see Table 10.1). This represents

Table 10.1   Value of Agricultural Production, 1980 and 1993 (percentage of GDP)

	At current prices		At constant 1962 prices	
	1980	1993	1980	1993
Agriculture and agroindustry	35.2	19.6	36.5	35.9
Crops	23.3	5.9	17.6	14.9
Principal export products	19.1	3.1	11.6	7.9
Coffee	16.4	2.4	8.9	6.8
Cotton	1.8	0.1	2.0	0.1
Sugar cane	0.9	0.6	0.7	1.0
Basic grains	2.6	2.0	3.9	4.8
Maize	1.4	1.0	2.5	2.9
Beans	0.4	0.5	0.4	0.7
Rice	0.3	0.1	0.5	0.5
Sorghum	0.5	0.3	0.5	0.6
Other crops	1.7	0.8	2.2	2.2
Animal husbandry and miscellaneous	4.5	3.0	7.9	8.6
Livestock raising	2.6	1.8	3.4	3.1
Forestry	0.4	0.1	0.8	0.8
Fishing	0.5	0.4	0.4	0.3
Apiculture	0.1	0.0	0.1	0.1
Poultry	1.0	0.6	3.3	4.3
Agroindustrial	7.4	10.8	10.9	12.5
Food products	4.8	7.2	7.1	9.1
Beverages	1.9	2.8	2.9	2.7
Tobacco	0.7	0.8	0.9	0.7

Source: BCR.

a marked decline from agriculture's share of GDP in 1980, when (including agroprocessing) the total stood at 35 percent.

The Deterioration of Real Prices in Agriculture

A marked deterioration in agriculture's intersectoral terms of trade, propelled by declines in the relative prices of coffee and basic grains, played the key role in this decline. In fact, when output is valued at constant 1962 prices (the year used as a base for Central Reserve Bank [BCR] estimates of "real" income), the reported share of the agricultural sector as a whole remained remarkably stable, at approximately 36 percent of GDP (see Table 10.1). By 1993 the price index for the agricultural sector relative to that of GDP had slipped to 75 percent of its 1989 level, and to only 35 percent of its 1980 level (see Figure 10.1 and Table 10.2).

In terms of foreign exchange, too, agriculture's relative significance diminished in the 1980s and early 1990s, particularly due to the increase in remittances from Salvadorans resident overseas. Nevertheless, exports

Figure 10.1   Relative Prices of Agricultural Goods Compared with Nonagricultural Goods and Services, 1970–1993 (1962 = 1)

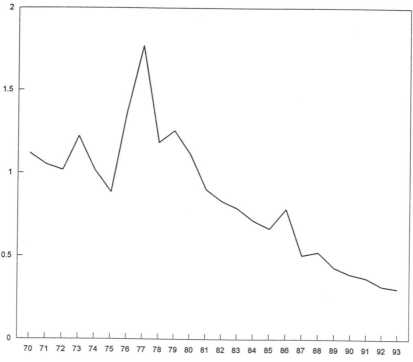

Source: USAID, from BCR.

Table 10.2   Indices of Implicit Prices of Agricultural Production and GDP, 1980–1993
(1962 = 100)

Year	Indices of implicit prices		Ratio of agriculture to GDP
	Agriculture	GDP	
1980	294.9	271.1	1.09
1981	267.4	286.6	0.93
1982	276.5	314.9	0.88
1983	297.3	351.6	0.85
1984	308.9	397.1	0.78
1985	351.5	478.7	0.73
1986	551.5	656.0	0.84
1987	435.3	748.0	0.58
1988	522.3	870.5	0.60
1989	515.3	1,014.5	0.51
1990	585.5	1,249.8	0.47
1991	621.7	1,405.2	0.44
1992	603.7	1,534.0	0.39
1993	668.8	1,764.5	0.38

Source: Central Reserve Bank, *Revista Trimestral,* various issues.

generated by agriculture, animal husbandry, and agroprocessing still ac-count for more than 50 percent of El Salvador's total export earnings (see Table 10.3). Among the country's exports, coffee continues to occupy first place: In 1989–1993 it accounted for 37 percent of total exports.

Agriculture, animal husbandry, and agroprocessing employ more than 50 percent of El Salvador's economically active population (FUSADES 1994). The agricultural and animal husbandry sector alone absorbs 34 per-cent of the labor force.

El Salvador's agricultural sector was severely affected by the politi-cal and economic crisis that gripped the country in the 1980s. The Ministry of Planning and Coordination of Economic and Social Development (MI-PLAN 1992b) estimated the total direct damages in the sector at 465 mil-lion colones, and the opportunity cost due to the reduction in cultivated area and yields at 4.38 billion colones. At the end of the decade the sector began a process of recovery to prewar output levels. During the period 1990–1993, the value added generated by agriculture, animal husbandry, and agroprocessing grew at 4.6 percent per year in real terms. The area, yield, and output of basic grains shared in this growth. With the exception of cotton, the production of export crops also rebounded (see Appendix Table A.9).

This recovery of production has not been sufficient, however, to arrest the slide in the share of the agricultural sector in nominal GDP, due to the continuing deterioration of relative prices.

In analyzing this deterioration, the literature on El Salvador has tended to emphasize the negative effects of currency overvaluation on the

Table 10.3   Value of Agricultural Exports, 1986–1993 (percentage of total exports)

	1986	1987	1988	1989	1990	1991	1992	1993
Total agriculture and agroindustry	84.4	73.9	73.4	61.3	63.1	61.5	53.7	53.7
Traditional	77.6	64.2	63.5	49.3	49.3	43.4	33.4	35.6
Coffee (various forms)	73.2	59.9	59.3	46.4	45.4	37.8	25.7	31.1
Unrefined sugar	3.4	2.0	3.1	2.7	3.6	5.5	7.5	4.3
Cotton	1.1	2.3	1.1	0.2	0.4	0.2	0.3	0.2
Nontraditional	6.8	9.8	9.9	12.0	13.8	18.1	20.2	18.1
Animal products								
Beef	0.0	0.3	0.4	0.7	0.4	—	—	0.1
Shrimp	2.3	3.5	2.6	2.0	2.5	3.5	3.4	3.6
Honey	0.3	0.3	0.1	0.2	0.2	0.3	0.5	0.3
Other	0.2	0.3	0.3	0.4	0.5	1.0	1.2	1.1
Vegetable products								
Fruit, fresh or dried	0.2	0.4	0.2	0.3	0.4	0.4	0.3	0.4
Sesame seed	0.2	0.1	0.7	1.0	1.9	3.1	1.7	1.0
Natural balsam	0.2	0.3	0.3	0.3	0.3	0.2	0.2	0.1
Other	1.2	1.7	1.1	0.9	1.2	1.1	1.5	1.1
Processed foods								
Bakery products	0.1	0.1	0.1	0.2	0.2	0.3	0.6	0.5
Other	1.1	1.5	2.1	2.7	2.7	4.5	7.1	7.5
Textiles								
Cotton thread	0.9	1.0	1.5	2.6	3.1	3.0	3.1	1.9
Cotton cloth	0.1	0.2	0.3	0.6	0.5	0.6	0.6	0.5
Total agriculture and agroindustry (millions of U.S. dollars)	637	437	447	305	367	362	321	393
Total exports (millions of U.S. dollars)	755	591	609	498	582	588	598	732

Source: BCR.

competitiveness of producers of tradeable goods in general. With exchange-rate overvaluation, agricultural products must compete on the domestic market with imported products that are artificially cheap, while agricultural exports become less remunerative. The impact of overvaluation is greatest for those productive activities that have the highest percentage of national value added in their cost composition.[1] According to estimates by Norton (1990), more than half of the decline in real prices in El Salvador's agricultural sector between 1978 and 1986 was caused by exchange-rate overvaluation.

The adjustment program begun in 1989 (MIPLAN 1989) implemented exchange-rate liberalization, which was expected to result in devaluation of the real exchange rate. It was assumed that devaluation would increase the profitability of agricultural production and thereby stimulate growth in the value of agricultural production (Norton 1990; Norton and Liévano 1988). In practice, however, the real exchange rate appreciated, driven by inflows of foreign exchange from remittances and external assistance (see Chapter 4).

A second element often cited as a factor in the deterioration of agricultural real prices is the asymmetrical tariff treatment given to agriculture and industry. According to calculations by Norton and Llort (1989), in the mid-1980s Salvadoran industry enjoyed effective protection of 27 percent, while agriculture faced a negative effective protection of 25 percent.

This situation has improved as a result of the tariff reductions carried out since 1989 in the context of adjustment. Despite these efforts, the tariff structure maintains some discrimination against the agricultural sector in favor of industrial production. Although many industrial outputs enjoy the maximum tariff protection levels, tariffs on industrial inputs are pegged at the minimum. This disadvantages agriculture, both by raising industrial output prices and by lowering the prices of imported inputs, some of which are substitutes for domestically produced agricultural goods. But the fact that the extent of tariff discrimination against agriculture has lessened in recent years means that this cannot be blamed for the further decline in relative prices.

A third factor that helps to explain the deterioration of real agricultural prices is the price liberalization undertaken as part of the adjustment program. Until 1989, agricultural price policy in El Salvador included a number of common interventionist measures: guaranteed prices for producers, consumer price controls, credit and input subsidies, and state marketing of agricultural products. After 1989 such interventions were abandoned, and price policy was revised so as to peg internal prices to international prices plus importation costs. A system of price categories implemented for imports of some basic grains cushioned the impact of international price fluctuations and facilitated the anti-inflationary management of local prices (Binswanger 1991).

The world market context, however, was a downward tendency of prices for primary commodities (CEPAL 1992, 1993c; FAO 1992, 1993). Hence, the narrowing of the differential between internal and external prices has significantly exacerbated the deterioration of real agricultural prices. The decline was especially dramatic in the case of coffee, the country's principal export crop. As international market prices sank to their lowest level since World War II, producer prices collapsed. By 1991/92, the real price (deflated by the CPI) received by Salvadoran growers was only 28 percent of its 1980/81 level, and only 20 percent of its peak level in 1985/86 (see Table 10.4). Real prices for basic grains also tumbled after 1989. By 1992/93, the real producer price for maize stood at 75 percent of its 1985/86 level, and the real producer price for beans stood at 70 percent of its 1985/86 level (see Table 10.5).[2]

There is no convincing reason, even in theory, to adopt a laissez-faire agricultural price policy in a world of market imperfections and instability. In practice, to do so is extremely risky. No industrialized country in the world surrenders its domestic agricultural prices to the dictates of the international market. On the contrary, the governments of industrialized

Table 10.4   Coffee Prices and Exports, 1980/81–1992/93

Harvest year	Price to producers		Exports		
	Nominal (colones/quintal)	Real[a]	Volume (millions of quintals)	Export price (dollars/quintal)	Value (millions of dollars)
1980/81	148.7	148.7	3.65	84.3	308.1
1981/82	167.0	145.4	3.53	105.2	371.0
1982/83	161.6	125.9	3.44	116.7	401.0
1983/84	182.7	125.8	3.73	126.4	471.0
1984/85	202.4	124.8	3.13	132.9	416.0
1985/86	405.0	204.2	3.45	162.9	562.3
1986/87	278.5	106.5	3.28	109.4	359.4
1987/88	349.5	106.9	2.46	130.9	321.9
1988/89	370.6	94.7	2.21	128.2	283.0
1989/90	390.3	84.1	3.38	77.4	261.5
1990/91	382.5	67.0	2.63	80.6	212.2
1991/92	267.4	40.9	2.84	58.6	166.7
1992/93			3.77	60.0	226.3

Source: Consejo Salvadoreño del Café.
Note: a. Nominal price deflated by CPI (1980/81 = 100).

Table 10.5   Prices of Maize and Beans, 1985/86–1992/93

Harvest year	International price of maize[a] (dollars/quintal)	Prices to producers (colones/quintal)			
		Maize		Beans	
		Nominal	Real[b]	Nominal	Real[b]
1985/86	4.63	26.0	26.0	84.7	84.7
1986/87	3.26	35.9	27.2	96.5	73.2
1987/88	4.07	37.1	22.5	207.3	125.8
1988/89	5.28	44.7	22.7	177.1	89.7
1989/90	5.00	59.4	25.4	195.0	83.3
1990/91	4.76	64.0	22.2	269.0	93.5
1991/92	4.96	71.1	21.6	188.5	57.3
1992/93	4.36	63.8		195.3	

Sources: Dirección General de Economía Agropecuaria; BCR.
Notes: a. International price corresponds to U.S. yellow maize no. 2, FOB Gulf of Mexico ports.
   b. Nominal price deflated by CPI (1985/86 = 100).

countries deploy a wide array of interventions to support producer prices and restrain domestic price fluctuations. The case for such policies in El Salvador is at least as compelling as it is in France, the United States, or Japan.

Nontraditional Agricultural Exports

Any policy for agricultural development in El Salvador is condemned to fail unless it results in significant increases in profitability in this sector. This requires not only a more favorable structure of prices, but also increased productivity. The latter can come about not only through increases in crop yields, but also through changes in the crop mix. The higher-value crops toward which production could be reoriented include nontraditional agricultural exports. This has considerable appeal in theory, but the practical risks involved should not be minimized.

The first risk is that of an adverse international context.[3] As noted earlier, the global economic context for agriculture has been characterized since the 1980s by a marked decline in relative prices. In the specific case of El Salvador, the fall in value of coffee exports despite increased export volume (see Table 10.4) provides a particularly dramatic illustration. But adverse price trends also help explain why efforts to diversify agricultural exports under the Caribbean Basin Initiative—including such nontraditional agricultural products as sesame, honey, melons, okra, broccoli, lemons, watermelons, cashew nuts, hog plums, myrtle, and natural balsam—did not significantly alter the composition of agroexports (see Table 10.3).

Second, technological and institutional difficulties hinder efforts to shift to production of more valuable crops, particularly in the case of small farmers who now cultivate basic grains. Sixty-eight percent of the maize, 73 percent of the beans, and 50 percent of the rice produced in 1989 were grown on farms 0.5 to 2 hectares in size (López Córdovez 1994, p. 32). The majority of the farmers growing basic grains have limited or no access to credit, little technical assistance, soils of marginal quality, and little storage capacity. In the absence of more extensive systems of credit and technical support, further efforts to reorient agriculture toward international trade are likely to benefit only those farmers who have a comparative advantage in terms of access to productive resources. This would reinforce the bimodal structure that has so long characterized Salvadoran agriculture, and that constitutes one of the country's fundamental weaknesses.

Third, intrasectoral restructuring toward nontraditional agricultural exports at the expense of staple grains could negatively affect the internal food supply, increasing the country's vulnerability to international supply fluctuations. The steep rise in imports of powdered milk and meat in 1992 and the shortage of beans in 1993 illustrate the risks in such a strategy.

The above concerns do not imply that some shift of agricultural resources toward nontraditional crops is not warranted, particularly in cases where there is scope for the creation of additional value added in agroprocessing. But they do imply a need for caution, and suggest that nontraditional exports should not be regarded as a panacea for the economic crisis of the agricultural sector.

The Agrarian Structure and the Case for Further Reform

The "agrarian question" historically has been a root cause of social conflict in El Salvador. To a large extent this continues to be true, despite partial escape valves in the form of out-migration, expansion of the informal sector of the economy, and the redistributive effects of the limited agrarian reforms undertaken in the 1980s. The focal point of the agrarian question has been land, but it also embraces access to other productive resources, including credit and technical assistance.

Land

The availability of arable land in El Salvador is approximately 0.7 hectare per rural inhabitant, or 2.1 hectares per person actively engaged in agriculture (CEPAL 1993a, p. 57). Under the agrarian reform process that began in 1980, approximately 295,000 hectares of land were redistributed, equal to almost one-fifth of the arable land. Phase I of the reform expropriated farms of more than 500 hectares. The 244 landowners affected were compensated with 30-year bonds. Phase II, which would have extended the reform to holdings of 100–500 hectares, including much of the country's coffee estates, was never implemented. Phase III attempted to transfer land titles to tenants on rented lands. Direct beneficiaries numbered slightly more than 85,000 peasant families, comprising 10 percent of the country's population (see Table 10.6). Roughly 70 percent of the redistributed land was organized into cooperatives.

Because the last agricultural census was published in 1971, it is difficult to document the effects of the agrarian reform and the civil war on El

Table 10.6   Beneficiaries of Land Reform in the 1980s

	Phase I	Phase III	Voluntary transfers[a]	Total
Families benefited	36,697	42,289	6,041	85,227
People benefited	194,494	259,183	36,850	490,527
Hectares	215,167	69,605	10,922	295,694
Hectares/family	5.86	1.63	1.81	3.47

Sources: OSPA-MAG (1992, Cuadro 7, p. 12, and Cuadro 107, p. 135); FINATA (1993, Cuadro 3–1, p. 8).
Note: a. Decree 839.

Salvador's agrarian structure. There have been two major attempts to gather the relevant data since the mid-1980s—one based on a survey of farmers, the other based on a survey of rural households—with somewhat conflicting results. The results of the first study, carried out by the Ministry of Agriculture in 1987, are summarized in Table 10.7. According to this study, as a result of the reform the average size of large agricultural holdings was reduced from 289 to 133 hectares (CEPAL 1993a, p. 62). Based on these results, some observers (for example, Seligson 1994, p. 22; Grindle 1986, pp. 134–136) have rated the Salvadoran experience as the most extensive "nonsocialist" agrarian reform in Latin America with the exception of Mexico.

Be that as it may, the success of the agrarian reform should not be exaggerated. Such changes as did occur in the 1980s were due not only to the reform, but also to the displacement of large numbers of families who migrated to provincial capitals, San Salvador, or abroad. Seligson's analysis of the second source of data—a 1991–1992 MIPLAN survey of rural households—indicates that the numbers of the land-poor, landless, and permanent wage workers have fallen since the 1971 census, both in absolute terms and as a fraction of the economically active agricultural population (see Table 10.8). During the same period, however, unemployed agricultural labor grew significantly in absolute and relative terms. Seligson estimates that in 1991/92, 34 percent of the economically active population were entirely landless and working as temporary day laborers, and 13 percent were landless and working as permanent wage workers.[4] A further 17 percent were land-poor, with access to less than one manzana (0.7 hectare).[5] In total, more than 370,000 adults, constituting 64 percent of the economically active agricultural population, had little or no land.[6]

Viewed in this context, the land-transfer program contained in the peace accords—which, if fully implemented, would provide land to some 47,500 beneficiaries—is clearly insufficient to solve the problem of rural landlessness. At most it could resolve the problem of lack of land for about 75,000 adults. This would still leave roughly 300,000 adults—more than half of the agricultural labor force—with little or no land, only one-quarter (77,000) of whom have permanent employment. This does not differ dramatically from the agrarian situation at the beginning of the war.

The picture is even less encouraging when one notes that the land-transfer program envisaged in the peace accords has been considerably delayed and is ultimately likely to reach a smaller number of beneficiaries. A lack of funds to finance land acquisition is often blamed for the delays, but in reality administrative bottlenecks, themselves a symptom of a lack of political resolve, have been the major impediments (see Chapter 5).

Agricultural Credit and Technical Assistance

Access to agricultural credit also has been a long-standing problem for the rural poor in El Salvador. Prior to 1989, rural credit policy was characterized

Table 10.7   Farm-Size Distribution, 1971 and 1987

Size of farm (hectares)	1971 agricultural census					1987 survey[a]				
	Farms		Area (hectares)[a]		Average area per farm (hectares)	Farms		Area (hectares)		Average area per farm (hectares)
	Number	% of all farms	Total	% of total area		Number	% of all farms	Total	% of total area	
Total	270,868	100.0	1,451,895	100.0	5.4	286,183	100.0	1,334,748	100.0	4.7
0.7–3.5	234,941	86.7	283,311	19.5	1.2	222,883	77.9	201,503	15.1	0.9
3.5–14	24,762	9.1	237,446	16.4	9.6	43,304	15.1	275,097	20.6	6.4
14–35	6,986	2.6	215,456	14.8	30.8	12,550	4.4	262,094	19.6	20.9
35–70	2,238	0.8	154,164	10.6	68.9	4,589	1.6	217,378	16.3	47.4
> 70	1,941	0.7	561,518	38.7	289.3	2,857	1.0	378,676	28.4	132.5

Sources: CEPAL (1993d, Table 14, p. 48). The 1971 census data are drawn in the source table from Ministry of Agriculture and Livestock, Agriculture and Livestock Sectoral Planning Office, Agrarian Reform Planning and Evaluation Project, "Encuesta sobre uso y tenencia de la tierra" [Survey of Land Tenure and Use], Vol. 1, January 1989.

Note: a. These data appear to exclude 40,233 farms of less than 0.7 hectares each—12,482 farms with new owners and 27,751 farms that are rented or held under other forms of land tenure.

by subsidized interest rates and by a highly complex structure of lines of credit (FUSADES 1994). At the same time, in response to the crisis that affected agriculture during the 1980s, the resources of the country's financial system were redirected to other activities considered less risky and more profitable. During the period 1980–1988, the real volume of credit granted to the agricultural sector shrank by 44 percent, and its share of total bank credit fell from 30 percent to 13.5 percent. With respect to the structure of credit by subsector, the available evidence shows a clear priority accorded to the financing of coffee cultivation, which absorbed more than 70 percent of the credit extended to the agricultural sector during the 1980s by commercial and mortgage banks (see also Cruz Letona 1991).

The lack of up-to-date and reliable data makes it difficult to analyze the extent to which the policies of credit deregulation and interest-rate liberalization under the adjustment program affected the allocation of financial resources to and within the agricultural sector.[7] The available evidence suggests that the major share of agricultural credit continues to be absorbed by coffee (see Table 10.9; see also Wenner and Umaña 1993, p. 50).

In general, the commercial banking system provides little credit to basic grains producers, while the Banco de Fomento Agropecuario directs a somewhat larger share of its lending to them (see Table 10.9). According to López Córdovez (1994, p. 32), the formal financial sector covers the credit needs of barely 20 percent of small farmers. In the absence of countervailing measures, the liberalization of interest rates and credit deregulation are likely to result in a further reduction of credit allocated to small producers, who have little access to financial services of any kind (see Chapter 9).

At the same time, the privatization of agricultural organizations and services concerned with the production and transfer of agricultural technology[8] could result in a decrease in technical assistance to small farmers, despite the fact that they are the producers who most need assistance to increase their productivity levels. Small farmers in El Salvador in general work with very low levels of technology and infrastructure (see Seligson et al. 1993, pp. 2–38). Almost 50 percent of farmers have no formal education, and more than 80 percent are functionally illiterate (McReynolds et al. 1989, p. 73). A consistent policy of investment in human capital could integrate the provision of technical assistance as one of its components (see Griffin 1989; de Janvry and Sadoulet 1989).

Agrarian Reform

Agrarian reform should be a high priority for the government of El Salvador and supporting international agencies for three reasons. First, it is the agrarian policy most likely to foster sustainable long-term growth of

Table 10.8 Agrarian Structure, 1961–1991

National totals	1961 census			1971 census			1991–1992 MIPLAN survey		
	Total	% of EANP	% of EAAP	Total	% of EANP	% of EAAP	Total	% of EANP	% of EAAP
Economically active national population (EANP)	807,092	100.0	—	1,166,479	100.0	—	1,781,582	100.0	—
EANP > 15 years of age[a]	727,736	90.2	—	1,043,334	89.4	—	1,633,993	91.7	—
Economically active agricultural population (EAAP) >15[b]	416,728	59.9	100.0	542,929	46.5	100.0	581,661	32.6	100.0
Landed[c]	118,687	16.3	28.5	78,167	6.7	14.4	136,171	8.3	23.4
Land-poor[d]	96,456	13.4	23.1	119,350	10.2	22.0	96,821	5.9	16.6
Landless (temporary day workers)[e]	115,161	15.7	27.6	207,116	17.8	38.1	198,309	12.1	34.1
Permanent wage workers[e]	51,498	7.0	12.4	92,640	7.9	17.1	77,001	4.7	13.2
Family laborers	34,926	3.8	8.4	45,606[f]	3.9	8.4	73,359	4.5	12.6
Unemployed EAAP[g]	22,008	3.0	5.3	33,994	2.9	6.3	58,293	3.6	10.0

Source: Seligson et al. (1993, p. 20), based on MIPLAN survey and census documents.

Notes: a. Census data for 1961 and 1971 are given in age groups of 10–14 and 15–19. Therefore, for these two censuses the 16-and-older group is computed by interpolation.

b. The census reports the data by economic activity in two ways: by branch (*rama*) and by occupation. These figures differ slightly from each other because not all of those who work in the agricultural branch have agricultural occupations, and some of those who work in branches other than agriculture have agricultural occupations (e.g., gardener). In this chapter, the data are based upon occupations rather than branch because the published census provides much finer breakdowns by occupation as opposed to branch. For example, the occupation breakdowns indicate specific occupations (workers versus farmers) and provide those breakdowns by age.

c. Includes 3,387 administrators for 1961 and 5,692 for 1971. The published 1961 census categorizes individuals as landed (*agricultores y ganaderos*) if their principal occupation is based on land they own or rent. These figures correspond very closely to the 1961 agricultural census, which finds 119,842 farms of 1 hectare or larger. Farms may have more than one economically active person, of course, but these are accounted for in the family labor, temporary worker, and permanent–wage worker categories below. For 1971 the census distinguishes between diversified and monoculture farms.

Table 10.8   Continued

d. The land-poor figures are drawn from the agricultural censuses. Note, however, that the census reports land in hectares, whereas all data in the MIPLAN survey are in manzanas. The 1961 census does not subdivide into smaller categories the listing of farms smaller than 1 hectare, but the MIPLAN data set includes all farms in the 1–4 manzana size in a single cohort. Therefore, in this table, for 1961 and 1971, land-poor are those with less than 1 hectare, whereas for the MIPLAN survey the land-poor are those with less than 1 manzana, or 0.7 hectare. The decline in 1991 of the land-poor, therefore, is partially a function of the smaller size limit used for that year. The land-poor data are taken from the agricultural censuses because the population census does not show the size of farm land held by the various occupational categories. No adjustment for the 10–15 age group has been made in the agricultural census data because the 1961 population census reports only 6 individuals aged 10–14 who are land owners (*agricultores y ganaderos*). The 1971 census reports no such individuals.

e. The published population census does not distinguish between permanent and temporary wage workers, but groups them both into the category of agricultural workers (*trabajadores agrícolas*). In order to make this important distinction here, the agricultural worker category (minus those younger than 16) is subdivided in the same proportion as the 1991 MIPLAN survey, which does allow for this distinction. In that survey, 30.9 percent of the agricultural workers were permanent day laborers and the remainder temporary. Furthermore, the MIPLAN survey found that 9.9 percent of the agricultural laborers (permanent and temporary combined) were simultaneously small landholders, owning 1 manzana or less of land. Therefore, in order not to double count these individuals as both land-poor and landless, 9.9 percent of the land-poor are subtracted from the agricultural census data. As a result, those who both own less than 1 hectare and are agricultural laborers are categorized as laborers in this table. Then, the remaining land-poor group is subtracted from the agricultural-worker category because these individuals are all subsumed in the worker category by the population census.

f. The 1971 population census did not include a separate category for family laborers, so the 1961 percentages were used to estimate the 1971 value.

g. Note that the MIPLAN numbers have been adjusted to reincorporate the unemployed. The MIPLAN data set allows the segregation of the unemployed from other workers, a procedure followed throughout this chapter. The census, however, does not allow this distinction, but includes the unemployed among the economically active population, providing only an overall total of unemployed for each major sector (e.g., agriculture). In order to allow direct comparison between the MIPLAN survey and the census data, the MIPLAN survey results are adjusted here to reintegrate the unemployed back into the occupation category they had when they were employed. Also note that the population census gives the total unemployed in the agricultural sector, but does not provide age breakdowns that would allow the exclusion of the unemployed younger than 16 years of age. It is unlikely that the 10–15-year-old group comprises a significant number of individuals, so the failure to exclude them does not greatly change the data.

Table 10.9   Agricultural Credit, 1990 and 1993 (millions of colones)

	Commercial-banking system		Banco de Fomento Agropecuario		FEDECREDITO
	1990	1993	1990	1993	1993
Total agricultural lending	1434	1675	654	1021	26
Major crops					
Maize	24	n.a.	94	70	7
Beans	3	n.a.	14	11	1
Rice	10	n.a.	19	21	1
Cotton	49	52	13	10	
Sugar cane	124	161	22	12	3
Coffee	1031	1075	164	234	
Livestock	19	n.a.	41	69	12

Sources: BCR; BFA; FEDECREDITO.
n.a. = data not available

the economy as a whole. Second, agrarian reform can increase efficiency in the agricultural sector itself by improving the structure of incentives. Third, asset redistribution is essential to raise the incomes of the rural poor.

We recognize that in El Salvador, as in most countries, agrarian reform is a controversial topic. The argument presented in this section is based on strictly economic analysis, not on a weighing of the political prospects for agrarian reform in the near term. We suspect, however, that the obstacles to reform, though by no means inconsequential, are less formidable than they were a decade or two ago. The de facto (if not de jure) reallocation of land wrought by the war, the loosening of ties to the land with the advent of new economic opportunities, and the democratization of the country's political order have all combined to create historic new opportunities. Our aim here is not to offer a blueprint for reform, but to present the economic case for a renewed debate on agrarian policies.

The links between agrarian reform and long-term growth are profound and complex. Recent empirical analyses have demonstrated the importance of a relatively egalitarian asset distribution as a precondition for high levels of investment and sustained growth. Cross-national analyses, using land distribution as a proxy for asset distribution more generally, provide direct evidence of the particular importance of relatively equal access to *land* for sustainable growth. The accumulated evidence overwhelmingly supports the conclusion that a very unequal landholding pattern poses a serious barrier to growth over the long run. In an analysis of the determinants of growth in 16 developing countries, including Korea, Taiwan,

Malaysia, and Thailand, Rodrik (1994) finds that the initial conditions of land distribution and primary education substantially explain the variation in subsequent growth rates. Similarly, Persson and Tabellini (1994) and Alesina and Rodrik (1994) find that the degree of land inequality is inversely associated with economic growth for larger samples of countries.

The World Bank study *The East Asian Miracle* notes that in the six high-performing Asian economies with significant agrarian sectors—Japan, Korea, Taiwan, Indonesia, Thailand, and Malaysia—three implemented extensive land reforms prior to the onset of rapid long-run growth: Japan, Korea, and Taiwan. Indonesia and Thailand already had traditional patterns of widely dispersed landholding. Only Malaysia had an agricultural sector characterized by significant concentration of landholdings, but in that case the availability of abundant land meant that this did not haunt the country's development (World Bank 1993b, p. 159).

A variety of causal explanations have been advanced regarding the relationship between the egalitarian distribution of assets and sustained development. Some stress the importance of political stability and state legitimacy for growth (World Bank 1993b); others suggest that more equal land distribution attenuates socially suboptimal primary-school enrollment rates (Birdsall, Ross, and Sabot 1995); others stress the diversion of public resources to ameliorate ongoing social conflict in inegalitarian countries (Alesina and Rodrik 1994).[9]

Whatever the precise mechanisms at work, the international evidence dramatically reveals the salutary effects of widely dispersed asset distribution for long-run growth. The clear implication of this research is that in El Salvador the present unequal distribution of land poses an obstacle to the long-term growth of the economy as a whole. Removing this obstacle is the first argument for a thoroughgoing agrarian reform.

A second argument for further land redistribution is that it will generate a realignment of individual incentives more consistent with efficiency and growth in agricultural productivity. Empirical data from throughout the world demonstrate the superior labor intensity, and hence land productivity, of owner-operated smallholdings compared to larger farms cultivated by means of wage labor or tenancy.[10] There is no reason to imagine that, with adequate institutions to ensure equal access to credit and technical assistance, El Salvador would violate this rule.

Furthermore, vesting rights of residual claimancy in the farmer working the land would increase the incentive for investment and adoption of soil-conservation practices. As secure owners of the land they till, the rural poor would for the first time have the secure prospect of reaping the returns to investments in the "natural capital" of their farms.

Agrarian reform would also decrease the incentive to use herbicides, chemical weed killers that endanger water purity and human health.

Herbicides are a substitute for labor in the control of weeds; hence the choice between herbicides and labor depends on their relative price. For small family farmers, labor is cheaper than it is for large farms for a variety of reasons.[11] For this reason, smaller farms are more likely to use labor instead of herbicides to control weeds, particularly if the prices of the latter are raised to capture more fully their external environmental costs. Moreover, small farmers are likely to put greater weight on the risks of occupational exposure to herbicides, because these fall on the farmers themselves and their family members, whereas larger landowners shift the risk to their laborers. In a study of coffee producers in Costa Rica, Boyce et al. (1994, p. 160) found that large farms (over 20 hectares) spend almost three times as much per hectare on herbicides as do small farms (under 5 hectares).[12] Again, there is no reason to expect otherwise in El Salvador.

The third compelling reason for continued agrarian reform is the political imperative to reduce rural poverty, coupled with the economic objective of doing so at a feasible cost. Even under current market conditions, owners of smallholdings in El Salvador receive significantly higher incomes than do tenant farmers, permanent wage laborers, or temporary day laborers (USAID 1993b; Seligson 1994). A recent study for the Inter-American Development Bank concludes:

> Policies to reduce poverty must, in addition to education, health, housing, support for employment creation and/or productivity increases of the poor, address other elements that produce and reproduce poverty and make the process of economic growth systematically unequal. Those other factors refer first to asset distribution (concentration of ownership), particularly of land, and secondly to economic structure, i.e., the labor intensity of production, the rural/urban terms of trade, etc. (Griffith-Jones et al. 1993, p. 89).

The poverty-reduction impact would not be confined to the direct beneficiaries of land redistribution. By increasing labor absorption, land reform would put upward pressure on rural wages and eventually on urban wages, helping to halt or reverse the real-wage decline of the past decade. The titling of assets to smallholders could also foster more productive use of remittance inflows, fueling private rural investment that would directly and indirectly benefit the poor. It must be emphasized, however, that these benefits are contingent on the restoration of a macroeconomic price environment more favorable to agriculture.

A nexus of complementarity among growth, poverty reduction, and the consolidation of peace is absolutely crucial to El Salvador's long-run economic future. In the agricultural sector, agrarian reform offers the surest route to capitalize on this complementarity.

Toward Sustainable Agricultural Development

Sustainable agricultural development is critical for El Salvador's economic future. As a supplier of food, a source of export earnings, and a market for nonagricultural products, the agricultural sector plays a key role in macroeconomic growth and stability. As the source of income and food for many of the poor, the sector's performance critically affects livelihood security. And as a provider of vital environmental services, the sector's importance to the country as a whole cannot be overstated.

The interrelated goals of macroeconomic growth and stability, sustainable livelihood security, and environmental sustainability will not be achieved by laissez-faire policies reliant solely on market forces. In a small, open economy, agricultural prices cannot safely be entrusted to world markets characterized by massive imperfections, pervasive government interventions, and chronic price instability.

Nor can the market be relied upon to generate an efficient and equitable agrarian structure: Oligarchic power historically has favored resource allocations that are both inequitable and inefficient, and the exercise of democratic power is necessary to yield superior outcomes. And environmental "externalities," by definition, trigger market failures; policy interventions are essential if individual economic decisions are to take account of social costs and benefits.

A range of alternative policies are therefore required. This section offers recommendations pertaining to agricultural price policy and agrarian reform, with a focus on steps that can and should be taken in the short run. The next chapter explores the complementary environmental policies needed to reorient El Salvador toward sustainable agricultural development.

Price Policies

As discussed in the first section, the low prices and low profitability currently faced by the Salvadoran agricultural sector are an outcome of exchange-rate overvaluation driven by remittances and external assistance, coupled with a residue of tariff discrimination against agriculture, and a policy of price liberalization that has transmitted the impact of adverse price trends in world markets. At the present conjuncture there is a strong economic case for a variety of measures to support producer prices:

- As will be argued further in Chapter 12, the tradeable-goods sector in general—including nontraditional manufactured exports as well as agriculture—would benefit from steps to counteract the current overvaluation of the exchange rate.

- A moderate increase in tariffs on imported food grains would redress current discrimination and insulate domestic farmers from the impact of dumping of agricultural surpluses by the industrialized countries.
- In the case of basic grains, there is a compelling case for direct interventions to raise producer prices above the current levels. This case is reinforced by four considerations in addition to those pertaining to the agricultural sector as a whole:

Social considerations. Basic grain production is a critical element in the livelihoods of the rural poor. Insofar as the rural poor are net sellers of grain, higher prices would benefit them. Price support for basic grains must be coupled, however, with steps to safeguard the food-purchasing power of poor net buyers of grains.

Political considerations. The economic viability of small-scale agricultural producers in general, and of land-transfer beneficiaries in particular, has crucial implications for the consolidation of the peace process in the medium and long term. If macroeconomic policies continue to yield an adverse price environment, it will simply be impossible for the majority of land-transfer beneficiaries to repay production loans, let alone the debt incurred for the acquisition of land itself.

Food security. Without a national capacity for basic-grains production, any country is highly vulnerable to international market fluctuations driven by unpredictable climatic and policy changes elsewhere. The need to limit exposure to this risk is one important rationale for the ubiquitous price interventions practiced by industrial countries.

Environmental considerations. Finally, as noted earlier and further elaborated in Chapter 11, it must be recognized that small-scale hillside farmers in El Salvador produce not only grain, but also critical environmental services via their impact on watershed hydrology. Price policy alone is not sufficient to address this problem, but compensation for the provision of environmental services constitutes one element in the set of investment, fiscal, and regulatory measures needed to confront the country's emerging environmental crisis.

Direct producer price supports would of course place demands on limited government resources. Targeting supports to the poor (most simply by limiting total support payments to any single producer) would limit the fiscal burden. Moreover, as noted in previous chapters, there is currently considerable scope for increasing tax revenues.

In sum, the need to get agricultural prices "right" should not be equated with allowing world market conditions coupled with overvalued exchange rates to dictate domestic prices. Economic, social, political, food-security, and environmental considerations all lead to the conclusion that current macroeconomic policy has produced the wrong prices for Salvadoran agriculture. El Salvador cannot affect world-market conditions, but it can take rational and prudent measures to prevent the decimation of its agricultural sector.

Agrarian-Reform Policies

Appropriate and politically feasible long-run agrarian-reform policies can emerge only through a serious national debate on the case for building a more equitable agrarian structure in El Salvador. For the reasons elaborated in the previous section, we believe that case to be very strong. Experience has demonstrated, however, that top-down reforms often fail to achieve their stated goals, and can exacerbate rather than ease social tensions. The democratization process now underway in El Salvador opens, for the first time in the nation's history, the possibility of a publicly accountable and participatory approach to the agrarian question.

In the short and medium run, however, a number of steps can be taken to redress the most glaring shortcomings of present policies:

• Alternative terms and conditions for retiring debts for land acquisition incurred by land-transfer-program beneficiaries should be devised. This debt is likely to prove unrepayable on current terms, and it undermines the creditworthiness of beneficiaries; moreover, the finance itself came to El Salvador in the form of grants. One option is an outright write-off of the debt. Another is to tie retirement of the debt to specific performance criteria, such as adoption of socially beneficial soil- and water-conservation practices.

• The present land-transfer program should be accelerated by reversing the logic of the process so that the "default option" is the transfer, rather than nontransfer, of the lands in question. Under the current system, transfers cannot be completed until all owners are identified and agree. This places an enormous burden on the administrative apparatus. Under the revised system, the onus would be upon the owners to come forward and to substantiate claims for compensation or retention of land ownership within a reasonable time period; if they fail to do so, the transfer would proceed.[13]

• Land-titling procedures should be greatly simplified. The recent success of *lotificadores* (housing developers) in titling large-scale developments may hold useful lessons in this regard. It is important that efficient procedures be put in place before the land-transfer program begins permanent titling.

• The "agrarian debts" of the cooperatives established under Phase I of the 1980 reform should be forgiven. These debts are not collectible at reasonable political or economic cost, and they pose significant obstacles to productive investment on some of the best properties in the country.

• Given the importance of rural organizations for articulating rural interests and for developing alternative marketing channels, cooperative holding of land should remain an option left to the decision of members, but should be subsidized (after the erasure of the agrarian debt) only where market failures provide a clear economic justification to do so.

• Properties in excess of 245 hectares in 1983 that were unconstitutionally transferred in subsequent years should be an exception to the voluntary nature of current and proposed reforms. The existence of such properties should be investigated by an interparty team of persons experienced in similar collaboration during the land-transfer program. Such investigation should include public hearings on contested properties to determine whether a legally divided holding is in fact managed as a single unit.

• Because tenancy and wage labor are inferior to family farms from a productivity standpoint, the development of an institutional environment that permits more equal access to capital and technology will create incentives for voluntary land transfers. This requires further steps to surmount the credit-market failures now impeding market-based redistribution of assets.

This chapter has focused on two central issues in El Salvador's agricultural sector: the macroeconomic price environment and agrarian reform. In addition, however, it is critical that agricultural policies take into account the environmental services provided by the sector to the economy as a whole. The next chapter examines this dimension in greater detail.

Notes

1. For discussion, see Harberger and Wisecarver (1988), Norton (1990), Norton and Liévano (1988), and Loehr and Núñez (1991).

2. Real producer prices for basic grains had already fallen in the early 1980s. According to data provided by the DGEA, the real prices of maize and beans in 1985/86 stood at 72 percent and 48 percent, respectively, of their 1980/81 levels.

3. For discussions, see López Córdovez (1987), Streeten (1987), Valdes and Pinckney (1989), Scandizzo (1992), Goldin and Winters (1992), Martin and Warr (1993), and Singh and Tabatabai (1993).

4. The 10 percent who were unemployed are distributed among these categories.

5. This estimate for the land-poor is quite conservative, given the very low threshold of 0.7 hectare.

6. If we were to exclude the permanent wage workers, as Seligson does in his own discussion of these data, the fraction is 51 percent. Given the high degree of poverty among even those permanently employed, we include them among the landless and land-poor.

7. For a discussion of the low reliability of data on the structure and levels of credit in El Salvador in recent years, see Loehr and Núñez (1991, pp. 48–52).

8. The most ambitious effort in this regard is the Project for Institutional Reform of the Agricultural and Animal Husbandry Sector. The World Bank approved a loan of $40 million for this project in March 1993, to which the government added $16.5 million.

9. For further references and discussion of the relationship between equity and growth, see Chapters 1 and 8 of this volume.

10. See Sen (1975), Berry and Cline (1979), and Netting (1993).

11. For example, family members may prefer to work on their own land, and thus be willing to do so even when the marginal product of their own labor is below the market wage; uncertainty of wage employment and the costs of a job search may drive a further wedge between the two; and family labor does not require the supervision costs of hired labor. For discussion of these and other factors in the inverse relation between farm size and labor intensity, see Sen (1975) and Boyce (1987).

12. Boyce et al. (1994) report the opposite correlation in the case of fungicides, nematicides, and insecticides, which complement rather than substitute for labor: Smaller farms used more.

13. CEPAL (1993d, p. 58) recommends two additional steps in this regard: (1) the government should state that all lands, or at least those in conflictive zones, are subject to expropriation, and (2) municipal governments should have the resources to issue land-transfer documents.

11

Environmental Degradation and Development Options

Deborah Barry and Herman Rosa

El Salvador entered the period of postwar reconstruction and development with enormous environmental handicaps that threaten to undermine both peace and economic stability. Yet the environmental dimension of El Salvador's future was excluded from the macroeconomic reform process begun in the late 1980s and from the political reforms spearheaded by the peace accords of 1992. This reflects the fact that the relationship of the environment to democratization and development has yet to be clearly recognized by policymakers in El Salvador and within the international organizations that supported these economic and political efforts.

This omission has led many policymakers to a dangerously inaccurate reading of the current and future capacity of the country's environment to sustain economic growth and promote improvement of social well-being. Conversely, explicit recognition of the interdependence between the economic, social, political, and environmental dimensions of development, and their inclusion into the broad policy framework for reconstruction, offers opportunities for addressing some of the causes of the past social conflict and can help to lay the grounds for sustainable development.

Water: The Picture Today

The territory of El Salvador has been degraded to the point at which the country's capacity to renew the most basic natural resource for any development option—water—is being lost. Past development patterns resulted in near total deforestation, widespread soil erosion, sedimentation of rivers, lakes, and reservoirs, and unchecked contamination of surface water. Together these processes are beginning to limit the availability of fresh water to meet domestic, industrial, agricultural, and energy needs. At the same time, demand for water is increasing in the postwar reconstruction period.

233

The deterioration of natural resources is most apparent in the rural areas, particularly in the north and east. The steepest slopes of the country are being cultivated out of sheer economic desperation, causing heavy increases in soil erosion and thus in the capacity to retain moisture. Many upland rivers are drying up, once year-round sources of water are now only seasonal at best, and fuelwood and water for family needs must be sought at greater distances from villages.

Continued degradation of the principal watersheds of the country is also jeopardizing future water supply for urban development. At the same time, the total neglect of environmental issues in urban growth (to a large degree attributable to political resistance to measures such as land-use regulation, zoning, control of industrial wastes, and increased spending for proper municipal waste disposal) is further damaging the water and energy supply through contamination, sedimentation, and reduced groundwater infiltration.

The loss of natural resources, or of their natural capacity to renew themselves, cannot be documented with precision, for even the collection of basic data has not taken place. But there is cause to fear that some losses could be approaching irreversibility.[1] Hillsides denuded of forest cover suffer from either agricultural "overuse," producing an increase in the loss of topsoil, or from highly degrading urbanization processes. Together these break down nature's capacity to regulate the impact of tropical rains, heavy surface-water flows, and groundwater infiltration. Increased downhill runoff leads to flooding, sedimentation, and the increased loss of fresh water to the sea.[2]

In the postwar period, access to water has emerged as a new source of social conflict, highlighting problems of availability and supply. Local disputes over user rights and responsibilities for water and the systems that protect it are on the rise.[3] Regional inequalities of water distribution are striking and may lead to serious interregional disputes as well: Sixty-four percent of potable water is consumed by the San Salvador Metropolitan Area (SSMA), which holds 26 percent of the population, while four eastern provinces with roughly the same percentage of the population enjoy access to only 5 percent of the country's potable water (Chavarría 1994). Yet plans for the expansion of water-delivery systems, hydropower generation, and economic growth continue to ignore the dynamic of land degradation that is undermining the capacity to deliver crucial services in the future. Present economic policies and the postwar reconstruction plans simply assume water availability, ignoring the degree of urban and rural land degradation, the negative dynamics of degradation that have been established, and their implications for national reconstruction.[4]

The threats to livelihoods and environment in the rural areas, above all in the northern and eastern sectors of the country, and the rapid and uncontrolled urbanization and concentration of population in southwestern El

Salvador, are inextricably related. Both socially and ecologically, the rural and urban landscapes are now linked together in a complex system of dependence on the country's natural-resource base. Social inequality and exclusion have forced the rural poor into either a greater dependence on the extraction of increasingly scarce natural resources for survival (fuelwood, water, and soils) or migration to urban areas in hope of increasing economic opportunities. El Salvador's development is swiftly approaching an environmentally determined limit at which future growth, regardless of the model or option, can no longer permit the current pattern and levels of rural poverty on the one hand, nor the current styles of rapacious urban development on the other.

Urban Growth and Environmental Degradation

El Salvador's population growth slowed significantly over the last 20 years as a result of increasing contraceptive prevalence and massive out-migration.[5] Indeed, rural areas in the north and the east have seen absolute population declines. Currently, it is the patterns of human settlement and production, rather than population growth per se, that are degrading the natural-resource base.

Census data from 1971 and 1992 reveal population declines in the northern and eastern sectors of the country, coupled with a dramatic increase in the southwest, where 64 percent of the population is now concentrated (see Figure 11.1). The SSMA is the area of maximum concentration, with 30 percent of the population residing in 3 percent of the national territory.

Where and how this concentration of population is occurring has important environmental impacts. Current patterns of rapid, massive, and totally unplanned urbanization are having a highly degrading impact. Much urban growth takes place at the expense of shade-coffee plantations. The ecological function of these "surrogate forests" has been to maintain the hydrological balances. The forests—coffee mixed with diverse other tree species that provide fruit, fodder, fuel, and wood as well as shade for the coffee—cover the surface of a chain of young volcanic mountains running along the southern corridor of the country. This fragile ecosystem depends on adequate land-surface conditions to capture rainwater in areas where the porous volcanic rock allows high levels of infiltration to replenish the underground reserves.

Uncontrolled urbanization is putting enormous pressure on the remaining forest and vegetative cover. Urban developers have operated with no effective zoning or land-use regulation whatsoever, employing radical practices of land terracing and landfill in the SSMA principally for high-income housing, shopping centers, and urban infrastructure.[6] Vegetative

Figure 11.1   Population Growth by Selected Zones, 1971–1992 (In millions)

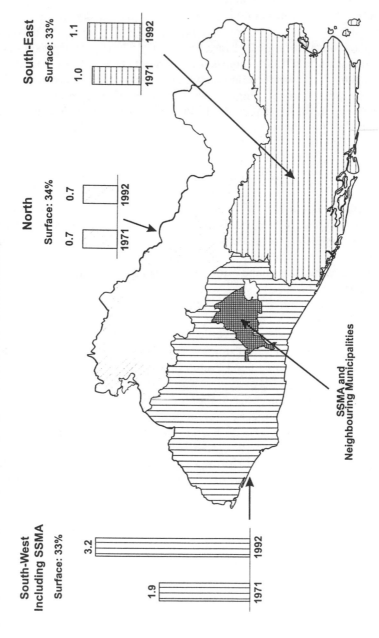

Source: PRISMA, based on Population Census

cover is replaced by an "urban cover" of asphalt and cement, which greatly reduces the infiltration capacity of these areas. Poorly designed urban housing projects on the steeper volcanic slopes cause increases in run-off, downhill flooding, and sedimentation, further limiting the capacity for groundwater recharge. At the same time, urbanization escalates the demand for water from these same groundwater reserves (Barry 1994).

The flight from misery in the north and east has meanwhile concentrated many of the rural poor in the southwest, creating a demand for small plots of land. Fueled also by remittances, the result has been "lotification," the division of surrounding rural properties into tiny plots.[7] Here, families build rudimentary shelters and usually continue to grow basic grains to satisfy minimal needs. The ensuing land clearance, together with the fact that a large percentage of the population has no alternative to firewood as their principal source of energy for cooking, leads to additional pressure on the forest cover.[8]

The picture is further complicated by the fact that the SSMA lies in the watershed of the Acelhuate River, which empties inland into the Cerrón Grande Reservoir, the largest artificial lake in the country, that is formed by the country's most important hydroelectric dam. Nearly 100 percent of urban liquid and solid wastes are directly or indirectly discharged untreated into this river. Industrial contamination is high, given that 88 percent of the industry concentrated in the SSMA during the war, and that there are no effective controls on industrial contamination of water systems. Three other large rivers—the Suquiapa, the Sucio, and the Quezalapa—also converge on the reservoir from the south, carrying untreated contaminants from smaller surrounding cities (see Figure 11.2).

The urban contamination not only threatens the biotic life of the Cerrón Grande Reservoir, but flows on to pollute the largest river in the country, the Lempa, which drains the reservoir to the sea. Together, these constitute 60 percent of the country's surface waters. In total, today nearly 90 percent of surface waters in the country are contaminated.[9] No studies have yet been done to ascertain the extent of contamination of groundwater sources.

The water problem is already becoming dramatic in the SSMA and some secondary cities. Despite the roughly 80 percent coverage of infrastructure for potable water, effective delivery is diminishing and water rationing is becoming a common practice. Over the last several years normal water delivery reached a maximum of 18 hours per day in wealthier neighborhoods, and only eight hours per day in more populated areas. Water has been further rationed lately, leaving many neighborhoods without water for days.

The SSMA has now begun to bring surface water from outside its own hydrological region in an attempt to augment its local (principally groundwater) supplies. Overland pumping is currently bringing water from the Lempa River, upstream from the contaminated Cerrón Grande Reservoir.

Figure 11.2   Selected Tributaries of the Lempa River

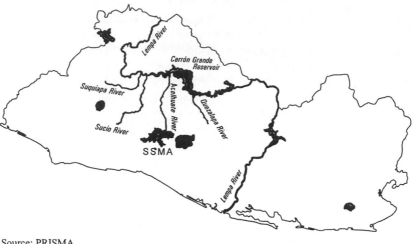

Source: PRISMA

However, high sediment loads in the river are damaging the pumping systems, again forcing rationing as a result of intermittent shutdowns. As electricity blackouts can no longer be blamed for those shutdowns, public understanding of the real causes of water shortages is growing.

Rural Livelihoods and Sustainability

An increase in basic-grains production on steeper and more marginal lands has accelerated erosion and thus sedimentation of rivers and lakes. The effects, as explained above, extend to urban areas. To address this problem it is necessary to analyze the situation of the rural poor from the perspective of their livelihoods and the sustainability of those livelihoods.[10]

The principal rural livelihood of concern here is that of the peasant producer. Though evolving over the last century (see Chapter 2), the basic profile of peasant livelihood has centered on two major activities: harvest labor in the major agroexport crops, notably coffee, cotton, and sugar cane, and the production of basic grains. Peasant families produce grains during the rainy season (May to October) and migrate at the beginning of the dry season to work in the harvest of the major export crops. The latter usually provides between three and four months' more income to several family members. This binomial relationship has functioned as the backbone of rural livelihoods for decades. Complementary activities involve direct use of natural resources, as in the case of firewood gathering.

Over the last 15 years, peasant livelihoods have been undermined by the civil war, the drop in international prices for export crops, and national economic policies (see Chapter 10). There was a concurrent and significant drop in harvest employment for the three major export crops (coffee, cotton, and sugar cane) for at least five consecutive harvest seasons, from 1984/85 through 1988/89. In the 1980s as a whole, roughly 50 percent of this seasonal employment (approximately 4 million person-days of work) was lost. As Figure 11.3 shows, all three crops provided less harvest employment, with cotton accounting for the greatest losses. This reflects the overall decline in cotton acreage, which has continued after the war.[11]

Nominal minimum harvest wages were kept constant for much of the 1980s in the face of significant inflation. Because actual harvest wages usually follow minimum wages, real wages fell sharply—by almost 70 percent between 1980 and 1988 (see Figure 11.4). The declines in both employment and wages together led to an enormous loss of harvest-wage income.

At the same time, there was a loss of income for peasants derived from grains production, as the prices of basic grains also fell significantly in real terms (see Figure 11.5 and Table 10.5).

Figure 11.3   Harvest Employment for Major Export Crops, 1979/80–1988/89 (Millions of person-days)

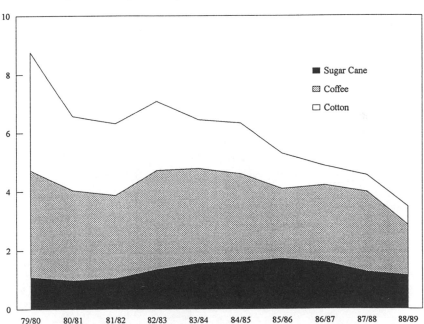

Source: PRISMA based on Population Census data.

Figure 11.4   Coffee-Harvest Minimum Wages, 1973–1993 (1978 = 100)

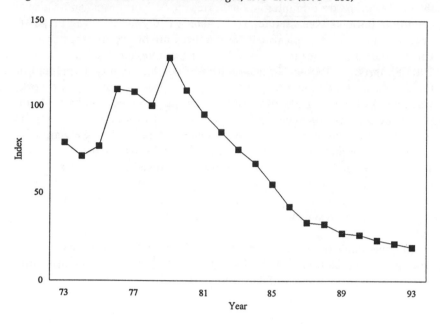

Source: PRISMA, based on Ministry of Economy data.

Figure 11.5   Indices of Real Prices of Corn and Beans, 1978–1993 (1978 = 100)

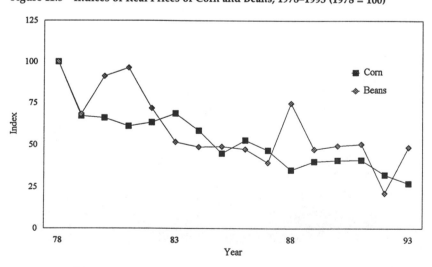

Source: PRISMA

It is still early to assess fully the long-term consequences of this massive loss of rural livelihoods. The short-term impacts included a dramatic increase in rural-urban migration and out-migration, and an increase in the surface area of basic-grains production despite falling prices (see Appendix Table A.8). In particular, corn acreage has expanded onto overused grazing lands and higher slopes best suited for forestry (Montoya 1991, pp. 8–17). Both are causing intensified soil erosion in the upper watersheds. In northern and eastern El Salvador, drinking water and firewood, two basic components of peasant livelihoods, are increasingly scarce and costly (in terms of time or money).[12]

Access to land is a key determining factor for rural livelihoods. As discussed in previous chapters, El Salvador's highly unequal structure of land tenure was partially modified by the land reform of the 1980s. However, recent studies (e.g., Seligson et al. 1993) indicate a return to pre-reform tendencies. Along with the increase in cultivation of marginal lands, *minifundismo* and the number of producers renting land appear to be on the rise.[13]

The social relations of land rental in rural El Salvador exacerbate myopic land use and pose a serious obstacle to the adoption of soil-conservation techniques. Tenancy is highly insecure because land is frequently leased for only one year. In the past, such short-term tenancies were related to the practice of shifting cultivation, so as to leave the land fallow after cropping. Today, however, one tenant is simply replaced by another, with the key motivation being landlord fears of the establishment of permanent land claims by the tenant. Moreover, tenants who do make land improvements are similarly suspected of attempting to lay claim to the land; hence they are often evicted when such actions are detected.

The environmental impacts of inequity and poverty are now undermining the common good of the country as a whole. The watersheds of northern El Salvador in particular constitute the "hydrological rearguard" for future development. Decreased water retention on eroded hillsides reduces the quantity and quality of surface-water flows to meet the dramatic rise in urban demand, coupled with the reduction in groundwater supply. Increased erosion and sedimentation also contribute to the siltation of the country's dam sites. Because hydropower accounts for nearly 50 percent of energy generation and is by far the cheapest energy source, this effect is of considerable national importance.[14]

The foregoing implies a need for a reconceptualization of the role of hillside agriculture in El Salvador. Hillsides, or *laderas,* are considered to be all terrain with more than a 15 percent slope. Hillside topsoil is not well suited to intensive tillage, yet it is precisely on these slopes that 86 percent of basic grains (corn, beans, and sorghum) are grown, as well as 87 percent of permanent crops (mostly coffee) and approximately 80 percent of pasture land (Lindarte and Benito 1993).

The production of basic grains on hillsides differs greatly from that of coffee in its environmental impact. With the current techniques, basic-grains production is highly degrading. Few soil-conservation techniques are applied. On the contrary, common practices include total clearing and burning of land for planting, intensive tillage, no contouring, no live or fence barriers, little use of cover crops and multicropping, high levels of agrochemical inputs, and the introduction of cattle during the dry season.

Shaded coffee, on the other hand, is usually grown with fruit trees and larger trees for top cover. Figure 11.6 shows the location of coffee forests. The coffee species grown have a longer lifetime than nonshaded coffee, requiring less replanting, thus causing less erosion. The coffee forest acts as a surrogate for original tropical forests by re-establishing several levels of vegetation, which break the rainfall's impact on topsoil, while root systems help to retain moisture. Some of the interplanted tree species also fix atmospheric nitrogen in the soils, and plant litter provides a source of natural fertilizer.

Although coffee in El Salvador has traditionally been grown on medium- to large-scale farms, small producers with less than 5 hectares accounted for 16 percent of coffee acreage in 1971 (see Table 11.1). In 1988, after the land reform, small producers together with the land-reform cooperatives accounted for 25 percent. Though both subsectors currently face serious difficulties, they provide a beginning for policy initiatives to encourage the cultivation of permanent crops by the rural poor.

Figure 11.6   Map of Coffee Areas

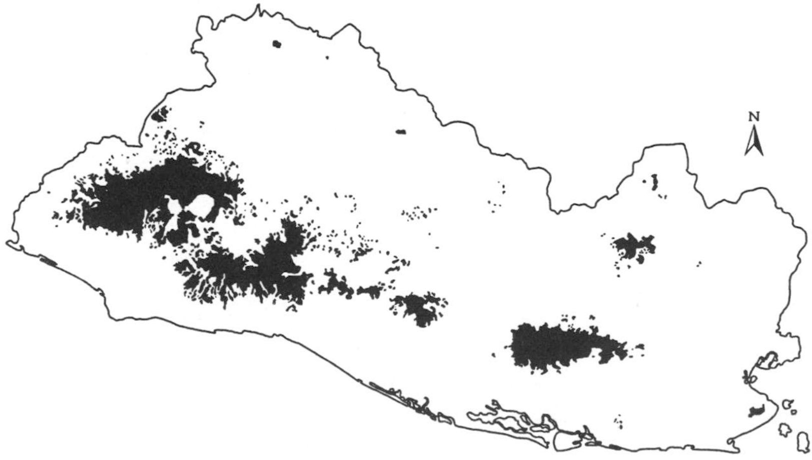

SOURCE: PRISMA Based on PROCAFE-GIS

Table 11.1   Distribution of Coffee Lands, 1971 and 1988

	1971		1988	
	Area (ha)	Distribution (%)	Area (ha)	Distribution (%)
Less than 5 hectares	24,019	16	29,466	15
5–20 hectares	23,807	16	22,044	11
20–50 hectares	30,047	20	42,767	21
50–100 hectares	24,942	17	48,834	24
More than 100 hectares	44,223	30	37,132	19
Land-reform cooperatives			19,738	10
Total	147,038	100	199,981	100

Source: PRISMA, based on PROCAFE-GIS.

Basic-grains production has traditionally been virtually synonymous with rural poverty. Whereas coffee growers are generally well endowed with access to infrastructure, technical assistance, and market information, basic-grains producers suffer from their absence. There is a critical need to provide much greater support to basic-grains producers. But that support must be couched within the recognition that hillside agriculture not only supplies food, but also provides critical hydrological services to the rest of the population.

Toward a Framework for Sustainability

The creation of a new framework for development, in which the environmental dimension is incorporated into economic logic, requires far-reaching reforms. Although we cannot attempt to set forth a comprehensive blueprint here, we consider the following steps to be critical.

First, at the macroeconomic level, recognition of environmental feedbacks into the functioning of the economy implies a need to incorporate the monetary valuation of environmental costs and benefits, both present and future, in investment planning. Valuation poses serious practical and theoretical problems, but the difficulty of such an exercise does not diminish its importance.[15] On this basis it would become possible to assess the economic rationale for investments in natural capital, including investments in soil and water conservation in hillside agriculture.

Second, policies to "reform the state" must include efforts to establish the necessary administrative capacity for environmental management. This includes the implementation of fiscal, regulatory, and investment policies. It would be sheer folly to imagine that market forces in the absence of state intervention will suffice to resolve the country's environmental crisis.

Third, at this stage several desirable areas for near-term policy initiatives are clear:

• The introduction of soil-conservation techniques, ecologically sound agricultural practices, and the restoration of vegetation cover (agroforestry) in hillside agriculture are urgent tasks. In the case of basic-grains producers this will require secure land tenure, well-designed monetary incentives to promote the adoption of these techniques by small producers, and timely access to appropriate technical assistance and inputs. This will in turn require a profound reorientation of institutions (including the Ministry of Agriculture and financial institutions), training and retraining of personnel, new designs for delivery systems, and redefinition of interaction with local agents.

• The administrative relationship of the state apparatus to territory must be restructured to take the watershed as the basis for soil and water conservation. This criterion is germane to the current state reforms promoting decentralization.

• There must be a coherent policy directed toward the coffee sector for maintaining or increasing the surface area of shade coffee nationally. The set of policies adopted should include measures to stimulate small agriculturalists to grow shade coffee and to enhance the sustainability of both cooperative and small-producer production, together with the appropriate policies for large growers.

• Land policy must embrace not only land tenure but also land use, through regulation and incentives. The design and effective implementation of urban land-use planning and zoning are urgent needs.

• Specific attention needs to be directed to the problem of energy resources, ranging from household and industrial use to the level of a national energy strategy. A coherent national development plan could strengthen the role of hydropower generation (based on environmentally sustainable practices), permitting a more sustainable balance between thermal, geothermal, and hydropower sources.

Finally, policy-oriented research on environmental problems must be accompanied by widespread dissemination of findings to stimulate public awareness and debate. A well-informed public, acting within a framework of democratic participation, provides crucial feedback to state interventions. Experience elsewhere convincingly demonstrates that without these political preconditions, government failures can be just as serious as market failures.

Notes

1. These include loss of biodiversity through destruction of tropical forest and fauna. This translates into a loss of many products (for example, timber, medicinal

sources, fertilizers and plant nutrients, etc.) and in many parts of the country the total destruction of tropical habitats.

2. When this process reaches a point of irreversibility it leads to what is termed "desertification," where the land left behind is of no value to humans and cannot be recuperated (Clarke 1993, pp. 1–4, 63).

3. Examples include disputes over surface-water bodies such as in Lake Jocotal; conflict over access to groundwater sources as in the struggle between the municipalities of Nauhuilingo and Sonsonate (El Pescadito de Oro); problems arising from contamination of public water sources as in Conchagua or Barrio Analco in Zacatecoluca; and conflict over uncontrolled flooding from uphill urban development in San Salvador as in Barrio Manzanares.

4. The World Bank's Natural Resources Management Study of January 1994 (World Bank 1994a) mentions in passing that existing deficits in surface-water supply are calculated on the basis of flawed and incomplete data, and thus tend to be underestimated. Only minimal mention is made of overdrafts on aquifers and of the continuing pressure on these groundwater sources from contamination and the paving over of infiltration areas in the greater San Salvador area. In a footnote the study acknowledges the lack of consideration of freshwater inputs for hydropower generation and coastal ecosystem maintenance. These problems do not make their way into the overall policy framework and project proposals.

5. The national fertility rate dropped 38 percent between 1978 and 1993 and further declines are expected. That fall, together with out-migration, is reflected by the changes in the intercensus (mean) annual population-growth rates, which dropped from 3.5 percent between 1961 and 1971 to 1.7 percent between 1971 and 1992. Current annual growth rates have been estimated by USAID (1994a) at 2.2 percent.

6. Previous legislation establishing "Ecological Protection Areas" for the purpose of guaranteeing aquifer surface recharge was simply ignored by housing and commercial developers (Barry 1994).

7. The precipitous drop in coffee prices also helped to open the way for lotification of coffee lands (Seligson et al. 1993).

8. Within San Salvador proper nearly 50 percent of the population cooks with firewood, and in the surrounding areas the figure is estimated to be 89 percent (Juárez 1993).

9. Part of this derives from the practice of using natural river flows to dilute contaminated water for reuse (Chavarría 1994).

10. "A livelihood comprises the capabilities, assets (stores, resources, claims and access) and activities required for a means of living: a livelihood is sustainable which can cope with and recover from stress and shocks, maintain or enhance its capabilities and assets, and provide sustainable livelihood opportunities for the next generation; and which contributes net benefits to other livelihoods at the local and global levels in the short and long term" (Chambers and Conway 1992, pp. 7–8). Following Chambers and Conway's definition of sustainable livelihoods, environmental sustainability concerns the external impact of livelihoods on other livelihoods at the local and larger level, immediately and over a longer time frame (for example, on-farm impacts and the downhill, regional, or national-level impacts over time). Social sustainability refers to whether a human unit (individual, household, or family) can maintain an adequate livelihood, and its internal capacity to withstand outside pressure (due to price changes, droughts, etc.).

11. The abandonment of cotton production in El Salvador is attributable in part to the "pesticide treadmill": Large doses of agrochemicals created pest resistance, demanding increased spraying, which raised production costs.

12. The price of firewood has increased from 400 percent to 1,200 percent over the last 10 years. Meanwhile, rural families in these areas must spend four to five times longer to haul water to their homes (Juárez 1993; USAID 1993c).

13. Due to inconsistent data it is impossible to establish precisely the magnitude of these trends. See Chapter 10 for discussion.

14. Current debates on energy strategies reflect a lack of consciousness of environmental concerns. Large discrepancies exist in estimates of the useful lifetime of the country's most important dam site, Cerrón Grande, varying from 12 to 112 years (Perdomo Lino 1994). Meanwhile, the government is in the early stages of planning the construction of another major dam (El Tigre) in an area where watersheds are seriously degraded. At the same time, privatization is stimulating interest in thermal (petroleum-based) generation, an option far more costly and highly vulnerable to fluctuations of international prices.

15. For discussions of practical problems in the economic valuation of environmental costs and benefits, see Repetto et al. (1989), Markandya (1991), and Munasinghe (1992). One theoretical problem of considerable potential importance in El Salvador is the sensitivity of conventional measures, based on willingness to pay, to the underlying distribution of income (see Boyce 1994).

12

Exports and
the Consolidation of Peace

Eva Paus

El Salvador's experience in the 1970s clearly demonstrates that export growth and economic growth are not sufficient to maintain peace in civil society. There can be no doubt that, after 12 years of civil war and the signing of the peace accords, significant improvements in distribution are key to the medium-term consolidation of peace. An *inclusive* distribution of the fruits of growth provides the link between export and economic growth and peace consolidation. Civil society will become more harmonious as poverty is reduced and income is distributed more equally.

In Chapter 8, Pastor and Conroy argue convincingly that there is no necessary trade-off between improved equality and economic growth. On the contrary, they can be mutually reinforcing, and in the case of El Salvador it is imperative that they be if social peace is to hold. To that end, it is critical that economic and export growth generate productive employment at livable incomes, and that government policies permit and foster inclusive growth.

To be sure, the export sector is but one element in the pursuit of sustained peace. Production for the domestic market, especially (but not limited to) the production of basic grains, government investment in infrastructure and social services, and a more extended social safety net all play a vital role in reducing poverty and increasing gainful employment. Yet, in a more open economy the export sector occupies a pivotal position in the generation of economic growth and, therefore, in the consolidation of peace.

The inability to generate new sources of foreign exchange was one of the main shortcomings of the import-substituting industrialization (ISI) model that was followed on a national and regional scale for most of the last 30 years. Starting in 1989, the Salvadoran government adopted structural adjustment measures with the goal of achieving a different and dynamic insertion of El Salvador's economy into the world economy. Increased exports were to provide the basis for renewed economic growth.

247

Reduction and simplification of tariff rates and market determination of exchange rates were intended to lead to a more efficient allocation of resources within and toward the tradeable-goods sector and thus to make the export sector the driving force of renewed economic growth.

Structural adjustment policies foster a surge in imports with a decline in tariffs, while export growth lags behind because of the time needed to acquire competitiveness. El Salvador is no exception in this regard. Figure 12.1 shows the surge in imports after 1989, while exports increased only slowly. To be sure, nontraditional exports (NTX) rose rapidly, but they started from such a low base that they could not keep up with higher imports. El Salvador's experience differed from that of many countries undergoing structural adjustment, in that rising imports were fueled and financed by the influx of foreign aid and, above all, by private remittances. The large foreign exchange inflow financed, and in this sense created, the trade deficit. This enabled the economy to grow at respectable rates in the midst of structural adjustment, avoiding the economic recession that often accompanies adjustment policies elsewhere.

Yet the underlying macroeconomic basis for El Salvador's growth remains insecure because remittances, and not export growth, have provided the underpinnings of growth in the last years. In the next few years, remittances and foreign aid may continue to grow, taper off gradually, or drop precipitously, but in the long run they will certainly prove to be temporary. When—not if—foreign aid and remittances decline, the economy will return to the stop-and-go cycles induced by foreign exchange scarcity and availability, unless a competitive and diversified export sector has

Figure 12.1   Merchandise Exports and Imports, 1980–1993

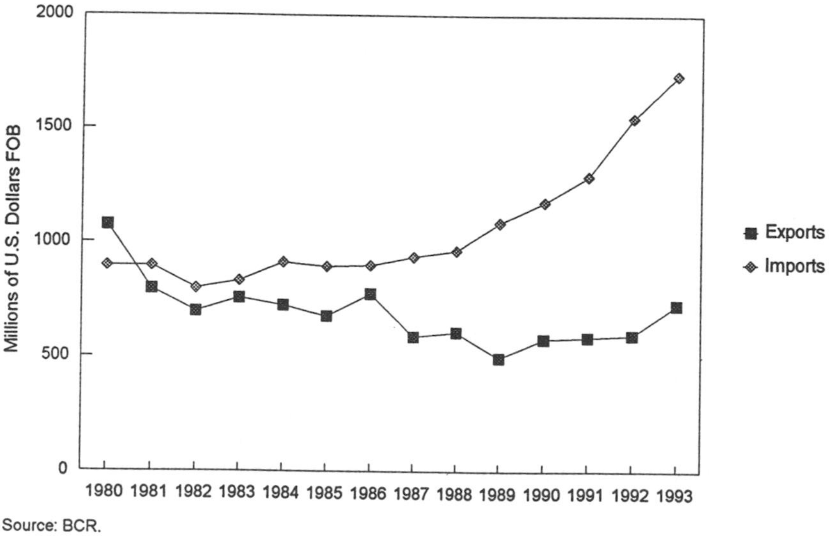

Source: BCR.

been developed to serve as a dynamic generator of foreign exchange. For that to materialize, however, the grace period provided by remittances and foreign aid has to be used expeditiously for economic restructuring to make production more efficient and competitive internationally, as well as to redress directly the distributional inequities that lead to extreme poverty and undermine long-run growth.

The new development model has to be based not only on nontraditional export growth (NTEG), but also on investment, both private and public. Together NTEG and investment will reduce the economy's dependence on the vagaries of the international coffee market and provide the basis for sustained economic growth, the benefits of which can be widely distributed.

The interaction between nontraditional export growth and investment in determining economic growth is important and complex. A large body of literature emphasizes the direct impact of export growth on economic growth, stressing higher productivity in the export sector and spillover effects for the rest of the economy (see, for example, Ram 1987; Balassa 1983; Feder 1983). Other economists highlight the importance of NTEG as a medium for higher imports of intermediate and capital goods. Not only do these contribute directly to ongoing capital accumulation, but—through embodied technology—they also allow for higher productivity growth (see, for example, Grossman and Helpman 1991; Esfahani 1991). In an extensive cross-country empirical study, Levine and Renelt (1992) found persuasive support for the argument that investment is the key route by which export growth leads to higher economic growth.[1] There is also an important feedback loop from investment to NTEG. For nontraditional exports to grow they have to be competitive in the international market. Through the generation of productivity increases, investment plays a key role in the achievement of such competitiveness.

The development of a competitive and dynamic export sector is one of the major challenges facing the Salvadoran economy today. This chapter analyzes the prospects for meeting that challenge and the key elements necessary to make exports a basis for future inclusive economic growth. After a brief description of El Salvador's trade structure in the next section, the second section analyzes the determinants of Salvadoran export growth. In the third section we discuss policies for effective structural adjustment so that export and economic growth will contribute to the consolidation of peace in El Salvador. The conclusions summarize the main dilemmas and challenges in this pursuit.

A Profile of El Salvador's Trade Sector

The main feature of El Salvador's export sector over the last decade has been a dramatic decline in the level and share of coffee exports, accompanied by a substantial increase in nontraditional exports. Exports to the Central American Common Market (CACM) have exhibited the most dynamic performance. Exports of manufactured goods, most of which are sold in the CACM, have grown rapidly, whereas exports of nontraditional agricultural goods have stagnated. Finally, *maquila* exports (that is, goods from export-processing zones) have risen considerably, too.

El Salvador's heavy dependence on coffee as the principal export commodity has long meant that fluctuations in the international coffee price have a decisive influence on overall export revenues and thus economic growth. During the 1980s this mono-export dependency had a disastrous impact on the country's merchandise exports. The volume of coffee exports fluctuated widely, partly in response to deteriorating prices and partly as a result of the abandonment of coffee-growing areas during the civil war. Export value declined from $1.075 billion in 1980 to $498 million in 1989. International coffee prices followed a steep, fairly steady downward trend, especially after 1986. The price per kilogram declined from a high of $4.56 in 1977 to a low of $1.21 in 1992. As a result, the share of coffee in total export value declined from nearly 60 percent in 1980 to less than 30 percent in 1993.

The performance of the other traditional exports has been varied. Exports of sugar and shrimp have fluctuated substantially around a basically stagnant level. Cotton exports have plummeted due to ecological destruction caused by the overuse of pesticides, and to the impacts of land reform and the civil war.

With the contraction of the Central American Common Market in the early 1980s, nontraditional exports declined. Yet, in contrast to traditional exports, they regained momentum after 1986. This growth was based principally on nontraditional manufactured exports (NTMX), as nontraditional agricultural exports (NTAX) showed little dynamism (see Figure 12.2). The key was nontraditional exports to the CACM, which grew rapidly, especially after 1990. Between 1990 and 1993, intra–Central American trade as a whole doubled, and Salvadoran NTX to the region jumped from $175 million to $310 million in 1993, which corresponds to roughly 70 percent of all NTX. In contrast, Salvadoran exports to non-CACM markets exhibited slow growth, particularly after 1989. Exports to the United States amounted to $218 million in 1993.

Dada Sánchez (1994) shows that the manufactured exports with the highest revealed comparative advantage in the late 1980s were pharmaceutical products, paper and cardboard, textiles and clothing articles, and shoes.[2] Table 12.1 confirms the importance of these products among the country's nontraditional exports. It also shows that, with the exception of textile and clothing products, manufactured exports are geared primarily to the CACM. Nontraditional agricultural exports, in contrast, go primarily to non-CACM countries, but their share in total NTX is small. There is no

Figure 12.2 Nontraditional Exports by Product Type and Destination, 1981–1993 (In U.S.$ millions)

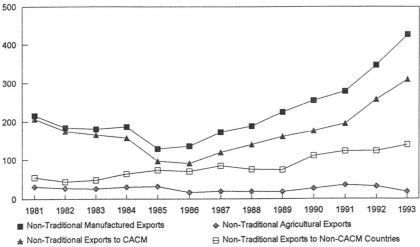

Non-Traditional Manufactured Exports ◆ Non-Traditional Agricultural Exports
▲ Non-Traditional Exports to CACM ⊟ Non-Traditional Exports to Non-CACM Countries

Source: BCR.

doubt that El Salvador's exports have become more diversified since the second half of the 1980s, in terms of product composition as well as market destination. Yet rising exports in a particular product line are not necessarily a reflection of broad-based competitiveness in that rubric when they are heavily dominated by one firm, as is the case for shoes, towels, and cardboard cartons.

In addition to manufactured exports to the CACM, maquila exports have been a dynamic source of export revenue in recent years (see Table 12.2). These consist principally of clothing items for the U.S. market. As in many other developing countries, maquila exports are recorded under exports of services rather than merchandise. Thus, they are not included in the figures discussed earlier. The gross value of maquila exports increased from $80 million in 1989 to $278 million in 1993, the equivalent of 16 percent and 40 percent of total merchandise exports in those years. Maquila assembly has been an important source of full-time employment for women, with total employment rising from 1,281 in 1985 to 10,771 in 1993. Yet, as in maquila operations in other countries, local sourcing is low, and thus the indirect employment effects are small. Domestic value added constitutes only around 25 percent of the export value.[3] In comparison, domestic value added for nontraditional exports is estimated to be 60 percent (Abrego 1994, p. 16).

With the elimination of nontariff barriers to imports and the reduction of tariff rates after 1989, imports have been rising rapidly (see Table 12.3). Whereas all import categories have witnessed substantial increases, the

Table 12.1   Structure of Nontraditional Exports, by Destination and Product, 1992 and 1993

	Product share in total NTX (%)		Non-CACM share in product exports (%)	
	1992	1993	1992	1993
Total	100.0	100.0	32.4	31.0
Honey	0.7	0.5	88.3	77.6
Fresh or dried fruit	0.5	0.6	99.9	99.9
Instant coffee	0.6	0.3	76.7	74.1
Sesame seeds	2.7	1.6	99.0	92.5
Sweets	1.3	1.6	2.7	3.1
Snack food	4.2	2.9	1.4	1.9
Gas oil, diesel	0.0	0.1	0.0	100.0
Lubricating oil	0.2	0.1	0.0	23.1
Medicine	7.8	7.5	29.4	30.9
Cosmetics	1.1	1.0	3.2	0.5
Soap	1.1	1.5	4.7	4.6
Detergent	2.2	2.0	0.0	0.0
Insecticide	1.5	1.2	11.0	14.1
Toilet paper	1.4	1.6	0.5	0.0
Cardboard cartons	6.4	6.6	27.8	30.6
Cotton thread	4.9	3.1	52.6	54.8
Synthetic textiles	4.0	3.7	34.1	28.0
Clothing	5.6	3.3	67.5	70.0
Sheets, towels, etc.	3.1	3.0	62.8	67.1
Shoes	3.3	3.0	16.5	24.3
Aluminum products	3.1	1.5	15.1	36.6
Agricultural tools	1.2	0.9	18.2	17.1
Refrigerators	1.5	1.4	0.0	0.0
Wires and cables	0.6	1.7	18.0	31.2
Other	41.0	42.7	30.7	18.2
Total (millions of U.S. dollars)	380.2	448.3	380.2	448.3

Source: BCR.

rise in capital-goods imports since 1990 is of particular importance. A decomposition by sector of demand shows, however, that only one-third of capital-goods imports went to the tradeable-goods sector (industry and agriculture). The principal destination for capital-goods imports was transportation (vehicles of various types and uses), with a share of around 45 percent.

The Determinants of Export Growth

The Structure of Incentives

Between 1989 and 1993 the share of exports of goods and nonfactor services in GDP varied between 13 and 15 percent. Over this period relative

Table 12.2 Indicators of Maquila Performance, 1985–1993

	1985	1986	1987	1988	1989	1990	1991	1992	1993
Employment	1,281	596	1,407	3,221	4,200	5,478	6,117	8,081	10,771
Investment (millions of U.S. dollars)	0.4	0.6	0.9	4.0	7.9	10.0	11.6	16.1	25.6
Net foreign exchange earnings (millions of U.S. dollars)	2.2	3.5	5.0	12.7	19.4	29.2	47.2	58.6	62.7

Source: PRIDEX.

Table 12.3 Structure of Imports, 1980–1993

	1980	1985	1989	1990	1991	1992	1993
Millions of U.S. dollars CIF							
Consumer goods	306.7	258.8	294.6	398.8	372.7	489.0	522.0
Intermediate goods	544.4	544.8	577.2	629.2	710.0	778.0	825.4
Capital goods	110.6	157.7	279.7	234.5	323.3	431.0	565.0
Total imports	961.7	961.3	1,161.3	1,262.5	1,406.0	1,699.0	1,912.2
Percentage distribution							
Consumer goods	31.9	26.9	25.4	31.6	26.5	28.8	27.3
Intermediate goods	56.6	56.7	49.7	49.8	50.5	45.8	43.2
Capital goods	11.5	16.4	24.1	18.6	23.0	25.4	29.5
Total	100	100	100	100	100	100	100
Percentage distribution of capital-goods imports by sector of demand							
Industry				30.3	27.6	28.2	30.2
Transportation				43.7	46.0	47.7	45.6
Agriculture				3.8	3.4	2.7	1.9
Construction				3.6	3.6	3.6	5.3
Other				18.6	19.4	17.8	17.1
Total				100	100	100	100

Source: BCR.

prices moved in favor of the nontradeable-goods sector. However, if relative prices had remained constant, the share of exports would have risen over the period as a result of considerable growth of export volumes in some categories, notably maquila exports. The performance of the non-traditional-export sector was affected by an incentive structure still biased against exports, the absence of productivity growth, declining real wages, a revitalization of the CACM, and imperfect knowledge about markets outside the CACM. The performance of the traditional-export sector was strongly affected by the decline in coffee prices.[4]

The exchange rate and trade taxes/subsidies play a critical role in determining relative prices, and with that the incentive structure for selling in the domestic market versus exporting. The evolution of the exchange rate determines the relative price of tradeables to nontradeables and is particularly important for the competitiveness of nontraditional exports in non-CACM markets. If the real exchange rate appreciates, then the prices of nontradeable goods are rising faster than the prices of tradeable goods, and producers have an incentive to expand output in the nontradeable sector. The structure of export tariffs and subsidies, on the other hand, shapes relative prices within the tradeable-goods sector between the import-competing sector and exports.

If the export sector is to play a central role in economic growth, then the anti-export bias of the ISI period has to be eliminated. In other words, the real exchange rate should not appreciate from its equilibrium value (whatever it might be), and the tariff and subsidy structure should be neutral between sales in the domestic market and sales abroad.

The exchange rate and trade policies pursued by the Cristiani government were intended to come closer to such a neutral incentive structure. Between 1989 and 1990 exchange rates were unified and then liberalized. Yet, the real exchange rate has become increasingly overvalued. The large nominal devaluation of the colón in 1990 led to only a temporary real devaluation against the U.S. dollar. By the end of 1993 the colón had again appreciated against the dollar by 21.5 percent in real terms. Salvadoran policymakers had to learn the same painful lessons about exchange-rate determination as many of their Latin American neighbors: A market-determined exchange rate will equilibrate the foreign exchange market and the balance of payments, but it will not necessarily maintain the competitiveness of the export sector. When capital inflows and remittances are the key determinants in the foreign exchange market, liberalization of the exchange rate will lead to an appreciation of the real exchange rate. The non-tradeable-goods sector becomes relatively more attractive for producers, and exporters' competitiveness in the international market declines.

The exchange-rate system in El Salvador after 1990 is more accurately characterized as a "dirty float" than as completely market determined. By sterilizing some of the inflow of foreign exchange through certificates of monetary stabilization (CEMS; for details see Chapter 9), the central bank of El Salvador has been successful in preventing an appreciation of the nominal exchange rate, but not of the real exchange rate. In comparison to 1988, the last year before restructuring policies were adopted, the relative price ratio between nontradeables and tradeables (agriculture and industry) was 20 percent higher in 1993. The price developments in the tradeable-goods sector were dominated by the low price increases in agriculture. Between 1988 and 1993 the cumulative increase in the GDP deflator was 127 percent for the broad agricultural sector (*agropecuario*), 208 percent for industry, and 214 percent for the total nontradeable-goods sector.

With respect to trade policies, the Cristiani government sought to reduce the anti-export bias implicit in the tariff/subsidy structure of the 1980s by lowering tariffs rather than increasing subsidies. After 1989, import procedures were simplified, various licenses and permits were eliminated, and the top tariff rate as well as the tariff range were reduced sharply. Between 1989 and 1994 the number of tariff rates declined from 25 to five, and the tariff range was reduced from 0–290 percent to 5–20 percent. The revitalization of the Central American Common Market (which was never abandoned formally), starting with a joint declaration of Central American presidents in Antigua, Guatemala, in June 1990, has led to the adoption of a common external tariff with a range from 5 to 20 percent.[5]

On the export side, the previous complex and ineffective scheme of export-promoting policies was replaced with a new, simplified system in early 1990. Inputs used in assembly production for exports (temporal admission regime, primarily for free-trade zones) are exempted from tariffs. A drawback scheme was established to compensate exporters for the remaining import duties. It entitles exporters to a cash payment equivalent to presently 6 percent of the Free on Board (FOB) value of exports (reduced from the original 8 percent).[6] And since the introduction of a value-added tax, exporters are also eligible for a reimbursement of these indirect taxes.

All three policies are permissible under the regulations of GATT, which El Salvador joined in December 1990. Although all exporters are eligible for the reimbursement of the value-added tax, only producers exporting to outside the CACM qualify for the drawback scheme. Apparently there are substantial delays, however, in the actual delivery of both compensating payments. A recent World Bank document (1993c, p. 30) estimates that over 30 percent of the accumulated value of duty drawbacks has not been reimbursed.

Abrego (1994) analyzes the extent to which the trade reforms have reduced the anti-export bias and shifted the incentives in favor of exporting. He calculates the relative prices of selling in the domestic market, selling to the CACM, and exporting to outside the CACM on a product level for 1993. Although the value of the relative price ratio changes depending on the indicator used (nominal protection, real effective protection, real effective exchange rate), they all indicate the same trends: (1) The anti-export bias of the prereform years has been reduced substantially, given that export incentives as a percentage of export value are basically unchanged and tariffs have been reduced. Nevertheless, the overall structure is still not neutral. (2) The effective rate of protection is higher for consumer goods than for intermediate and capital goods, thus providing a disincentive for domestic production of the latter. (3) There is considerable heterogeneity in the ratios of domestic to export prices for different products. Regardless of the type of measure, the incentive structure for agricultural and fishing products is basically neutral. The same is true for chemical products and cardboard for non-CACM exports. What is surprising is that some of the most successful nontraditional-export products showed the highest anti-export bias as measured by relative prices: textiles, shoes, and especially clothing. This suggests that these sectors have excessive protection and/or that different types of goods are produced for the domestic and the foreign markets.

It must be remembered, however, that the manufacturing sector is very heterogeneous in terms of productivity and competitiveness, so that "excessive protection" might not apply to substantial segments of a given industry. Furthermore, Abrego's calculations probably overstate the degree of protection for sales in the domestic market; there is a substantial difference between the legal and the actual tariff rates because of evasions and exemptions. In the late 1980s the average tariff rate was 23 percent, the import-weighted legal tariff rate was 11.4 percent, but the actual tariff rate (collected tariff revenue over import value) was only 6.5 percent (World Bank 1989a, p. 34).

In summary, the structure of incentives in El Salvador in 1995 does not provide sufficient support for a strategy in which the nontraditional-export sector is a key driving force. Changes in the tariff structure have reduced the bias against exports, in some cases making the incentive structure neutral between domestic sales and exports and in others maintaining a preference for the domestic market. At the same time, the development of the real exchange rate has turned the terms of trade against the tradeable-goods sector as a whole. Before addressing the question of whether and how the incentive structure can be changed, we will discuss the importance of other factors in determining export growth and competitiveness. These relate to costs, productivity, and market knowledge in the widest sense of the term.

Wage Developments

A real appreciation of the exchange rate indicates a loss in international competitiveness, on the assumption that the price indices used in the calculation of the real exchange rate are representative of the overall cost increases in the two countries. Because labor is an important cost factor, the development of labor costs can be used as an alternative indicator of cost performance.[7] Thus, we calculate a wage-adjusted real exchange rate (RER)—the nominal exchange rate adjusted for wage changes in El Salvador and the United States. Average wages for the total private sector were taken as a proxy for U.S. wages (United States Government 1994, p. 320). For Salvadoran wages two proxies were used: average wages for social security affiliates in the private sector (RER wage adjusted) and minimum wages for industrial and service workers in San Salvador (RER minimum-wage adjusted).

A comparison of the inflation-adjusted real exchange rate with the wage-adjusted real exchange rate reveals a dramatic divergence between the two (see Figure 12.3) since 1980. Following Latin American convention, a fall in the real exchange-rate index indicates an appreciation of the colón. In the first half of the 1980s the inflation-adjusted real exchange rate appreciated much more dramatically than the wage-adjusted real exchange rate. Following the nominal depreciation of the colón by 100 percent in 1985, the inflation-adjusted real exchange rate depreciated by nearly 50 percent. That depreciation had basically been eroded by 1989. The wage-adjusted real exchange rate, in contrast, depreciated by nearly 80 percent and remained fairly steady until 1989. Finally, with the depreciation of 1989–1990 and the subsequent dirty float, the inflation-adjusted real exchange rate repeated the earlier pattern, in that the initial real depreciation eroded quickly. The further depreciation of the wage-adjusted real exchange rate was eroded partially, but not fully, after 1990. In 1993 the inflation-adjusted real exchange rate was lower than in 1985, when it had been at the lowest point during the last 13 years. The wage-adjusted real exchange rate, in contrast, was still 80 to 90 percent higher than in 1985.

The typical economic story about the link between real wages and exchange-rate changes is that a real *devaluation* leads to a decline in real wages, as nominal wage increases are being held down in the aftermath of a nominal devaluation (see, for example, Pastor 1987). How, then, is it possible that in El Salvador real wages have been declining since 1980 while the real exchange rate was actually appreciating, and a million people left the country?

Although there are no detailed labor-market studies for all of the 1980s, the answer is fairly straightforward. Declining or stagnant economic growth

Figure 12.3   Inflation and Wage-Adjusted Real Exchange Rates, 1980–1993
(1985 = 100)

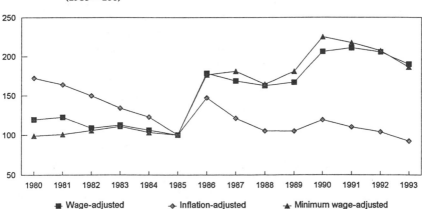

Source: See text.

per capita throughout the 1980s, combined with substantial internal migration due to the civil war, led to an excess supply of labor. The very same economic and political conditions gave little clout to unions. The minimum wage is set by the government, and as such it is an administered price reflecting not only the state of the labor market, but also the government's political priorities. Table 12.4 gives the development of various minimum wages and of the real average wage of workers in the formal private sector who were social security affiliates. It shows that after an initial widening, the ratio of wages of social security affiliates to minimum wages has held fairly steady at around 2.4 to 2.5. That suggests that minimum wages do play an indicative role in overall wage setting.

The fact that nominal wages increased much more slowly than output prices is one reason that companies could increase nontraditional exports in spite of adverse movement of the inflation-adjusted real exchange rate. That seems to have been particularly true for exports outside the CACM, principally textile and clothing items. In 1990 the wage level in those industries was substantially below the average in manufacturing, and real wages in clothing dropped by 30 percent between 1990 and 1993, in comparison to 10 percent for industry as a whole.[8]

The decline in real wages also must have played an important role in the survival of the import-competing sectors. The swift opening on the import side in conjunction with the overvaluation of the exchange rate is bound to lead to a decline of manufacturing value added. Firms that have become highly inefficient behind the protective walls of ISI are forced out under the onslaught of foreign competition. Concomitantly, the more competitive sectors are hampered in their expansion by the overvalued exchange rate as well as the time and other changes needed to gear production toward the international market. This has happened in a number of Latin American countries, where the competitive pressures of rapid import liberalization were greatly intensified by an overvalued exchange rate.[9]

Yet such a process of relative deindustrialization has not happened in El Salvador. By all accounts, bankruptcies have been negligible, and the manufacturing sector actually has increased its share of national output after 1989. The explanation for this is threefold: First, as noted earlier, effectively applied tariff rates were much lower than the official ones; second, there was considerable "water" in the earlier tariffs due to competition within the CACM; and third, decreases in real wages kept costs down.

Productivity Developments

In calculating a real exchange rate that adjusts for relative labor costs it would be more appropriate to use unit labor costs rather than wages. Unit labor costs reflect average wages per worker divided by productivity.

Table 12.4 Daily Real Minimum Wages, 1980–1993 (1985 = 100)

	1980	1981	1982	1983	1984	1985	1986	1987	1988	1989	1990	1991	1992	1993
Agricultural workers	198.3	172.7	154.6	136.7	122.3	100.0	114.0	93.4	90.5	82.9	74.2	73.1	68.3	68.5
Harvest workers														
coffee	198.3	172.7	154.5	136.7	122.3	100.0	75.8	60.7	51.0	49.1	40.5	41.6	37.4	31.5
sugar	163.5	172.7	154.6	136.7	122.3	100.0	75.8	60.7	51.1	50.6	41.6	42.8	38.5	32.4
cotton	157.3	172.7	154.6	136.7	122.3	100.0	75.8	60.7	51.1	49.2	40.6	41.7	37.5	31.6
Workers in agroindustry														
coffee	198.3	172.7	154.6	136.7	122.3	100.0	75.8	60.7	57.6	52.3	43.1	44.3	39.8	38.4
sugar	198.3	172.7	154.6	136.7	122.3	100.0	75.8	60.7	62.8	59.2	48.8	50.1	45.1	47.0
cotton	198.3	172.7	154.6	136.7	122.3	100.0	75.8	60.7	62.8	59.2	48.8	50.1	45.1	47.0
Industry and services														
San Salvador	157.9	146.2	130.8	115.6	114.4	100.0	86.7	70.1	66.0	59.7	54.0	53.0	53.7	53.7
Other areas	155.8	145.2	129.9	114.8	115.8	100.0	82.4	66.3	66.2	61.5	56.1	55.4	56.4	58.3
Commerce														
San Salvador	157.9	146.2	130.8	115.6	116.1	100.0	86.3	70.1	66.0	59.7	54.0	53.0	53.7	53.7
Other areas	155.8	145.2	129.9	114.8	116.0	100.0	82.4	66.3	66.2	61.5	56.1	55.3	56.4	58.3
Average monthly real wages for social security affiliates (private sector)	130.3	120.4	127.0	113.8	112.9	100.0	86.6	75.2	67.1	64.5	59.1	54.6	54.1	52.7
Ratio of average monthly wage in manufacturing (social security affiliates) to the minimum wage in San Salvador	1.8	1.9	2.2	2.3	2.2	2.3	2.3	2.5	2.4	2.5	2.5	2.5	2.4	2.3

Sources: Daily real minimum wage calculated on the basis of MIPLAN data; average monthly real wages of social security affiliates from IDB 1993a, p. 19, and IMF 1994b, p. 40.

Thus, what happens to unit labor costs depends on the development of wages on the one hand and productivity on the other.

Information on productivity developments in El Salvador in the 1980s is scarce. An IDB study (1993a, pp. 68–69) provides a graph showing fluctuating labor productivity in the industrial sector in the 1980s. It falls dramatically from 1980 to 1983, rises until 1989, and drops again from 1989 to 1991. The study concludes that productivity was falling overall, but that real wages were falling even faster, so that unit labor costs declined. Measuring total factor productivity in the reduced private sector (GDP excluding agriculture, housing, and the public sector), Harberger (1993a) finds continuous and considerable total factor productivity growth between 1982 and 1991. The calculated productivity growth occurred, however, in the context of a declining capital stock in the first half of the 1980s and a stagnant capital stock in the second half of the 1980s. Thus, productivity growth was not the reflection of increased investments and incorporation of new technology, but rather of reorganizations of the production process. In any case, both time series point in the same direction: to a decline in unit labor costs.

The wage-adjusted real exchange rate calculated earlier is an imperfect measure of cost developments. If productivity data had been included, the value of the index would have changed. With low but positive productivity growth in the United States and stagnant productivity in El Salvador, the overall trend toward depreciation of the labor-cost-adjusted real exchange rate would not have been reversed. Thus, insofar as Salvadoran exports retained their competitiveness despite appreciation, this was because real wages declined so dramatically.

The mirror image of declining real wages and a declining/stagnant capital stock, combined with an increase in output, is of course a rise in the rate of profit. The same Harberger study shows that the return to capital as a percentage of the capital stock increased steadily from 7 percent in 1980 to 33 percent in 1991 (the last year included in the study). These are average figures, and more disaggregated data are not available. It is likely that companies in the exporting sectors did not experience such a dramatic increase in the profit rate, because they have to operate in more competitive markets. If so, companies in the nontradeable-goods sector increased their profits even more, with relative prices moving in their favor, and external competition—by definition—virtually nonexistent.

Knowledge of Markets

Exports to the CACM have expanded much more rapidly than exports to the rest of the world, and they started doing so in the mid-1980s, before the restructuring policies were adopted. In most cases, the inflation-adjusted real exchange rate appreciated even more against the currencies of the other CACM member countries than against the U.S. dollar. Although the real-wage decline helped to keep costs down for CACM exports, there is no doubt that prior knowledge of the Central American Common Market and the exporting success there in the 1970s contributed to the renewal of CACM exports in the mid-1980s.

The flip side of the argument is that lack of information about other foreign markets deters domestic producers from exporting, or more precisely, from considering exporting to be a serious option for them. Salvadoran firms, especially—but not exclusively—small and medium-size ones, have indicated in surveys that their lack of information about foreign markets and export channels constitutes a serious obstacle to exporting. In addition to market ignorance, lack of knowledge about quality control and technical requirements are considered equally important deterrents (see, for example, Dada Sánchez 1994).

Effective Structural Adjustment: In Pursuit of Inclusive Export Growth

The structural adjustment measures implemented from 1989 onward have not made the export sector the growth pole of the economy. They have not led to a considerable shift of resources from the nontradeable- to the tradeable-goods sectors, nor to a restructuring of the tradeable-goods sector itself. The analysis in the previous section highlighted four important factors that have to be addressed if the export sector is to grow and if growth is to be inclusive.

The first factor is the "Dutch disease" phenomenon that, driven by large remittances and aid inflows, has maintained the bias against exports.[10] The second factor is the decline in real wages, which has allowed companies to maintain their competitiveness, yet contributed to a declining living standard of a large part of the population. At the same time, there can be no doubt that this decline has been counteracted to some extent by the influx of remittances. The third factor is the absence of productivity growth based on new technology and production processes. And the fourth factor is the lack of knowledge among producers, especially among the small and medium-size ones, of international markets, export channels, quality-control standards, and best-practice technologies.

Unless these trends are reversed, sustained and inclusive export-linked growth cannot be achieved. In our discussion of policies to reverse these trends, our starting point is the premise that political stability is key to economic growth, and that economic growth is not a sufficient condition to achieve political stability. Economic growth accompanied by growing distributional disparities and the marginalization of significant sectors of the population might lead to unrest in civil society and political instability. The latter, in turn, has negative consequences for economic growth.

The Salvadoran civil war in the 1980s made it amply clear that, in times of political instability, the uncertainty and risk attached to investment can become so large that most producers shy away from significant outlays on long-term capital investment. Political stability is thus a sine qua non for renewed investment and growth. A faithful implementation of the peace accords will go a long way in the establishment of goodwill and trust. Nevertheless, widespread poverty and unproductive employment, combined with the memories and divisions of the long armed conflict, require political leadership to strive for a greater degree of tolerance and harmony in civil society. Political leadership is required to bring about a consensus that inclusiveness must be a key element in renewed growth, and conversely that exclusion is anathema to maintaining political stability. To foster this consensus requires deliberate policies to increase real incomes in the various sectors of society. As will be discussed in more detail, these can mean real-wage increases in the context of productivity gains, and special policies to help small-scale producers face the risks of producing in a more competitive environment.

Changing the Incentive Structure: The Challenge of the Real Exchange Rate

In order to improve the competitive potential of the Salvadoran economy, policies must aim at maintaining a stable macroeconomic environment with a manageable fiscal deficit, a low rate of inflation, a stable exchange rate, and—most important for our discussion here—a relative price structure that does not discriminate against exports. The challenge is how to bring about a real depreciation of the exchange rate and how to make the incentives neutral between import-competing activities and exporting. The first point addresses the real exchange rate, and the second point the relative incentive structure embodied in trade tariffs and subsidies. We discuss each of them in turn.

Analysts of the manufactured-export success in developing countries disagree on a number of issues, such as the importance of controlled government intervention and the timing of import liberalization. Yet regardless of the economic paradigm to which they adhere, these analysts generally agree on one point: the critical importance of getting the exchange rate "right" (see, for example, Helleiner 1994; Leamer et al. 1994; World Bank 1991c, 1993c). This means having a fairly stable real exchange rate that restructures the economy toward the tradeable-goods sector. The South Korean government, for example, while deliberately distorting market prices in a number of different areas, did not allow an exchange rate with a bias against the tradeable-goods sector.

In El Salvador the inflow of remittances and aid has been very important in raising the living standards of the recipients. But they have clearly been a mixed blessing in their influence on the real exchange rate. Whereas they have raised the demand for tradeables/imports, they have raised the demand for nontradeables even more, thus leading to the relative price shift in favor of the nontradeable-goods sector (that is, real-exchange-rate appreciation) discussed earlier.

The increase in international reserves during the last couple of years has been helpful in preventing an appreciation of the nominal exchange rate, but sterilization was not on a large enough scale to prevent an appreciation of the real exchange rate. Sterilization cannot and should not be on a scale to maintain the real exchange rate, because of the limited market for CEMs in the short run, the implications for central-bank losses, and the possibility that interest-rate increases could bring forth a capital inflow that would counteract the sterilization attempt. A return to fixed exchange rates with the par value to the U.S. dollar set low enough to imply a significant real devaluation will not work as long as the forces driving the present real appreciation persist.

The only way to change these underlying dynamics is through an increase in demand for U.S. dollars. The most propitious circumstance for increasing growth is if a devaluation of the colón is brought about by increasing the demand for dollars through greater imports of investment goods (which accounted for 30 percent of total Salvadoran imports in 1993). Investment goods are, after all, the key element in bringing about industrial restructuring and productivity growth. Here we are faced with an apparent sequencing problem: A real depreciation is important for inducing producers to orient their production toward exporting and thus to import capital goods to become more competitive; but it is increased capital-goods imports that would bring about a depreciation of the colón in the first place. An overvalued real exchange rate does cheapen the cost of capital-goods imports. Yet by itself this is unlikely to have the desired impact on investment, since private producers invest only if they are convinced that they can sell their output.

To solve this conundrum and provide the initial impetus for larger imports of machinery, Salvadoran policymakers must (1) deploy other policy measures to make private investment attractive in spite of the exchange-rate overvaluation, and (2) strengthen tax revenues to finance public investment. Policy measures to increase the incentives for private investment in the tradeable-goods sector include government investment in infrastructure (for example, transportation and electricity) and government investment in human capital to increase labor productivity. These policies should be complemented with others that aim at reducing or eliminating market and coordination failures in different information markets related to exporting, which will be discussed in more detail. Because some of these actions might not bear fruit quickly enough to stimulate investment in the export sector, serious consideration should be given to investment tax credits as a short-term measure.

In addition to "crowding in" private investment, public investment can increase demand for dollars (to cover the associated import needs) and thereby put downward pressure on the exchange rate. However, the exchange-rate impact will occur only if public investment is financed by domestic resources, rather than by external loans. This provides a further compelling reason to raise the tax coefficient from its very low level at present. An added advantage of domestic financing of public investment is, of course, that it does not impose the future burden of negative net transfers on debt.

Even if the policy goal of real exchange-rate devaluation cannot be achieved in the short run, the adoption of policies that run counter to this goal in the medium term can and should be avoided. Fixing the nominal exchange rate and renouncing any attempt at sterilization through monetary policy would be anathema to export-cum-investment-led growth.[11]

Changing the Incentive Structure: Tariffs and Subsidies

In addition to aiming for a real devaluation of the colón, getting the incentives for exports right also involves trade policies, that is, eliminating the remaining export bias implied by the existing tariff/subsidy structure. That can be achieved in one of two ways: by eliminating tariffs and subsidies completely, or by making sure that subsidies and tariffs provide equal incentives for selling domestically or abroad with a positive level of subsidies and tariffs.

The main argument in favor of the first alternative is that exposure to international prices and competition forces companies to increase productivity in order to survive and thrive in the more competitive environment. The counterargument is that it takes time to become competitive, that the achievement of dynamic competitive advantages—the incorporation of technological change—requires initial protection from full-blown international competition. In other words, the original idea behind infant-industry protection is still considered valid, but any protection has to be relatively low and finite in time.

There is no empirical evidence to suggest that in developing countries the elimination of tariffs and subsidies is necessary for industrialization and long-term growth (see, for example, Rodrik 1994). On this point, Helleiner (1994, p. 17) summarizes the results of 14 careful and detailed country studies as follows: "There is virtually no evidence in these country studies of any direct link between the overall degree of protectionism in the import regime (as opposed to liberalized imports solely for exports) and manufactured export growth."[12]

That does not mean that tariff levels are unimportant. The successful East Asian countries, for example, had lower average protection rates than the Latin American or African countries. But if lowering tariffs below a certain level runs counter to long-run growth, then the remaining tariff structure has to be balanced by export subsidies.

Certain export subsidies are not permissible under the regulations of GATT, and run the risk of facing countervailing duties from the importing country. However, some export subsidies that correct for domestic price distortions are explicitly sanctioned by GATT.

The Final Act of the Uruguay Round contains new stipulations regarding the legitimacy of various types of subsidies. The agreement distinguishes between "prohibited" subsidies, "actionable" subsidies, and "nonactionable" subsidies. Prohibited subsidies refer to those that are in some form contingent upon export performance or domestic content requirements. Actionable subsidies are those that cause serious prejudice to the interests of another member, where "serious prejudice" is presumed to exist when the total subsidy exceeds 5 percent of the product's value. Nonactionable subsidies involve subsidies to industrial research and "precompetitive development activity."

There are, however, important exceptions for developing countries. They are exempted from the presumption of serious prejudice, and prohibited export subsidies can be phased out over time: five years for subsidies linked to domestic content requirements and 8 to 10 years for subsidies related to export performance.[13] The rules governing the imposition of countervailing duties against subsidized imports are equally important. Of particular relevance are the special rules for developing countries that state that countervailing investigations will be terminated (or not even initiated) in cases where the injury is negligible (the import value constitutes less than 4 percent of the injured country's total imports).

These rules leave a wide margin of flexibility for the Salvadoran government to use subsidies, if it chooses to do so. First, drawback schemes and reimbursement of indirect taxes are still allowed under the Uruguay agreement. Second, export performance requirements, which have proven to be very useful in the case of the East Asian success stories as well as in Brazil and Mexico (Shapiro 1993), can still be used for the next eight to 10 years. Finally, any subsidies that involve support to industrial research are nonactionable, and they comprise a potentially large and important area of incentives.

Export subsidies are not terribly useful, however, if producers do not have swift access to imports. An inefficient customs process, with lots of red tape and willful delays, presently presents an important obstacle. The customs office must be streamlined and made efficient so that domestic producers can meet their export obligations on time.

Regional Integration and Free-Trade Associations

El Salvador is using different tariff and subsidy structures for trade with CACM member countries on the one hand, and nonmember countries on the other. We will discuss further why it is important to maintain that differentiation in the short run, and how future free-trade agreements with Mexico and eventually the Western Hemisphere should be used to "discipline" regional exporters so as to transform them into global exporters.

The main rationale for the establishment of the Central American Common Market in the early 1960s was that ISI could be successful only on a scale larger than that provided by the small Central American countries individually.[14] In the 1960s and 1970s the customs union was rather successful in increasing intraregional trade and stimulating industrialization. In the 1980s, however, the CACM collapsed for basically two reasons: First, there was no institutionalized mechanism to compensate for the rather unequal distribution of the costs and benefits of the CACM, with Nicaragua and Honduras running a chronic balance-of-trade deficit with the other member countries. Second, regional import substitution never advanced to the phase of extraregional exports, so that each country remained dependent on its traditional exports as the main source for foreign exchange. Thus when traditional-export revenues declined in the early 1980s, the regional trade imbalances could no longer be financed. Debts accumulated, arrears built up, and countries adopted unilateral actions to lower their imports through renewed tariffs and quotas.[15]

In contrast to the situation 30 years ago, the present revitalization of the CACM is very much embedded in the context of general economic opening and the promotion of export-linked growth. It is widely accepted now that import substitution and export-linked growth are not mutually exclusive strategies. Rather, they can reinforce each other, if the incentive structure is specified properly. Increasing the market size from 5 million (El Salvador) to 26 million (CACM) allows for economies of scale that the domestic market in many product lines simply does not provide. It also increases competitive pressures and the possibilities for product differentiation.

An analogous argument can of course be made for the benefits of production for the international market, in comparison to which the CACM is minuscule. What makes production for the regional market different from—and in the short run in some areas preferable to—production for the international market is that it allows for learning effects in production and exporting with the benefit of some external protection. In addition, the geographical proximity among the Central American countries bestows a certain degree of natural protection to trade within the area, especially in products for which long-distance transportation is relatively costly (see Siri 1984, 1994). At the same time, the scope for rent seeking and entrenchment of protection can be limited by intraregional competition and by a credible joint commitment to gradual further lowering of the common tariff.

Production for the regional market can thus be seen as the route to efficient import substitution, concomitantly as a learning experience in exports, and as a first and sometimes necessary step toward exporting to outside the region. In other words, successful regional integration is an important goal in itself, and at the same time a stepping stone toward larger hemispheric integration and increased nontraditional exports to the world market.

The facts that all CACM member countries have adopted a much lower common external tariff than before and that their production structures are fairly similar, reduces the risk of large trade diversion. At the same time, however, trade creation is not the only, and maybe not even the most important, potential benefit from regional integration.[16] The dynamic effects of integration are often more important. The main factor here is an increase in capital formation as a result of larger capital mobility among the CACM member countries or due to increased foreign investment from nonmember countries. Many analyses of the impact of NAFTA on the Mexican economy found foreign-investment inflows to be much more important than increases in trade (see, for example, Brown, Deardorff, and Stern 1991). Similarly, in the case of Spain, Kehoe (1992, cited in Preusse 1994) argues that the large influx of direct foreign investment has been the country's largest benefit from joining the European Common Market.

To increase the likelihood that the benefits of regional integration will materialize, the Central American countries need to adopt a number of important policy measures:

1. The institutional structure must be made more efficient and coherent, with a few effective supranational institutions substituting for the present proliferation of institutions with overlapping or unclear areas of authority, and with more direct links between top-level decisionmaking and policy implementation on the ground.

2. Remaining barriers to intraregional trade, especially nontariff barriers, have to be reduced and eliminated. Of particular importance is the elimination of trade barriers for agricultural products, given that natural-resource-based industrial exports offer a high potential for dynamic comparative advantage, and regional sourcing should be encouraged to foster that potential.

3. Improvements in the intraregional transportation network should be a high priority. Potential locational advantages will not be fully realized unless there is an efficient system of intraregional transportation and communication.

4. There is a need for greater policy coordination among member governments so as to maintain a stable and low rate of inflation. Policy coordination is also advisable in regard to the incentive structure for attracting foreign investment in order to circumvent damaging competition in that respect.

5. The effective rate of protection of intermediate and capital goods should be equal to that of consumer goods, to avoid biases against their

regional production and against the choice of more labor-intensive technologies.

Figure 12.4 shows the development of net exports of CACM member countries since 1970. Different member countries of the CACM might well feel different degrees of urgency to implement the policies recommended here, given the variation among them in the relative importance of CACM exports in total exports. Exports to the CACM are most important for El Salvador and Guatemala and least important for Costa Rica and Honduras. In 1992 the share of the CACM in total exports was 35.5 percent for El Salvador (27.7 percent in 1978), 30.5 percent for Guatemala (23.4 percent in 1978), 18.1 percent for Nicaragua (22.6 percent in 1978), 9.4 percent for Costa Rica (21.9 percent in 1978), and 6.3 percent for Honduras (8.2 percent in 1978).

The distribution of net trade deficits and surpluses in the 1990s has not been much different from what it was in the 1970s. Guatemala and Costa Rica have again run large surpluses, and Nicaragua and Honduras have had deficits. After a decade of large trade deficits with the CACM, El Salvador has been coming closer to balance. Thus, one cause of the previous contraction of the CACM has not been eliminated.

The potential for learning effects in production and exporting on a regional scale justifies the protection from external competition. Nevertheless, it is critical that protection be temporary and phased out over a specified

Figure 12.4   Net Exports of CACM Member Countries to CACM, 1970–1993

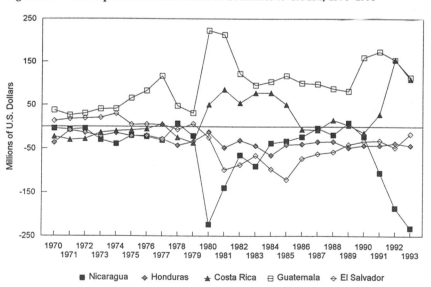

Source: Calculated from IMF Direction of Trade data tapes.

period so that producers are forced to become competitive not just regionally, but internationally as well. There are a number of ways to impose the discipline of a preannounced decline in protection. One candidate in the Salvadoran and Central American context is phased-in free trade with Mexico and possibly the Western Hemisphere.[17]

In January 1991 the Central American governments signed an agreement with Mexico in Tuxtla Gutiérrez to establish a free-trade zone by the end of 1996. Trade between El Salvador (and other Central American countries) and Mexico is currently very limited, with the exception of Mexican oil exports to the region.[18] At the same time, the gap in the level of development between Mexico and the Central American countries is sufficiently large to raise Central American fears of rapid deindustrialization if the doors are opened too rapidly to Mexican producers. NAFTA, however, considerably increases the pressure on Central American governments to negotiate a free-trade agreement with Mexico in order to avoid trade and investment diversion. Costa Rica's breakaway in the negotiations further intensifies the need for the Northern Triangle (El Salvador, Guatemala, and Honduras, more recently joined by Nicaragua) to come to a fairly swift, though not hasty, agreement with Mexico.[19]

Investment diversion resulting from NAFTA is at least as serious a concern for El Salvador as trade diversion. The latter would affect primarily clothing exports (Leamer et al. 1994; López 1993; United States International Trade Commission 1992). Because both Mexico and El Salvador enjoyed Generalized System of Preferences (GSP) status before the signing of NAFTA, and because many agricultural goods enter the United States tariff-free under GSP, trade diversion in agriculture is low. At the same time, NAFTA will erode the preference margin that El Salvador as a Caribbean Basin Economic Recovery Act (CBERA) beneficiary has enjoyed over Mexico. But the implications for El Salvador are not dramatic, for two reasons: First, El Salvador has taken little advantage of free access to the U.S. market under CBERA.[20] Second, most textile and clothing categories that are relevant for El Salvador have been excluded from CBERA since its inception in 1982.[21]

Trade diversion in the apparel sector will occur as a result of U.S. elimination of tariffs rather than quotas on Mexican textile and clothing exports.[22] El Salvador has never had any textile or clothing quotas on exports to the United States, with the exception of a quota on men's shirts established in 1994. Under the Final Act of the Uruguay Round, the Multifibre Agreement will be phased out over 10 years anyway. NAFTA parity for textiles and clothing for CBERA countries has been under consideration in the U.S. Congress, but whether such legislation will eventually be passed remains uncertain.[23]

Whereas the fallout from trade diversion will be relatively small for El Salvador, the diversion of foreign investment following NAFTA is potentially larger. The fear is that those foreign companies whose primary goal is to take advantage of low labor costs while having access to the U.S. market will now opt for Mexico rather than a Central American country. Given the very generous incentives that Central American countries already offer to foreign investors, there is little more these countries can do in that direction. By entering a free-trade agreement with Mexico, Central American countries can hope that a revitalized CACM will attract investment or coinvestment in projects that seek to take advantage of areawide sourcing, or others whose aim is to service the larger regional market.

Entering a free-trade agreement with Mexico in order to combat trade and investment diversion highlights the defensive nature of such an action from El Salvador's perspective. Yet it is crucial to recognize also the positive side: duty-free access to a market whose size is a multiple of the CACM. Even though El Salvador exports little to Mexico now, the certainty of unrestricted market access might lead to the development of larger exports in the future. In the study for the World Bank, Leamer et al. (1994) argue that a free-trade agreement between Central America and Mexico can benefit Central America, if the region can direct its exports of labor-intensive goods (mainly apparel and shoes) toward Mexico, while Mexico under NAFTA directs its exports to the United States.

Market access does not count for much, however, if a country is not in a position to take advantage of it. Just as El Salvador has not been able to increase its exports to the United States significantly under the Caribbean Basin Initiative (CBI), it has not taken advantage of the limited unilateral tariff preferences Mexico has extended since the early 1980s.[24] The anti-export bias and the civil war are important explanatory factors behind El Salvador's small exports to the United States and to Mexico. Yet even with political stability and an export-neutral incentive structure, market access is a necessary but not sufficient condition for successful export-linked growth.

With the announcement of the Enterprise for the Americas Initiative in June 1990 the United States proclaimed its intention to bring all Western Hemisphere countries together in one free-trade area. At the Miami Summit in December 1994, leaders of the Western Hemisphere countries agreed to establish an American Free Trade Area by the year 2005. In light of the political battle surrounding the passage of NAFTA in the U.S. Congress, it remains to be seen to what extent rhetoric will translate into actual free-trade agreements. For El Salvador, a free-trade agreement with the United States is desirable for the same reasons a free-trade area is desirable with Mexico: to avoid trade and investment diversion and to secure market access. In contrast to the Mexican market, however, the U.S. market is the single most important export market for El Salvador. Although CBI already provides unilateral access to the U.S. market (with the important exception of textiles and apparel), such preferential access can be revoked by equally unilateral action on the part of the United States. A free-trade agreement would put access to the U.S. market on a contractual basis and thus on a sounder footing. It would preclude the arbitrary use of anti-dumping and countervailing procedures, as occurred in the case of Salvadoran shirt exports in 1994.[25]

To maximize El Salvador's benefits from a free-trade agreement with Mexico (and possibly later with the United States/Western Hemisphere), a negotiated agreement has to ensure that asymmetry in development does not translate into asymmetry in benefits. Taking proper account of the asymmetric levels of development and competitiveness between the two countries means giving El Salvador sufficient time to face Mexican competition. A slower pace of import liberalization could either come on a general level or a product-specific level. Whereas the former is accepted by Venezuela and Colombia, the latter is preferred by Mexico. El Salvador is in dire need of sectoral-impact studies that can provide the informational basis for sector- or product-specific demands in free-trade negotiations.

From Wage Repression to Productivity Growth

Figure 12.5 summarizes the development of real wages and profit rates in El Salvador over the last decade. There can be no doubt that further reductions in the real wage are incompatible with the consolidation of peace. In addition, real-wage declines also are not desirable from the point of view of achieving lasting competitiveness. Seeking price competitiveness through wage reductions is a short-term and defensive strategy. In the global economy, increasing interdependence and rapid technological changes have intensified competition to such an extent that wage reductions will not likely be able to secure competitiveness beyond the short run. Even in the production of completely standardized goods, low labor costs in El Salvador will not continue to compensate for lower productivity, as technological changes increase productivity elsewhere, and as large suppliers with even lower wages, like China, aggressively enter the international market.

The worst-case scenario in Leamer's NAFTA-impact study (1994) is that China will prevent Mexico from capturing the U.S. market in labor-intensive commodities, which then in turn will prevent Central America from making inroads into the Mexican market. "Under this very pessimistic scenario," Leamer et al. (1994, p. 2) argue, "wages in Central America are set in Beijing, not in San José." Furthermore, growing intra-industry trade and product differentiation during the last two decades have made product quality and design increasingly important sources of competitiveness. The implication is not that production costs have ceased to play a role in competition, but rather that they only become decisive once product design, quality, and other nonprice determinants of competitiveness (for example, speedy and punctual delivery) are internationally competitive as well.

Figure 12.5   Real Profit Rate and Real Minimum Wage, 1980–1991

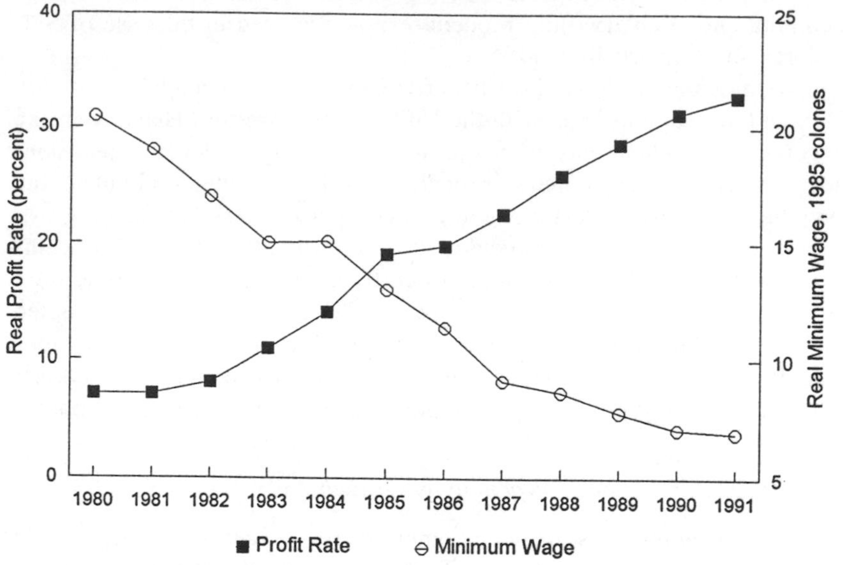

Source: Profit rate from Harberger (1993a, Table 6); nominal minimum wage from MIPLAN, CPI from BCR.

There is only one way to achieve and maintain competitiveness in a broad array of commodities *and* at the same time to prevent real-wage decline (or better, allow real-wage increases): sustained growth in productivity. Michael Porter (1990, p. 84) succinctly summarizes the link between competitiveness and productivity growth: "The only meaningful concept of competitiveness at the national level is productivity." Achieving inclusive export-linked growth thus poses the twin challenges of achieving sustained productivity growth and establishing a consensus in civil society that the fruits of this growth will be shared equitably.

The government has an important role to play in supporting productivity growth in the private sector. Access to information and technology at affordable prices is today a key element in the acquisition of competitiveness. The markets for knowledge and information are highly imperfect, however, and they would provide suboptimal quantities if left to their own devices. Private agents cannot appropriate all the returns to their investments in information and technology, and positive externalities are large (see, for example, Stiglitz 1989).

Producers need up-to-date information on a product level about prices, product quality, market conditions, and competitors in different foreign markets. At the same time, they need to be aware of, learn, and adapt to local circumstances the best-practice technologies available in other countries.

Whereas the acquisition of technological know-how in developing countries consists primarily of the diffusion and adaptation of technology developed elsewhere, producers might need help in the adaptation process itself. They also need incentives and support to find niches in product markets and the best technical ways to fill them.

There is little empirical evidence to suggest that nontraditional export-linked growth can be achieved and sustained without government policies to deal with market and coordination failures in information and knowledge (see, for example, Shapiro and Taylor 1990). In addition to the well-known and documented experiences of the East Asian "miracle" countries in this respect, there is ample evidence from other successful developing countries as well. Chile, for example, has been hailed as the example par excellence for the success of a purely market-based strategy. Yet its two most important nontraditional exports, fruit and wood, were critically influenced by product-specific government policies.[26] A 1993 World Bank study that analyzed successful experiences of nontraditional agricultural exports in nine developing countries found that in nearly all cases government intervention played an important role, through programs of technological investigation and technology transfer, product certification and inspection, and provision of better information (cited in von Hesse 1994).

Finally, El Salvador's own experience in the promotion of maquila production provides strong evidence of the importance of effective support in the areas of information, marketing, and technical know-how to promote nontraditional exports. The work of the Program for Promotion of Export Investment and Diversification (PRIDEX) in helping Salvadoran producers to establish market contacts abroad through promotional offices and participation in trade shows, and its help in bringing in technicians from abroad for training sessions in specific companies or industries, have been critical to the rapid growth of maquila exports.

We are putting emphasis on what one might call deliberate "competitiveness policies," because market liberalization by itself will not automatically lead to greater competitiveness. Getting the incentive structure right is not sufficient for an increase in productivity. First, as argued and shown earlier, a reduction in wages can be the short-run response to more intense competition. Second, just because productivity increases are necessary for survival does not mean that they will occur ipso facto. The alternative to lower wages and no productivity growth is simply extinction. In other words, allocative efficiency is not identical with productive efficiency, and the former does not automatically generate the latter.

The need for competitiveness policies in El Salvador has become all the more urgent in the context of the revitalization of the Central American Common Market, the negotiations with Mexico (and Colombia and Venezuela) about the establishment of a free-trade association, and the possibility of a free-trade agreement with the United States in the context of the Enterprise for the Americas Initiative and NAFTA.

Government intervention does not necessarily translate into direct and exclusive government action. On the contrary, limited government resources (financial and administrative) and the desire to minimize the potential for rent-seeking behavior often make other alternatives preferable. These include the building of public institutions that bring together the private and the government sectors as well as relevant academic resources, help in the establishment and strengthening of sector-specific private organizations, and special incentives (subsidies or tax exemptions) to encourage desired investment and export-promoting behavior. Close cooperation between the public and private sectors is absolutely vital in the endeavor to foster domestic capabilities for technology absorption and to set priorities in this respect. The government is no better than the private sector in "picking the winners." But it is better at coordinating efforts and stimulating activities, especially in new areas, and especially as a result of an ongoing dialogue between the public and private sectors.

On a general level, a number of important issues can be highlighted with respect to areas of comparative advantage and government policies in support of competitiveness:

1. *Maquila exports* cannot form the linchpin of export-led growth, because technology transfer is minimal, backward linkages are limited, and low wages are the basis for a temporary comparative advantage. Nevertheless, given their labor intensity, maquila exports do generate much-needed employment in the short run.

2. *Nontraditional agricultural exports with low value added* probably cannot provide the basis for export-led growth, given that their prices are highly volatile and often follow a downward trend. In a study of the key nontraditional agricultural exports (NTAX) from Central America in the period 1979–1988, Conroy (1989) found that they exhibited more international price volatility than the principal traditional export products (with the exception of sugar). Among the four NTAX studied (melons, cucumbers, cashews, and pineapples), only pineapples showed a rising price trend.

Schmitt's study (1993) on Salvadoran exports generally supports these findings. Over the period 1975–1992, the coefficient of variation of El Salvador's NTAX was 35.9, similar to that of sugar (35.8) and coffee (33.1), but substantially higher than that for nontraditional manufactured exports (NTMX) (21). The coefficient of variation measures the standard deviation of prices as a percentage of the average price. During the same period, the average annual change in the real unit price of NTAX was somewhat higher than that for NTMX (1.9 percent versus 1.3 percent) and substantially better than for traditional agricultural exports (–1 percent).

3. *Agricultural exports with high value added* play an important role in successful export-led growth. There is no doubt that El Salvador (like the rest of Central America) has climatic advantages that it should utilize. For the reasons outlined above, the emphasis should, however, be on the development of agroindustry—the creation of production chains based on natural resources. The promotion of such production chains requires different interventions at key points. At the one end, it requires support for the identification of specific market niches for processed natural resources. At the other end, it requires support measures to make it possible for subsistence and other small farmers to produce nontraditional agricultural products.

It is important that any special incentives are tied to performance and limited in time. That is clearly one of the lessons of past policy mistakes in Latin American industrial policy and of industrial policy in the successful East Asian countries. A final specification of special incentives also must follow a clear identification of their feasibility, in terms of both administrative capabilities and international legitimacy.

Conclusions

This chapter analyzed the key elements necessary to make exports a basis for future inclusive economic growth. Three dilemmas stand out that must be solved for the success of such a strategy. The first is the real overvaluation of the colón, which works against investments in export (and import-substitution) activities. The second is the need for government support on a micro level—competitiveness policies, as we called them here—given the state's limitations in terms of administrative capability. The third is the need to use export-linked growth to promote higher real wages, rather than relying on real-wage compression to stimulate exports.

To resolve these conundrums is a challenge, but the point is to recognize the challenge and act on it. With respect to the exchange rate the goal should be a real devaluation of the colón. We have recommended a number of policies to that end, including measures to stimulate private investment and domestically financed public investment.

Competitiveness policies can be effective only if their design does not outstrip administrative ability. But administrative limitations do not imply that inaction is the best course; rather, they imply a need to include the development of administrative capabilities among the goals of policy design. As Wade (1994, p. 76) remarks:

> Governments with weak capacity can begin with selective industrial policy on a modest scale, not attempting to pick winners from a long menu, but identifying what activities already going on in the country seem to be

doing well, analyzing what public policy should do (and stop doing) to foster those activities, and putting low-powered programs in place. There is a learning effect in bureaucracy as surely as in industry. If governments do not attempt to accelerate, even modestly, the acquisition of technological learning in important industries, they will not learn how to do so.

Our analysis highlights the importance of explicitly focusing on increasing the government's administrative capabilities, and establishing public institutions that bring together the private and government sectors around selected areas important to export success.

Regarding wages and export-linked growth, our argument is twofold. First, low real wages are neither necessary nor sufficient to secure competitiveness in international markets for nontraditional exports; other determinants—including the real exchange rate, the structure of incentives, productivity, and knowledge of markets—are far more important. Second, export-linked growth is necessary for sustained improvements in real wages in El Salvador. But this is not to say that it is sufficient: Deliberate policy measures are needed to ensure an equitable distribution of the benefits of growth. These include investments in human capital; complementary reforms discussed in other chapters in this volume, including reforms in the distribution of assets, fiscal policy, and access to finance; and the strengthening of democratic institutions so as to protect human rights, including the rights of labor.

Notes

1. The econometric results in Levine and Renelt (1992) show that when imports are substituted for exports in cross-country growth or investment regressions the coefficient estimates and standard errors are similar. When controlling for investment, the trade variable is no longer statistically significant in determining per capita economic growth.

2. "Revealed comparative advantage" compares a product's share in a country's exports with the same product's share in total world exports. If the former is greater than the latter, the country is said to have a revealed comparative advantage in that particular product.

3. This is not an unusual ratio. Kaplinsky (1993), for example, cites a similar figure for maquila operations in the Dominican Republic.

4. Siri (1984) found that during the 1960s and 1970s exports to Central America were mainly determined by the economic growth of trading partners, while traditional exports were primarily driven by world prices.

5. The tariff ceiling of 20 percent applies to imports of consumer goods produced in the region; the rate of 15 percent applies to consumer goods not produced in the region; the 10 percent rate applies to intermediate and capital goods produced in the region; and the 5 percent floor is applicable to intermediate and capital goods not produced in the region (Bulmer-Thomas 1993).

6. Exports of coffee, sugar, and cotton are excluded from the duty drawback scheme.

7. There are basically three sources of information about wages in El Salvador: minimum-wage data, wages of workers covered by social security, and wage information from the multipurpose household surveys. The surveys do not allow for the construction of a time series on wages, but they give useful information on the range of wages in a particular year.

8. These data are based on the average wages of workers affiliated with social security by industry (IMF 1994b, p. 86).

9. Chile in the second half of the 1970s is a case in point (Paus 1994b).

10. The "Dutch disease" refers to the adverse impact of a foreign exchange bonanza (derived in the original Dutch example from natural-gas exports) on the competitiveness of other industries in the tradeable-goods sector.

11. With the nominal exchange rate fixed, the performance of the real exchange rate depends on the relative magnitude of domestic versus international inflation. As long as the domestic inflation rate is higher than the international inflation rate (as is likely in the absence of sterilization), the real exchange rate becomes increasingly overvalued. The experience of the Southern Cone countries in the late 1970s showed that even when the nominal exchange rate is fixed, the domestic price level converges only slowly onto the international price level (see, for example, Paus 1994b; Foxley 1983). Argentina's experience over the last few years is a more recent case in point. Because the exchange rate between the austral and the U.S. dollar was fixed (at 1) in 1991, inflation in Argentina has remained above U.S. inflation. As a result, the austral has become increasingly overvalued in real terms.

12. The countries included in the study are Bangladesh, Brazil, Colombia, India, Korea, Mexico, Thailand, Turkey, Chile, Kenya, Malaysia, Peru, Sri Lanka, and Tanzania.

13. That period is reduced to two years if a country's export product accounts for more than 3.25 percent of world trade.

14. El Salvador, Guatemala, and Nicaragua signed the treaty for a common market in 1961, Honduras in 1962, and Costa Rica in 1963.

15. For a detailed discussion of the rise and fall of the CACM, see Bulmer-Thomas (1987, 1989).

16. Trade diversion refers to imports being switched from pretariff cheaper nonmember sources to member countries after the formation of a customs union. Trade creation refers to the production of one customs-union member being replaced by cheaper imports from another member.

17. For excellent discussions of the key issues involved in a free-trade association between Central American countries and Mexico or the United States, see Leamer et al. (1994), López (1993), Alas de Franco (1992), Saborio (1992), and Salazar-Xirinachs and Lizano (1992).

18. In 1993, El Salvador's exports to Mexico amounted to $16.3 million, the equivalent of 2.2 percent of total Salvadoran merchandise exports and 0.02 percent of Mexican imports.

19. Central American unity was broken with Costa Rica's negotiating a separate bilateral free-trade agreement with Mexico that was signed in April 1994. The member countries of the Northern Triangle have been negotiating jointly with

Mexico, though allowing for special bilateral provisions in the multilateral context.

20. El Salvador's exports to the United States under CBERA provisions were $22.2 million in 1988 and $26.5 million in 1993. By way of comparison, the respective figures for Honduran exports to the United States are $56.2 million and $127.4 million, for Costa Rican exports $141.1 million and $387.7 million, and for Guatemalan exports $77.3 million and $207.3 million (United States International Trade Commission 1994, p. 27).

21. The Caribbean Basin Initiative (CBI), the informal name for CBERA, was launched in 1982 and extended indefinitely in 1990. Under the CBI, most tariff categories enjoy duty-free entry into the United States. Although some of the products excluded originally have since been moved to duty-free status, most footwear and textile and apparel items continue to be excluded.

22. NAFTA will not affect those Salvadoran clothing exports to the United States that enter under the HTS (harmonized tariff schedule) subheading 9802.00.80 (formerly TSUS item 807.00)—imported assembled products of U.S. components.

23. Bills proposing NAFTA parity for textiles and apparel for CBI countries were attached to the omnibus bill in the U.S. Congress to ratify the Final Act of the Uruguay Round. In the political wrangling preceding the midterm elections in November 1994, however, they were dropped from the bill. In early 1995, new bills for NAFTA parity were introduced in the House and the Senate. They include a broader range of products, but have more stringent conditions attached, such as certified compliance with rules regarding intellectual property rights.

24. In the context of the Treaty of Montevideo in 1980 (which established the Latin American Integration Association), Latin American countries signed Acuerdos Bilaterales de Alcance Parcial (ABAP). Mexico extended unilateral tariff preferences to El Salvador for 271 products. López (1993, p. 33) shows that El Salvador has taken little advantage of this preferential treatment. Slightly less than 10 percent of the country's exports to Mexico benefited from the ABAP, in contrast to over 80 percent for Honduras and Costa Rica.

25. After very rapid export growth of men's shirts from El Salvador to the United States, the U.S. government imposed unilaterally a quantitative restriction in the summer of 1994. The Salvadoran government took the case to the textile-monitoring organization in Geneva, which ruled that the United States had not *demonstrated* market injury and that it should rescind the quota imposition. The United States rescinded the restraint, but then negotiated quantitative limitations on men's shirts with the government of El Salvador.

26. Recognizing Chile's potential for fruit exports, CORFO (the government's development corporation) initiated a program of national fruit development in the early 1960s, with investments in agricultural research, subsidized credit, technical assistance, and export subsidies (Jarvis 1991; Figueroa 1990). Similarly, the government fostered the forestry sector through generous incentives (Echenique 1990; Gwynne 1993).

13

Conclusions and Recommendations

James K. Boyce

The interdependence of peace and development is widely acknowledged. Yet there has been little systematic discussion of how economic policy should be reshaped in the special circumstances of a country emerging from civil war. In El Salvador both the government and the international financial institutions (IFIs) have pursued essentially the same macroeconomic-stabilization and structural adjustment policies they would have followed had the country never been at war. Too often, recognition of the interdependence between peace and development has been translated into the precept that if the peace process were allowed to interfere with economic policy, both would fail.

This study argues, in contrast, that *unless* the peace process is allowed to reshape economic policy, both will fail. We do not suggest that sound economic policies are unnecessary, nor that they should be sacrificed to political expediency. Rather we maintain that the soundness of policies can be ascertained only in light of the political economy of the peace process.

Principal Findings

The principal findings of this study are as follows:

1. *External resource availability has not been the binding constraint on the implementation of the peace accords; rather, the key constraint has been political will.* El Salvador will continue to require substantial external assistance in coming years. But this assistance must be accompanied by "peace conditionality," that is, a willingness to make assistance conditional on specific measures to implement the accords and consolidate the peace.

2. *The foreign exchange bonanza arising from remittances presents an opportunity that is being squandered; in the long run this may worsen*

279

prospects for growth. Remittances from the roughly 20 percent of Salvadorans who now live abroad provide crucial foreign exchange, income, and governability cushions. But they cannot be expected to last forever. At the same time, remittances have allowed policymakers to postpone needed reforms, and their impact on the real exchange rate has moved relative prices against exports and import substitutes. Unless more vigorous steps are taken now to increase investment, reduce poverty, and promote the production of tradeable goods, the eventual diminution of remittances will leave behind a weak economy and a fragile social peace.

3. *Without policies to redress inequity in the distribution of wealth and power, El Salvador can achieve neither prosperity nor peace.* Greater economic equity and greater political equity (or democratization in the broad sense of the term) will foster higher rates of investment, a more productive labor force, political and economic stability, and the successful functioning of markets and the state. Growth and equity are not contradictory objectives, one of which must be traded off against the other. In El Salvador, pursuing both together is not only possible but imperative.

4. *Current development policy in El Salvador is environmentally unsustainable.* The diminishing quantity and quality of the country's hydrological resources pose a particularly grave threat to livelihoods and to future economic growth. Steps are urgently needed to incorporate environmental costs and benefits into land-use decisions.

Main Policy Recommendations

The study offers policy recommendations for the short, medium, and long terms. The short-term recommendations focus on measures to complete the implementation of the peace accords. The medium-term recommendations focus on policies to escape from the current macroeconomic trap and move toward more equitable development. The long-term recommendations focus on policies to promote sustainable growth and consolidate the economic basis of peace.

Short-Term Policy Recommendations

1. Military expenditure should be reduced in the next two years to its prewar fraction of the gross domestic product, that is, to 0.7 percent of GDP. The "peace dividend" from the end of the war has yet to be fully realized. The resources freed through military-expenditure reductions should be allocated to priority programs mandated by the peace accords.

2. The tax coefficient should be raised and the incidence of taxation made more progressive. The tax-to-GDP ratio should be increased to 15 percent (which is closer to but still below the regional norm) in the next

three years. Efforts should be continued to improve income-tax collection from high-income individuals. In addition, the government should consider further taxes on the transactions of high-income individuals, for example, sales taxes on purchases of luxury goods (or tariffs in the case of luxury goods that are exclusively imported) and on high-value property transfers.

3. Adequate domestic resources should be committed on a priority basis to the strengthening of democratic institutions, including the National Civilian Police, and strict measures should be implemented to prevent human-rights abuses. The necessary resources should be mobilized through expenditure shifting (including reductions in military expenditure) and increased tax revenues. The prevention of human-rights abuses remains a critical element in the consolidation of the peace process.

4. Steps should be taken to streamline and expedite the land-transfer program mandated by the peace accords. These steps include: (a) placing the onus on landowners to initiate and substantiate claims for compensation or retention of land ownership within a reasonable time period, after which transfers would proceed; (b) altering the terms for retiring debt for land acquisition incurred by beneficiaries; and (c) simplification of procedures for the granting of land titles.

5. External-assistance actors, including the IFIs, should be willing to provide direct assistance for the strengthening of democratic institutions. IFI lending for this purpose would translate concern for "good governance" into action, broadening the concept of economically relevant infrastructure to include democratic institutions.

6. External-assistance actors, including the IFIs, should exercise peace conditionality through formal performance criteria and/or informal policy dialogue. Access to external resources should be made conditional on implementation of the peace accords and related policies, including those recommended under points 1 to 4.

Medium-Term Policy Recommendations

1. Military expenditure should be further reduced in the next five years to a fraction of GDP similar to that in Mexico or Costa Rica, that is, 0.3–0.4 percent. The savings thereby released should be reallocated to public investment, including investment in human capital through health and education programs.

2. Further appreciation of the real exchange rate should be prevented, but new policies are needed to achieve this goal. In recent years the influx of remittances (and to a lesser extent external assistance) has appreciated the real exchange rate, shifting relative prices against tradeable goods, including exports and agriculture. The central bank's effort to sterilize this inflow—by buying dollars and issuing high-interest bonds to soak up

colones—discourages private investment and may attract further inflows of short-term capital. Alternative policies include: (a) using required reserves rather than open-market operations to absorb liquidity; (b) nurturing a market in government bonds to channel savings into public investment rather than into central-bank liabilities; and (c) pegging deposit interest rates only just above inflation, so as to keep real interest rates positive but low. A long-term policy to use accumulating reserves more efficiently is suggested in the following subsection (point 2).

3. Prudential regulation of banks should be tightened to reduce the risk of future financial crises. The banking system was recently privatized and is currently expanding rapidly. The superintendent of financial services needs the power and political insulation to mandate greater loan-loss provisioning by banks and to take over or liquidate banks threatened with insolvency. Higher reserve requirements should be used to discourage the rapid accumulation of foreign-currency liabilities.

4. Agrarian policy should consolidate the achievements of past reforms and encourage family farms. Measures to these ends include: (a) identification and expropriation (with due compensation) of properties in excess of 245 hectares in 1983 that were unconstitutionally transferred in subsequent years; (b) the development of an institutional environment to facilitate voluntary land transfers to family farms, including more equitable access to technical assistance, infrastructure, inputs, and credit; and (c) the forgiveness of the agrarian debt of the cooperatives established under Phase I of the 1980 agrarian reform.

5. Land-use incentives and regulations should be deployed to sustain and restore hydrological resources. These include: (a) the implementation of effective urban land-use planning and zoning; (b) incentives for soil conservation in hillside agriculture; (c) policies to maintain and increase acreage under shade coffee; and (d) a territorial reorganization of state institutions to make the watershed the administrative basis for land-use policies.

Long-Term Policy Recommendations

1. Increased public investment, particularly in human capital, is crucial to the long-run goal of inclusive growth. El Salvador's public investment and primary-school enrollment both are exceptionally low. Well-planned public investment can "crowd in" private investment.

2. The appreciation of the real exchange rate should be reversed through policies to increase demand for dollars through greater imports of investment goods. The most propitious way to depreciate the real exchange rate in the long term is to increase public and private investment and with it the demand for foreign currency to buy capital and intermediate goods.

3. The development of a second tier of smaller-scale financial institutions would both encourage local savings and provide credit based on knowledge of local conditions and borrowers. External assistance may facilitate this with training and capital requirements, but credit-channeling programs should be eschewed.

4. Producer prices for basic grains should be supported through direct subsidies, tariff protection, and/or incentives tied to appropriate environmental practices. Relative prices for basic grains, which are mostly grown by small farmers, have deteriorated drastically due to real-exchange-rate appreciation, residual tariff discrimination against agriculture, and liberalization that has transmitted adverse world price trends (driven in part by producer price supports elsewhere) to the domestic market. Interventions to counter these forces are justified on social, political, food-security, and environmental grounds.

5. Policies to "reform the state" should include efforts to establish the necessary administrative capacity for environmental management, including analysis of environmental costs and benefits, their integration into the planning process, and the implementation of fiscal, regulatory, and investment policies. In this respect, reform clearly cannot be synonymous with downsizing.

6. Further reforms to create a more equitable and efficient agrarian structure should be placed on the agenda for national policy debate. Such reforms can foster long-term growth in the economy as a whole, contribute substantially to the reduction of poverty, and help to consolidate the peace. Two crucial caveats are in order, however: First, agrarian reforms can succeed only if they are designed and implemented with public accountability and participation. The democratization process enhances the prospects for this approach. Second, the long-term viability of agrarian reforms will hinge on complementary policies to improve relative prices for agriculture and to promote environmental restoration.

7. Employment-guarantee programs should be expanded to reduce poverty and to mobilize labor for productive infrastructure and environmental-restoration projects. By setting the wage offered at appropriate levels, such programs can be highly successful in targeting benefits to some of the poorest strata of the labor force.

8. Nontraditional exports should be supported through appropriate government policies. Wage repression is neither necessary nor sufficient for competitiveness. In addition to measures to redress exchange-rate overvaluation, increase complementary public investment, and improve the productivity of the labor force, export-promotion policies should include: (a) support for technological change, for example, through improved access to information and vocational training; (b) measures to improve the efficiency of the customs office and ensure swift access to imported inputs; (c) continued participation in the revitalized Central American Common Market;

(d) steps to improve knowledge of product markets; and (e) selective incentives strictly tied to performance and limited in time.

The implementation of these policy recommendations would greatly enhance the prospects for a successful adjustment toward peace in El Salvador.

In a world of proliferating civil conflicts, the relevance of the issues analyzed in this study is not confined to a single country. The short-run problems of financing the costs of peace and building new democratic institutions, and the medium- and long-run problems of realizing the powerful complementarities among growth, equity, and the consolidation of peace, will recur in many settings in coming years. It is our hope that the hard-won lessons of the Salvadoran experience will ease the difficult process of postconflictual transition elsewhere.

Statistical Appendix

Table A.1   Central America: Human Development Indicators, 1992

	El Salvador	Costa Rica	Guatemala	Honduras	Nicaragua	Latin America and Caribbean
Life expectancy	65.2	76.0	64.0	65.2	65.4	67.7
Adult literacy	74.6	93.2	56.4	74.9	78.0	87
Female	70	93	48	73	n.a.	84
Male	80	93	65	78	n.a.	88
Mean years of schooling	4.2	5.7	4.1	4.0	4.5	5.4
Female	4.0	5.6	3.8	3.8	4.3	5.2
Male	4.4	5.8	4.4	4.1	4.7	5.5
GNP per capita U.S.$ (1991)	1,090	1,870	940	590	400	2,480
Real GDP per capita PPP$ (1991)	2,110	5,100	3,180	1,820	2,550	5,360
Human Development Index	0.543	0.848	0.564	0.524	0.583	0.757
HDI ranking	112	39	108	115	106	—
Population in absolute poverty (%)	51	29	71	37	20	40
Rural	75	34	74	55	19	61
Urban	20	24	66	14	21	30
Population with access to (%):						
Health services	60	97	50	66	n.a.	88
Safe water	47	92	60	78	54	79
Sanitation	58	97	50	67	52	70
Population per doctor	1,560	1,030	2,270	3,130	1,670	1,210
Population per nurse	1,040	490	910	3,130	3,340	3,610
Pupil-teacher ratio						
Primary	40	32	38	34	24	27
Secondary	28	19	n.a.	15	12	15
Percentage completing primary education	24	79	36	34	41	45
Public expenditure as % of GNP						
On education	1.8	4.6	1.4	4.6	n.a.	4.2
On health	2.6	5.6	2.1	2.9	6.7	2.4
On military	2.9	0.5	1.1	1.2	9.0	1.7

Source: UNDP 1994d.
n.a. = data not available

Table A.2a   Gross Domestic Product at Current Prices, 1970–1993 (millions of colones)

	1970	1971	1972	1973	1974	1975	1976	1977	1978	1979
By sector of origin										
Gross domestic product	2,571	2,704	2,882	3,324	3,944	4,478	5,706	7,167	7,692	8,607
Primary production	735	733	733	942	1,006	1,036	1,622	2,382	2,057	2,518
Agriculture and related										
sectors	731	729	728	937	999	1,028	1,614	2,374	2,049	2,508
Mining	4	4	4	6	7	7	8	8	8	10
Secondary production	596	640	708	756	907	1,107	1,238	1,480	1,656	1,842
Manufacturing	485	519	563	605	707	831	933	1,047	1,205	1,338
Construction	72	80	102	107	146	219	216	327	320	337
Utilities	39	40	43	43	54	57	90	107	131	167
Services	1,240	1,331	1,442	1,627	2,030	2,335	2,845	3,304	3,979	4,248
Transportation and										
communications	128	132	140	148	173	188	211	243	291	292
Commercial services	544	587	644	728	965	1,112	1,412	1,601	1,936	2,005
Financial services	58	62	66	97	104	128	157	234	260	286
Housing	95	100	107	118	142	172	192	227	285	318
Public administration	200	219	239	266	338	384	486	571	719	784
Other services	216	231	247	271	308	351	388	429	489	562
Percentage composition										
Gross domestic product	100.0	100.0	100.0	100.0	100.0	100.0	100.0	100.0	100.0	100.0
Primary production	28.6	27.1	25.4	28.3	25.5	23.1	28.4	33.2	26.7	29.3
Agriculture and related										
sectors	28.4	27.0	25.3	28.2	25.3	23.0	28.3	33.1	26.6	29.1
Mining	0.2	0.2	0.2	0.2	0.2	0.2	0.1	0.1	0.1	0.1
Secondary production	23.2	23.7	24.6	22.7	23.0	24.7	21.7	20.7	21.5	21.4
Manufacturing	18.8	19.2	19.5	18.2	17.9	18.6	16.3	14.6	15.7	15.5
Construction	2.8	3.0	3.5	3.2	3.7	4.9	3.8	4.6	4.2	3.9
Utilities	1.5	1.5	1.5	1.3	1.4	1.3	1.6	1.5	1.7	1.9
Services	48.2	49.2	50.0	48.9	51.5	52.1	49.9	46.1	51.7	49.4
Transportation and										
communications	5.0	4.9	4.8	4.4	4.4	4.2	3.7	3.4	3.8	3.4
Commercial services	21.1	21.7	22.3	21.9	24.5	24.8	24.7	22.3	25.2	23.3
Financial services	2.2	2.3	2.3	2.9	2.6	2.9	2.7	3.3	3.4	3.3
Housing	3.7	3.7	3.7	3.6	3.6	3.8	3.4	3.2	3.7	3.7
Public administration	7.8	8.1	8.3	8.0	8.6	8.6	8.5	8.0	9.3	9.1
Other services	8.4	8.5	8.6	8.1	7.8	7.8	6.8	6.0	6.4	6.5

1980	1981	1982	1983	1984	1985	1986	1987	1988	1989	1990	1991	1992	1993[a]
8,917	8,646	8,966	10,152	11,657	14,331	19,763	23,141	27,366	32,230	41,057	47,792	54,961	66,356
2,491	2,119	2,089	2,176	2,338	2,631	3,996	3,237	3,848	3,825	4,664	4,963	5,265	5,814
2,480	2,106	2,075	2,161	2,320	2,611	3,969	3,198	3,801	3,767	4,599	4,881	5,167	5,690
11	13	14	15	18	21	27	38	47	58	65	82	99	125
1,834	1,835	1,882	2,159	2,474	3,118	4,051	5,252	6,158	7,426	9,512	11,348	13,272	16,446
1,339	1,359	1,382	1,572	1,837	2,346	3,086	4,045	4,809	5,836	7,647	8,957	10,348	12,639
306	284	301	343	355	437	547	710	815	984	1,072	1,310	1,640	2,073
189	192	200	244	281	335	418	497	535	606	793	1,082	1,284	1,734
4,591	4,693	4,995	5,817	6,846	8,582	11,716	14,652	17,360	20,979	26,881	31,481	36,424	44,095
314	328	347	412	481	613	816	1,061	1,206	1,416	1,897	2,274	2,678	3,298
2,038	2,028	2,089	2,510	2,995	3,898	5,627	7,275	8,721	10,832	14,187	16,751	19,664	24,299
302	295	331	358	392	442	564	640	779	795	924	1,171	1,445	1,863
384	412	471	538	630	747	939	1,182	1,520	1,893	2,366	2,721	3,068	3,500
917	944	1,050	1,177	1,366	1,603	1,977	2,207	2,385	2,714	3,232	3,578	3,860	4,330
637	687	708	823	982	1,278	1,794	2,286	2,749	3,330	4,275	4,986	5,710	6,804
100.0	100.0	100.0	100.0	100.0	100.0	100.0	100.0	100.0	100.0	100.0	100.0	100.0	100.0
27.9	24.5	23.3	21.4	20.1	18.4	20.2	14.0	14.1	11.9	11.4	10.4	9.6	8.8
27.8	24.4	23.1	21.3	19.9	18.2	20.1	13.8	13.9	11.7	11.2	10.2	9.4	8.6
0.1	0.1	0.2	0.1	0.2	0.1	0.1	0.2	0.2	0.2	0.2	0.2	0.2	0.2
20.6	21.2	21.0	21.3	21.2	21.8	20.5	22.7	22.5	23.0	23.2	23.7	24.1	24.8
15.0	15.7	15.4	15.5	15.8	16.4	15.6	17.5	17.6	18.1	18.6	18.7	18.8	19.0
3.4	3.3	3.4	3.4	3.0	3.0	2.8	3.1	3.0	3.1	2.6	2.7	3.0	3.1
2.1	2.2	2.2	2.4	2.4	2.3	2.1	2.1	2.0	1.9	1.9	2.3	2.3	2.6
51.5	54.3	55.7	57.3	58.7	59.9	59.3	63.3	63.4	65.1	65.5	65.9	66.3	66.5
3.5	3.8	3.9	4.1	4.1	4.3	4.1	4.6	4.4	4.4	4.6	4.8	4.9	5.0
22.9	23.5	23.3	24.7	25.7	27.2	28.5	31.4	31.9	33.6	34.6	35.1	35.8	36.6
3.4	3.4	3.7	3.5	3.4	3.1	2.9	2.8	2.8	2.5	2.2	2.5	2.6	2.8
4.3	4.8	5.3	5.3	5.4	5.2	4.8	5.1	5.6	5.9	5.8	5.7	5.6	5.3
10.3	10.9	11.7	11.6	11.7	11.2	10.0	9.5	8.7	8.4	7.9	7.5	7.0	6.5
7.1	7.9	7.9	8.1	8.4	8.9	9.1	9.9	10.0	10.3	10.4	10.4	10.4	10.3

(continues)

Table A.2a   Continued

	1970	1971	1972	1973	1974	1975	1976	1977	1978	1979
By sector of final demand										
Gross domestic product	2,571	2,704	2,882	3,332	3,944	4,478	5,706	7,167	7,692	8,607
Gross domestic expenditure	2,564	2,758	2,854	3,432	4,275	4,709	5,779	7,117	8,405	8,622
Consumption expenditures	2,223	2,336	2,446	2,823	3,383	3,719	4,659	5,439	6,570	7,066
Private sector	1,948	2,061	2,138	2,474	2,954	3,218	3,973	4,634	5,574	5,933
Public sector	276	275	307	349	429	501	686	805	996	1,133
Gross domestic investment	341	422	408	609	892	990	1,120	1,679	1,834	1,556
Gross fixed capital formation	308	359	474	521	718	1,031	1,145	1,521	1,652	1,512
Private sector	236	264	346	377	508	674	791	995	1,202	990
Public sector	72	96	128	144	210	357	354	525	449	522
Changes in inventories	33	62	−66	88	174	−40	−26	158	182	44
Net exports	7	−54	28	−101	−332	−232	−73	50	−713	−15
Exports of goods and nonfactor services	639	666	839	998	1,278	1,480	2,028	2,735	2,328	3,182
Imports of goods and nonfactor services	631	720	811	1,099	1,610	1,711	2,101	2,686	3,041	3,197
Net factor payments	−21	−25	−27	−38	−53	−69	−17	−72	−130	−60
Gross national product at market prices	2,550	2,679	2,855	3,294	3,891	4,409	5,689	7,095	7,562	8,547
Percentage composition										
Gross domestic product	100.0	100.0	100.0	100.0	100.0	100.0	100.0	100.0	100.0	100.0
Gross domestic expenditure	99.7	102.0	99.0	103.0	108.4	105.2	101.3	99.3	109.3	100.2
Consumption expenditures	86.5	86.4	84.9	84.7	85.8	83.1	81.7	75.9	85.4	82.1
Private sector	75.7	76.2	74.2	74.3	74.9	71.9	69.6	64.7	72.5	68.9
Public sector	10.7	10.2	10.7	10.5	10.9	11.2	12.0	11.2	12.9	13.2
Gross domestic investment	13.2	15.6	14.2	18.3	22.6	22.1	19.6	23.4	23.8	18.1
Gross fixed capital formation	12.0	13.3	16.5	15.6	18.2	23.0	20.1	21.2	21.5	17.6
Private sector	9.2	9.7	12.0	11.3	12.9	15.0	13.9	13.9	15.6	11.5
Public sector	2.8	3.5	4.4	4.3	5.3	8.0	6.2	7.3	5.8	6.1
Changes in inventories	1.3	2.3	−2.3	2.6	4.4	−0.9	−0.5	2.2	2.4	0.5
Net Exports	0.3	−2.0	1.0	−3.0	−8.4	−5.2	−1.3	0.7	−9.3	−0.2
Exports of goods and nonfactor services	24.8	24.6	29.1	30.0	32.4	33.0	35.5	38.2	30.3	37.0
Imports of goods and nonfactor services	24.5	26.6	28.1	33.0	40.8	38.2	36.8	37.5	39.5	37.1
Net factor payments	−0.8	−0.9	−0.9	−1.1	−1.3	−1.5	−0.3	−1.0	−1.7	−0.7
Gross national product at market prices	99.2	99.1	99.1	98.9	98.7	98.5	99.7	99.0	98.3	99.3

Source: USAID, from BCR.
Note: a. Estimated values.

1980	1981	1982	1983	1984	1985	1986	1987	1988	1989	1990	1991	1992	1993[a]
8,917	8,646	8,966	10,152	11,657	14,331	19,763	23,141	27,366	32,230	41,057	47,792	54,961	66,356
8,835	9,244	9,477	10,702	12,448	15,415	20,628	24,786	29,138	35,605	45,641	53,699	63,570	75,943
7,652	8,013	8,291	9,478	11,054	13,860	18,009	21,926	25,637	30,373	40,791	47,093	54,527	64,911
6,405	6,644	6,877	7,871	9,184	11,640	15,206	18,744	22,153	26,443	36,141	41,821	48,738	58,420
1,247	1,369	1,415	1,607	1,869	2,220	2,803	3,181	3,484	3,930	4,649	5,272	5,789	6,491
1,183	1,231	1,185	1,224	1,394	1,554	2,619	2,861	3,501	5,232	4,851	6,606	9,043	11,032
1,210	1,173	1,130	1,180	1,336	1,723	2,593	3,158	3,456	4,293	4,834	6,435	8,763	10,988
575	539	585	716	881	1,251	2,091	2,481	2,607	3,169	3,904	5,226	6,762	8,583
636	634	545	464	455	473	502	677	848	1,124	930	1,209	2,001	2,405
−27	58	56	44	59	−169	26	−297	45	938	17	171	280	44
82	−597	−510	−550	−791	−1,084	−865	−1,646	−1,772	−3,375	−4,584	−5,908	−8,609	−9,587
3,046	2,307	2,042	2,486	2,536	3,199	4,875	4,395	4,327	4,261	6,528	7,055	7,459	9,074
2,964	2,904	2,553	3,036	3,327	4,283	5,740	6,040	6,099	7,636	11,113	12,963	16,068	18,662
−128	−149	−229	−370	−343	−354	−472	−525	−509	−568	−775	−822	−485	−360
8,789	8,498	8,737	9,782	11,314	13,977	19,291	22,616	26,857	31,662	40,282	46,970	54,476	65,996
100.0	100.0	100.0	100.0	100.0	100.0	100.0	100.0	100.0	100.0	100.0	100.0	100.0	100.0
99.1	106.9	105.7	105.4	106.8	107.6	104.4	107.1	106.5	110.5	111.2	112.4	115.7	114.4
85.8	92.7	92.5	93.4	94.8	96.7	91.1	94.7	93.7	94.2	99.4	98.5	99.2	97.8
71.8	76.8	76.7	77.5	78.8	81.2	76.9	81.0	80.9	82.0	88.0	87.5	88.7	88.0
14.0	15.8	15.8	15.8	16.0	15.5	14.2	13.7	12.7	12.2	11.3	11.0	10.5	9.8
13.3	14.2	13.2	12.1	12.0	10.8	13.3	12.4	12.8	16.2	11.8	13.8	16.5	16.6
13.6	13.6	12.6	11.6	11.5	12.0	13.1	13.6	12.6	13.3	11.8	13.5	15.9	16.6
6.4	6.2	6.5	7.0	7.6	8.7	10.6	10.7	9.5	9.8	9.5	10.9	12.3	12.9
7.1	7.3	6.1	4.6	3.9	3.3	2.5	2.9	3.1	3.5	2.3	2.5	3.6	3.6
−0.3	0.7	0.6	0.4	0.5	−1.2	0.1	−1.3	0.2	2.9	0.0	0.4	0.5	0.1
0.9	−6.9	−5.7	−5.4	−6.8	−7.6	−4.4	−7.1	−6.5	−10.5	−11.2	−12.4	−15.7	−14.4
34.2	26.7	22.8	24.5	21.8	22.3	24.7	19.0	15.8	13.2	15.9	14.8	13.6	13.7
33.2	33.6	28.5	29.9	28.5	29.9	29.0	26.1	22.3	23.7	27.1	27.1	29.2	28.1
−1.4	−1.7	−2.6	−3.6	−2.9	−2.5	−2.4	−2.3	−1.9	−1.8	−1.9	−1.7	−0.9	−0.5
98.6	98.3	97.4	96.4	97.1	97.5	97.6	97.7	98.1	98.2	98.1	98.3	99.1	99.5

Table A.2b   Gross Domestic Product at Constant 1962 Prices, 1970–1993 (millions of colones)

	1970	1971	1972	1973	1974	1975	1976	1977	1978	1979
By sector of origin										
Gross domestic product	2,394	2,504	2,646	2,759	2,958	3,123	3,247	3,444	3,665	3,602
Primary production	631	654	664	676	746	792	729	755	860	891
Agriculture and related sectors	627	651	660	672	741	787	725	751	857	887
Mining	4	4	4	4	5	5	4	4	4	4
Secondary production	547	588	635	656	702	777	822	906	935	908
Manufacturing	438	469	487	520	552	578	629	662	691	657
Construction	64	71	94	77	86	128	116	157	147	144
Utilities	45	49	54	59	64	71	78	88	97	108
Services	1,216	1,262	1,347	1,427	1,511	1,554	1,695	1,782	1,869	1,802
Transportation and communications	128	130	136	141	164	173	196	214	223	209
Commercial services	566	576	613	657	682	709	770	803	829	760
Financial services	51	52	60	68	76	78	88	102	104	106
Housing	90	93	99	103	107	110	114	118	123	127
Public administration	183	199	214	223	243	244	274	288	320	332
Other services	198	212	224	234	239	240	253	257	271	268
Annual growth rates (in percent)										
Gross domestic product		4.6	5.7	4.3	7.2	5.6	4.0	6.1	6.4	-1.7
Primary production		3.7	1.5	1.8	10.3	6.2	-7.9	3.5	13.9	3.6
Agriculture and related sectors		3.8	1.5	1.8	10.2	6.3	-7.9	3.6	14.0	3.6
Mining		-2.8	11.3	6.6	17.3	-6.8	-11.3	-8.4	-0.4	3.1
Secondary production		7.5	7.9	3.3	7.0	10.6	5.9	10.2	3.2	-2.9
Manufacturing		7.0	3.8	6.7	6.3	4.7	8.7	5.2	4.5	-5.0
Construction		10.6	33.0	-17.5	10.7	49.3	-9.4	35.5	-6.4	-2.1
Utilities		8.6	11.3	8.9	8.4	9.9	10.4	12.7	10.1	11.5
Services		3.8	6.7	5.9	5.9	2.9	9.1	5.1	4.9	-3.6
Transportion and Communications		1.2	5.0	3.6	16.5	5.4	13.1	9.6	4.2	-6.5
Commercial Services		1.9	6.5	7.1	3.7	4.0	8.6	4.3	3.1	-8.3
Financial Services		1.7	15.2	13.6	11.6	2.6	13.6	15.0	2.3	2.1
Housing		3.1	6.7	3.5	3.5	3.5	3.5	3.5	3.5	3.5
Public Administration		9.1	7.1	4.6	8.9	0.2	12.5	5.1	11.1	3.7
Other Services		6.9	6.0	4.4	2.0	0.7	5.2	1.4	5.5	-0.8
Percentage composition										
Gross domestic product	100.0	100.0	100.0	100.0	100.0	100.0	100.0	100.0	100.0	100.0
Primary production	26.4	26.1	25.1	24.5	25.2	25.4	22.5	21.9	23.5	24.7
Agriculture and related sectors	26.2	26.0	25.0	24.4	25.0	25.2	22.3	21.8	23.4	24.6
Mining	0.2	0.1	0.1	0.2	0.2	0.1	0.1	0.1	0.1	0.1

1980	1981	1982	1983	1984	1985	1986	1987	1988	1989	1990	1991	1992	1993[a]
3,289	3,017	2,848	2,870	2,936	2,994	3,013	3,094	3,144	3,177	3,285	3,401	3,580	3,762
845	791	754	730	755	747	724	739	732	736	790	790	861	866
841	788	751	727	751	743	720	735	728	731	786	785	856	860
4	4	4	4	4	4	4	4	5	5	5	5	6	6
803	722	671	688	691	719	737	766	793	812	821	869	929	1,015
586	525	481	491	497	515	528	544	561	574	592	620	658	709
111	94	90	92	87	91	93	104	112	116	101	112	125	138
106	102	100	105	108	113	116	118	120	121	128	137	146	168
1,641	1,504	1,422	1,452	1,490	1,528	1,552	1,588	1,619	1,629	1,674	1,742	1,790	1,881
194	173	161	171	176	179	180	183	187	189	201	215	228	247
625	532	468	478	487	490	491	498	500	517	533	556	580	620
103	93	99	99	100	103	104	107	109	99	101	105	110	120
130	134	137	140	142	144	145	149	153	156	160	165	169	174
342	346	356	366	385	412	430	447	463	458	465	479	472	476
248	227	201	198	200	201	202	205	208	211	215	223	231	244
−8.7	−8.3	−5.6	0.8	2.3	2.0	0.6	2.7	1.6	1.1	3.4	3.5	5.3	5.1
−5.2	−6.4	−4.7	−3.2	3.3	−1.1	−3.1	2.1	−0.9	0.5	7.3	0.0	9.0	0.6
−5.2	−6.4	−4.7	−3.2	3.3	−1.1	−3.1	2.1	−1.0	0.5	7.4	0.0	9.0	0.5
3.0	−2.6	0.0	−2.6	2.7	0.0	2.6	12.8	6.8	4.3	−8.2	11.3	11.8	12.5
−11.6	−10.2	−7.0	2.4	0.6	4.0	2.5	3.9	3.5	2.4	1.1	5.9	6.9	9.2
−10.8	−10.4	−8.4	2.0	1.3	3.7	2.5	3.0	3.0	2.5	3.0	4.9	6.0	7.8
−22.6	−15.4	−4.1	2.0	−5.7	4.6	2.6	11.5	7.9	3.6	−12.8	10.1	12.0	10.3
−1.9	−3.1	−2.5	5.0	2.7	5.0	2.5	2.0	1.8	0.8	5.6	7.2	6.6	14.8
−8.9	−8.4	−5.4	2.1	2.6	2.6	1.6	2.4	1.9	0.7	2.8	4.0	2.8	5.1
−7.2	−10.9	−6.5	6.0	2.8	1.8	0.5	1.8	2.0	1.2	6.3	7.0	6.1	8.2
−17.7	−14.9	−12.0	2.1	1.9	0.5	0.3	1.4	0.4	3.4	3.1	4.2	4.3	7.0
−3.3	−9.3	5.8	0.2	1.0	3.0	1.5	2.4	2.0	−9.5	2.0	4.0	5.3	8.8
2.5	2.9	2.6	2.0	1.6	1.5	0.3	2.6	2.8	2.4	2.5	2.8	2.8	3.0
2.9	1.2	3.0	2.8	5.0	7.0	4.5	4.0	3.4	−1.1	1.6	3.1	−1.6	0.9
−7.6	−8.6	−11.5	−1.1	1.0	0.2	0.5	1.5	1.4	1.5	1.8	3.8	3.8	5.5
100.0	100.0	100.0	100.0	100.0	100.0	100.0	100.0	100.0	100.0	100.0	100.0	100.0	100.0
25.7	26.2	26.5	25.4	25.7	24.9	24.0	23.9	23.3	23.2	24.0	23.2	24.1	23.0
25.6	26.1	26.4	25.3	25.6	24.8	23.9	23.7	23.1	23.0	23.9	23.1	23.9	22.9
0.1	0.1	0.1	0.1	0.1	0.1	0.1	0.1	0.1	0.2	0.1	0.1	0.2	0.2

(continues)

Table A.2b   Continued

	1970	1971	1972	1973	1974	1975	1976	1977	1978	1979
Secondary production	22.9	23.5	24.0	23.8	23.7	24.9	25.3	26.3	25.5	25.2
Manufacturing	18.3	18.7	18.4	18.8	18.7	18.5	19.4	19.2	18.9	18.2
Construction	2.7	2.8	3.5	2.8	2.9	4.1	3.6	4.6	4.0	4.0
Utilities	1.9	2.0	2.1	2.1	2.2	2.3	2.4	2.5	2.6	3.0
Services	50.8	50.4	50.9	51.7	51.1	49.8	52.2	51.8	51.0	50.0
Transportation and										
Communications	5.3	5.2	5.1	5.1	5.5	5.5	6.0	6.2	6.1	5.8
Commercial Services	23.6	23.0	23.2	23.8	23.0	22.7	23.7	23.3	22.6	21.1
Financial Services	2.1	2.1	2.3	2.5	2.6	2.5	2.7	2.9	2.8	2.9
Housing	3.8	3.7	3.8	3.7	3.6	3.5	3.5	3.4	3.3	3.5
Public Administration	7.6	8.0	8.1	8.1	8.2	7.8	8.4	8.4	8.7	9.2
Other Services	8.3	8.4	8.5	8.5	8.1	7.7	7.8	7.4	7.4	7.5

By Sector of the Final Demand

Gross domestic product	2393.6	2508.8	2646.0	2779.8	2958.4	3122.8	3247.0	3443.7	3664.8	3601.7
Gross domestic expenditure	2443.1	2567.3	2659.2	2938.0	3101.8	3145.1	3480.3	4034.9	4165.8	3767.6
Consumption expenditures	2155.0	2217.2	2331.6	2513.1	2566.4	2664.4	2948.3	3271.2	3379.8	3161.5
Private sector	1903.7	1980.6	2054.0	2203.5	2268.8	2340.7	2573.6	2878.0	2943.3	2714.2
Public sector	251.3	236.6	277.6	309.6	297.6	323.7	374.7	393.2	436.5	447.3
Gross domestic investment	288.1	350.1	327.6	424.9	535.4	480.7	532.0	763.7	786.0	606.1
Gross fixed capital formation	259.1	293.6	385.8	351.0	401.5	519.1	535.0	677.4	695.5	586.7
Private sector	195.6	209.3	272.0	245.7	281.0	320.3	355.1	430.8	495.3	371.2
Public sector	63.5	84.3	113.8	105.3	120.5	198.8	179.9	246.6	200.2	215.5
Changes in inventories	29.0	56.5	−58.2	73.9	133.9	−38.4	−3.0	86.3	90.5	19.4
Net exports	−49.5	−58.5	−13.2	−158.2	−143.4	−22.3	−233.3	−591.2	−501.0	−165.9
Exports of goods and										
nonfactor services	510.1	554.4	649.8	625.0	666.6	747.1	676.5	597.2	719.7	979.9
Imports of goods and										
nonfactor services	559.6	612.9	663.0	783.2	810.0	769.4	909.8	1188.4	1220.7	1145.8
Net factor payments	−19.6	−23.4	−24.5	−31.4	−39.7	−47.9	−9.7	−34.7	−62.1	−25.3
Gross national product										
at market prices	2374.0	2485.4	2621.5	2748.4	2918.7	3074.9	3237.3	3409.0	3602.7	3576.4

Annual growth rates (in percent)

Gross domestic product	3.0	4.8	5.5	5.1	6.4	5.6	4.0	6.1	6.4	−1.7
Gross domestic expenditure		5.1	3.6	10.5	5.6	1.4	10.7	15.9	3.2	−9.6
Consumption expenditures		2.9	5.2	7.8	2.1	3.8	10.7	11.0	3.3	−6.5
Private sector		4.0	3.7	7.3	3.0	3.2	10.0	11.8	2.3	−7.8
Public sector		−5.8	17.3	11.5	−3.9	8.8	15.8	4.9	11.0	2.5
Gross domestic investment		21.5	−6.4	29.7	26.0	−10.2	10.7	43.6	2.9	−22.9
Gross fixed capital formation		13.3	31.4	−9.0	14.4	29.3	3.1	26.6	2.7	−15.6
Private sector		7.0	30.0	−9.7	14.4	14.0	10.9	21.3	15.0	−25.1
Public sector		32.8	35.0	−7.5	14.4	65.0	−9.5	37.1	−18.8	7.6
Changes in inventories										

1980	1981	1982	1983	1984	1985	1986	1987	1988	1989	1990	1991	1992	1993[a]
24.4	23.9	23.6	24.0	23.6	24.0	24.5	24.8	25.2	25.6	25.0	25.6	25.9	27.0
17.8	17.4	16.9	17.1	16.9	17.2	17.5	17.6	17.8	18.1	18.0	18.2	18.4	18.8
3.4	3.1	3.2	3.2	3.0	3.0	3.1	3.4	3.6	3.7	3.1	3.3	3.5	3.7
3.2	3.4	3.5	3.7	3.7	3.8	3.8	3.8	3.8	3.8	3.9	4.0	4.1	4.5
49.9	49.8	49.9	50.6	50.7	51.0	51.5	51.3	51.5	51.3	51.0	51.2	50.0	50.0
5.9	5.7	5.7	6.0	6.0	6.0	6.0	5.9	5.9	5.9	6.1	6.3	6.4	6.6
19.0	17.6	16.4	16.7	16.6	16.4	16.3	16.1	15.9	16.3	16.2	16.3	16.2	16.5
3.1	3.1	3.5	3.4	3.4	3.4	3.5	3.4	3.5	3.1	3.1	3.1	3.1	3.2
4.0	4.4	4.8	4.9	4.8	4.8	4.8	4.8	4.9	4.9	4.9	4.8	4.7	4.6
10.4	11.5	12.5	12.8	13.1	13.7	14.3	14.5	14.7	14.4	14.1	14.1	13.2	12.6
7.5	7.5	7.0	6.9	6.8	6.7	6.7	6.6	6.6	6.6	6.5	6.5	6.5	6.5
3289.3	3016.9	2847.7	2870.4	2935.6	2993.6	3012.5	3093.5	3143.8	3177.0	3285.0	3401.0	3580.1	3761.7
3330.2	3112.3	2875.9	2868.1	2971.6	3059.4	3140.1	3153.5	3259.9	3436.1	3304.0	3462.8	3663.1	3795.7
2918.1	2716.1	2520.1	2542.5	2636.3	2742.8	2755.5	2785.1	2823.3	2848.7	2914.2	2985.2	3058.1	3153.0
2495.7	2278.8	2084.6	2113.7	2175.3	2250.6	2244.9	2259.2	2284.3	2316.0	2376.6	2424.2	2496.1	2583.1
422.4	437.3	435.5	428.8	461.0	492.2	510.6	525.9	539.0	532.7	537.6	561.0	562.0	569.9
412.1	396.2	355.8	325.6	335.3	316.6	384.6	368.4	436.6	587.4	389.8	477.6	605.0	642.7
422.3	376.7	338.7	313.5	320.8	353.6	380.1	414.7	430.2	469.2	388.0	461.2	577.8	638.8
189.4	161.3	163.7	178.0	199.4	241.9	285.8	306.8	305.1	318.5	293.8	350.9	413.5	466.6
232.9	215.4	175.0	135.5	121.4	111.7	94.3	107.9	125.1	150.7	94.2	110.3	164.3	172.2
−10.2	19.5	17.1	12.1	14.5	−37.0	4.5	−46.3	6.4	118.2	1.8	16.4	27.2	3.9
−40.9	95.4	−28.2	2.3	−36.0	−65.8	−127.6	−60.0	−116.1	−259.1	−19.0	−61.8	−83.0	−34.0
837.6	690.4	588.4	698.1	674.4	648.1	566.4	636.6	576.8	476.1	718.9	707.4	786.9	900.6
878.5	785.8	616.6	695.8	710.4	713.9	694.0	696.6	692.9	735.2	737.9	769.2	869.9	934.6
−47.0	−51.9	−72.7	−104.5	−86.3	−73.9	−72.0	−70.1	−58.5	−56.0	−62.0	−58.5	−31.6	−20.4
3242.3	2965.0	2775.0	2765.9	2849.3	2919.7	2940.5	3023.4	3085.3	3121.0	3223.0	3342.5	3548.5	3741.3
−8.7	−8.3	−5.6	0.8	2.3	2.0	0.6	2.7	1.6	1.1	3.4	3.5	5.3	5.1
−11.6	−6.5	−7.6	−0.3	3.6	3.0	2.6	0.4	3.4	5.4	−3.8	4.8	5.8	3.6
−7.7	−6.9	−7.2	0.9	3.7	4.0	0.5	1.1	1.4	0.9	2.3	2.4	2.4	3.1
−8.1	−8.7	−8.5	1.4	2.9	3.5	−0.3	0.6	1.1	1.4	2.6	2.0	3.0	3.5
−5.6	3.5	−0.4	−1.5	7.5	6.8	3.7	3.0	2.5	−1.2	0.9	4.4	0.2	1.4
−32.0	−3.9	−10.2	−8.5	3.0	−5.6	21.5	−4.2	18.5	34.5	−33.6	22.5	26.7	6.2
−28.0	−10.8	−10.1	−7.4	2.3	10.2	7.5	9.1	3.7	9.1	−17.3	18.9	25.3	10.6
−49.0	−14.8	1.5	8.7	12.0	21.3	18.1	7.3	−0.6	4.4	−7.8	19.4	17.8	12.8
8.1	−7.5	−18.8	−22.6	−10.4	−8.0	−15.6	14.4	15.9	20.5	−37.5	17.1	49.0	4.8

(continues)

Table A.2b Continued

	1970	1971	1972	1973	1974	1975	1976	1977	1978	1979
Net exports										
Exports of goods and										
nonfactor services		8.7	17.2	–3.8	6.7	12.1	–9.4	–11.7	20.5	36.2
Imports of goods and										
nonfactor services		9.5	8.2	18.1	3.4	–5.0	18.2	30.6	2.7	–6.1
Net factor payments		19.5	4.8	27.9	26.5	20.6	–79.7	257.8	78.8	–59.3
Gross national product										
at market prices		4.7	5.5	4.8	6.2	5.4	5.3	5.3	5.7	–0.7
Percentage composition										
Gross domestic product	100.0	100.0	100.0	100.0	100.0	100.0	100.0	100.0	100.0	100.0
Gross domestic expenditure	102.1	102.3	100.5	105.7	104.8	100.7	107.2	117.2	113.7	104.6
Consumption expenditures	90.0	88.4	88.1	90.4	86.7	85.3	90.8	95.0	92.2	87.8
Private sector	79.5	78.9	77.6	79.3	76.7	75.0	79.3	83.6	80.3	75.4
Public sector	10.5	9.4	10.5	11.1	10.1	10.4	11.5	11.4	11.9	12.4
Gross domestic investment	12.0	14.0	12.4	15.3	18.1	15.4	16.4	22.2	21.4	16.8
Gross fixed capital formation	10.8	11.7	14.6	12.6	13.6	16.6	16.5	19.7	19.0	16.3
Private sector	8.2	8.3	10.3	8.8	9.5	10.3	10.9	12.5	13.5	10.3
Public sector	2.7	3.4	4.3	3.8	4.1	6.4	5.5	7.2	5.5	6.0
Changes in inventories	1.2	2.3	–2.2	2.7	4.5	–1.2	–0.1	2.5	2.5	0.5
Net exports	–2.1	–2.3	–0.5	–5.7	–4.8	–0.7	–7.2	–17.2	–13.7	–4.6
Exports of goods and										
nonfactor services	21.3	22.1	24.6	22.5	22.5	23.9	20.8	17.3	19.6	27.2
Imports of goods and										
nonfactor services	23.4	24.4	25.1	28.2	27.4	24.6	28.0	34.5	33.3	31.8
Net factor payments	–0.8	–0.9	–0.9	–1.1	–1.3	–1.5	–0.3	–1.0	–1.7	–0.7
Gross national product										
at market prices	99.2	99.1	99.1	98.9	98.7	98.5	99.7	99.0	98.3	99.3

Source: USAID, from BCR.
Note: a. Estimated values.

1980	1981	1982	1983	1984	1985	1986	1987	1988	1989	1990	1991	1992	1993[a]
–14.5	–17.6	–14.8	18.6	–3.4	–3.9	–12.6	12.4	–9.4	–17.5	51.0	–1.6	11.2	14.4
–23.3	–10.6	–21.5	12.8	2.1	0.5	–2.8	0.4	–0.5	6.1	0.4	4.2	13.1	7.4
86.3	10.3	40.1	43.9	–17.4	–14.4	–2.6	–2.5	–16.6	–4.3	10.8	–5.7	–46.0	–35.4
–9.3	–8.6	–6.4	–0.3	3.0	2.5	0.7	2.8	2.0	1.2	3.3	3.7	6.2	5.4
100.0	100.0	100.0	100.0	100.0	100.0	100.0	100.0	100.0	100.0	100.0	100.0	100.0	100.0
101.2	103.2	101.0	99.9	101.2	102.2	104.2	101.9	103.7	108.2	100.6	101.8	102.3	100.9
88.7	90.0	88.5	88.6	89.8	91.6	91.5	90.0	89.8	89.7	88.7	87.8	85.4	83.8
75.9	75.5	73.2	73.6	74.1	75.2	74.5	73.0	72.7	72.9	72.3	71.3	69.7	68.7
12.8	14.5	15.3	14.9	15.7	16.4	16.9	17.0	17.1	16.8	16.4	16.5	15.7	15.2
12.5	13.1	12.5	11.3	11.4	10.6	12.8	11.9	13.9	18.5	11.9	14.0	16.9	17.1
12.8	12.5	11.9	10.9	10.9	11.8	12.6	13.4	13.7	14.8	11.8	13.6	16.1	17.0
5.8	5.3	5.7	6.2	6.8	8.1	9.5	9.9	9.7	10.0	8.9	10.3	11.5	12.4
7.1	7.1	6.1	4.7	4.1	3.7	3.1	3.5	4.0	4.7	2.9	3.2	4.6	4.6
–0.3	0.6	0.6	0.4	0.5	–1.2	0.1	–1.5	0.2	3.7	0.1	0.5	0.8	0.1
–1.2	–3.2	–1.0	0.1	–1.2	–2.2	–4.2	–1.9	–3.7	–8.2	–0.6	–1.8	–2.3	–0.9
25.5	22.9	20.7	24.3	23.0	21.6	18.8	20.6	18.3	15.0	21.9	20.8	22.0	23.9
26.7	26.0	21.7	24.2	24.2	23.8	23.0	22.5	22.0	23.1	22.5	22.6	24.3	24.8
–1.4	–1.7	–2.6	–3.6	–2.9	–2.5	–2.4	–2.3	–1.9	–1.8	–1.9	–1.7	–0.9	–0.5
98.6	98.3	97.4	96.4	97.1	97.5	97.6	97.7	98.1	98.2	98.1	98.3	99.1	99.5

Table A.2c   National Accounts and Government Revenue and Expenditure, 1970–1993
(in millions of current colones)

	1970	1971	1972	1973	1974	1975	1976	1977	1978	1979
GDP	2,571	2,704	2,882	3,332	3,944	4,478	5,706	7,167	7,692	8,607
Private consumption	1,948	2,061	2,138	2,474	2,946	3,283	3,973	4,634	5,574	5,933
Gross fixed capital formation	308	359	474	521	719	1,031	1,145	1,521	1,652	1,512
Increase/decrease (–) in stocks	33	62	–66	88	174	–40	–26	158	183	45
Government consumption	276	275	308	349	429	501	686	805	996	1,133
Exports	639	666	839	998	1,279	1,480	2,028	2,735	2,328	3,182
Imports	631	720	811	1,099	1,610	1,711	2,101	2,686	3,041	3,197
Net factor income/ payments abroad	–21	–25	–27	–38	–53	–69	–17	–72	–130	–60
GNP	2,550	2,679	2,855	3,294	3,891	4,409	5,689	7,095	7,562	8,547
Government accounts										
Expenditure	283	328	351	391	542	606	827	1,077	1,184	1,280
Revenue	284	298	327	403	488	581	805	1,257	1,048	1,171
Net lending	0	0	0	0	0	0	0	0	–14	13
Deficit (–) or surplus	1	–30	–24	12	–54	–25	–21	180	–122	–122
Financing	–1	30	24	–12	54	25	22	–180	122	122
Net domestic borrowing	–6	21	7	–40	5	3	25	–90	54	73
Net foreign borrowing	7	8	15	35	62	15	23	0	36	28
Use of cash balances	–2	2	2	–7	–13	7	–27	–89	33	21

As a percentage of GDP

	1970	1971	1972	1973	1974	1975	1976	1977	1978	1979
GDP	100.0	100.0	100.0	100.0	100.0	100.0	100.0	100.0	100.0	100.0
Private consumption	75.7	76.2	74.2	74.3	74.7	73.3	69.6	64.7	72.5	68.9
Gross fixed capital formation	12.0	13.3	16.5	15.6	18.2	23.0	20.1	21.2	21.5	17.6
Increase/decrease (–) in stocks	1.3	2.3	–2.3	2.6	4.4	–0.9	–0.5	2.2	2.4	0.5
Government consumption	10.7	10.2	10.7	10.5	10.9	11.2	12.0	11.2	12.9	13.2
Exports	24.8	24.6	29.1	30.0	32.4	33.0	35.5	38.2	30.3	37.0
Imports	24.5	26.6	28.1	33.0	40.8	38.2	36.8	37.5	39.5	37.1
Net factor income/payments abroad	–0.8	–0.9	–0.9	–1.1	–1.3	–1.5	–0.3	–1.0	–1.7	–0.7
GNP	99.2	99.1	99.1	98.9	98.7	98.5	99.7	99.0	98.3	99.3
Government accounts										
Expenditure	11.0	12.1	12.2	11.7	13.8	13.5	14.5	15.0	15.4	14.9
Revenue	11.0	11.0	11.3	12.1	12.4	13.0	14.1	17.5	13.6	13.6
Net lending	0.0	0.0	0.0	0.0	0.0	0.0	0.0	0.0	–0.2	0.1
Deficit (–) or surplus	0.0	–1.1	–0.8	0.4	–1.4	–0.6	–0.4	2.5	–1.6	–1.4
Financing	0.0	1.1	0.8	–0.3	1.4	0.6	0.4	–2.5	1.6	1.4
Net domestic borrowing	–0.2	0.8	0.2	–1.2	0.1	0.1	0.4	–1.3	0.7	0.8
Net foreign borrowing	0.3	0.3	0.5	1.1	1.6	0.3	0.4	0.0	0.5	0.3
Use of cash balances	–0.1	0.1	0.1	–0.2	–0.3	0.1	–0.5	–1.2	0.4	0.2

Source: IMF, *International Financial Statistics.*

1980	1981	1982	1983	1984	1985	1986	1987	1988	1989	1990	1991	1992	1993
8,917	8,647	8,966	10,152	11,657	14,331	19,763	23,141	27,366	32,230	41,057	47,792	54,853	66,239
6,405	6,644	6,877	7,871	9,184	11,640	15,206	18,744	22,153	26,729	36,141	41,821	48,799	58,588
1,210	1,173	1,130	1,180	1,336	1,723	2,594	3,158	3,456	4,293	4,834	6,435	8,594	10,726
−27	58	56	44	59	−169	26	−297	45	646	17	171	280	44
1,247	1,369	1,415	1,607	1,869	2,220	2,803	3,181	3,484	3,930	4,649	5,273	5,789	6,438
3,046	2,307	2,042	2,486	2,536	3,199	4,875	4,395	4,327	4,267	6,538	7,055	7,459	8,998
2,964	2,904	2,553	3,036	3,327	4,283	5,740	6,040	6,099	7,636	11,113	12,963	16,068	18,555
−128	−149	−229	−370	−343	−354	−471	−525	−509	−568	−775	−822	−481	544
8,789	8,498	8,737	9,782	11,314	13,977	19,292	22,616	26,857	31,662	40,282	46,970	54,373	65,695
1,422	1,582	1,695	1,571	1,821	2,150	2,723	3,023	3,096	3,307	3,855	4,928	7,254	8,387
1,029	1,068	1,091	1,258	1,574	1,902	2,822	2,981	2,928	2,631	3,853	4,072	5,716	7,203
3	36	4	11	136	−55	57	−128	7	55	25	329	301	186
−397	−549	−607	−324	−382	−193	42	86	−175	−731	−27	−1,185	−1,839	−1,370
397	549	607	324	382	193	−42	−86	175	731	27	—	—	—
429	501	437	296	342	142	33	−17	254	690	191	—	—	—
22	61	124	39	32	1	−84	104	302	259	−90	—	—	—
−54	−13	47	−10	9	49	9	−172	−381	−219	−74	—	—	—
100.0	100.0	100.0	100.0	100.0	100.0	100.0	100.0	100.0	100.0	100.0	100.0	100.0	100.0
71.8	76.8	76.7	77.5	78.8	81.2	76.9	81.0	80.9	82.9	88.0	87.5	89.0	88.4
13.6	13.6	12.6	11.6	11.5	12.0	13.1	13.6	12.6	13.3	11.8	13.5	15.7	16.2
−0.3	0.7	0.6	0.4	0.5	−1.2	0.1	−1.3	0.2	2.0	0.0	0.4	0.5	0.1
14.0	15.8	15.8	15.8	16.0	15.5	14.2	13.7	12.7	12.2	11.3	11.0	10.6	9.7
34.2	26.7	22.8	24.5	21.8	22.3	24.7	19.0	15.8	13.2	15.9	14.8	13.6	13.6
33.2	33.6	28.5	29.9	28.5	29.9	29.0	26.1	22.3	23.7	27.1	27.1	29.3	28.0
−1.4	−1.7	−2.6	−3.6	−2.9	−2.5	−2.4	−2.3	−1.9	−1.8	−1.9	−1.7	−0.9	0.8
98.6	98.3	97.4	96.4	97.1	97.5	97.6	97.7	98.1	98.2	98.1	98.3	99.1	99.2
16.0	18.3	18.9	15.5	15.6	15.0	13.8	13.1	11.3	10.3	9.4	10.3	13.2	12.7
11.5	12.4	12.2	12.4	13.5	13.3	14.3	12.9	10.7	8.2	9.4	8.5	10.4	10.9
0.0	0.4	0.0	0.1	1.2	−0.4	0.3	−0.6	0.0	0.2	0.1	0.7	0.5	0.3
−4.4	−6.4	−6.8	−3.2	−3.3	−1.3	0.2	0.4	−0.6	−2.3	−0.1	−2.5	−3.4	−2.1
4.5	6.4	6.8	3.2	3.3	1.3	−0.2	−0.4	0.6	2.3	0.1	—	—	—
4.8	5.8	4.9	2.9	2.9	1.0	0.2	−0.1	0.9	2.1	0.5	—	—	—
0.2	0.7	1.4	0.4	0.3	0.0	−0.4	0.4	1.1	0.8	−0.2	—	—	—
−0.6	−0.2	0.5	−0.1	0.1	0.3	0.0	−0.7	−1.4	−0.7	−0.2	—	—	—

Table A.3   **Balance of Payments, 1970–1993 (millions of U.S. dollars)**

	1970	1971	1972	1973	1974	1975	1976	1977	1978	1979
Current account (excluding exceptional financing)	9	−14	12	−44	−134	−93	24	31	−286	21
Trade balance (FOB)	41	18	52	19	−58	−18	64	113	−149	178
Exports	236	244	302	358	464	533	745	974	802	1,132
Imports	−195	−226	−250	−340	−522	−551	−681	−861	−951	−955
Services and transfers	−33	−32	−40	−62	−76	−75	−40	−82	−136	−156
Other goods, services, and income	−47	−49	−52	−76	−95	−103	−69	−121	−188	−208
Private unrequited transfers	12	16	9	12	17	25	24	30	45	45
Official unrequited transfers	2	1	3	2	1	2	5	9	6	6
Capital account	13	31	42	55	103	132	86	44	340	−49
Foreign investment	4	7	7	6	20	13	31	19	27	−16
Direct	4	7	7	6	20	13	13	19	23	−10
Portfolio	0	0	0	0	0	0	18	1	4	−6
Other capital	9	24	35	49	83	119	55	25	313	−33
Long-term	1	7	56	29	75	101	42	19	138	74
Short-term	8	17	−20	21	8	18	13	6	175	−107
Capital account plus current account	22	17	54	12	−31	39	109	75	55	−28
Net errors and omissions	−20	−31	−39	−24	−58	−34	−25	−34	−29	−106
Overall balance	1	−15	15	−12	−89	5	84	41	25	−134
Financing	−1	15	−15	12	89	−5	−84	−41	−25	134
Exceptional	1	8	0	2	104	25	0	0	30	0
Liabilities constituting foreign authorities' reserves	0	0	0	0	0	0	0	0	0	0
Reserve assets	5	3	−13	21	−36	−30	−78	−26	−55	134
Credit from fund and fund-administered resources	−7	4	−2	−11	21	0	−6	−15	0	0

Source: IMF, *International Financial Statistics.*

1980	1981	1982	1983	1984	1985	1986	1987	1988	1989	1990	1991	1992	1993
31	−250	−120	−148	−189	−189	−17	−68	−129	−330	−235	−213	−195	−118
178	−100	−100	−74	−189	−216	−124	−349	−356	−592	−600	−706	−961	−1,035
1,075	798	700	758	726	679	778	590	611	498	580	588	598	732
−897	−898	−800	−832	−914	−895	−902	−939	−967	−1,090	−1,180	−1,294	−1,559	−1,767
−148	−150	−20	−74	0.0	27	107	281	227	262	365	493	766	917
−197	−210	−227	−225	−173	−156	−142	−54	−119	−127	−106	−133	−85	−87
17	39	88	97	118	129	150	180	202	208	324	470	709	823
32	21	119	54	55	54	100	154	143	181	146	156	142	181
25	151	175	93	19	−3	46	−59	52	106	−10	−61	−4	87
5	−6	−2	28	12	12	21	18	17	13	2	25	15	16
6	−6	−1	28	12	12	24	18	17	13	2	25	15	16
−1	0	−1	0	0	0	−3	0	0	0	0	0	0	0
20	157	177	64	7	−16	25	−77	35	93	−12	−87	−20	70
105	176	154	183	22	45	−2	−55	12	126	0	−3	—	—
−84	−19	23	−119	−15	−61	27	−22	23	−33	−12	−83	—	—
56	−99	55	−55	−169	−192	29	−127	−77	−225	−245	−274	−199	−32
−318	−59	−62	−50	−52	23	−142	7	−107	126	270	126	66	90
−262	−158	−7	−106	−222	−169	−113	−120	−184	−98	25	−148	−134	59
262	158	7	106	222	169	113	120	184	98	−25	148	134	−59
155	74	14	135	215	190	176	203	165	202	129	78	225	53
5	36	−36	−6	14	6	−19	−1	0	0	0	0	0	0
68	11	−37	−40	−1	0	14	−37	30	−98	−148	70	−92	−112
33	37	65	17	−5	−27	−58	−45	−11	−5	−5	0	0	0

Table A.4   External Debt and Net Transfers, 1970–1993 (millions of U.S. dollars)

	1970	1971	1972	1973	1974	1975	1976	1977	1978	1979
Total debt stocks	182	206	252	244	360	412	480	723	910	886
Long-term debt	176	195	243	244	338	391	466	507	581	608
Public and publicly										
guaranteed	88	93	109	107	176	196	263	266	330	408
Official creditors	70	74	88	95	104	145	189	240	309	391
Multilateral	41	43	51	54	60	78	95	128	178	226
IBRD	25	24	22	24	29	41	49	56	65	80
IDA	8	8	14	16	16	17	18	19	21	24
Other	8	11	15	14	15	20	28	53	92	122
Bilateral	30	31	37	41	43	67	94	112	131	166
Private creditors	17	18	22	12	72	51	74	26	21	17
Bonds	3	3	6	6	6	6	2	0	0	0
Commercial banks	14	15	16	6	67	26	41	10	8	7
Other	0	0	0	0	0	19	30	16	13	10
Private nonguaranteed	88	102	133	138	163	196	203	241	251	201
Short-term debt	0	0	0	0	0	0	0	216	329	278
Total creditors	—	0	0	0	0	0	0	216	329	278
Interest arrears on										
long-term debt	—	0	0	0	0	0	0	0	0	0
Use of IMF credit	7	11	10	0	22	21	15	0	0	0
Debt Flows										
Disbursements (On long-term										
debt and IMF credit)	31	57	83	46	167	132	135	136	135	90
Long-term debt	31	48	74	46	140	132	135	136	135	90
Public and publicly										
guaranteed	8	17	22	15	88	67	88	57	77	90
Official creditors	6	8	16	13	14	46	47	57	77	90
Multilateral	5	5	10	8	11	21	20	36	54	53
IBRD	1	1	1	4	8	13	9	9	11	17
IDA	0	0	5	1	0	1	2	1	2	3
Other	3	4	5	3	3	6	10	26	41	32
Bilateral	2	2	6	5	4	25	27	21	23	37
Private creditors	1	9	6	2	74	21	41	1	0	0
Bonds	0	0	3	0	0	0	0	0	0	0
Commercial banks	1	9	3	2	74	2	30	0	0	0
Other	0	0	0	0	0	19	11	1	0	0
Private nonguaranteed	24	32	53	31	53	65	47	79	58	0
IMF purchases	0	9	10	0	27	0	0	0	0	0
Principal repayments (On long-term										
debt and IMF credit)	27	35	38	54	52	80	67	115	65	63
On long-term debt	22	30	27	43	46	80	61	95	60	63
Public and publicly										
guaranteed	6	12	7	16	19	47	22	54	12	13
Official creditors	3	4	4	5	6	4	4	5	7	8
Multilateral	3	3	3	4	4	3	3	3	4	5
IBRD	2	2	2	3	2	2	1	2	2	3
IDA	0	0	0	0	0	0	0	0	0	0
Other	1	1	1	1	2	1	1	2	2	2
Bilateral	0	1	1	1	1	1	1	2	3	3

1980	1981	1982	1983	1984	1985	1986	1987	1988	1989	1990	1991	1992
911	1,130	1,443	1,740	1,826	1,854	1,848	1,971	1,983	2,068	2,137	2,174	2,131
659	851	1,107	1,507	1,590	1,660	1,659	1,735	1,729	1,855	1,928	2,072	2,028
499	704	974	1,385	1,476	1,555	1,576	1,665	1,674	1,815	1,902	2,051	2,017
487	690	878	1,159	1,275	1,395	1,456	1,576	1,585	1,667	1,734	1,864	1,848
258	323	380	492	519	611	668	732	724	775	784	839	860
87	98	105	106	95	119	140	167	155	142	140	189	182
27	27	27	26	26	26	25	25	24	24	23	23	22
144	198	248	359	398	466	503	541	544	609	620	627	656
229	366	497	667	756	784	789	845	860	893	950	1,024	987
12	14	96	227	201	160	120	89	89	148	168	187	169
0	0	25	38	29	19	10	0	0	0	0	0	0
8	6	58	170	156	121	91	71	68	111	127	151	135
4	8	14	19	17	20	19	18	21	37	41	36	34
161	147	134	122	114	104	83	70	55	39	26	21	12
220	212	206	94	111	84	127	214	243	208	209	102	103
220	212	206	94	111	82	123	209	234	185	203	96	89
0	0	0	0	0	2	4	5	9	23	6	6	14
32	67	129	139	125	111	62	22	11	5	0	0	0
149	277	370	396	278	206	139	131	143	236	109	278	108
110	239	304	379	278	206	139	131	143	236	109	278	108
110	232	295	377	278	206	139	131	143	236	109	278	108
105	228	221	335	241	191	138	131	125	171	79	188	106
36	75	70	124	67	77	44	35	54	78	44	102	88
10	15	11	7	11	14	3	3	13	1	2	56	11
3	1	0	0	0	0	0	0	0	0	0	0	0
23	59	58	117	56	63	41	32	41	78	42	46	77
69	153	152	211	174	115	94	96	71	93	35	85	18
5	4	74	41	37	15	1	1	18	65	30	90	1
0	0	25	13	1	1	1	0	0	0	0	0	0
3	0	43	23	35	9	0	0	11	50	25	90	0
2	4	6	6	1	5	1	1	7	15	5	0	1
0	7	9	2	0	0	0	0	0	0	0	0	0
40	38	66	17	0	0	0	0	0	0	0	0	0
35	38	55	108	136	164	194	171	124	101	123	166	135
35	38	55	108	131	137	136	125	114	96	118	165	135
17	18	32	94	123	127	115	111	99	80	104	161	125
8	16	30	48	62	72	73	80	82	73	93	92	107
5	9	13	12	15	20	29	33	32	32	56	52	61
3	4	4	6	5	8	7	8	11	9	15	12	13
0	0	0	0	0	0	1	1	1	0	1	1	1
2	5	8	6	10	12	21	24	21	23	40	39	47
3	7	17	35	47	52	44	47	50	40	37	40	46

(continues)

Table A.4   Continued

	1970	1971	1972	1973	1974	1975	1976	1977	1978	1979
Private creditors	3	8	3	12	13	43	18	49	5	5
Bonds	0	0	0	0	0	0	4	2	0	0
Commercial banks	3	8	3	12	13	43	15	32	2	2
Other	0	0	0	0	0	0	0	15	3	3
Private nonguaranteed	16	18	21	27	28	33	39	41	48	50
IMF repurchases	5	5	11	10	6	0	6	21	5	0
Net flows on long-term debt and IMF	4	22	45	−7	116	52	68	21	70	27
(Disbursements − principal repayments)										
Net flows on short-term debt	0	0	0	0	0	0	0	0	0	0
Net flows on all debt	4	22	45	−7	116	52	68	21	70	27
Interest repayments	9	10	11	15	17	20	27	32	37	41
On long-term debt	9	10	11	15	17	19	26	31	37	41
Public and publicly guaranteed	4	4	4	4	5	7	14	15	18	21
Official creditors	2	3	3	3	4	5	9	11	15	18
Multilateral	2	2	2	3	3	4	5	6	8	10
IBRD	1	1	1	2	2	3	3	4	5	6
IDA	0	0	0	0	0	0	0	0	0	0
Other	0	1	1	1	1	1	1	2	2	4
Bilateral	0	1	1	1	1	1	4	5	7	8
Private creditors	1	1	1	1	1	2	5	4	3	3
Bonds	0	0	0	0	0	0	0	0	0	0
Commercial banks	1	1	1	1	1	2	3	3	1	1
Other	0	0	0	0	0	0	2	1	1	2
Private nonguaranteed	6	6	7	10	12	12	12	16	19	21
On short-term debt	—	0	0	0	0	0	0	0	0	0
IMF charges	0	0	0	0	0	2	1	0.6	0	0
Net transfers on debt	−5	13	34	−22	99	32	40	−11	33	−14
(Net flows − interest payments)										

Source: World Bank, *World Debt Tables,* various issues.

1980	1981	1982	1983	1984	1985	1986	1987	1988	1989	1990	1991	1992
10	2	3	46	62	55	42	31	17	8	11	69	19
0	0	0	0	10	10	10	10	0	0	0	0	0
2	2	3	45	50	44	30	19	14	7	9	66	16
8	0	0	1	2	1	2	2	3	1	2	3	3
18	20	22	14	8	10	21	14	15	16	14	5	9
0	0	0	0	6	27	58	46	10	5	5	0	0
114	239	315	288	142	42	−54	−40	19	135	−14	113	−27
0	0	0	0	0	−29	41	86	25	−49	18	−107	−7
114	239	315	288	142	13	−13	46	44	86	4	5	−34
61	55	75	94	100	94	92	89	78	68	84	82	83
35	39	44	69	78	81	81	83	72	60	75	72	79
24	30	36	62	76	73	73	81	67	56	72	69	78
22	28	33	44	49	58	65	70	59	50	62	56	67
11	13	16	18	21	30	36	38	33	31	50	39	41
7	7	7	8	6	8	10	11	12	10	14	11	14
0	0	0	0	0	0	0	0	0	0	0	0	0
4	6	9	10	15	22	26	27	22	21	35	28	27
11	14	17	26	28	27	29	32	26	29	13	18	26
2	2	3	18	27	15	8	10	8	6	9	13	10
0	0	0	3	4	3	2	1	0	0	0	0	0
1	1	1	14	21	11	5	7	6	4	8	11	8
1	1	2	1	2	2	2	3	2	2	2	2	2
11	9	8	7	3	8	7	2	6	4	3	2	1
25	15	27	17	14	6	6	5	6	8	9	10	4
0	1	4	7	8	7	5	2	0	0	0	0	0
53	184	240	194	41	−81	−105	−43	−35	18	−81	−77	−117

Table A.5   Structure of Government Revenue, 1970–1992 (millions of colones)

	1970	1971	1972	1973	1974	1975	1976	1977	1978	1979
Revenue and grants	286.7	294.9	341.0	399.0	484.0	561.7	806.9	1,174.0	1,009.9	1,188.7
Revenue	286.0	294.0	340.0	399.0	483.8	561.0	806.8	1,173.9	1,009.9	1,188.7
Current revenue	277.7	294.0	331.0	395.0	483.7	561.0	806.7	1,173.7	1,009.9	1,187.0
Tax revenue	264.0	280.0	304.0	383.8	461.8	550.0	777.9	1,139.9	984.0	1,169.0
On income, profits,										
capital gains	40.8	46.0	50.0	64.0	81.8	121.0	142.0	168.0	205.0	190.0
On property	25.6	24.7	23.5	31.7	30.5	36.0	49.0	75.0	86.0	85.0
On goods and services										
(domestic)	89.8	79.0	84.8	133.0	163.0	188.0	231.0	272.9	291.0	322.8
On international trade										
and transactions	108.0	106.0	119.0	154.0	186.0	204.0	355.0	623.0	401.0	571.0
Other										
Nontax revenue	15.0	17.0	19.8	16.0	19.0	22.6	28.0	37.5	37.5	41.5
Entrepreneur and										
property income		7.0	6.5	8.6	9.8	11.0	15.7	23.0	7.0	10.0
Fees, etc.		8.5	7.6	6.0	7.6	9.5	10.6	11.9	19.5	19.0
Fines and forfeits			3.9	1.0	1.6	1.5	1.8	2.0	9.0	10.7
Other		1.5	1.8				0.1	0.1	1.3	1.5
Capital revenue	8.7		9.0	3.8	0.1		0.1	0.2		1.2
Sales of fixed capital assets				0.9	0.1		0.1	0.1		1.2
Sales of land and intangible										
assets	8.7		9.0	1.3				0.1		
Capital transfers from										
nongovernment sources				1.6						
Total grants	0.3	0.3	0.8	0.3	0.2	0.5	0.1	0.1		
From abroad			0.8	0.3	0.2	0.5	0.1	0.1		
From other levels of national										
government										

Source: IMF, *Government Financial Statistics.*

1980	1981	1982	1983	1984	1985	1986	1987	1988	1989	1990	1991	1992
1,016.0	1,085.0	1,085.0	1,213.0	1,701.0	2,439.7	2,919.0	3,077.8	2,960.7	2,777.7	3,953.0	4,783.0	5,605.8
1,015.7	1,084.7	1,085.0	1,213.0	1,541.0	1,939.8	2,829.8	2,687.0	2,815.0	2,677.0	3,350.0	4,271.0	5,262.0
1,014.0	1,084.0	1,085.0	1,209.9	1,537.0	1,939.0	2,827.0	2,687.0	2,815.0	2,677.0	3,348.8	4,254.0	5,261.9
989.0	1,002.0	963.0	1,101.0	1,371.0	1,698.8	2,743.9	2,554.0	2,622.8	2,509.9	3,246.0	4,119.0	4,915.7
235.0	226.0	221.0	240.8	272.9	317.0	564.8	575.7	593.0	599.0	744.0	983.8	1,072.0
76.9	71.0	74.0	77.0	80.6	102.9	105.0	161.0	202.0	189.0	211.0	286.9	331.0
302.0	381.8	387.9	497.7	637.0	736.0	893.0	1,103	1,232.9	1,218.8	1,517	1,934.8	2,602
375.0	323.0	279.0	278.0	372.0	533.0	1,169.0	702.0	594.7	450.0	729.0	877.9	892.0
			7.0	7.6	9.3	10.8	11.7	0.0	52.0	44.0	35.8	18.0
45.0	100.0	131.5	122.6	199.0	200.7	250.9	155.8	177.0	105.0	111.0	234.0	343.0
13.5	14.5	27.0	22.0	110.0	101.0	145.7	37.8	128.0	50.0	46.0	67.0	178.0
15.6	57.9	87.0	93.8	82.9	85.7	95.9	103.7	34.8	43.6	48.0	82.7	111.7
12.8	25.0	3.0	3.0	3.8	4.0	4.8	6.5	7.9	6.0	7.0	11.6	11.7
3.4	2.2	13.0	3.4	2.5	9.4	4.5	7.8	6.4	4.8	9.0	73.0	42.0
1.2	0.1		3.1	3.5	0.3	2.4	0.1			1.3	16.9	0.4
1.2	0.1		1.9	3.5	0.3	2.4	0.1			0.2	0.3	0.3
		1.2								1.1		0.1
											16.6	
0.6	0.4		0.2	159.9	499.9	89.0	390.0	145.0	100.0	603.0	512.0	343.0
0.6	0.4		0.2	159.9	499.9	89.0	390.0	145.0	100.0	603.0	512.0	266.0
												77.0

Table A.6   Structure of Government Expenditure, 1970–1992 (millions of colones)

	1970	1971	1972	1973	1974	1975	1976	1977	1978	1979
Total expenditure	298	319	366	411	493	602	837	998	1,119	1,270
General public services	71	75	79	74	96	113	134	171	181	224
Defense	16	19	24	27	29	34	45	62	76	118
Public order and safety	—	—	—	—	—	—	—	—	—	—
Education	67	79	78	105	131	143	176	211	231	249
Health	33	37	40	43	51	49	77	98	99	110
Social security and welfare	2	19	22	24	22	22	27	29	42	54
Housing and community amenities	2	5	6	10	11	11	25	37	36	25
Recreation, culture, religious affairs	1	1	0	0	3	15	15	14	22	15
Economic affairs and services	39	47	53	69	98	140	245	245	250	309
Agriculture, forestry, fishing, hunting	15	18	9	30	47	49	102	74	75	59
Mining, manufacturing, construction	—	—	0	—	–	—	0	1	1	1
Fuel and energy	2	3	17	16	15	17	20	14	20	26
Transportation and communications	12	11	20	16	24	51	91	100	103	133
Other	10	15	6	6	12	23	32	55	51	89
Other	33	11	20	13	14	15	17	11	55	28

As a percentage of GDP

	1970	1971	1972	1973	1974	1975	1976	1977	1978	1979
Total expenditure	11.60	11.81	12.71	12.34	12.51	13.47	14.68	13.94	14.55	14.77
General public services	2.76	2.76	2.73	2.22	2.43	2.53	2.35	2.39	2.35	2.60
Defense	0.60	0.69	0.84	0.81	0.74	0.76	0.78	0.87	0.99	1.37
Public order and safety	—	—	—	—	—	—	—	—	—	—
Education	2.59	2.91	2.72	3.15	3.32	3.20	3.09	2.95	3.00	2.90
Health	1.27	1.37	1.39	1.28	1.29	1.10	1.35	1.36	1.29	1.28
Social security and welfare	0.07	0.70	0.75	0.71	0.56	0.49	0.47	0.41	0.55	0.63
Housing and community amenities	0.07	0.17	0.22	0.29	0.27	0.25	0.44	0.52	0.47	0.29
Recreation, culture, religious affairs	0.04	0.02	0.00	0.00	0.07	0.33	0.25	0.20	0.29	0.17
Economic affairs and services	1.52	1.73	1.83	2.07	2.49	3.13	4.30	3.42	3.25	3.59
Agriculture, forestry, fishing, hunting	0.60	0.65	0.31	0.91	1.19	1.11	1.79	1.03	0.98	0.69
Mining, manufacturing, construction	—	—	—	—	—	—	0.01	0.01	0.01	0.01
Fuel and energy	0.07	0.11	0.59	0.47	0.37	0.38	0.34	0.19	0.26	0.31
Transportation and communications	0.45	0.39	0.69	0.48	0.62	1.14	1.60	1.40	1.34	1.55
Other	0.39	0.56	0.21	0.18	0.30	0.51	0.56	0.77	0.66	1.03
Other	1.28	0.40	0.69	0.39	0.36	0.33	0.30	0.15	0.72	0.32

Source: IMF, *Government Financial Statistics.*

1980	1981	1982	1983	1984	1985	1986	1987	1988	1989	1990	1991	1992
1,531	1,614	1722	1,708	2,087	2,674	2,474	2,863	3,024	3,321	3,976	4,906	6,077
240	233	250	254	305	351	399	208	213	235	272	532	761
134	170	205	270	512	543	709	768	777	925	974	1,010	974
—	—	—	—	—	—	—	272	284	349	357	410	445
303	288	290	283	323	387	431	489	516	585	643	706	778
137	135	123	143	169	156	185	211	216	245	310	378	446
51	61	64	58	76	76	89	86	88	106	127	145	205
32	26	18	20	21	15	23	47	45	66	89	70	79
28	26	22	20	22	8	18	31	29	31	55	63	90
321	398	362	364	385	337	559	396	531	497	665	937	1,178
88	114	146	140	142	88	92	105	108	136	215	264	160
1	2	2	2	2	1	2	8	8	3	3	5	5
20	8	2	3	5	3	4	1	70	1	1	91	302
105	154	153	162	178	151	230	215	279	275	306	362	528
105	120	59	56	56	92	231	65	66	81	140	214	182
45	98	172	146	189	176	265	241	243	287	326	527	1,102
17.18	18.68	19.22	16.83	17.91	18.66	12.52	12.37	11.05	10.30	9.69	10.27	11.10
2.69	2.70	2.79	2.50	2.62	2.45	2.02	0.90	0.78	0.73	0.66	1.11	1.39
1.50	1.97	2.29	2.66	4.39	3.79	3.59	3.32	2.84	2.87	2.37	2.11	1.78
—	—	—	—	—	—	—	1.18	1.04	1.08	0.87	0.86	0.81
3.40	3.33	3.24	2.79	2.77	2.70	2.18	2.11	1.89	1.82	1.57	1.48	1.42
1.54	1.56	1.37	1.41	1.45	1.09	0.94	0.91	0.79	0.76	0.76	0.79	0.81
0.57	0.71	0.71	0.57	0.65	0.53	0.45	0.37	0.32	0.33	0.31	0.30	0.37
0.36	0.30	0.20	0.20	0.18	0.10	0.12	0.20	0.16	0.20	0.22	0.15	0.14
0.31	0.30	0.25	0.20	0.19	0.06	0.09	0.13	0.11	0.10	0.13	0.13	0.16
3.60	4.61	4.04	3.59	3.30	2.35	2.83	1.71	1.94	1.54	1.62	1.96	2.15
0.99	1.32	1.63	1.38	1.22	0.61	0.47	0.45	0.39	0.42	0.52	0.55	0.29
0.01	0.02	0.02	0.02	0.02	0.01	0.01	0.04	0.03	0.01	0.01	0.01	0.01
0.23	0.09	0.03	0.03	0.04	0.02	0.02	0.00	0.25	—	—	0.19	0.55
1.18	1.78	1.71	1.60	1.53	1.05	1.16	0.93	1.02	0.85	0.75	0.76	0.96
1.18	1.39	0.66	0.55	0.48	0.64	1.17	0.28	0.24	0.25	0.34	0.45	0.33
0.51	1.13	1.92	1.44	1.62	1.23	1.34	1.04	0.89	0.89	0.79	1.10	2.01

Table A.7   **Total Approved Credit from Banking System, by Sector, 1985–1993 (millions of colones)**

	1985	1986	1987	1988	1989	1990	1991	1992	1993
Agriculture	976	908	1,070	938	1,303	1,434	2,001	3,007	3,539
Mining	5	3	5	13	7	0	5	2	11
Manufacturing	667	864	1,034	1,256	1,163	1,762	2,685	4,964	4,766
Construction	239	257	229	283	252	180	440	1,639	2,600
Utilities	13	7	2	3	2	15	5	.4	7
Commerce	3,606	4,078	3,233	4,588	6,780	5,810	5,731	7,419	6,199
Transport	33	53	46	51	51	48	161	254	478
Services	143	128	143	208	195	150	206	525	589
Refinancing	717	775	758	864	1,000	977	980	1,210	1,003
Other	7	1	2	8	2	14	9	78	20
Total	6,407	7,074	6,520	8,212	10,756	10,390	12,223	19,102	19,212

Percentage of total

	1985	1986	1987	1988	1989	1990	1991	1992	1993
Agriculture	15.2	12.8	16.4	11.4	12.1	13.8	16.4	15.7	18.4
Mining	0.1	0.0	0.1	0.2	0.1	0.0	0.0	0.0	0.1
Manufacturing	10.4	12.2	15.9	15.3	10.8	17.0	22.0	26.0	24.8
Construction	3.7	3.6	3.5	3.4	2.3	1.7	3.6	8.6	13.5
Utilities	0.2	0.1	0.0	0.0	0.0	0.1	0.0	0.0	0.0
Commerce	56.3	57.6	49.6	55.9	63.0	55.9	46.9	38.8	32.3
Transport	0.5	0.7	0.7	0.6	0.5	0.5	1.3	1.3	2.5
Services	2.2	1.8	2.2	2.5	1.8	1.4	1.7	2.7	3.1
Refinancing	11.2	11.0	11.6	10.5	9.3	9.4	8.0	6.3	5.2
Other	0.1	0.0	0.0	0.1	0.0	0.1	0.1	0.4	0.1
Total	100.0	100.0	100.0	100.0	100.0	100.0	100.0	100.0	100.0

Source: BCR.

Table A.8 Area, Yield, and Output of Major Crops, 1970–1993

	1970	1971	1972	1973	1974	1975	1976	1977	1978	1979	1980	1981	1982	1983	1984	1985	1986	1987	1988	1989	1990	1991	1992	1993
Coffee																								
Area	130	141	140	146	146	146	147	147	147	180	185	170	161	186	186	164	164	160	161	151	174	186	164	172
Yield	992	1122	1071	786	1366	1000	1002	968	894	998	894	882	908	833	892	724	849	881	747	772	901	773	989	960
Output	129	159	150	115	199	146	148	143	132	180	165	150	146	155	166	119	139	141	120	117	156	144	162	165
Sugar cane																								
Area	28	30	31	33	36	38	42	41	41	37	34	28	32	41	48	40	42	42	34	37	37	43	48	49
Yield	52441	62947	71813	73492	81503	78947	76202	77548	77482	86816	64794	68501	74803	72992	65417	84912	75698	75698	80923	70393	72243	89663	95154	94490
Output	1463	1888	2226	2398	2953	3000	3170	3200	3200	3214	2207	1916	2372	2984	3140	3429	3185	3179	2736	2582	2673	3813	4563	4630
Maize																								
Area	206	230	210	202	211	214	234	245	252	276	292	259	239	242	242	253	257	279	282	276	282	307	321	305
Yield	1765	1640	1167	2004	1668	1779	1464	1550	2145	1896	1806	1882	1734	1835	2103	1954	1695	2051	2086	2102	2189	1645	1970	2098
Output	363	377	245	406	353	381	342	380	540	523	527	487	414	443	509	495	436	572	588	581	616	504	632	640
Sorghum																								
Area	124	136	126	119	127	131	125	132	133	143	119	116	119	111	116	114	120	125	122	120	129	123	149	143
Yield	1186	1150	1159	1316	1029	1114	1253	1143	1321	1118	1172	1195	1044	1113	1216	1159	1229	208	1241	1233	1244	1323	1468	1442
Output	147	156	146	156	131	146	156	151	176	160	140	138	124	123	141	133	148	26	151	148	161	163	219	207
Beans																								
Area	36	40	36	45	51	52	53	53	53	55	52	50	56	56	58	58	61	59	67	64	63	77	80	73
Yield	827	865	806	834	655	708	758	643	819	845	760	753	687	750	841	593	825	415	837	686	957	869	780	947
Output	30	35	29	37	34	37	40	34	43	47	40	37	38	42	49	35	50	24	56	44	60	67	62	69
Cotton																								
Output	46	55	69	71	74	78	65	67	74	72	65	41	40	41	30	30	18	11	10	9	7	4	4	4
Beef																								
Cattle (1,000 head)	1241	1253	1265	1008	1009	1062	1109	1283	1333	1387	1440	1211	1106	954	937	980	1050	1024	1144	1176	1193	1243	1276	1345
Beef and veal meat	19	21	26	26	32	33	31	33	34	30	28	28	30	30	30	21	22	19	22	28	28	24	23	26

Source: FAO, *Food Production Yearbook*, various issues.
Units: Area, 1,000 ha; Yield, kg/ha; Output, 1,000 metric tons

Table A.9   Merchandise Exports, 1970–1993 (millions of U.S. dollars FOB)

	1970	1971	1972	1973	1974	1975	1976	1977	1978	1979
Total exports (FOB)	236.1	243.9	301.7	358.4	464.5	533.0	744.7	973.3	801.8	1,132.6
Traditional exports	154.6	150.6	193.5	220.0	288.2	354.0	518.8	718.3	513.7	799.2
Coffee	119.1	106.2	130.1	156.8	192.1	187.0	404.4	605.6	385.6	675.2
Cotton	23.2	29.0	38.6	36.4	48.2	74.5	62.0	75.7	98.4	84.6
Sugar	7.0	9.4	18.0	17.8	39.6	82.1	40.5	26.4	18.9	26.8
Shrimp	5.3	6.0	6.8	9.0	8.3	10.4	11.8	10.5	10.7	12.6
Nontraditional exports	81.5	93.4	108.2	138.4	176.4	179.0	225.9	255.1	288.1	333.4
CACM	73.6	81.0	93.3	113.2	149.9	141.8	176.1	211.7	233.6	266.6
To other markets	7.9	12.4	14.9	25.2	26.5	37.2	49.8	43.4	54.5	66.8
Percentage composition										
Traditional exports	65.5	61.7	64.1	61.4	62.0	66.4	69.7	73.8	64.1	70.6
Coffee	50.4	43.5	43.1	43.8	41.4	35.1	54.3	62.2	48.1	59.6
Cotton	9.8	11.9	12.8	10.2	10.4	14.0	8.3	7.8	12.3	7.5
Sugar	3.0	3.9	6.0	5.0	8.5	15.4	5.4	2.7	2.4	2.4
Shrimp	2.2	2.5	2.3	2.5	1.8	2.0	1.6	1.1	1.3	1.1
Nontraditional exports	34.5	38.3	35.9	38.6	38.0	33.6	30.3	26.2	35.9	29.4
CACM	31.2	33.2	30.9	31.6	32.3	26.6	23.6	21.7	29.1	23.5
To other markets	3.3	5.1	4.9	7.0	5.7	7.0	6.7	4.5	6.8	5.9

Source: USAID.

1980	1981	1982	1983	1984	1985	1986	1987	1988	1989	1990	1991	1992	Prel. 1993
1,075.3	797.9	699.6	758.1	725.9	695.1	755.0	590.9	608.8	497.5	581.5	588.0	597.5	731.7
726.0	537.0	481.9	550.2	505.0	525.7	593.6	386.4	393.5	252.8	296.2	272.1	217.2	282.3
615.2	452.6	402.6	443.0	449.8	463.7	546.8	351.5	358.0	228.6	260.2	219.5	151.2	225.2
84.6	53.6	45.2	55.4	9.1	29.0	4.5	2.3	0.3	0.7	1.3	0.7	1.5	0.2
13.4	14.8	15.9	40.1	25.9	23.2	25.3	12.1	19.2	13.5	20.3	32.0	44.7	31.1
12.8	16.0	18.2	11.7	20.2	9.8	17.0	20.5	16.0	10.0	14.4	19.9	19.8	25.8
349.3	260.9	217.7	207.9	220.9	169.4	161.3	204.5	215.3	244.7	285.3	315.9	380.3	449.4
295.8	206.5	174.2	164.9	157.2	95.7	91.0	119.6	139.8	160.6	175.0	193.7	257.3	310.2
53.5	54.4	43.5	43.0	63.7	73.7	70.3	84.9	75.5	84.1	110.3	122.2	123.0	139.2
67.5	67.3	68.9	72.6	69.6	75.6	78.6	65.4	64.6	50.8	50.9	46.3	36.4	38.6
57.2	56.7	57.5	58.4	62.0	66.7	72.4	59.5	58.8	45.9	44.7	37.3	25.3	30.8
7.9	6.7	6.5	7.3	1.3	4.2	0.6	0.4	0.0	0.1	0.2	0.1	0.3	0.0
1.2	1.9	2.3	5.3	3.6	3.34	3.4	2.0	3.2	2.7	3.45	5.4	7.5	4.3
1.2	2.0	2.6	1.5	2.8	1.4	2.3	3.5	2.6	2.0	2.5	3.4	3.3	3.5
32.5	32.7	31.1	27.4	30.4	24.4	21.4	34.6	35.4	49.2	49.1	53.7	63.6	61.4
27.5	25.9	24.9	21.8	21.7	13.8	12.1	20.2	23.0	32.3	30.1	33.0	43.1	42.4
5.0	6.8	6.2	5.7	8.8	10.6	9.3	14.4	12.4	16.9	19.0	20.8	20.6	19.0

Table A.10 Merchandise Imports, 1984–1994 (millions of U.S. dollars)

	1984	1985	1986	1987	1988	1989	1990	1991	1992	1993	1994
Total imports (CIF)	977.5	961.3	934.9	994.1	1,006.7	1,161.3	1,262.5	1,406.0	1,698.5	1,912.2	2,067.0
Consumer goods	276.5	258.8	207.0	240.5	258.2	294.6	398.8	372.7	489.1	522.0	578.8
Nondurables	238.5	210.9	181.8	208.4	224.9	258.0	361.3	322.0	417.8	440.8	495.2
Durables	38.0	47.9	25.2	32.1	33.3	36.6	37.5	50.7	71.3	81.2	83.6
Raw materials	568.8	544.8	453.4	501.3	496.2	577.2	629.2	710.0	778.4	825.4	868.1
Agriculture	57.3	75.5	41.2	39.1	35.9	52.2	58.0	67.7	70.8	70.2	78.2
Of which: fertilizers	25.0	39.5	24.7	27.3	23.5	32.5	29.8	30.2	30.2	33.7	38.0
Industry	454.6	417.5	363.2	394.3	390.5	414.4	486.4	547.4	606.4	630.1	654.3
Of which: petroleum imports	130.3	133.2	82.0	104.3	81.0	87.0	121.8	126.8	128.2	123.0	120.5
Construction materials	50.6	46.2	44.0	60.5	63.3	98.9	78.3	85.9	90.6	111.0	120.4
Other	6.3	5.6	5.0	7.4	6.5	11.7	6.5	9.0	10.6	14.1	15.2
Capital goods	132.2	157.7	224.5	252.3	252.3	279.7	234.5	323.3	431.0	564.8	620.1
Agriculture	13.0	13.5	10.3	13.2	8.0	9.2	8.9	11.1	11.8	10.9	14.2
Industry	42.6	43.3	58.7	72.4	79.1	77.4	71.1	89.2	121.4	170.5	184.8
Transport	53.4	67.9	123.6	123.9	121.8	141.5	102.6	148.9	205.5	257.4	273.4
Construction	5.2	6.2	6.4	10.6	11.2	17.0	8.3	11.5	15.4	29.6	30.6
Other	18.0	26.8	25.5	32.2	32.2	34.6	43.6	62.6	76.9	96.4	117.1
Not elsewhere classified[a]	—	—	50.0	—	—	9.8	—	—	—	—	—
Percentage composition											
Total imports (CIF)	100.0	100.0	100	100	100.0	100.0	100.0	100.0	100.0	100.0	100.0
Consumer goods	28.3	26.9	22.1	24.2	25.6	25.4	31.6	26.5	28.8	27.3	28.0
Nondurables	24.4	21.9	19.4	21.0	22.3	22.2	28.6	22.9	24.6	23.1	24.0
Durables	3.9	5.0	2.7	3.2	3.3	3.2	3.0	3.6	4.2	4.2	4.0

(continues)

Table A.10 Continued

	1984	1985	1986	1987	1988	1989	1990	1991	1992	1993	1994
Raw materials	58.2	56.7	48.5	50.4	49.3	49.7	49.8	50.5	45.8	43.2	42.0
Agriculture	5.9	7.9	4.4	3.9	3.6	4.5	4.6	4.8	4.2	3.7	3.8
Of which: fertilizers	2.6	4.1	2.6	2.7	2.3	2.8	2.4	2.1	1.8	1.8	1.8
Industry	46.5	43.4	38.8	39.7	38.8	35.7	38.5	38.9	35.7	33.0	31.7
Of which: petroleum imports	13.3	13.9	8.8	10.5	8.0	7.5	9.6	9.0	7.5	6.4	5.8
Construction materials	5.2	4.8	4.7	6.1	6.3	8.5	6.2	6.1	5.3	5.8	5.8
Other	0.6	0.6	0.5	0.7	0.6	1.0	0.5	0.6	0.6	0.7	0.7
Capital goods	13.5	16.4	24.0	25.4	25.1	24.1	18.6	23.0	25.4	29.5	30.0
Agriculture	1.3	1.4	1.1	1.3	0.8	0.8	0.7	0.8	0.7	0.6	0.7
Industry	4.4	4.5	6.3	7.3	7.9	6.7	5.6	6.3	7.1	8.9	8.9
Transport	5.5	7.1	13.2	12.5	12.1	12.2	8.1	10.6	12.1	13.5	13.2
Construction	0.5	0.6	0.7	1.1	1.1	1.5	0.7	0.8	0.9	1.5	1.4
Other	1.8	2.8	2.7	3.2	3.2	3.0	3.5	4.5	4.5	5.0	5.7

Source: USAID, from BCR and IMF staff estimates.
Note: a. Includes emergency relief after the earthquake of 1986 and donations in late 1989.

Table A.11 Consumer Price Index by Major Categories, 1980–1993

End of period	Weights	1980	1981	1982	1983	1984	1985	1986	1987	1988	1989	1990	1991	1992	1993
General	100.0	100.0	111.7	126.7	145.4	159.6	210.6	274.5	328.4	388.3	479.4	572.1	628.1	753.6	844.7
Foodstuffs	41.6	100.0	114.4	127.1	149.7	165.6	211.2	275.1	337.1	440.2	583.7	693.1	778.0	959.7	1,163.1
Nonfood	58.4	100.0	110.4	126.5	143.3	156.7	210.3	274.3	324.2	363.1	428.9	513.5	555.5	653.7	690.4
Clothing	7.1	100.0	120.2	140.1	159.2	174.4	231.9	314.4	340.7	360.6	396.1	437.3	459.4	535.0	562.9
Housing	23.0	100.0	103.0	121.9	136.3	146.3	214.6	270.6	324.8	326.1	347.7	445.7	471.5	504.5	525.7
Miscellaneous	28.3	100.0	111.4	125.9	138.4	153.0	194.0	254.7	302.2	332.4	389.4	448.3	475.2	584.1	623.8
Annual percentage changes															
General			11.7	13.4	14.8	9.8	32.0	30.3	19.6	18.2	23.5	19.3	9.8	20.0	12.1
Foodstuffs			14.4	11.1	17.8	10.6	27.5	30.3	22.5	30.6	32.6	18.7	12.2	23.4	21.2
Nonfood			10.4	14.6	13.3	9.4	34.2	30.4	18.2	12.0	18.1	19.7	8.2	17.7	5.6
Clothing			20.2	16.5	13.6	9.6	33.0	35.6	8.4	5.8	9.9	10.4	5.1	16.5	5.2
Housing			3.0	18.4	11.8	7.4	46.7	26.1	20.0	0.4	6.6	28.2	5.8	7.0	4.2
Miscellaneous			11.4	12.9	10.0	10.5	26.8	31.3	18.6	10.0	17.1	15.1	6.0	22.9	6.8

Source: USAID, from General Directorate of Statistics and Census and BCR.

Table A.12 Minimum Real Wages, 1989–1993
Index, 1978=100

	1989	1990	1991	1992	Prelim. 1993
Agricultural workers	36.6	33.9	33.5	30.1	31.3
Harvest					
Coffee	27.2	26.4	23.0	20.7	19.2
Sugar cane	36.7	35.5	31.0	27.9	31.8
Cotton	32.7	31.7	27.7	24.9	28.9
Full-time					
Coffee	38.9	37.7	32.9	29.6	29.4
Sugar cane	28.4	27.5	24.0	21.6	23.4
Cotton	27.3	26.4	23.1	20.7	22.5
Other activities in San Salvador					
Industry and services	41.0	38.6	37.8	39.0	37.8
Commerce	39.9	37.5	36.7	37.9	36.7

Source: CEPAL.

Acronyms, Units of Measure, and Spanish Terms

Acronyms

ANEP	Asociación Nacional de la Empresa Privada
ANSP	Academia Nacional de Seguridad Pública
ARENA	Alianza Republicana Nacional
BCR	Banco Central de Reserva de El Salvador
BFA	Banco de Fomento Agropecuario
BID	Banco Interamericano de Desarrollo (IDB)
BMI	Banco Multisectorial de Inversiones
CACM	Central American Common Market
CATIE	Centro Agronómico Tropical de Investigación e Enseñanza
CBERA	Caribbean Basin Economic Recovery Act
CEA	Comisión Especial Agraria
CEM	Certificado de Estabilización Monetaria
CG	Consultative Group
CENTA	Centro Nacional de Tecnología Agropecuaria y Forestal
CEPAL	Comisión Económica para América Latina y el Caribe (ECLAC)
CIF	Cost, Insurance, Freight
CONAMA	Consejo Nacional del Medio Ambiente
CONARA	Comisión Nacional para la Restauración de Areas
COPAZ	Comisión Nacional para la Consolidación de la Paz
CREDIAMPES	Servicio Crediticio de la Asociación de Medianos y Pequeños Empresarios Salvadoreños
DGEA	Dirección General de Economía Agropecuaria
ECLAC	Economic Commission for Latin America and the Caribbean (CEPAL)
FAO	Food and Agriculture Organization
FEDECREDITO	Federación de Cajas de Crédito

317

FIGAPE	Fondo de Financiamiento y Garantía para la Pequeña Empresa
FINATA	Financiera Nacional de Tierras Agricolas
FIS	Fondo de Inversión Social
FOB	Free on Board
FOSEP	Fondo Salvadoreño para Estudios de Preinversión
FMLN	Frente Farabundo Martí para la Liberación Nacional
FUSADES	Fundación Salvadoreña para el Desarrollo Económico y Social
GAO	General Accounting Office
GATT	General Agreement on Tariffs and Trade
IDB	Inter-American Development Bank (BID)
IFI	International Financial Institution
IICA	Instituto Interamericano de Cooperación para la Agricultura
IMF	International Monetary Fund
ISI	Import-Substitution Industrialization
MAG	Ministerio de Agricultura y Ganadería
MAGDALEÑA	Proyecto Madera y Leña
MEA	Municipios en Acción
MERCOMUN	Mercado Común Centroamericano
MIPLAN	Ministerio de Planificación y Coordinación del Desarrollo Económico y Social
NAFTA	North American Free Trade Agreement
NFPS	Nonfinancial Public Sector
NGO	Nongovernmental Organization
NTAX	Nontraditional Agricultural Export
NTEG	Nontraditional Export Growth
NTMX	Nontraditional Manufactured Export
NTX	Nontraditional Export
OEA	Organización de los Estados Americanos
ONUSAL	Organización de las Naciones Unidas, Misión para El Salvador
OSPA-MAG	Oficina Sectorial de Planificación Agropecuaria, Ministerio de Agricultura y Ganadería
PCN	Partido de Conciliación Nacional
PDC	Partido Demócrata Cristiana
PN	Policia Nacional
PNC	Policia Nacional Civil
PREALC	Programa Regional del Empleo para América Latina y el Caribe
PRIDEX	Programa de Inversión y Diversificación de Exportaciones
PRN	Plan de Reconstrucción Nacional

PRUD	Partido Revolucionario de la Revolución Democratica
ROCAP	Regional Office for Central America and Panama
SEMA	Secretaría Ejecutiva del Medio Ambiente
SRN	Secretaría para la Reconstrucción Nacional
SSF	Superintendencia de Servicios Financieros
SSMA	San Salvador Metropolitan Area
TSE	Tribunal Suprema Electoral
UCA	Universidad Centroamericana
UNDP	United Nations Development Programme
USAID	United States Agency for International Development

Units of Measure

1 billion = 1,000 million
1 colón = 0.114 U.S. dollars as of 1 January 1995
1 quintal = 100 lbs.
1 manzana = 0.7 hectare

Spanish Terms

concertación—agreement, process of agreement
ejido—community-owned farmland
financiera—bank that offers only savings or time deposits (like a U.S. savings and loan)
latifundio—large agricultural estate
minifundio—small farm, generally too small to support a family
tenedor—holder, generally in the sense of one farming but not necessarily owning land

Bibliography

Abdallah, K. W. (1995) "*GFS Yearbook* Highlights Trends in Fiscal Balance, Military Spending," *IMF Survey* Vol. 24, no. 5, pp. 66–76.

Abrego, L. (1994) "El Salvador: Régimen de incentivos a las exportaciones y desempeño exportador," San Salvador: UCA (mimeo).

Adams, D. W., ed. (1992) *Informal Finance in Low-Income Countries*. Boulder: Westview Press.

Adams, D. W., and Von Pischke, J. D. (1992) "Micro-Enterprise Trading Programs: Déjà Vu," *World Development*, Vol. 10, pp. 1463–1470.

Agency for International Development, *see* USAID

Ahluwalia, M. S. (1976) "Income Distribution and Development: Some Stylized Facts," *American Economic Review*, Vol. 66, pp. 128–135.

AID, *see* USAID

Alas de Franco, C. (1992) "Intercambio comercial entre México y Centro América: Perspectivas de la confirmación de una zona de libre comercio en la región," Instituto de Investigaciones Económicas y Sociales, Universidad Centroamericana (Documentos de Trabajo, Documento no. 92-1).

Alesina, A., and Drazen, A. (1991) "Why Are Stabilizations Delayed?" *American Economic Review*, Vol. 8, no. 5, pp. 1170–1188.

Alesina, A., and Perotti, R. (1993) "Income Distribution, Political Instability, and Investment." Cambridge, Mass.: National Bureau of Economic Research (Working Paper no. 4486, October).

Alesina, A., and Rodrik, D. (1994) "Distributive Policies and Economic Growth," *Quarterly Journal of Economics*, Vol. CIX, no. 436, Issue 2, pp. 465–490.

Amsden, A. (1989) *Asia's Next Giant: South Korea and Late Industrialization*. New York: Oxford University Press.

Amsden, A. (1990) "Third World Industrialization: 'Global Fordism,' or a New Model?" *New Left Review*, no. 182, pp. 5–31 (July–August).

Amsden, A. (1994) "Why Isn't the Whole World Experimenting with the East Asian Model to Develop?" *World Development*, Vol. 22, no. 4, pp. 627–633.

Anderson, T. (1971) *Matanza: El Salvador's Communist Revolt of 1932*. Lincoln, Neb.: University of Nebraska Press.

ANEP (1992) "Tres años de gestión macroeconómica: logros y dificultades," *Revista Unidad Empresarial*, May–June.

ANEP (1993) "Reflexiones sobre la intermediación y política financiera," *Unidad Empresarial*, July–August.

ANEP (1994) "Síntesis de la gestión macroeconómica 1989–1994," *Unidad Empresarial*, March–April.

Arestis, P., and Demetriades, P. (1993) "Financial Liberalisation and Economic Development: A Critical Exposition," in S. Frowen, ed., *Money and Banking: Issues for the 21st Century.* New York: St. Martin's Press.

Asociación Nacional de la Empresa Privada, *see* ANEP

Associated Press (1994) "U.S. to Ax Salvadoran Program," wire story, 28 November.

Baer, W., and Conroy, M. E., eds. (1993) *Latin America: Privatization, Property Rights, and Deregulation I.* Proceedings of the Fall 1992 conference of the Latin America 2000 Project. Special Issue of the *Quarterly Review of Economics and Finance*, published as a monograph. Greenwich, Conn.: JAI Press.

Baer, W., and Conroy, M. E., eds. (1994) *Latin America: Privatization, Property Rights, and Deregulation II.* Proceedings of the Fall 1993 conference of the Latin America 2000 Project. Special issue of the *Quarterly Review of Economics and Finance*, published as a monograph. Greenwich, Conn.: JAI Press.

Balassa, B. (1983) "Exports, Policy Choices, and Economic Growth in Developing Countries after the 1973 Oil Shock," *Journal of Development Economics,* Vol. 18, pp. 23–35 (May–June).

Ball, N. (1992) *Pressing for Peace: Can Aid Induce Reform?* Washington, D.C.: Overseas Development Council (Policy Essay no. 6).

Ball, N. (1993) "Development Aid for Military Reform: A Pathway to Peace." Washington, D.C.: Overseas Development Council (Policy Focus Paper no. 6).

Banco Central de Reserva de El Salvador, *see* BCR

Banco Interamericano de Desarrollo, *see* IDB

Barraza, B. (1994) "El conflicto por El Espino: Dónde está el estado?" *Prisma Boletín*, no. 7, pp. 7–10.

Barry, D. (1993) "Una herencia de AID en El Salvador: Andamiaje institucional empresarial en la sociedad civil," *Prisma Boletín*, no. 2, pp. 1–4 (2 October).

Barry, D. (1994) "El aquifero de San Salvador," *Prisma Boletín*, no. 7, pp. 1–6.

Bayoumi, T., Hewitt, D., and Schiff, J. (1993) "Economic Consequences of Lower Military Spending: Some Simulation Results," International Monetary Fund, Fiscal Affairs Department and Research Department (Working Paper 93/17; March).

BCR (1980) *Memoria anual de labores.* San Salvador: BCR

BCR (1989) *Memoria anual de labores.* San Salvador: BCR.

BCR (1994a) "Programa monetario y financiero 1994," *Boletín Económico,* Vol. 6, no. 68 (February).

BCR (1994b) *Directorio y Servicios de Instituciones del Sistema Financiero de El Salvador 1994.* San Salvador: BCR.

Bell, C. (1988) "Credit Markets and Interlinked Transactions," in H. Chenery and T. N. Srinivasan, eds., *Handbook of Development Economics.* Amsterdam: North Holland, pp. 763–830, vol. 1.

Belt, J., and Lardé de Palomo, A. (1994a) *El Salvador: Política social y combate a la pobreza.* Unpublished manuscript.

Belt, J., and Lardé de Palomo, A. (1994b) "El Salvador: Transition Towards Peace and Participatory Development," USAID/El Salvador, 25 October (mimeo).

Beretta, G. (1989) "Joaquín Villalobos: Los puntos sobre las ies," *Pensamiento Propio*, Vol. 7, no. 57, pp. 13–17 (January–February).

Berg, A., and Sachs, J. (1988) "The Debt Crisis: Structural Explanations of Country Performance," *Journal of Development Economics*, Vol. 29, pp. 271–306.

Bernstein, B., and Broughton, J. (1994) "Adjusting to Development: The IMF and the Poor," *Finance and Development*, September 1994, pp. 42–45.

Berry, R. A., and Cline, W. (1979) *Agrarian Structure and Productivity in Developing Countries*. Baltimore: Johns Hopkins University Press.

Binswanger, H. (1991) *El Salvador: Alternativa para una nueva política de granos básicos*. San Salvador: UNAT-RUTA-Banco Mundial.

Birdsall, N., and Sabot, R. (1994) "Inequality as a Constraint on Growth in Latin America," *Development Policy: Newsletter on Policy Research,* Office of the Chief Economist, Inter-American Development Bank, September, pp. 1–5.

Birdsall, N., Ross, D., and Sabot, R. (1995) "Inequality and Growth Reconsidered." Typescript, February.

Blejer, M. I., and Khan, M. S. (1984) "Government Policy and Private Investment in Developing Countries," *International Monetary Fund Staff Papers*, Vol. 31 (June), pp. 379–403.

Bouman, F., and Hospes, O., eds. (1994) *Financial Landscapes Reconstructed*. Boulder: Westview Press.

Bourguignon, F., de Melo, J., and Morrison, C. (1991) "Poverty and Income Distribution During Adjustment: Issues and Evidence from the OECD Project." *World Development*, Vol. 19, no. 11, pp. 1485–1508.

Bowles, P. (1987) "Foreign Aid and Domestic Savings in Less Developed Countries: Some Tests for Causality," *World Development*, Vol. 15, no. 6, pp. 789–796.

Bowles, S., and Gintis, H. (1990) "Contested Exchange: New Microfoundations for the Political Economy of Capitalism," *Politics and Society* Vol. 18, no. 2.

Boyce, J. K. (1987) *Agrarian Impasse in Bengal*. Oxford: Oxford University Press.

Boyce, J. K. (1992) "La fuga de capitales en América Central entre 1971–1987: Una estimación cuantitativa," *Cuadernos de Política Económica* (Heredia, Costa Rica: Universidad Nacional Autónoma), no. 6 (December).

Boyce, J. K. (1994) "Inequality as a Cause of Environmental Degradation," *Ecological Economics* 11, pp. 169–178.

Boyce, J. K., and Segura, O. (1993) "Inversión en capital natural y humano en los paises en desarrollo," *Presencia* 19, pp. 2–11.

Boyce, J. K., Fernández González, A., Fürst, E., and Segura Bonilla, O. (1994) *Café y desarrollo sostenible*. Heredia, Costa Rica: Editorial Fundación UNA.

Briones, C. (1991) "Economía informal en el gran San Salvador," in Pérez Sainz and R. Menjívar, eds., *Informalidad urbana en Centroamérica: entre la acumulación y la subsistencia*. FLACSO/Editorial Nueva Sociedad.

Brown, D., Deardorff, A., and Stern, R. (1991) "A North American Free Trade Agreement: Analytical Issues and a Computational Assessment," University of Michigan (mimeo).

Browning, D. (1971) *El Salvador: Landscape and Society*. Oxford: Oxford University Press.

Buergenthal, T. (1994) "The United Nations Truth Commission for El Salvador," *Vanderbilt Journal of Transnational Law,* Vol. 27, no. 3, pp. 497–544.

Bulmer-Thomas, V. (1987) *The Political Economy of Central America Since 1920.* Cambridge: Cambridge University Press.
Bulmer-Thomas, V. (1988) *Studies in the Economics of Central America.* New York: St. Martin's Press (London: Macmillan).
Bulmer-Thomas, V. (1989) "Can Regional Import Substitution and Export-Led Growth Be Combined?" in G. Irvin and S. Holland, eds., *Central America: The Future of Economic Integration.* Boulder: Westview Press, pp. 67–88.
Bulmer-Thomas, V. (1993) "Strategy and Policy Recommendation for Central American Integration," Inter-American Development Bank (mimeo).
Burke, M. (1976) "El sistema de plantación y la proletarización del trabajo agrícola en El Salvador," *Estudios Centroamericanos,* Vol. 31, no. 335–336, pp. 473–486.
Buttari, J. J. (1992) "Economic Policy Reform in Four Central American Countries: Patterns and Lessons Learned," *Journal of Interamerican Studies and World Affairs,* Vol. 34, no. 1 (Spring), pp. 179–214.
Byrne, H. (1994) "The Problem of Revolution: A Study of Strategies of Insurgency and Counter-Insurgency in El Salvador's Civil War, 1981–1991," doctoral dissertation in Political Science, University of California at Los Angeles.
Byrne, H. Forthcoming. *El Salvador's Civil War: A Study of Revolution.* Boulder: Lynne Rienner Publishers.
Calvo, G. (1991) "The Perils of Sterilization," *IMF Staff Papers,* Vol. 38.
Cardoso, E. (1991) "Privatization Fever in Latin America," *Challenge,* Vol. 34, no. 5 (September/October), pp. 35–41.
Cardoso, E., and Helwege, A. (1992) "Below the Line: Poverty in Latin America," *World Development,* Vol. 20, no. 1, pp. 19–37.
Carrington, T. (1994) "Poor Lands Try to Cope With Residue of War: Their Leftover Armies," *Wall Street Journal,* 12 December, pp. A1, A8.
CENITEC (1993) "Propuesta de un programa económico-social de consenso para El Salvador," *Política Económica,* Vol. 17.
Center for Information, Documentation and Research Support (CIDAI) (1995) "Editorial: Demobilized Soldiers Mobilize," *Proceso,* no. 647, 1 February.
Central Reserve Bank of El Salvador, *see* BCR
Centro de Investigaciones Tecnológicas y Científicas, *see* CENITEC
CEPAL (1976) *Tenencia de la tierra y desarrollo rural en Centroamérica.* San José, Costa Rica: EDUCA.
CEPAL (1980) *Anuario estadístico de América Latina, 1979.* New York: United Nations.
CEPAL (1992) *Tendencias recientes de los precios internacionales de los productos tradicionales de exportación de Centroamérica y principales repercusiones económicas.* Mexico: CEPAL.
CEPAL (1993a) *La economía salvadoreña en el proceso de consolidación de la paz.* Mexico: CEPAL (LC/MEX/R.414/Rev.1, 29 June 1993).
CEPAL (1993b) *El impacto económico y social de las migraciones en Centroamérica.* Santiago, Chile: CEPAL (Estudios e Informes de la CEPAL).
CEPAL (1993c) *Centroamérica: productos tradicionales de exportación. Situación y perspectivas.* Mexico: CEPAL.
CEPAL (1993d) "Economic Consequences of Peace in El Salvador," 30 August.

CEPAL (1994) "Inflación y estabilización en Centroamérica." Mexico City: CEPAL, Sección de Desarrollo Económico.

Chambers, R., and Conway, G. (1992) "Sustainable Rural Livelihoods: Practical Concepts for the 21st Century," *Institute of Development Studies: Discussion Paper* no. 296, pp. 7–8.

Chavarría, H. (1994) "Actualización de la situación hidrológica de El Salvador." Unpublished report for Prisma, San Salvador, November.

Childers, E., and Urquhart, B. (1994) *Renewing the United Nations System.* Uppsala: Dag Hammarskjold Foundation; New York: Ford Foundation.

Cho, Y. J. (1986) "Inefficiencies from Financial Liberalization in the Absence of Well Functioning Equities Markets," *Journal of Money, Credit, and Banking,* Vol. 18, no. 1 (May).

Cho, Y. J., and Khatkhate, D. (1989) *Lessons of Financial Liberalization in Asia.* Washington, D.C.: World Bank (World Bank discussion paper 50).

Christensen, G. (1993) "The Limits to Informal Financial Intermediation," *World Development,* Vol. 21, no. 5, pp. 721–731.

Clarke, R. (1993) *Water: The International Crisis.* Cambridge, Mass.: MIT Press.

Cline, W. R. (1983) "Economic Stabilization in Developing Countries: Theory and Stylized Facts," in J. Williams, ed., *IMF Conditionality.* Washington, D.C.: Institute for International Economics.

Colindres, E. (1977) *Fundamentos económicos de la burguesía salvadoreña.* San Salvador: UCA Editores.

Collier, P. (1994) "Demobilization and Insecurity: A Study in the Economics of the Transition from War to Peace," *Journal of International Development,* Vol. 6, no. 3, pp. 343–351.

Comisión Económica para América Latina y el Caribe, *see* CEPAL

Conable, B. (1991) "Growth—Not Guns," *Washington Post,* 24 December, p. A13.

Congressional Research Service (CRS) (1989) *El Salvador, 1979–1989: A Briefing Book on U.S. Aid and the Situation in El Salvador.* Washington, D.C.: Library of Congress, Congressional Research Service, Foreign Affairs and National Defense Division (28 April).

Conroy, M. (1989) "The Diversification of Central American Exports: Chimera or Reality?" Paper presented at the XV International Congress of the Latin American Studies Association (Miami, 4–6 December 1989).

Conroy, M. E., and Glasmeier, A. (1993) "Unprecedented Disparities, Unparalleled Adjustment Needs: Winners and Losers on the NAFTA Fast Track," *Journal of Interamerican Studies and World Affairs,* Vol. 34, no. 4, (Winter 1992–1993), pp. 1–37.

Conroy, M. E., and Glasmeier, A. (1995) "Industrial Strategies, the Newly Industrializing Economies, and New International Trade Theory in Latin America," *Environment and Planning A ,* Vol. 27, pp. 1–10.

Corden, M. (1984) "Booming Sector and Dutch Disease Economics: Survey and Consolidation," *Oxford Economic Papers.*

Cornia, G. A., Jolly, R., and Stewart, F., eds. (1987) *Adjustment With a Human Face.* Oxford: Clarendon Press.

Creative Associates International, Inc. (1991) "Program Options for Reintegrating Ex-Combatants into Civilian Life." Submitted to USAID/El Salvador, San Salvador, 26 April (Contract no. 519-0281-C-00-1014-00).

Crossette, B. (1995) "El Salvador Seeks Aid To Rebuild," *International Herald Tribune,* 6 January, p. 8.

Cruz Letona, R. (1991) *Realidad y perspectivas de la banca de fomento agrícola en El Salvador.* San Salvador: Dirección de Investigadores Económicas y Sociales, Centro de Investigaciones Tecnológicas y Científicas (Cuadernos de Investigación no. 8).

Cuevas, C. E., Graham, D. H., and Paxton, J. A. (1991) *El sector financiero informal en El Salvador.* San Salvador: FUSADES (Documentos de Trabajo no. 29).

Dada Sánchez, H. (1978) *La economía de El Salvador y la integración centroamericana: 1945–1960.* San Salvador: UCA Editores.

Dada Sánchez, H. (1994) "El Sector manufacturero en El Salvador: Competitividad y potencial de expansión de las exportaciones," *Política Económica,* no. 22, pp. 1–28 (January–February).

Dalton, J. J. (1994) "Military Budget May Be Made Public," *Excelsior* (Mexico City), 21 September, p. 2A.

de Janvry, A. (1981) *The Agrarian Question and Reformism in Latin America.* Baltimore: Johns Hopkins University Press.

de Janvry, A., and Sadoulet, E. (1989) "Investment Strategies to Combat Rural Poverty: A Proposal for Latin America," *World Development,* Vol. 17, no. 8, pp. 1203–1221.

de Soto, A. (1994) "Foreword," in T. Whitfield, *Paying the Price: Ignacio Ellacuría and the Murdered Jesuits of El Salvador.* Philadelphia: Temple University Press.

de Soto, A., and del Castillo, G. (1994a) "Obstacles to Peacebuilding," *Foreign Policy,* Vol. 94 (Spring), pp. 69–83.

de Soto, A., and del Castillo, G. (1994b) "El Salvador: Still Not a Success Story," June (mimeo).

Deere, C. D., and Diskin, M. (1984) *Rural Poverty in El Salvador: Dimensions, Trends, and Causes.* Geneva: International Labour Office (ILO) (World Employment Programme Research Working Paper WEP 10-6/WP64).

Díaz Alejandro, C. (1985) "Good-bye Financial Repression, Hello Financial Crash," *Journal of Development Economics,* Vol. 19, pp. 1–24.

Dimas Quintanilla, J. (1994) *Sistemas de financiamiento rural en El Salvador.* San Salvador: Unidad Regional de Asistencia Técnica (Proyecto CAM/89/001, Ejecutado por el Banco Mundial).

Dornbusch, R. (1980) *Open Economy Macroeconomics.* New York: Basic Books.

Dornbusch, R. (1990) "From Stabilization to Growth," *National Bureau of Economic Research Working Paper,* no. 3302. Cambridge, Mass.: National Bureau of Economics Research.

Dornbusch, R. (1992) "The Case for Trade Liberalization in Developing Countries," *Journal of Economic Perspectives,* Vol. 6, no. 1, pp. 69–86.

Durham, W. (1979) *Scarcity and Survival in Central America: The Ecological Origins of the Soccer War.* Stanford: Stanford University Press.

Dussel Peters, E., and Kim, K. S. (1992) "From Liberalization to Economic Integration: The Case of Mexico." Paper presented at the XVII International Congress of the Latin American Studies Association, Los Angeles, Calif. (September).

Dymski, G., and Pastor, M. (1990) "Misleading Signals, Bank Lending, and the Latin American Debt Crisis," *International Trade Journal*, Vol. 6, no. 2.

Echenique, J. (1990) "Las dos caras de la agricultura y las políticas posibles," *Proposiciones*, no. 18 (Santiago, Ediciones Sur).

Echeverri-Gent, J. (1988) "Guaranteed Employment in an Indian State," *Asian Survey*, Vol. 28, pp. 1294–1310.

Economic Commission for Latin America and the Caribbean (ECLAC), *see* CEPAL

Economist Intelligence Unit (1993) *Guatemala, El Salvador: Country Report* (second quarter).

Economist Intelligence Unit (1994) *Guatemala, El Salvador: Country Report* (first quarter).

Edwards, S. (1989) "The International Monetary Fund and the Developing Countries: A Critical Evaluation," NBER Working Paper no. 2909. Cambridge, Mass.: National Bureau of Economic Research.

Edwards, S. (1993) "Openness, Trade Liberalization, and Growth in Developing Countries," *Journal of Economic Literature*, Vol. 31, no. 3 (September), pp. 1358–1393.

El Salvador Information Project (1994) "Summary of Concerns," 19 October.

El Salvador Information Project (1995) "Summary of Concerns" (electronic publication), 25 February.

El Salvador, Ministerio de Planificación y Coordinación del Desarrollo Económico y Social, *see* MIPLAN

El Salvador, Presidencia de la Republica, *see* Presidencia de la República

El Salvador, Secretaria de Reconstrucción Nacional, *see* SRN

Engerman, S. L., and Sokoloff, K. L. (1994) "Factor Endowments, Institutions, and Differential Paths of Growth Among New World Economies: A View from Economic Historians of the United States." Cambridge, Mass.: National Bureau of Economic Research, Historical Paper no. 66, December.

Esfahani, H. (1991) "Exports, Imports, and Economic Growth in Semi-industrialized Countries," *Journal of Development Economics*, Vol. 35, no. 1, pp. 93–116.

FAO (1992) *Situación y perspectivas de los productos básicos, 1991–1992. Situación del mercado mundial de productos básicos y comercio exterior internacional*. Rome: FAO.

FAO (1993) *Situación y perspectivas de los productos básicos, 1992–1993*. Rome: FAO.

Feder, G. (1983) "On Exports and Economic Growth," *Journal of Development Economics*, Vol. 12, pp. 59–73 (February–April).

Feuerlein, W. (1954) *Proposals for the Further Economic Development of El Salvador*. New York: United Nations.

Figueroa, I. (1990) *Chile: Ventajas comparativas dinámicas generadas en los sectores fruticola y forestal*. Santiago: ILPES (Document RLA/86/029).

FINATA (1993) *FINATA: Diagnostico y su proyección*. San Salvador: FINATA.

FMLN (1989) "Hacia una revolución democrática en El Salvador," *Pensamiento Propio*, Vol. 4, no. 60 (May), pp. 1–8.

FMLN (1990) "Position of the FMLN on Ending Militarism, Reaching a Cease-Fire and Advancing to an Unarmed Democracy," 17 August.

Food and Agriculture Organization, *see* FAO

Foxley, A. (1983) *Latin American Experiments in Neoconservative Economics.* Berkeley, Calif.: University of California Press.

Frente Farabundo Martí para la Liberación Nacional, *see* FMLN

Frieden, J. (1992) *Debt, Development, and Democracy: Modern Political Economy and Latin America, 1965–85.* Princeton, N.J.: Princeton University Press.

Fry, M. (1988) *Money, Interest, and Banking in Economic Development.* Baltimore: Johns Hopkins University Press.

Fuentes Meléndez, M., and Cuéllar Aguilar, N. (1993a) *Los intermediarios financieros no oficiales en El Salvador: Un estudio de casos.* San Salvador: Dirección de Investigadores Económicas y Sociales, Centro de Investigaciones Tecnológicas y Científicas (Cuadernos de Investigación no. 15, March).

Fuentes Meléndez, M., and Cuéllar Aguilar, N. (1993b) *Los intermediarios financieros no oficiales en El Salvador.* San Salvador: PRISMA (July).

Fundación Flor de Izote (1995) *Report from El Salvador,* Vol. 6, no. 11 (13–20 March).

Fundación Salvadoreña para el Desarrollo Económico y Social, *see* FUSADES

Funkhouser, E. (1990) "Mass Emigration, Remittances, and Economic Adjustment: The Case of El Salvador in the 1980s." Paper presented at the National Bureau of Economic Research Conference on Immigration, Cancún, Mexico, 16 January.

FUSADES (1993) "Martes económico," *La Prensa Gráfica,* 9 February.

FUSADES (1994) "Una propuesta de desarrollo agropecuario 1994–2000: El financiamiento del sector," *Informe Económico Semanal,* Vol. 22. San Salvador.

Gallagher, M. (1993) "Reforma tributaria amplia en El Salvador," *Revista Económica y Social* (UCA).

Galor, O., and Zeira, J. (1993) "Income Distribution and Macroeconomics," *Review of Economic Studies,* Vol. 60, pp. 35–52.

GAO (1985) *Providing Effective Economic Assistance to El Salvador and Honduras: A Formidable Task.* Washington, D.C.: GAO (GAO/NSIAD-85-82, July).

GAO (1993) *Foreign Assistance U.S. Support for Caribbean Basin Assembly Industries.* Washington, D.C.: GAO.

GAO (1994) *El Salvador: Implementation of Post-War Programs Slower Than Expected.* Report to the Chairman, Subcommittee on Western Hemispheric Affairs, Committee on Foreign Affairs, House of Representatives. Washington, D.C.: GAO.

General Accounting Office, *see* GAO

Gibb, T., and Smyth, F. (1990) "El Salvador: Is Peace Possible?" Washington, D.C.: Washington Office on Latin America (mimeo, April).

Golden, T. (1992) "The Salvadorans Make Peace in a 'Negotiated Revolution,'" *New York Times,* 5 January, p. E3.

Goldin, I., and Winters, A., eds. (1992) *Open Economies: Structural Adjustment and Agriculture.* Cambridge: Cambridge University Press.

González Orellana, M. (1994) "Tipo de cambio y desarrollo económico en El Salvador." San Salvador: FUSADES (mimeo).

Gordon, S. (1989) *Crisis política y guerra en El Salvador.* Mexico City: Siglo XXI.

Government of El Salvador (1992) *Acuerdos de Chapultepec.* Secretaria Nacional de Comunicaciones.

Government of El Salvador (1995) *Acuerdos de paz: costos y déficit financiero.* San Salvador.

Greene, J., and Villanueva, D. (1991) "Private Investment in Developing Countries: An Empirical Analysis," *IMF Staff Papers,* Vol. 38, no. 1 (March), pp. 33–58.

Gregory, P. (1992) "Income Distribution in El Salvador," report for USAID/El Salvador under contract no. 519-0177-C-00-203-00, 29 September.

Griffin, K. (1970) "Foreign Capital, Domestic Savings and Economic Development," *Bulletin of the Oxford Institute of Economics and Statistics,* Vol. 32, no. 2, pp. 99–112.

Griffin, K. (1978) *International Inequality and National Poverty.* London: Macmillan.

Griffin, K. (1989) *Alternative Strategies for Economic Development.* New York: St. Martin's Press.

Griffith-Jones, S., Singer, H., Puyana, A., and Stevens, C. (1993) *Assessment of the IDB Lending Programme, 1979–92.* Sussex, U.K.: Institute of Development Studies, Sussex University.

Grindle, M. (1986) *State and Countryside: Development Policy and Agricultural Policy in Latin America.* Baltimore: Johns Hopkins University Press.

Grossman, G., and Helpman E. (1991) *Innovation and Growth in the Global Economy.* Cambridge, Mass.: MIT Press.

GTZ (1989) "Estudio sobre la estimación de los parámetros nacionales en El Salvador." Asistencia de GTZ a MIPLAN, San Salvador, January (Gesellschaft für Technische Zusammenarbeit, Federal Republic of Germany).

Guido Véjar, R. (1980) *El ascenso del militarismo en El Salvador.* San Salvador: UCA Editores.

Gwynne, R. N. (1993) "Nontraditional Export Growth and Economic Development: The Chilean Forestry Sector Since 1974," *Bulletin of Latin American Research,* Vol. 12, no. 2, pp. 147–169.

Haggard, S., and Kaufman, R. (1989) "The Politics of Stabilization and Structural Adjustment," in J. Sachs, ed., *Developing Country Debt and the World Economy.* Chicago: National Bureau of Economic Research.

Happe, N., and Wakeman-Linn, J. (1994) "Military Expenditure and Arms Trade: Alternative Data Sources," International Monetary Fund, Policy Development and Review Department, February.

Harberger, A. C. (1993a) "Measuring the Components of Economic Growth in El Salvador: Methods and Initial Results." San Salvador: FUSADES (29 May, mimeo).

Harberger, A. C. (1993b) "Las exportaciones y el tipo de cambio real en El Salvador." San Salvador: FUSADES (October, mimeo).

Harberger, A. C., and Wisecarver, D. (1988) *Guidelines for Development: Suggestions for Economic Policy Reform in El Salvador.* San Salvador: FUSADES.

Hartmann, B., and Boyce, J. K. (1983) *A Quiet Violence.* London: Zed Books.

Helleiner, G. (1994) "Introduction," in G. K. Helleiner, ed., *Trade Policy and Industrialization in Turbulent Times.* London and New York: Routledge, pp. 1–36.

Hewitt, C. (1991) "La economía política del maíz en México," *Comercio Exterior,* Vol. 41, no. 10, pp. 955–970.

Hewitt, C., ed. (1992) *Reestructuración económica y subsistencia rural: El maíz y la crisis de los ochenta.* Mexico: El Colegio de México.

Hewitt, D. P. (1991) "Military Expenditure: International Comparison of Trends." Washington, D.C.: International Monetary Fund (Fiscal Affairs Department, Working Paper 91/54, May).

Hinds, M. (1994) "El Régimen de Cambio." San Salvador: FUSADES (mimeo, "Memorandum para Roberto Orellana, Presidente, BCR, 5 de Enero 1994").

Holiday, D., and Stanley, W. (1993) "Building the Peace: The Role of the United Nations in El Salvador," *Journal of International Affairs,* Winter 1992–1993.

IDB (1987) *El Salvador: Informe socioeconómico.* Washington, D.C.: IDB (mimeo).

IDB (1993a) *El Salvador: Informe socioeconómico.* Washington, D.C. (Informe no. DES-13, June).

IDB (1993b) "El Salvador: Global Credit Program for Microenterprises." Washington, D.C.: IDB (ES-0037).

IMF (1991a) *El Salvador. Staff Report for the 1991 Article IV Consultation and Request for Stand-By Arrangement.* Limited distribution document. Washington, D.C. (November).

IMF (1991b) "The Fund and Poverty Issues: A Progress Report," *Development Issues, Presentations to the 39th Meeting of the Development Committee.* Washington, D.C.: IMF, Development Committee Pamphlet no. 26, pp. 29–34.

IMF (1992) "Aide-mémoire." Limited distribution document. Washington, D.C. (July).

IMF (1994a) *El Salvador. Staff Report for the 1994 Article IV Consultation and Midterm Review Under the Stand-By Arrangement.* Limited distribution document. Washington, D.C.: IMF (September).

IMF (1994b) *El Salvador—Recent Economic Developments.* Washington, D.C.: IMF (IMF Staff Country Report no. 94/10, November 1994).

IMF Survey (1994) "IMF Helps Developing Countries Achieve Sustainable Growth," 27 June, pp. 208–210.

IMF Survey (1995) "East Asian Economic Miracle," 6 March, pp. 65, 78–80.

INCAP (Institute of Nutrition of Central America and Panama) (1976) "Evaluación nutricional de la población de Centroamérica y Panamá: El Salvador." Guatemala City: INCAP.

Jarvis, L. S. (1991) "Chilean Fruit Development Since 1973: Manipulating the Cornucopia to What End?" Paper presented at the XVI International Congress of the Latin American Studies Association," Washington, D.C. (4–6 April).

Jepma, C. J. (1994) *Inter-nation Policy Co-ordination and Untying of Aid.* Aldershot, U.K.: Avebury.

Johnson, K. (1993) "Between Revolution and Democracy: Business Elites and the State in El Salvador During the 1980s." Ph.D. dissertation, Tulane University.

Johnson, O., and Salop, J. (1980) "Distributional Aspects of Stabilization Programs in Developing Countries," *IMF Staff Papers,* Vol. 27 (March), pp. 1–23.

Jones, E., and Taylor, L. (1991a) "Evaluación de la restauración/reconstrucción de la infraestructura para el Plan de Recuperación Nacional del Gobierno de El Salvador. Volumen I, informe narrativo," Development Associates, Inc., consultants' report to USAID (September).

Jones, E., and Taylor, L. (1991b) "Infrastructure Restoration/Reconstruction Assessment for the Government of El Salvador National Recovery Plan, 1991. Volume II, Appendices," Development Associates, Inc., consultants' report to USAID (September).

Juárez, M. (1993) "Estado presente y futuro de la producción y consumo de leña en El Salvador," Turrialba, Costa Rica, and USAID Regional Office for Central America and Panama.

Kan, S.A. (1993) "Military Expenditures by Developing Countries: Foreign Aid Policy Issues." Washington, D.C.: Library of Congress, Congressional Research Service (3 November).

Kaplinsky, R. (1993) "Export Processing Zones in the Dominican Republic: Transforming Manufactures into Commodities," *World Development*, Vol. 21, no. 11, pp. 1851–1865.

Karl, T. L. (1985) "After La Palma: The Prospects for Democratization in El Salvador," *World Policy Journal,* Vol. 2, no. 2 (Spring).

Karl, T. L. (1989) "Negotiations or Total War: Salvador Samayoa Interviewed by Terry Karl," *World Policy Journal,* Vol. 6, no. 2, pp. 321–355 (Spring).

Karl, T. L. (1992) "El Salvador's Negotiated Revolution," *Foreign Affairs,* Vol. 71, no. 2, pp. 147–164.

Kaufman, D., and Lindauer, D. L. (1984) *Income Transfers within Extended Families to Meet Basic Needs: The Evidence from El Salvador.* Washington, D.C.: World Bank (World Bank Staff Working Papers no. 644).

Kaufman, R., and Stallings, B. (1991) "The Political Economy of Latin American Populism," in R. Dornbusch and S. Edwards, *The Macroeconomics of Populism in Latin America.* Chicago: University of Chicago Press, pp. 15–44.

Kehoe, T. J. (1992) "Assessing the Impact of North American Free Trade." Paper presented at the 31st European Seminar of the European Association of Agricultural Economists, Frankfurt, 7–9 December.

KPMG Peat Marwick (1990) *Proyecto para el mejoramiento y modernización del Ministerio de Hacienda de la República de El Salvador.* Washington, D.C. (Final report prepared for USAID/El Salvador and the Ministry of the Treasury.)

Krugman, P., and Taylor, L. (1978) "Contractionary Effects of Devaluation," *Journal of International Economics,* Vol. 8, no. 3.

Kuznets, S. (1955) "Economic Growth and Income Inequality," *American Economic Review*, Vol. 45 (March), pp. 1–28.

Ladman, J. R., et al, (1986) *Final Report. Rural Savings Mobilization/Agricultural Credit Project.* Washington, D.C.: Center for Development Information and Evaluation, Agency for International Development (Contract no. 519-0263-C-00-5475).

Lago, R. (1991) "The Illusion of Pursuing Redistribution Through Macropolicy: Peru's Heterodox Experience (1985–1990)," in R. Dornbusch and S. Edwards, eds., *The Macroeconomics of Populism in Latin America.* Chicago: University of Chicago Press.

Lall, S. (1994) "The East Asia Miracle: Does the Bell Toll on Industrial Policy?" *World Development*, Vol. 22, no. 4, pp. 645–654.

Larraín, F. (1994) "Exchange Rates and Reserve Management with Large Capital Inflows," in G. Bell and W. Rhodes, co-chairmen, *Latin American Capital Flows: Living with Volatility.* Washington, D.C.: Group of Thirty.

Leamer, E., Guerra, A., Kaufman, M., Boris Segura, B. (1994) *Central America and the North American Free Trade Agreement.* Washington, D.C.: World Bank, Latin American and the Caribbean Regional Office (September).

Lecaillon, J., Paukert, F., Morrisson, C., and Germidis, D. (1984) *Income Distribution and Economic Development: An Analytical Survey.* Geneva: International Labour Office.

Leiderman, L., and Reinhart, C. (1994) "Capital Flows to Latin America," in G. Bell and W. Rhodes, co-chairmen, *Latin American Capital Flows: Living with Volatility.* Washington, D.C.: Group of Thirty.

Levine, R., and Renelt, D. (1992) "A Sensitivity Analysis of Cross-Country Growth Regressions," *American Economic Review,* Vol. 82, no. 4, pp. 942–963.

Lindarte, E., and Benito, C. (1993) *Sostenibilidad y agricultura de laderas en Centroamérica.* San José, Costa Rica: IICA.

Lindo, H. (1990) *Weak Foundations: The Economy of El Salvador in the Nineteenth Century.* Berkeley: University of California Press.

Loehr, W., and Núñez, R. (1991) *El Salvador: An Assessment of the Impact of Recent Policy Changes on Agriculture.* APAP II Technical Report no. 127. Cambridge, Mass.: Abt Associates.

López Córdovez, L. (1987) "Crisis, Adjustment Policies and Agriculture," *CEPAL Review,* no. 33, pp. 7–28.

López Córdovez, L. (1994) *Marco normativo de la política de desarrollo agrícola y rural sustentable en El Salvador.* Santiago, Chile: United Nations Food and Agriculture Program (FAO).

López, J. R. (1993) *El tratado de libre comercio México–El Salvador.* San Salvador: FUSADES.

López, J. R., and Seligson, M. A. (1989) "Remittances and Small Business Development in El Salvador." Report prepared for the Commission for the Study of International Migration and Cooperative Economic Development (October).

Lungo, M. (1994) *Una alternativa para San Salvador.* San Salvador: FLACSO.

Lungo, M., and Oporto, F. (1994) *San Salvador: Estadísticas básicas.* San Salvador: FLACSO/Proyecto El Salvador.

Markandya, A. (1991) *The Economic Appraisal of Projects: The Environmental Dimension.* Washington, D.C.: Inter-American Development Bank, Projects Analysis Department; London: University College.

Martin, W., and Warr, P. (1993) "Explaining the Relative Decline of Agriculture: A Supply-Side Analysis for Indonesia," *World Bank Economic Review,* Vol. 7, no. 3, pp. 381–401.

McKinnon, R. I. (1973) *Money and Capital in Economic Development.* Washington, D.C.: Brookings Institution.

McKinnon, R. I. (1988) "Financial Liberalization in Retrospect: Interest Rate Policies in LDS's," in G. Ranis and T. Shultz, eds., *The State of Development Economics: Progress and Perspectives.* New York: Basil Blackwell.

McKinnon, R. I. (1991) *The Order of Economic Liberalization.* Baltimore: Johns Hopkins University Press.

McNamara, R. S. (1992) "The Post Cold-War World: Implications for Military Expenditures in the Developing Countries," *Proceedings of the World Bank Annual Conference on Development Economics, 1991.* Washington, D.C.: World Bank, pp. 95–125.

McReynolds, S., Johnston, T., Gore, P., and Francis, J. (1989) *The 1989 El Salvador Agricultural Land Use and Land Tenure Study.* Washington, D.C.: National Cooperative Business Center.

Mena, D. (1976) "Inversión extranjera y grupos económicos en El Salvador." Paper presented at the second Central American Sociology Congress, Panama.

Méndez G., J. C., and Abrego, L. (1994) *Estudio del sistema tributario y arancelario de El Salvador*. San Salvador (April).

Menjívar, O. (n.d., probably 1978) "Estructura, desarrollo y crisis del modelo de capital: El Salvador: 1948–1976," *Cuadernos de Ciencias Sociales*. San Salvador: UCA

Menjívar, R. (1980) *El Salvador: El eslabón más pequeño*. San José, Costa Rica: EDUCA.

Menjívar, R. (1982) *Formación y lucha del proletariado industrial salvadoreño*. San José, Costa Rica: EDUCA.

Ministerio de Planificación y Coordinación del Desarrollo Económico y Social, *see* MIPLAN

MIPLAN (1989) *Plan de desarrollo económico y social 1989–1994*. San Salvador.

MIPLAN (1991a) "Plan de recuperación económica y social nacional, volumen 1," San Salvador (September).

MIPLAN (1991b) "Marco global del plan de recuperacion económica y social nacional," San Salvador (7 August).

MIPLAN (1991c) "Plan de reconstrucción nacional, versión preliminar revisada, volumen 1" (November).

MIPLAN (1991d) "The Government's Economic and Social Program, 1989–1994. Report to the First Consultative Group Meeting," Paris, 15–16 May.

MIPLAN (1992a) "Plan de reconstrucción nacional, resumen ejecutivo" (February).

MIPLAN (1992b) *Plan de Reconstrucción Nacional (PRN)*, Vol. I (March). San Salvador: MIPLAN.

MIPLAN (1993a) "Consolidating the Peace Through National Reconstruction and Poverty Alleviation: Report to the Consultative Group Meeting" (Paris, 1 April 1993). San Salvador: MIPLAN.

MIPLAN (1993b) "Priority Technical Assistance Requirements" (1 April).

Montes, S. (1987) *El Salvador: 1987: Salvadoreños refugiados en Estados Unidos*. San Salvador: Instituto de Investigaciones, Universidad Centroamericana.

Montgomery, T. S. (1995) *Revolution in El Salvador: From Civil Strife to Civil Peace*. Second edition. Boulder: Westview.

Montoya, A. (1991) *El agro salvadoreño antes y después de la reforma agraria*. San Salvador: DIES/CENITEC.

Morris, F., et al. (1990) *Latin America's Banking Systems in the 1980s: A Cross-Country Comparison*. Washington, D.C.: World Bank (Discussion Papers no. 81).

Mosley, P. (1985) "The Political Economy of Foreign Aid: A Model of the Market for a Public Good," *Economic Development and Cultural Change*, Vol. 32, no. 2, pp. 373–393.

Mosley, P., Harrigan, J., and Toye, J. (1991) *Aid and Power: The World Bank and Policy-based Lending. Volume 1: Analysis and Policy Proposals*. London and New York: Routledge.

Munasinghe, M. (1992) "Environmental Economics and Valuation in Development Decisionmaking." Washington, D.C.: World Bank, Environment Working Paper no. 51, February.

Munck, G. (1993) "Beyond Electoralism in El Salvador: Conflict Resolution Through Negotiated Compromise," *Third World Quarterly,* Vol. 14, no. 1, pp. 75–93.

Murillo Salinas, J. (1974a) "Breve panorama de la situación habitacional en El Salvador," *Estudios Centroamericanos,* pp. 308–309.

Murillo Salinas, J. (1974b) "Los tipos de vivienda predominante en la ciudad de San Salvador y sus alrededores," *Estudios Centroamericanos,* pp. 308–309.

Murray, K., with Coletti, E., and Spence, J. (1994) *Rescuing Reconstruction: The Debate on Post-War Economic Recovery in El Salvador.* Cambridge: Hemisphere Initiatives (May).

Nelson, J., and Eglinton, S. (1992) *Encouraging Democracy: What Role for Conditioned Aid?* Washington, D.C.: Overseas Development Council, Policy Essay no. 4.

Nelson, J., and Eglinton, S. (1993) *Global Goals, Contentious Means: Issues of Multiple Aid Conditionality.* Washington, D.C.: Overseas Development Council, Policy Essay no. 10.

Netting, R. M. (1993) *Smallholders, Householders: Farm Families and the Ecology of Intensive, Sustainable Agriculture.* Stanford: Stanford University Press.

New York Times (1994) "Salvadorans See Future Imperiled by U.S. Immigration Move," 4 December, p. A27.

North, L. (1985) *Bitter Grounds: Roots of Revolt in El Salvador.* Westport, Conn.: Lawrence Hill.

Norton, R. (1990) *An Assessment of the Recent Agricultural Policy Reforms in El Salvador.* San Salvador: USAID.

Norton, R., and Liévano, M. (1988) *Food Imports, Agricultural Policies and Agricultural Development in El Salvador, 1960–1987.* Washington, D.C.: Robert Nathan Associates.

Norton, R., and Llort, M. (1989) *Una estrategia para la reactivación del sector agropecuario en El Salvador.* San Salvador: FUSADES.

Orellana Merlos, C. (1992) "Migración y remesas: una evaluación de su impacto en la economía salvadoreña," *Política Económica,* Vol. 1, no. 11, pp. 2–23.

Organisation for Economic Cooperation and Development (OECD) (1985) *Twenty-Five Years of Development Cooperation: A Review.* Paris: OECD.

OSPA-MAG (1992) *XI Evaluación del proceso de Regorma Agraria.* San Salvador: Ministerio de Agricultura y Ganadería.

Overseas Development Council (ODC) (1994) "Informe Preliminar del Equipo Nacional de El Salvador" (August).

Paige, J. M. (1993) "Coffee and Power in El Salvador," *Latin American Research Review,* Vol. 28, no. 3, pp. 7–40.

Pastor, M. (1987) "The Effects of IMF Programs in the Third World," *World Development,* Vol. 15, no. 2, pp. 249–262.

Pastor, M. (1991) "Bolivia: Hyperinflation, Stabilisation, and Beyond," *Journal of Development Studies,* Vol. 27, no. 2 (January), pp. 211–237.

Pastor, M. (1992a) "Inversión privada y el 'efecto arrastre' de la deuda externa en America Latina," *El Trimestre Economico,* Vol. LIX, no. 1 (January–March), pp. 107–151.

Pastor, M. (1992b) *Inflation, Stabilization, and Debt: Macroeconomic Experiments in Peru and Bolivia.* Boulder: Westview Press.

Pastor, M., and Dymski, G. (1990) "Debt Crisis and Class Conflict in Latin America," *Review of Radical Political Economics,* Vol. 22, no. 1.

Pastor, M., and Hilt, E. (1993) "Private Investment and Democracy in Latin America," *World Development*, Vol. 21, no. 4 (April), pp. 489–508.

Pastor, M., and Wise, C. (1992) "Peruvian Economic Policy in the 1980s: From Orthodoxy to Heterodoxy and Back," *Latin American Research Review,* Vol. XXVII, no. 2.

Paukert, F. (1973) "Income Distribution at Different Levels of Development: A Survey of Evidence," *International Labor Review*, Vol. 108, pp. 97–125.

Paus, E. (1994a) "Capital-Labor Relations and Income Distribution in Latin America in the Eighties." Paper presented at the XVII Congress of the Latin American Studies Association, Atlanta, 10–12 March.

Paus, E. (1994b) "Economic Growth Through Neo-liberal Restructuring? Insights from the Chilean Experience," *Journal of Developing Areas,* Vol. 28, pp. 31–56 (October).

Pearce, J. (1986) *Promised Land: Peasant Rebellion in Chalatenango, El Salvador.* London: Latin America Bureau.

Pelupessy, W. (1988) "Dos modelos de política económica y el reajuste en El Salvador" (mimeo).

Perdomo Lino, F. (1994) *El suelo, la erosión y la sedimentación en El Salvador.* Unpublished report for PRISMA San Salvador (October).

Pérez Sainz and Menjívar, R., eds. (1991) *Informalidad urbana en Centroamérica: Entre la acumulación y la subsistencia.* FLACSO/Editorial Nueva Sociedad.

Pérez, W. (1994) "Políticas de competitividad," *Revista de la CEPAL,* no. 53, pp. 49–58 (August).

Permanent Secretariat of the General Treaty on Central American Economic Integration, *see* SIECA

Persson, T., and Tabellini, G. (1994) "Is Inequality Harmful for Growth?" *American Economic Review,* Vol. 84, no. 3, pp. 600–621.

PNUD, *see* UNDP

Polak, J. (1991) "The Changing Nature of IMF Conditionality." Princeton: Princeton University, Essays in International Finance, no. 184, September.

Popkin, M. (1994) "Justice Delayed: The Slow Pace of Judicial Reform in El Salvador." Washington, D.C., and Boston: Washington Office on Latin America and Hemisphere Initiatives.

Popkin, M., Vickers, G., and Spence, J. (1993) *Justice Impugned: The Salvadoran Peace Accords and the Problem of Impunity.* Cambridge: Hemisphere Initiatives (June).

Porter, M. (1990) "The Competitive Advantage of Nations," *Harvard Business Review,* no. 2, pp. 73–93.

PREALC (1977) *Situación y perspectivas del empleo en El Salvador.* Santiago, Chile: International Labour Organization.

Preusse, Heinz G. (1994) "Regional Integration in the Nineties—Stimulation or Threat to the Multilateral Trading System?" *Journal of World Trade,* Vol. 28, no. 4, pp. 147–164.

Proceso (1995a) *Proceso,* no. 649 (15 February). San Salvador: Centro de Información, Documentación y Apoya a la Investigación.

Proceso (1995b) *Proceso,* no. 653 (15 March). San Salvador: Centro de Información, Documentación y Apoya a la Investigación.

Programa Regional del Empleo para America Latina y el Caribe, *see* PREALC.

Prosterman, R., and Riedinger, J. (1987) *Land Reform and Democratic Development*. Baltimore: Johns Hopkins University Press.

Przeworski, A., and Limongi, F. (1993) "Political Regimes and Economic Growth," *Journal of Economic Perspectives*, Vol. 7, no. 3 (Summer), pp. 51–70.

Ram, R. (1987) "Exports and Economic Growth in Developing Countries: Evidence from Time-Series and Cross-Section Data," *Economic Development and Cultural Change,* Vol. 36, no. 1, pp. 51–72.

Ramos, J. (1986) *Neoconservative Economics in the Southern Cone of Latin America, 1973–1983.* Baltimore: Johns Hopkins University Press.

Ravallion, M. (1991) "Reaching the Rural Poor Through Public Employment: Arguments, Evidence, and Lessons from South Asia," *World Bank Research Observer*, Vol. 6, no. 2, pp. 153–175.

Reisen, H., and von Trotsenberg, A. (1988) *Developing Country Debt: The Budgetary and Transfer Problem.* Paris: OECD Development Centre.

Repetto, R., Magrath, W., Wells, M., Beer, C., and Rossini, F. (1989) *Wasting Assets: Natural Resources in the National Income Accounts.* Washington, D.C.: World Resources Institute.

Rivera Campos, R. (1988) "La inflación en El Salvador," *Revista Realidad Económico Social.* San Salvador: UCA Editores.

Rivera Campos, R. (1994) "Los Determinantes Financieros y No Financieros de la Inversión," San Salvador, January (mimeo).

Rivera Campos, R., and Gallagher, M. (1994) *El gasto público y el estado moderno.* Manuscript, 19 September.

Rodrik, D. (1989) "Promises, Promises: Credible Policy Reform via Signalling," *Economic Journal*, no. 99, pp. 756–772.

Rodrik, D. (1991) "Policy Uncertainty and Private Investment in Developing Countries," *Journal of Development Economics*, no. 36, pp. 229–242.

Rodrik, D. (1994) "King Kong Meets Godzilla: The World Bank and *The East Asian Miracle*," in A. Fishlow et al., *Miracle or Design: Lessons from the East Asian Experience.* Washington, D.C.: Overseas Development Council, pp. 13–53.

Rosa, H. (1993a) *AID y las transformaciones globales en El Salvador.* Managua: CRIES.

Rosa, H. (1993b) "El Banco Mundial y el futuro del ajuste estructural en El Salvador," *Prisma Boletín*, 3–4 December (San Salvador).

Rosa, H., and Segovia, A. (1989) "Financiamiento externo, deuda y transformación de la estructura productiva de El Salvador en la década de los ochenta: El papel de Estados Unidos," *Revista Realidad Económico-Social*, Vol. 2, no. 3.

Rosales, O. (1994) "Política industrial y fomento de la competitividad," *Revista de la CEPAL,* no. 53 (August), pp. 59–69.

Rosenthal, G. (1982) "Principales rasgos de la evolución de las economías centroamericanas desde la posguerra," in *Centroamérica: Crisis y política internacional.* Mexico City: Siglo XXI, pp. 19–38.

Russell, P. (1984) *El Salvador in Crisis.* Austin, Tex.: Colorado River Press.

Saborio, S. (1992) "U.S.–Central America Free Trade," in S. Saborio and contributors, *The Premise and the Promise: Free Trade in the Americas.* Washington, D.C: Overseas Development Council, pp. 195–216.

Saca, N. (1987) "Políticas de estabilización económica en países subdesarrollados: Un modelo aplicado a la economía salvadoreña," *Boletín de Ciencias Económicas y Sociales,* Vol. 10, no. 3.

Saca, N., and Rivera, R. (1987) "Política de estabilización y deuda externa en El Salvador," *Boletín de Ciencias Económicas y Sociales,* Vol. 10, no. 5.

Sachs, J. (1985) "External Debt and Macroeconomic Performance in Latin America and East Asia," *Brookings Papers on Economic Activity,* Vol. 2, (1985), pp. 523–573.

Sachs, J. (1987) "Trade and Exchange Rate Policies in Growth-Oriented Adjustment Programs," in V. Corbo, M. Goldstein, and M. Khan, eds., *Growth-oriented Adjustment Programs.* Washington, D.C.: World Bank, pp. 291–325.

Salazar-Xirinachs, J., and Lizano, E. (1992) "Free Trade in the Americas: A Latin American Perspective," in S. Saborio and contributors, *The Premise and the Promise: Free Trade in the Americas.* Washington, D.C.: Overseas Development Council, pp.75–93.

Salinas, A.D.R., Cerén Dueñas, A.V., and Cardoza López, S. (1993) *Informe técnico: Crédito para el pequeño agricultor de escasos recursos en area de laderas, fragiles y de altas pendientes.* San Salvador: FAO (Proyecto FAO/TCP/ELS/2251, 16 August).

Scandizzo, P. (1992) "Trade Liberalization and Agricultural Prices," *Journal of Policy Modeling,* Vol. 14, no. 5, pp. 561–582.

Schmitt, J. (1993) "Export Promotion in El Salvador: Is 'Getting the Prices Right' Enough?" Center for Economic Performance Working Paper no. 396 (London School of Economics, October).

Schoultz, L. (1989) "The Responsiveness of Policy and Institutional Reform to Aid Conditionality," in W. Ascher and A. Hubbard, eds., *Central American Recovery and Development.* Durham: Duke University Press.

Secretaria de Reconstruccion Nacional, *see* SRN

Segovia, A. (1991) "Los desequilibrios macroeconómicos en El Salvador." *Política Económica,* Vol 1, no. 6, pp. 2–33.

Segovia, A. (1994a) "La economía política del ajuste en una economía pequeña: La experiencia de El Salvador" (mimeo).

Segovia, A. (1994b) "La implementación de los acuerdos de paz y las reformas económicas en El Salvador," San Salvador (June).

Segovia, A. (1994c) "La privatización en El Salvador: Avances y estado actual de la discusión." Fundación Ebert, San Salvador (mimeo).

Segovia, A., and Pleitez, W. (1988) "Los efectos de una devaluación en la economía salvadoreña en el marco de un proceso de estabilización y reactivación," *Revista Presencia* (CENITEC), no. 2.

Segura, O., and Boyce, J. K. (1994) "Investing in Natural and Human Capital in Developing Countries," in A. Jansson et al., eds., *Investing in Natural Capital: The Ecological Economics Approach to Sustainability.* Washington, D.C.: Island Press, pp. 470–489.

Seligson, M. (1994) "Thirty Years of Transformation in the Agrarian Structure of El Salvador." Department of Political Science, University of Pittsburgh (mimeo).

Seligson, M., Thiesenhusen, W., Childress, M., and Vidales, R. (1993) *El Salvador Agricultural Policy Analysis and Land Tenure Study.* Cambridge, Mass.: Abt Associates (APAP II Technical Report no. 133; "Prepared for Agricultural Policy Analysis Project, Phase II (APAP II) and USAID/El Salvador").

Sen, A. (1975) *Employment, Technology and Development.* Oxford: Clarendon Press.

Serven, L., and Solimano, A. (1993) "Debt Crisis, Adjustment Policies, and Capital Formation in Developing Countries: Where Do We Stand?" *World Development,* Vol. 21, no. 1, pp. 127–140.

Shapiro, H. (1993) Automobiles: From Import Substitution to Export Promotion in Brazil and Mexico," in D. B. Yoffie, ed., *Beyond Free Trade: Firms, Governments, and Global Competition.* Cambridge, Mass.: Harvard University Press, pp. 193–248.

Shapiro, H., and Taylor, L. (1990) "The State and Industrial Strategy," *World Development,* Vol. 18, no. 6, pp. 861–878.

SIECA (1973a) *El desarrollo integrado de Centroamérica en la presente década.* Buenos Aires: INTAL.

SIECA (1973b) *Perspectivas para el desarrollo y la integración de la agricultura en Centroamérica.* Guatemala: United Nations Food and Agriculture Organization.

Singh, A., and Tabatabai, H., eds. (1993) *Economic Crisis and Third World Agriculture.* Cambridge: Cambridge University Press.

Siri, G. (1984) *El Salvador and Economic Integration in Central America.* Lexington: Lexington Books.

Siri, G. (1994) "Situación y problemática de la integración de los transportes en Centroamérica," Organizacion de los Estados (mimeo, May).

Siri, G., and Abelardo Delgado, P. (1995) "Uso productivo de las remesas familiares en El Salvador," FUSADES (January).

Sisson, C. (1986) "Fund-supported Programs and Income Distribution in LDCs," *Finance and Development,* Vol. 23, no. 1 (March), pp. 33–36.

Sorto, F. (1995) "El estado actual de la reforma financiera en El Salvador y sus perspectivas," San Salvador (mimeo).

Sorto, F., and Segovia, A. (1992) "La reforma financiera de ARENA: ¿Hacia dónde se dirige la privatización de la Banca?" *Política Económica,* no. 12 (CENITEC).

Spence, J., Dye, D. R., and Vickers, G. (1994) *El Salvador: Elections of the Century: Results, Recommendations and Analysis.* Cambridge: Hemisphere Initiatives.

Spence, J., and Vickers, G. (1994) *A Negotiated Revolution? A Two Year Progress Report on the Salvadoran Peace Accords.* Cambridge: Hemisphere Initiatives.

Spence, J., Vickers, G., and Dye, D. (1995) *The Salvadoran Peace Accords and Democratization: A Three Year Progress Report and Recommendations.* Cambridge: Hemisphere Initiatives.

SRN (1992a) "Plan de Reconstrucción Nacional (Fase de Contingencia)," San Salvador (February).

SRN (1992b) "Plan de Reconstrucción Nacional, Informe de Avance," San Salvador (August).

SRN (1992c) "Programa de apoyo a la reinserción de los ex-combatientes del FMLN" (8 September).

SRN (1993a) "Plan de Reconstrucción Nacional" (May).

SRN (1993b) "Plan de Reconstrucción Nacional Informe de Avance: Convenio 'Paz y Recuperación Nacional'" (December).

SRN (1994) "Participación de las ONGs en el Plan de Reconstruccion Nacional" (July).

Stanley, W. (1993) *Risking Failure: The Problems and Promise of the New Civilian Police Force in El Salvador.* Cambridge and Washington, D.C.: Hemisphere Initiatives and Washington Office on Latin America.

Stanley, W. (1995) "International Tutelage and Domestic Political Will: Lessons from El Salvador's Civilian Police Project," *Studies in Comparative International Development*, Vol. 30, no. 1 (May).

Stewart, F. (1987) "Alternative Macro Policies, Meso Policies, and Vulnerable Groups," in G. A. Cornia, R. Jolly, and F. Stewart, *Adjustment with a Human Face*. Oxford: Clarendon Press, pp. 147–164.

Stiglitz, J. E. (1986a) "The New Development Economics," *World Development*, Vol. 14, no. 2.

Stiglitz, J. E. (1986b) "The Wage-Productivity Hypothesis: Its Economic Consequences and Policy Implications for LDC's," National Bureau of Economic Research Working Paper no. 1976.

Stiglitz, J. E. (1989) "Markets, Market Failures, and Development," *American Economic Review,* Vol. 79, no. 2, pp. 197–203.

Stiglitz, J. E. (1991) *Government, Financial Markets, and Economic Development.* National Bureau of Economic Research Working Paper no. 3669, Cambridge, Mass.

Stiglitz, J. E. (1992) "Introduction: S&L Bail-Out," in J. Barth and D. Brumbaugh, eds., *The Reform of Federal Deposit Insurance.* New York: Harper Collins.

Stiglitz, J. E. (1993) "The Role of the State in Financial Markets" (mimeo).

Stiglitz, J. E., and Weiss, A. (1981) "Credit Rationing in Markets with Imperfect Information," *American Economic Review*, Vol. 71., no. 3, pp. 393–410.

Streeten, P. (1987) *What Price Food? Agricultural Price Policies in Developing Countries.* New York: St. Martin's Press.

Taylor, C., and Jodice, D. (1983) *World Handbook of Political Social Indicators.* New Haven: Yale University Press.

Taylor, L. (1983) *Structuralist Macroeconomics: Applicable Models for the Third World.* New York: Basic Books.

Taylor, L. (1988) *Varieties of Stabilization Experience.* Oxford: Clarendon Press.

Taylor, L. (1989) "Gap Disequilibria: Inflation, Investment, Saving and Foreign Exchange," Working Paper 76 (Helsinki, Finland: World Institute for Development Economics Research, United Nations University).

Taylor, L. (1993) "Stabilization, Adjustment, and Reform," in L. Taylor, ed., *The Rocky Road to Reform: Adjustment, Income Distribution and Growth in the Developing World.* Cambridge, Mass.: MIT Press.

Torres Rivas, E. (1969) *Interpretación del desarrollo social centroamericano.* San José, Costa Rica: EDUCA.

Truth Commission for El Salvador (1993) *From Madness to Hope: The Twelve-Year War in El Salvador.* New York and San Salvador: United Nations.

Tun Wai, U., and Wong, C. (1982) "Determinants of Private Investment in Developing Countries," *Journal of Development Studies,* Vol. 19 (1982), pp. 19–36.

UN General Assembly (1994) *Asistencia para la reconstrucción y el desarrollo de El Salvador: Informe del Secretario General* (Document no. A/49/562).

UN General Assembly and Security Council (1994) "The Situation in Central America: Procedures for the Establishment of a Firm and Lasting Peace and Progress in Fashioning a Region of Peace, Freedom, Democracy, and Development: Note by the Secretary-General" (Document no. A/49/281 S/1994/886, 28 July).

UN Security Council (1994a) "Letter dated 20 March 1994 from the Secretary-General Addressed to the President of the Security Council" (S/1994/361, 30 March).

UN Security Council (1994b) "Report of the Secretary-General on the United Nations Observer Mission in El Salvador" (S/1994/561, 11 May).

UN Security Council (1994c) "Letter dated 24 May 1994 from the Secretary-General Addressed to the President of the Security Council" (S/1994/612, 24 May).

UN Security Council (1994d) "Note by the Secretary-General" (S/1994/886, 28 July).

UN Security Council (1994e) "Report of the Secretary-General on the United Nations Observer Mission in El Salvador" (S/1994/1000, 26 August).

UN Security Council (1994f) "Report of the Secretary-General on the United Nations Observer Mission in El Salvador" (S/1994/1212, 31 October).

UNDP (1992) "Informe de Misión Interagencial de los Organismos del Sistema de las Naciones Unidas Para el Plan de Reconstrucción Nacionale de El Salvador," El Salvador (March).

UNDP (1993) *Launching New Protagonists in Salvadoran Agriculture: The Agricultural Training Programme for Ex-Combatants of the FMLN.* San Salvador (December).

UNDP (1994a) *Technical and Financial Cooperation with El Salvador as Reported by Donors (1992–1995).* San Salvador: UNDP (January).

UNDP (1994b) "Illustrated Annual Report, 1993," San Salvador, El Salvador Field Office (January).

UNDP (1994c) "Programa de apoyo a la reinserción económica de líderes y mandos medios del FMLN," San Salvador (March). (Proyectos ELS/93/006 y ELS/93/012; "Informe de Avances y Evaluación.")

UNDP (1994d) *Human Development Report 1994.* New York: Oxford University Press.

Unidad de Análisis de Políticas Agropecuarias, Ministerio de Agricultura y Ganadería (UAP-MAG) (1991) *Estrategia y políticas para el desarrollo del sector agropecuario 1991–94.* San Salvador.

United Nations Development Programme, *see* UNDP

United Nations Economic Commission for Latin America and the Caribbean, *see* CEPAL

United Nations Food and Agriculture Organization, *see* FAO

United Nations, *see* UN

United States Agency for International Development, *see* USAID

United States Government (1994) *Economic Report of the President.* Washington, D.C.

United States House of Representatives, Arms Control and Foreign Policy Caucus (1990) "Barriers to Reform: El Salvador's Military Leaders" (21 May).

United States International Trade Commission (USITC) (1992) *Potential Effects of a North American Free Trade Agreement on Apparel Investment in CBERA Countries.* Washington, D.C. Publication no. 2541.

United States International Trade Commission (USITC) (1994) *Impact of the Caribbean Basin Economic Recovery Act on U.S. Industries and Consumers.* Ninth Report 1993. Washington, D.C. USITC Publication 2813.

USAID (1977) *Agricultural Sector Assessment: El Salvador.* San Salvador: USAID/El Salvador (mimeo).

USAID (1989) *Environmental and Natural Resource Management in Central America: A Strategy for A.I.D. Assistance.* USAID Bureau for Latin America and the Caribbean. USAID/ROCAP.

USAID (1992) "FY 1992 Policy Reform Support," Program Assistance Approval Document.

USAID (1993a) "Memorandum from Charles E. Costello (Dir/USAID) to Maureen Dugan regarding the GAO Draft Report: 'El Salvador, Implementation of Post War Programs Slower than Expected'" (20 October).

USAID (1993b) *FY 1993 ESF Economic and Democratic Reform Program. Program Assistance Approval Document.* USAID/El Salvador.

USAID (1993c) "Protección del Medio Ambiente Salvadoreño (PROMESA) Project Document," USAID/El Salvador.

USAID (1993d) "El Salvador: Selected Economic Data" (ESDAT: LAC/DPP (3/03/03).

USAID (1994a) "El Salvador Action Plan FY-1995–96," USAID/El Salvador.

USAID (1994b) *FY 1994 ESF Modernization of the State Program Assistance Approval Document.* USAID/El Salvador.

USAID (1994c) "Concept Paper: Equitable Rural Economic Growth Activity," USAID/El Salvador (13 May).

Valdes, A., and Pinckney, T. (1989) "Trade and Macroeconomic Policies' Impact on Agricultural Growth: Evidence To-Date," *Eastern Africa Economic Review,* Vol. 5, no. 1, pp. 42–61.

van Wijnbergen, S. (1986) "Aid, Export Performance and the Real Exchange Rate: An African Dilemma," Macroeconomics Division, Development Research Department, World Bank (mimeo, October).

Vickers, G. (1992). "El Salvador: A Negotiated Revolution," *Report on the Americas* (North American Congress on Latin America), Vol. 25, no. 5 (May).

von Hesse, M. (1994) "Políticas públicas y competitividad de las exportaciones agricolas," *Revista de la CEPAL,* no. 53, pp. 129–146.

Wade, R. (1994) "Selective Industrial Policies in East Asia: Is *The East Asian Miracle* Right?" in A. Fishlow et al., *Miracle or Design: Lessons from the East Asian Experience.* Washington, D.C.: Overseas Development Council.

Washington Office on Latin America (WOLA) (1993) *Reluctant Reforms: The Cristiani Government and the International Community in the Process of Salvadoran Post-War Reconstruction.* Washington, D.C.: WOLA (June).

Washington Office on Latin America (WOLA) (1994) "Recent Setbacks in the Police Transition," *El Salvador Peace Plan Update 3.*

Weiss Fagen, P. (1995) "El Salvador: Lessons in Peace Consolidation," in T. Farer, ed., *Beyond Sovereignty: Collectively Defending Democracy in the Americas.* Baltimore: Johns Hopkins Press.

Wenner, M. D., and Umaña, R. (1993) *Agricultural Credit Market Assessment in El Salvador: Preliminary Report.* Bethesda, Md.: Abt Associates Inc. (Agricultural Policy Analaysis Project, Phase II, USAID, APAP II Technical Report no. 130, February 1993).

White, A. (1973) *El Salvador.* New York: Praeger Publishers.

Whitfield, T. (1994) *Paying the Price: Ignacio Ellacuría and the Murdered Jesuits of El Salvador.* Philadelphia: Temple University Press.

Williams, R. (1986) *Export Agriculture and the Crisis in Central America.* Chapel Hill: University of North Carolina Press.

Williamson, J. (1990) "The Progress of Policy Reform in Latin America," in J. Williamson, ed., *Latin American Adjustment: How Much Has Happened.* Institute for International Economics. Washington, D.C. (April).

Wilson, E. (1978) "La crisis de la integración nacional en El Salvador," in G. Véjar and R. Menjívar, eds., *El Salvador de 1840 a 1935: Estudiado y analizado por extranjeros*. San Salvador: UCA Editores.

Wisecarver, D. (1989) *El tamaño e influencia del sector público en la economía salvadoreña*. San Salvador: FUSADES (Documento de trabajo 1).

Wolf, D. H. (1992) "ARENA in the Arena: Factors in the Accommodation of the Salvadoran Right to Pluralism and the Broadening of the Political System." Paper presented to the United Nations Observers Mission in El Salvador (ONUSAL), 20 January. La Jolla, Calif.: University of California, San Diego, Department of Political Science.

Wood, E. (1995) "Agrarian Social Relations and Democratization: The Negotiated Resolution of El Salvador's Civil War." Doctoral dissertation, Stanford University.

World Bank (1979) *El Salvador: Cuestiones y perspectivas demográficas*. Washington, D.C.: World Bank.

World Bank (1980) *El Salvador: An Inquiry into Urban Poverty*. Washington, D.C.: World Bank.

World Bank (1983) *El Salvador: Updating Economic Memorandum*. Washington, D.C. (Report no. 4054-ES, January.)

World Bank (1986) *El Salvador: Country Economic Memorandum*. Washington, D.C.: World Bank.

World Bank (1988) *Adjustment Lending: An Evaluation of Ten Years*. Washington, D.C.: World Bank.

World Bank (1989a) *El Salvador: Country Economic Memorandum*. Washington, D.C.: World Bank (Latin America and Caribbean Regional Office, Country Department II, Report no. 7818-ES, 14 August).

World Bank (1989b) *World Development Report 1989*. New York: Oxford University Press.

World Bank (1991a) "Bank Work on Military Expenditure." Internal management note (circulated under the title "Military Expenditure," Sec. M91-1563, and subsequently incorporated into Operational Directive 2.00, Annex B, 6 December).

World Bank (1991b) "Military Expenditure: Statement by Vice President and General Counsel." Internal management note, Sec. M91-1563/1 (13 December).

World Bank (1991c) *World Development Report 1991*. Washington, D.C.: World Bank.

World Bank (1991d) "Workers' Benefits from Bolivia's Emergency Social Fund," LSMS Working Paper no. 77.

World Bank (1992a) "El Salvador: SAL II Identification Mission Aide-Mémoire" (mimeo, 11 June).

World Bank (1992b) *Consultative Group for El Salvador, Washington, D.C., March 23, 1992: Chairman's Report of Proceedings* (Report no. ES 92-10, 11 May).

World Bank (1992c) "El Salvador: Recent Economic Developments and Key Challenges." Prepared for the Consultative Group Meeting for El Salvador, Washington, D.C., 23 March.

World Bank (1992d) *Governance and Development*. Washington, D.C.: World Bank.

World Bank (1993a) "Agricultural Sector Reform and Investment Project." Washington, D.C.: World Bank (Staff Appraisal Report, Agriculture Operations Division Department II, Latin American and Caribbean Regional Office, Report no. 10933-ES, 1 March).

World Bank (1993b) *The East Asian Miracle: Economic Growth and Public Policy.* Oxford: Oxford University Press.

World Bank (1993c) *Report and Recommendation of the International Bank for Reconstruction and Development to the Executive Directors on a Proposed Second Structural Adjustment Loan (SAL) of US $50 million to the Republic of El Salvador.* Washington, D.C: World Bank (Report no. P-6108-ES, 23 August).

World Bank (1993d) *Consultative Group for El Salvador, Paris, France, April 1, 1993: Chairman's Report of Proceedings.* Washington, D.C.: World Bank (Report no. ES 93-3).

World Bank (1994a) *El Salvador: Natural Resources Management Study.* Washington, D.C.: World Bank (Agriculture and Natural Resources Operations Division, Latin America and Caribbean Region, Report no. 12355-ES, 21 January).

World Bank (1994b) *El Salvador: The Challenge of Poverty Alleviation.* Washington, D.C.: World Bank (Report no. 12315-ES, 9 June).

World Bank (1994c) *Governance: The World Bank's Experience.* Washington, D.C.: World Bank.

World Bank (1994d) *World Development Report 1994.* New York: Oxford University Press.

Yariv, D., and Curtis, C. (1992) "After the War: A Preliminary Look at the Role of U.S. Aid in the Post-War Reconstruction of El Salvador." Washington, D.C.: Foreign Aid Monitoring Project Investigative Report (December).

Yariv, D., and Curtis, C. (1993) "Después de la guerra: Una mirada preliminar al papel de la ayuda militar de EE.UU. en la reconstrucción de postguerra en El Salvador," *Estudios Centroamericanos,* Año XLVIII, no. 531–532 (January–February).

Younger, S.D. (1992) "Aid and the Dutch Disease: Macroeconomic Management When Everybody Loves You," *World Development,* Vol. 20, no. 11, pp. 1587–1597.

About the Contributors

Carlos Acevedo is a Guatemalan-Salvadoran philosopher and economist who has published extensively on social and economic issues in Central America. Since 1983 he has taught at the Universidad Centroamericana (UCA) in San Salvador, where he has also served as subdirector of the Centre of Information, Documentation and Investigation (CIDAI) and a member of the editorial board of the journal *Estudios Centroamericanos*. After earning his licenciatura in philosophy at the Universidad Iberoamericana in Mexico, he received a licenciatura in economics from the UCA and a master's degree in economics from Duke University. He is currently working toward a doctorate in economics at Vanderbilt University.

Deborah Barry, an economic geographer and social scientist, is director of PRISMA (Programa Salvadoreño de Investigación sobre Desarrollo y Medio Ambiente, the Salvadoran Program for Research on Development and the Environment) in San Salvador.

James K. Boyce is professor and chair of the Department of Economics at the University of Massachusetts, Amherst. He is author of *The Philippines: The Political Economy of Growth and Impoverishment in the Marcos Era,* written for the OECD's research program on Economic Choices before the Developing Countries, and coauthor of *Café y Desarrollo Sostenible.*

Michael E. Conroy is program officer in the Ford Foundation Office for Mexico and Central America. Prior to joining the foundation he taught economics at the University of Texas, Austin, specializing in Latin American economics and the economics of sustainable development. He has served as president of the board of directors of the Central America Resource Center in Austin, now known as the Human Rights Documentation Exchange. He has also served on the executive boards of the Latin American Studies Association, Policy Alternatives for the Caribbean and Central

America (PACCA), and the Latin American and Caribbean Economic Association.

Colin Danby, a doctoral candidate in economics at the University of Massachusetts, Amherst, teaches at Dickinson College in Carlisle, Pennsylvania. He has worked with the Central America Information Office, the Honduras Information Center, and Policy Alternatives for the Caribbean and Central America.

Manuel Pastor, Jr., is associate professor of economics and director of the International and Public Affairs Center at Occidental College in Los Angeles, California. He is the author of *The International Monetary Fund and Latin America: Economic Stabilization and Class Conflict* and of *Inflation, Stabilization, and Debt: Macroeconomic Experiments in Peru and Bolivia.* His articles on Latin American political economy have appeared in various journals, including *International Organization, World Development, Journal of Development Economics,* and *Latin American Research Review.*

Eva Paus is professor of economics at Mount Holyoke College in Massachusetts. She has published widely in the area of economic development, with a particular focus on industrialization strategies, nontraditional export growth, international competitiveness, and the distributional consequences of different development strategies in Latin America. She has served as a consultant to UNIDO and UNDP.

Herman Rosa, an economist and electrical engineer, is senior researcher and editor at PRISMA (Programa Salvadoreño de Investigación sobre Desarrollo y Medio Ambiente, the Salvadoran Program for Research on Development and the Environment) in San Salvador.

Alexander Segovia, a Salvadoran economist, earned his licenciatura from the Universidad Centroamericana in San Salvador and his master's degree at Oxford University. He is currently pursuing a doctorate in economics at the University of London. He is the author of numerous articles and works on the Salvadoran economy.

Elisabeth J. Wood is assistant professor of politics at New York University and an academy scholar at Harvard University's Academy for International and Area Studies. She received her doctorate from Stanford University in 1995 and is currently completing a book on the transformation of agrarian social relations and the resolution of the war in El Salvador.

Index

Accountability, 9, 10
Acevedo, Carlos, 19–29, 209–230
Ad Hoc Commission, 80, 92
Adjustment: consequences of, 43–45; costs of, 45–46, 82; economic, 52, 119–124; external, 46; fiscal, 43–45, 47, 147, 175*n10;* implementation, 59; interest rate, 36; lending, 52*tab;* neoliberal, 52; policy, 43, 50*n27,* 51; salary, 49*n14;* social costs, 51, 56, 78, 84; structural, 1, 4, 9, 55, 61, 63–65, 70*n1,* 78, 82, 84, 140, 148, 155–156, 157, 158*tab,* 162–165, 209–230, 247, 248, 261–275
Agriculture: competitive exclusion in, 20; diversification in, 21; employment in, 46, 213; farm size, 23*tab,* 220*tab;* incentives for, 20; investment in, 20; production, 23*tab,* 48*n6;* profitability of, 211–218; real prices in, 212–217; reconstruction costs, 45*tab;* subsistence, 11, 21, 22, 28; training programs, 90, 96, 100
Agroexports, 19, 20, 21, 22, 25, 27, 28, 47, 187, 188, 210
Aid: channeling, 139; commitments, 130–131, 134–135; competition for, 136; as complement to domestic resources, 129; conditionality, 129, 137, 140–150, 153*n14;* constraints on, 136; development, 152*n6,* 152*n9;* donor priorities, 135; economic, 12; external, 107, 130–140, 169, 215, 227; food, 136, 152*n7,* 153*n11;* foreign, 37, 41, 43, 49*n18,* 50*n28,* 180, 194, 249; impediments to, 137–138; international, 60, 69; military, 12, 13; official, 41, 46, 130–140, 152*n9,* 161; reverse leverage in, 148, 149; trade-related, 138; from United States, 37, 38*tab,* 41
Alliance for Progress, 28

Allianza Republicana Nacional (ARENA), 13, 14, 54, 74, 76, 77, 82, 85, 97, 101
American Free Trade Area, 270
ANSP. *See* National Academy of Public Security
Arbitrage, 186, 205*n3*
ARENA. *See* Allianza Republicana Nacional
Argentina: currency board in, 205*n16;* exchange rate in, 156, 277*n11;* liberalization in, 179
Armed Forces of National Resistance (FARN), 29
Atlacatl Battalion, 77, 80
Austerity, 35, 36, 37, 43, 46
Authoritarianism, 27–29, 47

Balance of payments, 25, 41, 129, 138, 140, 169, 296*tab*
Balance of power, 4–5, 102, 129
Banco Central de Reserva (BCR), 34–35, 60, 180, 181, 186, 200, 205*n10*
Banco de Fomento Agropecuario (BFA), 187, 193, 198, 207*n19,* 221, 224*tab*
Banco Hipotecario, 193
Banco Multisectorial de Inversiones (BMI), 188, 194, 195
Banking: Certificates of Monetary Stabilization, 181, 182, 183, 205*n9,* 205*n10,* 254, 263; commercial, 177, 187, 188, 192, 197, 199, 204*n1,* 221, 224*tab;* deregulation of, 177; development, 3, 136, 137, 141, 178, 192, 193–195, 197, 205*n2;* laws, 199; liberalization, 197; liquidity in, 180, 181, 185*tab,* 187; nationalization of, 34, 42, 187, 207*n18;* oligopoly, 66–67; privatization in, 63, 193; reform, 192, 194; regional, 3; regulation, 178, 181, 192, 198, 282; reserves, 181*fig,* 182*tab,* 187; rural, 192, 193

BCR. *See* Banco Central de Reserva
BFA. *See* Banco de Fomento Agropecuario
BMI. *See* Banco Multisectorial de Inversiones
Bolivia: exchange rate in, 156; hyperinflation in, 175*n10;* labor market regulations in, 176*n23;* liberalization in, 176*n25;* stabilization in, 176*n25*
BPR. *See* People's Revolutionary Bloc
Bush, George, 76

CACM. *See* Central American Common Market
Calderón Sol, Armando, 65, 95, 96, 101, 102, 125, 131, 134
Canada, 131*tab*
Capital: access to, 20, 230; accounts, 205*n3;* accumulation, 57, 205*n13,* 249; assets, 41; fixed, 26, 197; flight, 33, 48*n5,* 49*n13,* 49*n17,* 157, 164, 168; foreign, 32, 111, 164, 177, 205*n3;* formation, 53, 159, 267; goods, 25, 32, 63, 66, 157, 252, 255, 263, 267; human, 2, 5, 7–9, 45, 71*n8,* 88, 104*n15,* 114, 168, 171, 221, 263, 282; inflows, 111, 205*n13,* 254, 263; internationalization of, 55; investment, 196, 262; markets, 28; mobility, 267; movement, 48*n5,* 179; natural, 2, 5, 7–9, 225, 243; operating, 171; outlays, 159; physical, 5, 7–9; private, 15, 53, 110; quicksilver, 183; short-term, 164, 177, 183, 282; social, 114; spending, 122; stock, 260; working, 183, 196, 197
Caribbean Basin Economic Recovery Act, 269
Caribbean Basin Initiative (CBI), 217, 270, 278*n21*
Catholic Relief Services, 97
CBI. *See* Caribbean Basin Initiative
CEMs. *See* Certificates of Monetary Stabilization
Central American Common Market, 20, 49*n10,* 51, 54, 63, 67, 70*n6,* 71*n9,* 250, 251, 253, 255, 258, 260, 261, 265, 266, 267, 268, 270, 273, 283
Central Reserve Bank. *See* Banco Central de Reserva
Certificates of Monetary Stabilization (CEMs), 181, 182, 183, 205*n9,* 205*n10,* 254, 263
Chapultepec Accord (1992), 2, 13, 15, 53, 73, 79, 120
Chile: lending fraud in, 180; liberalization in, 179
China, 7
Christian Democratic Party (PDC), 37, 50*n21,* 101
Clinton, Bill, 71*n13,* 145

Coffee, 187; export nationalization, 33, 34, 42; growing areas, 242*fig,* 243*tab;* harvest wages, 240*fig;* historical background, 19–21; oligarchy, 20, 21; prices, 216*tab,* 250, 253; production, 19–21, 23*tab;* yields, 30*n2*
Comisión Económica para América Latina y el Caribe, 42
Commission for the Restoration of Areas (CONARA), 86
Communist Party, 12, 29, 29*n1*
Conable, Barber Jr., 145, 154*n24*
CONARA. *See* Commission for the Restoration of Areas
Conflict: civil, 3, 12, 19; economic roots of, 19–21; political, 15, 34; social, 1, 2, 167, 168, 234
Consultative Group for El Salvador, 86, 88, 91, 130, 131, 136, 153*n17*
Cooperatives, 42, 218, 229
COPAZ. *See* National Commission for the Consolidation of Peace
Corruption, 10, 101
Costa Rica: agricultural income, 24*tab;* immigration from El Salvador, 30*n9;* inflation rates, 28*tab;* life expectancy, 285*tab;* literacy rates, 285*tab;* military expenditures, 154*n19;* trade surpluses, 268
Cotton, 21, 23*tab,* 30*n2,* 187, 250
Credit, 96, 163, 177; access to, 20, 84, 97, 198, 217, 221; agricultural, 14, 90–91, 96, 97, 102, 132*tab,* 202, 207*n19,* 209, 219, 221, 224*tab;* allocation of, 179, 188, 195, 197; availability of, 33, 37, 67, 84; from banking system, 192*tab;* channeling, 103, 163, 178, 187, 188, 193, 194, 197, 200, 204, 207*n26;* commercial, 197; concessional, 201; costs, 90*tab,* 183; deregulation, 221; distribution, 207*n18;* domestic, 182*tab,* 188*fig;* expansion, 181; extensions, 102; formal sector, 195; guarantees, 201; informal, 195–197; internal, 34; for land purchase, 83; lines of, 194, 221; markets, 6, 171, 183, 202; for microenterprises, 91, 195, 196; misallocation of, 178, 183; networks, 209; official, 112; policy, 66, 84, 120, 202, 205*n2,* 219, 221; private sector, 40; production, 96; provision of, 178; rationing, 164; real, 67, 221; rural, 219; standby, 36; subsidies, 10, 215; supply, 35; tax, 263; trade, 195; unions, 194, 200
Crime, 14, 94, 95, 97, 98, 99, 104*n21*
Cristiani, Alfredo, 13, 15, 19, 51, 76, 79, 92, 94, 144, 254, 255
Currency: appreciation, 63, 161, 177, 180, 185, 205*n13,* 205*n15,* 254, 257, 260;

black market, 34; board, 65–66, 205*n16;*
circulating, 181; convertible, 53;
depreciation, 175*n14,* 257; devaluation,
31, 40, 41, 158, 185, 186, 205*n15,*
205*n16,* 207*n26,* 254, 263, 264;
exchange, 55; foreign, 25, 32, 34, 35, 41,
46, 49*n17,* 180, 181, 186; hard, 138;
interventions, 67; local, 138, 180;
overvaluation, 56, 213, 275; reserves, 25;
scarcity of, 35; sources, 41; speculative
runs on, 205*n16*

Dalton, Roque, 29
Debt: accumulation, 266; agrarian, 229;
crises, 152*n3,* 160; domestic, 186;
external, 127*n12,* 298*tab;* foreign, 117,
168; forgiveness, 50*n18,* 117, 152*n3,* 229;
internal, 127*n12;* public, 127*n12,* 152*n3;*
restructuring, 127*n12;* service, 33, 117,
135, 152*n3*
Deferred Enforced Departure program, 61,
71*n13*
Deforestation, 233
Deindustrialization, 258, 269
Democratization, 2, 9–10, 19, 47–48, 75, 85,
224
Development, 1; agricultural, 227–230; aid,
152*n6,* 152*n9;* asymmetrical, 271;
banking, 3, 136, 137, 141, 178, 187, 192,
193–195, 197, 205*n2;* community, 78;
economic, 42, 142, 148, 167, 173;
environmental, 233–244; financial, 177;
human, 88, 103; industrial, 20, 50*n21;*
institutional, 178; long-term, 123; and
nontraditional exports, 42; policy,
207*n28,* 280; productivity, 258, 260–261;
projects, 87, 136; real-estate, 183,
205*n13;* regional, 97; sustainable, 7, 178,
204, 227–230; urban, 235, 245*n3*
Drought, 31, 71*n11,* 121, 127*n12*
Duarte, José Napoleon, 12, 13
"Dutch disease," 67–68, 72*n21,* 261, 277*n10*

Earthquakes, 31, 41
Economic adjustment, 52
Economic aid. *See* aid
Economic crises, 20, 31, 32–41, 47, 213
Economic development, 42, 142, 148, 167,
173
Economic diversification, 211,
Economic growth, 2, 19, 20, 22, 27, 51, 73,
101, 118, 124, 156, 168, 225, 247, 248,
249, 261
Economic indicators, 62*tab*
Economic inefficiency, 30*n4*
Economic inequality, 12, 75, 82
Economic infrastructure, 43, 45
Economic justice, 73

Economic liberalization, 55, 68
Economic modernization, 66
Economic policy, 1, 2–5, 3, 33–41, 37, 42,
79, 82, 101, 239
Economic reform, 12, 15, 47
Economic restructuring, 42, 43, 55, 249
Economic stabilization, 4, 19, 47, 60–61,
122, 141–144, 155, 280
Economic stagnation, 35
Economic theory, 2, 3
Economic Commission for Latin America
and the Caribbean, 141–142
Economic Support Fund, 136, 148, 152*n7,*
152*n11*
Economy: competitive, 63; international, 20;
market, 71*n15;* modernization of, 63;
open, 58, 101; political, 201; of scale, 27,
163, 176*n20,* 266; structure of, 3;
wartime, 31–48
Education, 285*tab;* financing, 50*n24;* and
growth rates, 16*n6;* higher, 16*n1;*
investment in, 6, 172; primary, 5, 7, 16*n6,*
168, 171, 225, 285*tab;* reconstruction
costs, 45*tab;* relation to income, 6; role in
growth, 6–7; spending, 6, 16*n1,* 43,
119*tab,* 127*n15,* 144, 154*n24,* 285*tab*
EEC. *See* European Economic Community
Elections, 2, 9, 13, 17*n16,* 20, 29, 75–76,
80, 90*tab,* 91–92, 100–101
Electoral Tribunal, 101, 104*n24*
El Salvador: agrarian structure, 11;
agricultural income, 24*tab;* defense
budget, 118*tab,* 127*n11;* domestic
investment in, 7, 16*n7;* economic crisis,
32–41; economic growth, 19, 20, 22, 27;
education enrollment in, 7; education
spending, 6; financial sector in, 177–204;
fiscal deficits, 37*fig;* funding priorities,
90*tab;* government budgets, 119*tab;* gross
domestic product growth, 36*fig;* gross
national product, 4; heads of state, 22*tab;*
immigration to United States, 61;
inflation rates, 28*tab;* life expectancy,
285*tab;* literacy rates, 24, 285*tab;* living
standards, 24, 26; migration to United
States, 30*n9;* occupational structure,
46*tab,* 47; reliance on external resources,
32, 34, 37, 41–42, 51, 64, 65, 71*n8,* 111,
112–114 130, 248, 262–263; trade sector
in, 249–252
Emergency Plan (1980), 34
Employment: in agriculture, 213; of
children, 46; declines in, 34, 239;
domestic, 54; guarantees, 89, 172, 283;
harvest, 239*fig;* increasing, 247; in
manufacturing sector, 26, 27; maquila,
251, 253*tab;* public sector, 37, 41, 46,
48*n6,* 66; seasonal, 22; unproductive, 262

Enterprise for the Americas Initiative, 270, 274
Environment: conservation incentives, 225–226; focus on, 170; funding priorities, 90*tab;* restoration of, 172; sustainability in, 210
Environmental conservation, 225–226, 233–244; and income equality, 8; pest management, 8; pollution control, 8; soil, 8; water, 8, 10, 233–235, 245*n3*
Equity: and adjustments, 157; alternative policies for, 170–173; economic, 280; and efficiency, 155; and growth, 5–7, 16*n3,* 280; political, 280; social, 75, 82, 155, 156, 163, 164, 167
ERP. *See* People's Revolutionary Army
European Economic Community (EEC), 131*tab,* 132–133*tab,* 140, 149, 152*n2,* 267
Exchange: controls, 36, 179; currency, 55; foreign, 15, 32, 33, 34, 35, 37, 41, 47, 48*n2,* 48*n3,* 53, 55, 60, 107, 124, 161, 162, 172, 177, 210, 211, 215, 247, 249, 266, 279–280; gap, 107; generation of, 247, 249; market, 49*n17;* parallel market, 36; securities, 205*n11;* stability, 34; stock, 58
Exchange rate, 39*tab,* 159, 185, 253; appreciation, 64, 70*n6,* 254, 256, 281, 282; changes, 257; competitive, 156; controlled, 165; convertible, 65; depreciation, 37, 40, 41, 65, 124, 262; devaluation, 67; "dirty float," 58, 254, 257; evolution of, 254; fixed, 41, 53, 65, 66, 67, 142, 156, 157, 205*n16,* 263, 277*n11;* flexible, 58; fluctuations, 71*n11;* freezing, 68; inflation-adjusted, 174*n7,* 257, 258; liberalization, 214, 254; manipulative, 205*n15;* market determination, 248; nominal, 177, 256, 277*n11;* official, 49*n10;* overvaluation, 17*n18,* 60, 63, 214, 227, 228, 254, 258, 263; parallel, 49*n10;* pegged, 161; policy, 57, 64, 66, 161, 183, 205*n2;* real, 51, 60, 61*fig,* 64, 67, 70*n6,* 161, 175*n9,* 175*n16,* 214, 215, 254, 256, 257, 258, 260, 262–264, 281, 282; single, 40, 55, 57; stability, 41, 55, 57, 262; unified, 254; wage-adjusted, 256, 257*fig,* 260
Export(s): agricultural, 19, 20, 21, 22, 25, 27, 28, 57, 141, 187, 188, 193, 210, 214*tab,* 217–218, 250, 273, 274, 275; bias against, 261; channels, 261; competitiveness, 52, 60, 142, 161, 183, 205*n14,* 248, 254; composition, 54*tab;* diversification, 47, 65, 217, 251; duties, 58; earnings, 171, 213; extraregional, 266; growth, 247, 252–275; incentives,

10; industrial, 57, 267; infrastructure, 52, 68; managed, 63; manufactured, 25, 250; maquila, 250, 251, 253, 273, 274; markets, 28; merchandise, 248*fig;* nontraditional, 42, 51, 54*tab,* 57, 62*tab,* 63, 70*n6,* 210, 214*tab,* 217–218, 227, 248, 249, 250, 251*fig,* 252*tab,* 253, 254, 256, 258, 267, 273, 274, 283; and peace consolidation, 247–276; prices, 33, 239; primary, 32; processing zones, 250; promotion, 57, 138, 161, 180, 255; subsidies, 162, 265; taxes, 40, 112–114, 115*tab;* traditional, 54*tab,* 70*n6,* 214*tab,* 274, 276*n4;* undervaluation of, 48*n5*

FAPU. *See* United Front for Popular Action
Farabundo Martí for National Liberation (FMLN), 2, 12, 13, 14, 17*n12,* 19, 29, 74, 75, 76, 77, 78, 79, 80, 81, 82, 85, 87, 89, 91, 92, 95, 101, 104*n10*
FARN. *See* Armed Forces of National Resistance
FEDECACES. *See* Federación de Asociaciones Cooperativas de Ahorro y Crédito de el Salvador
FEDECREDITO. *See* Federaciónde Cajas de Crédito
Federación de Asociaciones Cooperativas de Ahorro y Crédito de el Salvador (FEDECACES), 200
Federaciónde Cajas de Crédito (FEDECREDITO), 193, 194
FIGAPE. *See* Fondo de Financiamiento y Garantía para la Pequeña Empresa
Financial institutions, international. *See* International financial institutions.
Financial institutions, local, 199–201
Financieras, 188, 193*tab*
FMLN. *See* Farabundo Martí for National Liberation
Fondo de Financiamiento y Garantía para la Pequeña Empresa (FUSADES), 193
Food and Agriculture Organization, 202, 207*n28*
Foundation for Economic and Social Development, 42, 55, 72*n20,* 125
"Fourteen Families," 11, 17*n11*
FPL. *See* Popular Liberation Forces
Free-rider problem, 135, 136–137
Free-trade zones, 52, 63, 66, 101, 255
FUSADES. *See* Foundation for Economic and Social Development

Generalized System of Preferences, 98, 269
General Treaty of Economic Integration (1960), 20
Germany: aid to El Salvador, 131*tab,* 132–133*tab,* 152*n2;* loan cofinancing, 138

Goulding, Marrack, 93
Government of National Unity, 36
Gross domestic product, 36*fig,* 55, 60,
62*tab,* 285*tab,* 286–289*tab;* agricultural
share in, 211, 212, 213*tab;* decline in, 34;
domestic credit in, 188*fig;* education
spending, 144; investment in, 109*tab;*
military expenditures, 144, 153*n19;*
monetary aggregates in, 184*fig;* savings
in, 108, 112*tab;* and tax revenues, 114
Gross national product, 4, 168, 285*tab*
Growth: economic, 19, 20, 22, 27, 51, 73,
101, 107, 118, 124, 125, 156, 167–168,
175*n15,* 225, 247, 248, 249, 261; and
education, 6–7, 16*n6;* and environmental
degradation, 235, 237–238; and equity,
5–7, 16*n3,* 280; export, 42, 56, 59, 247,
252–275; and foreign exchange, 32; long-
term, 167, 224; macroeconomic, 210;
market, 20; population, 235, 236*fig,*
245*n5;* productivity, 260, 271–275; rates,
67; real, 62*tab;* slowing, 159; sustained,
72*n20,* 73, 224; urban, 234, 235, 237–238
Guatemala: agricultural income, 24*tab;*
inflation rates, 28*tab;* life expectancy,
285*tab;* literacy rates, 285*tab;* military
expenditures, 154*n19;* trade surpluses,
268

Health care: financing, 50*n24;*
reconstruction costs, 45*tab;* spending, 43,
119*tab,* 127*n15,* 144, 285*tab*
Herbicides, 225–226, 231*n12*
Honduras: agricultural income, 24*tab;* aid
from United States, 152*n8;* domestic
investment in, 16*n8;* immigration, 24, 28,
30*n9;* inflation rates, 28*tab;* life
expectancy, 285*tab;* literacy rates,
285*tab;* military expenditures, 154*n19;*
trade deficits, 266, 268
Housing, 89, 100, 132*tab;* assistance, 13;
developers, 229; emergency, 96; and land
use, 235; reconstruction costs, 45*tab;*
standards, 24; urban, 237

Import(s), 62*tab;* barriers, 251; capital
goods, 25, 252, 263; competition, 165;
control of, 49*n10;* dependence on, 26;
lowered levels of, 34; merchandise,
248*fig,* 310*tab;* permits, 35; prior-deposit
requirements, 35; restrictions, 161, 162;
structure, 253*tab;* taxes, 112–114, 115*tab;*
technological, 25
Income: agricultural, 24, 28, 161; classes,
157, 164; concentration, 35; and demand
for education, 6; distribution, 2, 5, 9, 10,
15, 20, 27, 47, 52, 56, 66, 123, 155, 156,
157, 159, 160, 163, 165, 166, 167–168,

175*n13,* 247; inequality, 2, 6, 15, 20, 159,
167, 176*n25;* inequality of, 114; losses,
239; national, 211; real, 156, 212;
redistribution, 6; remittance, 70*n7;* rural,
224; taxes, 40
Indonesia: land distribution in, 225;
liberalization in, 179
Industrialization, import-substitution, 24–27,
247, 258, 266
Inflation, 4, 19, 27, 28*tab,* 31, 32, 33, 34,
35, 39*tab,* 40*fig,* 41, 46, 48*n2,* 51, 55, 60,
66, 71*n11,* 121, 122, 124, 141, 142, 156,
158, 161, 162, 180, 183, 205*n14,* 239;
conflict-driven, 167; domestic, 277*n11;*
and exchange rate, 174*n7;* and foreign
exchange, 48*n2,* 48*n3;* international,
277*n11;* policy, 48*n3;* seasonal, 48*n3*
Infrastructure, 90*tab,* 124, 131, 133*tab;*
access to, 243; assistance, 137; basic,
104*n15;* deficient, 63; economic, 43, 45;
emphasis on, 87, 88; employment in, 172;
export, 52, 68; financing for, 88*tab;*
foreign, 48*n5;* investment, 25, 172, 247,
263; local, 57; physical, 1, 21, 86, 137,
138, 139; production, 100; projects, 129,
135; provision of, 110; public, 47;
reconstruction, 84; rehabilitation, 11;,
repair, 1, 31; social, 43, 45, 100, 139;
spending, 107, 175*n12;* urban, 235
Institutions: capacity of, 93; change to, 3;
democratic, 1, 2, 9, 13, 15, 85, 88, 117,
118, 137, 147, 150, 151, 281; domestic,
74; economic, 42; financial, 1, 3, 4,
52*tab,* 63; formal sector, 177, 198;
informal, 177, 197; international, 47, 51,
52*tab;* lending, 47; local, 201;
nongovernmental, 42; political, 42, 79;
strengthening, 9, 13, 15, 88, 117, 118,
137, 147
Inter-American Court of Human Rights, 99
Inter-American Development Bank, 52*tab,*
126*n6,* 130, 131*tab,* 132–133*tab,* 140,
144, 145, 147, 154*n28*
Interest rates, 63, 158, 163, 182, 205*n3;*
active, 40; adjustment, 36; concessional,
188, 201; domestic, 177, 179, 180; and
financial stability, 183, 185–186; foreign,
177, 180; formal sector, 185*fig;*
liberalization, 221; market, 207*n28;*
nominal, 183, 185; overvalued, 48*n5;*
passive, 40; positive, 198; real, 33;
reduction in, 37; restrictions, 58, 188;
subsidized, 221
International Criminal Investigation and
Training Act Program, 137
International financial institutions, 63, 122,
123, 137, 142–143, 145, 147, 150, 152*n3,*
156; policymaking in, 4; political stances

of, 3; stabilization policies, 1; structural adjustment policies, 1

International Monetary Fund, 3, 4, 34, 36, 37, 48*n8*, 52*tab*, 60, 70*n4*, 73, 119, 121, 122, 126*n6*, 144, 147, 153*n15*, 156, 157, 173, 174*n5*, 205*n7*; aid conditionality, 140; Development Committee, 146; Executive Board, 120, 123; Memorandum on Economic Policies, 120; standby lending, 141, 153*n15*

Investment: agricultural, 20; biases, 72*n19*; capital, 196, 262; confidence, 66; consolidation of, 103; curtailment of, 36; declines in, 34; deregulation, 156; direct, 111; diversion, 269, 270; domestic, 7, 16*n7*, 41, 57, 62*tab*, 67, 109*tab*; in education, 6, 172; environmental, 8; financing for, 110, 112; foreign, 66, 67, 68, 111, 267, 269; in gross domestic product, 109*tab*; historical trends, 108–112; in human capital, 2, 5, 7–9, 171, 221, 263, 282; incentives, 263; industrial, 194; infrastructure, 25, 172, 247, 263; long-term, 262; natural capital, 243; need for stability in, 110; opportunities, 197–198; for peace, 88*tab*; in physical capital, 5, 7–9; private, 10, 33, 34, 53, 62*tab*, 63, 65, 108, 110, 111*fig*, 112, 118, 159, 160, 168, 172, 175*n12*, 226, 249, 263, 264, 282; productive, 63, 65, 67, 69; public, 10, 33, 34, 36, 40, 41, 44, 46, 47, 62*tab*, 65, 68, 108, 110, 111*fig*, 112, 122–123, 125, 135, 159, 171, 172, 175*n11*, 175*n12*, 249, 263, 264, 282; quicksilver, 158; reductions in, 40; risk in, 262; rural, 226; short-term, 158; social, 52*tab*, 54; speculative, 63; stability, 101; stimulation of, 5

Italy, 131*tab*, 152*n2*

Japan: aid to El Salvador, 131*tab*, 132–133*tab*; land reform in, 7, 225

Joint Group, 93

Korea: economic growth in, 224; exchange rate in, 262; land reform in, 7, 225; liberalization in, 179; state intervention in, 68

Labor: agricultural, 20, 219; cheap, 11, 20; costs, 20, 256, 258, 260, 270; family, 23, 226, 231*n11*; intensity, 225, 226, 271, 274; law, 98; markets, 166, 176*n23*, 258; migratory, 22; organizations, 27, 29, 98; peasant, 238–243; policy, 82; productivity, 260, 263; rural, 172; seasonal, 11, 22; shortages, 46; supply, 258; underutilization of, 23, 30*n4*; unrest,

101; unskilled, 166; urban, 27, 172; wage, 226, 230, 230*n6*, 231*n11*

Labor Council, 101

Laderas, 241

Land: access to, 20, 157, 241; acquisition costs, 88*tab*; arable, 21, 218; for arms exchange, 14; clearing, 242; communal, 11, 20; concentration, 20, 21, 22, 168; control of, 20; degradation, 234; distribution, 3, 5, 168, 171–172, 225; eviction from, 11; expropriation of, 11, 20; lotification, 237, 245*n7*; market prices, 89; overuse, 241; ownership of, 157, 166, 209; policy, 244; productivity, 7, 225; redistribution, 82; reform, 4, 7, 149, 167, 241, 250; rental, 241; shortages, 24; takeovers, 75; tenure, 28, 78, 166, 205*n2*, 209, 241, 244; titling, 95, 100, 229; transfer, 2, 13, 14, 80, 82, 83, 89, 90, 95, 96, 97, 100, 102, 103*n5*, 104*n10*, 129, 145, 149, 151, 193, 203, 219, 228, 229, 230, 281; underutilization of, 23, 30*n4*, 30*n5*; urban, 9, 26; use, 210, 235, 241, 244, 282

Land Bank, 95, 96, 104*n13*, 132*tab*

Latifundia, 11, 20, 21, 30*n5*

Law of Free Competition, 67

Law on the Protection and Assurance of Public Order (1977), 29

Lending, 34, 135; access to, 163; adjustment, 52*tab*; agricultural, 90–91; commercial, 204*n1*; direct, 151; domestic, 205*n3*; emphasis on social sector, 147; foreign, 178, 201, 205*n3*; funding for, 201; guarantees, 199; international, 47; and investment, 110; markets, 195; official, 110; and poverty, 6; production, 228; refinancing, 188; risky, 179–180; short-term, 195; speculative, 205*n13*; structural adjustment, 141. *See also* Aid

Liberalization, 51, 57, 58, 69, 205*n3*; banking, 197; domestic, 162–163; economic, 55, 68; exchange-rate, 214, 254; financial, 4, 163, 177, 179–187; import, 258, 262, 271; interest rate, 221; market, 53, 162, 163, 273; policy, 36; price, 227; trade, 4, 66, 141, 142, 162, 163, 165, 179

Malaysia: economic growth in, 225; land distribution in, 225

Market(s): access to, 21, 163, 269, 270; black, 34, 39*tab*, 49*n17*, 55; capital, 28; competition, 163, 260; control of, 10; credit, 6, 171, 183, 202; domestic, 20, 210, 214, 247, 254, 255, 256, 266; economy, 71*n15*; efficiency, 157; exchange, 36, 49*n17*; export, 28;

financial, 6, 9, 164, 205*n3*, 207*n28;*
foreign, 164, 256, 261; foreign exchange,
254; free, 36, 162; growth of, 20;
imperfections, 9; international, 32, 82,
163, 227, 249, 258, 261, 266; knowledge
of, 260–261; labor, 166, 176*n23,* 258;
lending, 195; liberalization, 53, 162, 163;
official, 37, 39*tab;* parallel, 37, 39*tab,* 40;
power, 10; recovery of, 54; regional, 54,
82, 266, 270; regulations, 176*n23;* role of,
5; wage, 176*n24*
Martí, Farabundo, 12, 29*n1*
Martínez, Maximiliano, 21
Matanza, the (1932), 12, 20–21
McNamara, Robert, 5, 145
MEA. *See* Municipalities in Action
Mexico: agrarian reform in, 219; domestic
investment in, 16*n8;* economic growth in,
175*n15;* exchange rate in, 156;
immigration from El Salvador, 30*n9;*
military expenditures, 154*n19;*
privatization in, 164
Miami Summit (1994), 270
Microenterprises, 91, 132*tab,* 172, 195,
196
Migration, 31, 50*n28,* 235, 245*n5,* 258; to
Honduras, 24, 28, 30*n9;* internal, 45, 46;
mass, 47, 50*n22;* to United States, 45;
urban, 26, 45, 47, 241
Military: aid, 12, 13, 145; civilian control
of, 74, 77, 80; crisis, 53–54; expenditures,
3, 4, 35–36, 37–38, 41, 43, 110, 118, 125,
127*n15,* 140, 144–147, 151, 153*n18,*
153*n19,* 154*n20,* 154*n24,* 170, 280, 281,
285*tab;* purge of, 13, 14, 92, 102;
reductions, 78; reform, 77, 79, 148;
regimes, 28–29; repression, 30*n10;*
restructuring, 92; rural control, 80;
stalemate, 2, 75
Minifundia, 11, 20, 21, 22
Ministry of Planning and Coordination of
Economic and Social Development, 86,
87, 207*n21*
Molina, Arturo Armando, 28, 29
Municipalities in Action (MEA), 86, 87,
132*tab*

NAFTA. *See* North American Free Trade
Agreement
National Academy of Public Security
(ANSP), 81, 90*tab,* 94, 99, 132*tab*
National Civilian Police, 13, 14, 78, 81,
88*tab,* 90*tab,* 93, 94, 95, 97, 99, 102,
104*n20,* 118, 132*tab,* 137, 139, 149, 281
National Commission for the Consolidation
of Peace (COPAZ), 78, 80, 83
National Counsel for the Defense of Human
Rights, 81, 90*tab,* 93, 99

National Counsel for the Judiciary, 99
National Guard, 20, 78, 80, 92
Nationalization, 12, 34; banking, 34, 42,
187, 207*n18*
National Judicial Council, 81, 93
National Reconstruction Program (PRN),
59, 70*n2,* 82, 83, 84, 86, 87, 88, 90*tab,*
91, 97, 108, 122, 131, 136, 143, 153*n12,*
169
Neoliberalism, 13, 52, 63, 74
Netherlands, 131*tab*
New York Accord (1991), 78, 81, 83, 94
Nicaragua, 85, 97, 104*n9,* 139; agricultural
income, 24*tab;* domestic investment in,
16*n8;* immigration from El Salvador,
30*n9;* inflation rates, 28*tab;* life
expectancy, 285*tab;* literacy rates,
285*tab;* peace negotiations in, 54; trade
deficits, 266, 268
Nongovernmental organizations, 42, 84, 87,
90, 97, 139, 153*n13,* 193, 195, 197, 200
North American Free Trade Agreement
(NAFTA), 176*n20,* 267, 269, 270, 274,
278*n22,* 278*n23*
Norway, 131*tab,* 137

ONUSAL. *See* Organización de las
Naciones Unidas, Misión para El
Salvador
Operation Guardian, 98
Organización de las Naciones Unidas,
Misión para El Salvador (ONUSAL), 92,
93, 94, 97, 98, 105*n25*
Organization for Economic Cooperation and
Development, 16*n3,* 152*n6*

Party of National Conciliation, 29
PDC. *See* Christian Democratic Party
Peace: accords, 79–84; agreement, 2;
conditionality, 15, 124, 140–150;
consolidation of, 5–10, 15, 73, 123, 137,
142, 178, 226, 247–276; costs of, 1, 85,
107, 122; domestic effects of, 54; and end
of Cold War, 15; financing for, 1, 4,
88*tab,* 107, 117*tab,* 119–123, 132–133*tab,*
134*tab,* 142, 143; fiscal targets, 119–123;
implementation of, 14, 85, 91–101;
international assistance for, 85, 86, 89;
negotiations, 75–79; political
commitments, 85; and reconstruction,
73–103; resources for, 1; social, 247;
terms of, 75–79
Pensions, 66, 132*tab*
People's Revolutionary Arm (ERP)y, 29
People's Revolutionary Bloc (BPR), 29
Pesticides, 8, 21, 231*n12,* 246*n11*
Plan for Economic and Social Development,
28

Police: Atlacatl Battalion, 77, 80; civilian, 77, 92; counterinsurgency, 80; National Guard, 20; paramilitary, 2, 12, 13, 29; rural, 20; standards for conduct, 99; state security, 29; Treasury, 78, 80, 92. *See also* National Civilian Police.

Policy: adjustment, 43, 50*n27*, 51; agrarian, 282; agricultural, 205*n2*, 210; anti-cyclical, 34, 46; anti-inflation, 48*n3*; competitiveness, 273; counterreaction, 168; credit, 66, 84, 120, 202, 205*n2*, 219, 221; development, 207*n28*, 280; distributional implications, 156–165; economic, 1, 2–5, 33–41, 42, 79, 82, 101, 239; exchange-rate, 57, 64, 66, 161, 183, 205*n2*; fiscal, 3, 47, 177; foreign, 49*n12*; formation, 168; immigration, 52, 61; implementation, 267; industrial, 171; labor, 82; land, 244; leverage, 201; liberalization, 36; macroeconomic, 51–70, 75, 155–173, 211–218; monetary, 3, 120, 179–187; price, 215, 216, 227–228; product-specific, 273; protectionist, 25; public, 194; real-sector, 204; recommendations, 280–284; redistributive, 10; reform, 176*n30*, 188; social, 65, 126; spending, 35; stabilization, 33, 41, 44, 51; structural adjustment, 248; tariff, 25, 151; tax, 205*n2*; trade, 205*n2*, 255, 264; wage, 82, 205*n2*; "Washington consensus," 156, 157, 162

Political access, 159
Political activism, 42
Political assassinations, 93
Political bargaining, 74
Political change, 11
Political conflict 15, 34
Political crises, 55, 110, 213
Political democracy, 75, 101
Political economy, 201
Political equity, 280
Political inequality, 12
Political instability, 124
Political institutions, 79
Political legitimacy, 7, 29
Political opposition, 29, 56, 137
Political parties, 2, 12, 50*n21*, 74, 76, 81
Political power, 21, 76, 159
Political reform, 9, 12, 77, 80–81, 101
Political repression, 12
Political stability, 6, 7, 10, 31, 50*n19*, 141–144, 160, 167, 261, 262, 270, 280
Political structure, 20
Political tensions, 78, 89
Political violence, 76, 93, 98–99
Popular Liberation Forces (FPL), 29, 92
Poverty, 5, 51, 82, 156, 157, 173, 262; alleviation, 13, 64, 90*tab*, 103, 129, 131,

132*tab*, 140, 155, 172, 226, 247; extreme, 43, 58, 64, 69, 72*n20*, 156, 249; income levels in, 27; increase in, 43; indexes, 51; lack of access to resources in, 6, 157; patterns of, 100; reduction, 58, 68; rural, 22, 24, 50*n21*, 56, 100, 196–197, 210, 226, 228, 237, 285*tab*; urban, 43, 56, 64, 64*tab*, 285*tab*

Power: balance of, 4–5, 13, 102, 129; coffee oligarchy, 20; democratic, 227; distribution of, 2, 9, 10, 13, 15, 165; exercise of, 10; groups, 47; inequities in, 10–11, 19, 159; market, 10; oligarchic, 227; political, 21, 76, 159; purchasing, 20; state, 65, 79

Price(s), 163; agricultural, 160, 174*n5*, 212*fig*, 213*tab*, 216; changes, 174*n7*; commodity, 21; competitiveness, 271; consumer, 215, 312*tab*; controls, 50*n27*, 58, 165, 215; declining, 12, 20, 33, 57, 214; distortions, 265; domestic, 159, 160, 162, 217, 228; establishing, 35; fluctuations, 215, 217; food, 32; freezing, 36, 49*n14*; guarantees, 215; increases, 71*n11*; international, 27, 28, 162, 215, 239, 264; market, 89; noncompetitive, 163; policy, 215, 216, 227–228; producer, 205*n2*, 215, 217, 227, 228, 230*n2*; property, 205*n13*; real, 212–217, 214, 215; regulation, 37, 49*n9*; relative, 71*n18*, 157, 158, 162, 167, 213, 253, 254; restraints, 163; stability, 27, 227

PRIDEX. *See* Program for Promotion of Export Investment and Diversification

Privatization, 9, 51, 57, 58, 63, 66, 69, 141, 164, 172, 179, 193, 221, 246*n14*

PRN. *See* National Reconstruction Program

Production: agricultural, 23*tab*, 48*n6*, 211*tab*, 213*tab*, 215; assembly, 255; coffee, 19–21, 23*tab*; consumer goods, 26; costs, 66, 271; credit, 96; declining, 34; domestic, 24, 247, 255, 261; efficiency, 249; expansion, 171; factors of, 68, 178, 205*n14*, 209; food, 35; industrial, 215; infrastructure, 100; lending, 228; local, 25, 205*n14*; maquila, 273; regional, 267–268; rural, 238; sectors of, 157–158; structures, 267

Productivity: agricultural, 225; of agroexport economy, 23; development, 258, 260–261; gains in, 262; growth, 249, 260, 271–275; increasing, 217; investment, 63, 65, 67, 69; labor, 260, 263; land, 7, 225; manufacturing, 32, 256

Program for Promotion of Export Investment and Diversification (PRIDEX), 273

Pro-Patria Party, 29

Protectionism, 25, 58, 215, 255, 256, 264, 266, 267

Reagan, Ronald, 12, 76, 148
Recession, 37, 57, 248
Reform, 167–168; agenda, 92; agrarian, 9, 12, 28, 30n8, 34, 35, 42, 47, 50n21, 76, 78, 82, 83, 123, 166, 171–172, 187, 218–226; banking, 192, 194; constitutional, 81, 99; costs of, 4, 86, 88tab, 90tab; economic, 12, 15, 47, 65–68, 123; electoral, 81, 101; fiscal, 58; judicial, 2, 13, 81, 88tab, 90tab, 92, 93, 147, 148; land, 4, 7, 149, 167, 241, 250; military, 77, 79, 148; neoliberal, 13; obstacles to, 224; pension, 66; policy, 176n30, 188; political, 9, 12, 77, 80–81, 101; program, 53–57; public-security, 80–81; socioeconomic, 79, 81–84; state, 4, 243; structural, 34, 35, 42, 47, 76, 123–124; tariff, 58; tax, 40, 43, 46, 51, 107, 112–114, 125, 126n5; trade, 51, 255
Remittances, 15, 32, 41, 49n17, 50n28, 51, 55–57, 64, 67–68, 69, 70n2, 70n7, 71n12, 107, 110, 111, 124, 126n2, 161, 180, 215, 227, 248, 249, 261, 262, 279–280
Rent seeking, 10, 68, 163, 171, 266, 274
Repression, 12, 29, 30n10
Resources: academic, 274; access to, 217; aggregate, 151; allocation, 162, 179, 227, 248; domestic, 1, 4, 60, 102, 105n28, 107–126, 135, 138, 139, 143, 144, 151, 281; energy, 244; external, 15, 17n18, 32, 34, 37, 41–42, 59, 64, 65, 111, 120, 123, 129–151, 142, 279; financial, 37; human, 59; local, 201; mobility of, 68; mobilization of, 1, 4, 60, 102, 105n28, 107–126, 143; natural, 234, 235, 238; physical, 44; public, 126n1, 225; reallocation, 4; redirection of, 54; transfer, 82
Revolutionary Party of Democratic Unity, 29
Rights: human, 2, 9, 10, 13, 77, 79, 80, 81, 92–93, 99, 137, 148, 151, 281; to life, 99; property, 3, 10, 75, 168; protecting, 9, 10
Romero, Archbishop Oscar, 12
Romero, Carlos Humberto, 29, 30n10

Savings, 178; capacity, 197; clubs, 196–197; domestic, 107, 108, 109tab, 111, 112tab, 126n2, 197; external, 57; foreign, 109tab, 110, 111, 112, 113fig, 126n3, 197; and gross domestic product, 108, 109tab; historical trends, 108–112; informal, 207n23; local, 178, 198; national, 63, 109tab, 111, 112, 113fig, 126n2, 126n3, 126n4; opportunities, 197–198; private,

108, 109tab, 112, 126n3; promotion of, 66; public, 109tab, 112; rural, 198. *See also* Resources, domestic
Secretariat of National Reconstruction (SRN), 86–87, 89, 97
Sector, agricultural, 160, 209–230; bimodal, 21–24; efficiency in, 224; profitability of, 211–218
Sector, financial, 177–204; liberalization of, 4; privatization in, 141
Sector, formal, 46tab; credit in, 195; interest rates, 183, 185fig
Sector, informal, 46tab, 160; employment in, 46; lending in, 196
Sector, manufacturing: employment in, 26, 27; growth of, 25; productivity of, 32, 256
Sector, private: accumulation, 63; alliance with government, 54; credit availability, 37, 40, 195; size of, 3; wages in, 44fig, 256, 258
Sector, public: credit availability, 37; deficits, 36, 127n14; employment in, 37, 41, 46, 48n6, 66; financing, 40; restructuring, 58; size of, 3; spending in, 16n1, 35, 43, 46, 54, 107, 175n12; wages in, 43, 44fig
Sector, service, 26, 64, 72n19; employment in, 46
Sector, subsistence, 22
Servicio Crediticio de la Asociación de Medianos y Pequeños Empresarios Salvadoreños, 200
Soccer War (1969), 24
Social benefits, 35, 176n24, 210
Social capital, 114
Social changes, 11, 27
Social classes, 157
Social conflict, 1, 2, 19–21, 167, 168, 225, 234
Social costs, 210, 227
Social crises, 19, 31, 47
Social dislocation, 47
Social disparities, 27
Social equity, 75, 82, 155, 156, 159, 163, 164, 167
Social infrastructure, 43, 45, 100, 139
Social instability, 124
Social investment, 54
Social organization, 29
Social peace, 247
Social policy 65, 126
Social protest, 29
Social restructuring, 19, 42
Social security, 4, 258, 277n7, 277n8
Social services, 46, 247,
Social spending 40, 41, 43, 44, 46, 107, 118, 123, 125, 126, 160

Social stability, 47, 53, 108, 124, 160, 196
Social tensions, 22, 56, 134, 142, 168
Social wage, 165, 176n24
Social welfare, 4, 65, 164
Social Investment Fund, 132tab
Spain, 94, 99, 131tab, 137, 267
Special Agrarian Commission, 83
SRN. *See* Secretariat of National
    Reconstruction
Stabilization, 36, 40, 48n8, 50n27, 55,
    60–61, 73, 157, 158tab; conventional,
    156–161; and distribution, 158–161;
    economic, 4, 19, 47, 123–124, 141–144,
    155; investment, 21; macroeconomic, 1,
    31, 140; orthodox, 156–161; policy, 3, 33,
    41, 44, 51; political, 141–144; role in
    reform, 4; short-run, 3; social cost, 56
Stagflation, 32
State: and agroexport model, 19–20; alliance
    with private sector, 54; capacity, 47;
    interventions, 3, 9, 68, 163, 227, 273,
    274; legitimacy, 225; modernization of, 9;
    power, 79; privatization in, 9; reduction in
    size, 63, 69; reform, 243; revenue raising,
    112, 113; role in economy, 48n6; security
    forces, 29; shrinking, 163, 165; spending,
    41; in structural adjustment, 9; weakening
    in, 47
Sterilization, 180–183, 254, 263, 277n11,
    281
Structural adjustment, 1, 55, 61, 63–65,
    70n1, 140, 148, 155–156, 157, 158tab,
    209–230, 247, 248, 261–275;
    consequences of, 43–46; costs of, 82; and
    distribution, 162–165; in long-run growth,
    4; modernization of state in, 9; social
    costs, 78, 84; state intervention in, 9
Subsidies, 50n27, 149, 159, 162, 230, 253,
    254, 255, 262, 264–265, 274; actionable,
    265; credit, 215; for environmental
    conservation, 8; to higher education,
    16n1; input, 215; interest rates, 221;
    nonactionable, 265; prohibited, 265
Sugar, 21, 23tab, 34, 42, 187
Superintendencia de Servicios Financieros,
    198–199
Supreme Electoral Tribunal, 81
Sweden, 131tab, 137

Taiwan: economic growth in, 224; land
    reform in, 225; liberalization in, 179;
    state intervention in, 68
Tariff(s), 71n9, 162, 228, 255, 258, 262,
    264–265, 270; asymmetrical, 215;
    ceilings, 276n5; discretionary application
    of, 25; discrimination, 227; policy, 25,
    151; reductions, 66, 248, 251; reform, 58;
    removing, 163; structure of, 254

Tax(es): advantages, 25; collection, 4, 151,
    281; on consumption, 40; corporate,
    112–114; credits, 263; direct, 41, 58, 114;
    evasion, 66, 114; exemptions, 40,
    112–114, 274; export, 40, 112–114,
    115tab; fraud, 112–114; import, 112–114,
    115tab; income, 40, 112–114, 115tab,
    151; increases, 134, 135, 158, 159;
    indirect, 114, 255; modernization, 125; on
    net worth, 112–114; policy, 205n2;
    progressive, 151, 171, 280; ratios, 112,
    114, 115tab, 116fig; reform, 43, 46, 51,
    107, 112–114, 126n5; regressive, 58, 114,
    125, 159, 171, 175n10; revenue, 59fig;
    sales, 115tab, 159, 281; sovereignty,
    49n16; structure, 125; trade, 253; value-
    added, 58, 66, 71n11, 112–114, 117, 121,
    126n7, 159, 175n10, 255
Technical assistance, 14, 88, 96, 97, 99, 171,
    217, 219, 221, 244
Technocratic insulation, 9, 10
Technology, 163; absorption, 274; access to,
    230, 272fig; best-practice, 261; change of,
    8; embodied, 249; imported, 25; transfer,
    273
Thailand: economic growth in, 225; land
    reform in, 225
Trade: agreements, 20; balance, 161;
    barriers to, 267; creation, 267; credit, 195;
    deficits, 51, 57, 62tab, 158, 248, 268;
    deregulation, 156; diversion, 267, 269,
    270, 277n16; free, 20, 52, 63, 66, 255,
    265–271, 273, 274; imbalances, 266;
    international, 171, 217, 277n13; intra-
    industry, 271; intraregional, 49n10, 67,
    250, 266, 267; liberalization, 4, 66, 141,
    142, 162, 163, 165, 179; policy, 205n2,
    255, 264; reform, 51; regional, 266;
    tariffs, 262; taxes, 253; terms of, 33, 212,
    226; unions, 67
Treasury Police, 78, 80, 92
Truth Commission, 17n16, 77, 81, 92, 93,
    99
Turkey, 179

Unemployment, 20, 27, 48n7, 51, 142, 159,
    176n24, 219, 230n4
Unions, 17n14, 82, 258; credit, 200;
    customs, 266; trade, 67
United Front for Popular Action (FAPU), 29
United Nations, 14, 17n16, 73, 74, 75, 77,
    85, 89, 94, 99, 100, 102, 123, 137;
    Development Programme, 84, 87, 89, 90,
    94, 97, 105n25, 130, 131tab, 139;
    Economic Commission for Latin America
    and the Caribbean, 141–142; General
    Assembly, 131; Joint Group, 93; Security
    Council, 105n29

United States, 12, 74, 99; aid to El Salvador, 37, 38*tab,* 41, 42, 50*n20,* 76, 85, 89, 94, 130, 132–133*tab,* 135, 136, 145, 148–150, 152*n7;* Arms Control and Disarmament Agency, 154*n19;* commitment to peace, 85; debt forgiveness, 117, 152*n3;* Deferred Enforced Departure program, 61, 71*n13;* foreign policy, 49*n12;* Generalized System of Preferences, 98, 269; immigration from El Salvador, 30*n9,* 45, 52, 61; immigration policy, 61, 161; markets in, 21; military aid to El Salvador, 12, 13; policy on El Salvador, 13, 148–150
United States Agency for International Development (USAID), 38*tab,* 40, 41, 42, 44, 50*n24,* 51, 71*n15,* 86, 89, 91, 95, 102, 122, 126*n6,* 136, 137, 145, 153*n13,* 172, 187
Urbanization, 9, 26, 234, 235, 237
Uruguay, 179
USAID. *See* United States Agency for International Development

Wage(s), 30*n3,* 56–57, 161, 277*n7,* 277*n8;* adjustment of, 49*n14;* agricultural, 175*n16;* declining, 12, 159, 253, 261;

depression, 166; developments, 256–258; farm, 23; freezing, 35, 36, 49*n9,* 175*n15;* harvest, 239; increases, 37, 41; market, 176*n24;* minimum, 258, 259*tab,* 272*fig,* 313*tab;* negotiations, 84; policy, 82, 205*n2;* private sector, 256, 258; public sector, 43; real, 28, 43, 44*fig,* 46, 57, 82, 174*n8,* 175*n9,* 239, 253, 257, 260, 261, 271, 313*tab;* repression, 271–275; rural, 226; social, 165, 176*n24;* structure, 20; urban, 26, 226
War, civil: and business closures, 35*tab;* causes, 52; change from, 11; costs of, 35, 45*tab;* debilitating effects of, 10–11; demobilization in, 13, 14; economic policy after, 5–10; economy during, 31–48; environmental damage from, 9; historical background, 19–29; military stalemate in, 2, 75; origins of, 12, 15; peace accord, 2; reconstruction, 45*tab,* 54; social costs of, 41, 50*n20*
Wealth: concentration of, 25, 35; inequities in, 2, 6, 15
World Bank, 3, 5, 48*n6,* 51, 52*tab,* 70*n1,* 73, 91, 122, 131*tab,* 140, 141, 143, 144, 145, 146, 152*n3,* 153*n17,* 156, 157, 168, 173, 225, 255; Natural Resources Resources Management Study, 245*n4;* Structural Adjustment Loan, 138

About the Book

Economic policy during a postwar adjustment toward peace confronts special challenges. Short-term policy must promote not only macroeconomic, but also political stabilization, mobilizing resources and political will for immediate needs such as the reintegration of ex-combatants into civil society and the strengthening of democratic institutions. Long-term policy must aim to achieve not only macreconomic balance, but also equity, or balance in the distribution of income and wealth; balanced investment in human, natural, and physical capital; and democratization in the broad sense of a more balanced distribution of power.

This volume, written by a team of distinguished scholars at the invitation of the United Nations Development Programme, analyzes the tensions between economic policy and peace building in El Salvador, and draws lessons for postconflict transitions elsewhere.

James K. Boyce is professor of economics at the University of Massachusetts, Amherst. His previous books include *Café y Desarrollo Sostenible, The Philippines: The Political Economy of Growth and Impoverishment in the Marcos Era*, and *Agrarian Impasse in Bengal* (winner of the 1990 Edgar Graham Book Prize).